# SEASONS PAST

*Also available by the same author*

CRICKET – A WAY OF LIFE
THE CRICKETER BOOK OF CRICKET DISASTERS AND BIZARRE RECORDS
THE CRICKETER BOOK OF CRICKET ECCENTRICS
AND ECCENTRIC BEHAVIOUR

# SEASONS PAST

## THE CRICKETER DIARIES OF
### JOHN ARLOTT · ALAN GIBSON · TONY LEWIS · MIKE BREARLEY ·
### · PETER ROEBUCK ·

*EDITED BY CHRISTOPHER MARTIN-JENKINS*

**STANLEY PAUL**
*London Melbourne Sydney Auckland Johannesburg*

*Stanley Paul & Co. Ltd*

*An imprint of Century Hutchinson Ltd*
*62-65 Chandos Place, London WC2N 4NW*
*Century Hutchinson (Australia) Pty Ltd*
*16-22 Church Street, Hawthorn, Melbourne, Victoria 3122*
*Century Hutchinson (NZ) Ltd*
*32-34 View Road, Glenfield, Auckland 10*
*Century Hutchinson (SA) Pty Ltd*
*PO Box 337, Bergvlei 2012, South Africa*

*First published 1986*
© *Lennard Books Ltd/The Cricketer 1986*

Printed and bound in Great Britain by
Butler & Tanner Ltd, Frome, Somerset
Filmset by Metro Filmsetting, London
Made by Lennard Books Ltd
Mackerye End, Harpenden, Herts AL5 5DR
Editor Michael Leitch
Designed by David Pocknell's Company Ltd

Cataloguing in Publication Data
Seasons past.
1. Cricket – History – 20th century
I. Martin-Jenkins, Christopher
796.35′8′0924 GV913

ISBN 0 09 163850 X

# CONTENTS

# INTRODUCTION

*DIARIES have long been a most valuable source of history. These Journals of the Season are no exception. They are more in the style of the Venerable Bede than of the venerated but not always venerable Samuel Pepys. In other words, they are more chronicles of events than personal indulgences. This said, however, each of the distinguished diarists who accepted the Editor of* The Cricketer's *invitation to write their accounts of the past 19 cricket seasons in Britain (having written for* The Scotsman *I am trained not to write England instead of Britain) has his own distinctive style and method.*

*To take the work of John Arlott, Tony Lewis, Alan Gibson, Mike Brearley and Peter Roebuck together in the same volume is to sample quite a feast. And it is a varied feast. Arlott, with great authority, and Gibson, with imagination and literary relish, wrote from the press-box (or, in Gibson's case, quite often from one of the bars or tents beside the County grounds). The three player-writers all put pen to paper in the dressing-room. Lewis is colourful, sympathetic and always ready to share a smile with his readers. Brearley is superbly lucid and analytical;*

*Roebuck is the most original of the lot: it will be fascinating to see if his quick wit and taste for the unconventional can be used in his role as Somerset captain to get the best out of the brilliantly talented and not quite-so-talented players around him. He believes his cricket writing has actually helped his cricket career, giving him more confidence and a reason to think carefully about the game he chose to make his profession.*

*Arlott and Gibson are too well established and too widely appreciated to need any introductory boost. It was the former who received the first invitation to write a diary for* The Cricketer's *Winter Annual, strictly observing the rules laid down by E.W. Swanton that each week was to be written up as soon as it had passed, with no opportunity for adjustments in hindsight. This is what diaries should be. They prove that no mortal is an infallible judge or observer. But the famous five have done well to make so few misjudgments as they went along. Gathered together, their work represents a fascinating cricket history of the last two decades, viewed from subtly different perspectives. I do hope you will enjoy it.*

*Christopher Martin-Jenkins*

# — 1967 —

*ALRESFORD: APRIL*

This journal is a record of the cricket season of 1967, set down every Friday. Each entry will be sent to the printer at the end of the week it covers and no subsequent alteration will be possible. Its purpose is to give a perspective view of the summer's cricket – if only because so many of us tend to recall the events of August more sharply than those of May. It will, however, have another attraction – it will enable readers to note the writer's errors of judgment and to proclaim (with the benefit of hindsight) that they made no such mistakes.

## NEW FACES AND A COLD WET START
### APRIL 29–MAY 5

Tony Greig – an unknown quantity in May 1967.

ON the first Saturday of the season, the changing shape of cricket history was reflected by the appearance of two Barbadians (Keith Boyce, of Essex, and John Shepherd, of Kent), a South African (Tony Greig, of Sussex), a Kenyan (Sheikh Basharat Hassan, of Notts), and a Pakistani (Mohammed Younis, of Surrey), all newly qualified to appear in the County Championship.

*Interesting that Greig should be described as a "South African". Younis became better known as Younis Ahmed.*

Bishen Bedi, who had begun his Test career against the West Indies at Calcutta earlier in the year.

The match between Worcestershire and the touring side marks general acceptance of cricket having positively begun and, memory insists, invariably produces bad weather. The Nawab of Pataudi on the one side, Jack Flavell and Jim Standen on the other, were fortunate enough to be confined to their beds with tonsillitis. The remainder suffered viciously cold, wet, windy weather. D'Oliveira made 174 not out, his highest score in first-class cricket, on the opening day when Bedi, a slow left-arm bowler, took three wickets, and bowled with a puzzling flight and some occasionally sharp spin to a steady length.

One of the season's awaited acquisitions, surely, appeared in Tony Greig, the tall South African who, in his first Championship match for Sussex, played an innings of 156 against Lancashire with such power and grace as to prompt comparison with Dexter.

## SOME EVIL WICKETS AND A SAD RETIREMENT
### MAY 6–12

A week that began in storm, stoked up to high summer heat and thunder by its end. In most of the week-end games there was time to make up after Saturday's rain and there were some valiant, if not all successful, attempts to contrive finishes. For Leicestershire, who beat Hampshire on what used to be reckoned a fast bowlers' pitch at Portsmouth, Lock performed a hat-trick with the last two wickets of the first innings and one with his first ball of the next. Birkenshaw, who has not yet redeemed his early promise as an off-spinner since he moved from Yorkshire, was Lock's worthy partner in the bowling out of Hampshire for 122 in the first innings, which proved the decisive phase of the match.

*"Birky", in fact, was to flourish with Leicestershire and his MCC touring days were not far off.*

During the Wednesday round of matches, superb summer weather was punctuated by rain which produced some evil wickets. Barrington and Mike Smith continued in steady batting form and Lock – 13 wickets for 116 in the match – was the effective bowler in the defeat of Glamorgan which kept Leicestershire level with Hampshire and Middlesex at the top of the sketchy early Championship table. Kent beat the Indians, who showed ambitious strokes but no experience of bad wicket play in the otherwise successful experiment of a May fixture at Canterbury. Bailey saved Essex from defeat with a stern defensive innings – which was no surprise – and Oxford beat Somerset by nine wickets – which was.

The saddest news of the week was that David Larter of Northants, long regarded as a "white hope" of English fast bowlers, announced his retirement from the game after yet another breakdown. There were times when he came near to the highest class but always some injury cut him back on the edge of real achievement.

## TOUGH TIMES FOR GROUNDSMEN
### MAY 13–19

THE week began with the second round of the Gillette Cup – which met a break in its hitherto remarkable luck with the weather – and ended in such gales that only one of the round of Championship matches was completed.

Bert Lock, the former Oval groundsman, first holder of the office of inspector of pitches, has been busy, conscientious and helpful. Not all captains have been satisfied with the pitches they have played on – particularly those of their opponents – but it is hard to withhold sympathy from groundsmen. In the earlier part of the year, as one of them said, "The wind wouldn't let the grass grow" and since the season started the rain has given them few opportunities to prepare or protect wickets as they would like.

A bleak scene at Trent Bridge.

## CLOSE EARNS HIS CAPTAINCY
### MAY 20–26

SURELY there has never before been such a miserably cold and wet month of May. Of 43 Championship fixtures thus far, there have been finishes in only 13: in this week 15 Championship and two tourists' matches yielded clear results. It is some consolation that, while such a run could have shattered most counties' finances before the last war, it cannot have any effect on the newer sources of payment – television and radio fees, supporters' club donations and the vastly greater subscription revenue. It is sufficient, however, to cast doubts on the wisdom of the counties in rejecting the suggestion of fewer fixtures in May and more in September when, certainly, playing hours would have to be 11 a.m. to 6 p.m. but when weather is rarely so bad as in the past few weeks and an increasing number of people are still on holiday.

The Indians, in such weather and conditions as few of them have ever experienced, have made something of a mark with their spin bowling: Prasanna and Bedi against MCC at Lord's, Prasanna, Chandrasekhar and Bedi in the Glamorgan match – the first ever played on the new ground at Sophia Gardens, Cardiff – all performed capably. But their batsmen, apart from the ebullient Engineer, look justifiably unhappy. Only Milburn for MCC made runs at any speed or with any confidence on a heavy pitch: it will be difficult for the selectors to leave him out of the Test team on his present form.

On Monday, during the MCC-India match, it was announced that Brian Close will captain England for the three-match series with India. He earned the appointment last August when he captained the side that beat the West Indies: although the rubber had already been lost, much self-respect and enthusiasm were regained by that result.

Later in the week – in fact a couple of days after their deliberations – the Registration Committee (appointed by MCC at the request of the counties) refused Barry Knight's application for special registration to play for Leicestershire and ruled that he must serve a two-year residential period before he can play in Championship matches for his new county. The inference to be drawn is that the counties are utterly determined that nothing like the transfer system in Association football shall ever exist in English cricket. The basic motive – to maintain county ties – is admirable; from time to time, however, individuals may have to suffer for it.

*Knight was in fact playing for Leicestershire one year later – not two.*

County Championship (as at May 23)

| | P | Pts |
| --- | --- | --- |
| 1 Hampshire | 5 | 42 |
| 2 Leicestershire | 6 | 30 |
| 3 Yorkshire | 5 | 28 |
| 4 Middlesex | 2 | 24 |

Barry Knight, who was to play no Championship cricket in 1967.

The latest news tonight is that Lancashire have stated that there will be no play *tomorrow* – Saturday – at Old Trafford when the Lancashire-Yorkshire fixture should have started. In the entire history of the Roses Match such an advance cancellation is unprecedented – like this damnable weather.

## DELUGE AT OLD TRAFFORD BUT A HAPPY CROWD AT LORD'S
### MAY 27–JUNE 2

THE Saturday of the new, anonymous Spring Bank Holiday – with all the traditional Whit fixtures – was completely washed out: not a ball was bowled in any one of the ten games. Someone calculated that this dismal day brought the season's tally to 52 utterly blank days out of a scheduled 202. Sunday and Monday were a little better but the damage had been done. The Yorkshire-Lancashire match – the unlucky Geoff Pullar's Benefit – was abandoned without a ball being bowled. Indeed the deluge upon Old Trafford was so heavy that the match with the Indians, arranged for June 3 – a *week* later – was transferred to Southport.

Understandably, not a single match in the week-end round yielded a finish. It has been, we are told, the wettest May for 194 years: no one disputes the statement.

The Monday crowd at Lord's was a happy one, seeming to cherish its cricket and, as the week grew warmer and drier, the atmosphere at matches was unmistakably happy.

The Indians had a sorry time of it against Surrey. Only Hanumant Singh – who saved them from an innings defeat – Engineer and, to markedly lesser degree, Kunderan and Borde of their batsmen batted even moderately convincingly. Pocock, who grows in capability week by week, bowled well against them: but not quite so well as they made it appear. They play off-spin with what an English professional would regard as naïveté.

It would be hard to dispute that the best finger-spinner in England at the moment is Tony Lock. This season, too, he must have dealt out more physical embraces than any other man in the history of cricket: a good catch or a valuable wicket for Leicestershire prompts him to transports of delight and affection and,

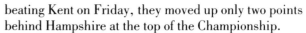

beating Kent on Friday, they moved up only two points behind Hampshire at the top of the Championship.

The team for the First Test – at Headingley – to be announced on Sunday, has been picked with an eye beyond this summer to the tour of West Indies. Presumably Close, Graveney, D'Oliveira, Murray and Higgs are certainties: Milburn ought to be: Snow – currently bowling faster than ever before – Amiss, Edrich, Price and – on past evidence – Boycott are probables: but Bob Barber is, apparently, not available. There is talk of Pocock being chosen: he should have a good future: but is he a better bowler now – or likely to be next winter in the West Indies – than David Allen?

*The off-spinner actually chosen was Ray Illingworth, whose Indian Summer was about to start, aided by the fact that his Yorkshire colleague, Brian Close, was now captain of England.*

It is a sad thought that three of the four best batsmen in England – assuming Graveney to be the other – Mike Smith, Colin Cowdrey and Ken Barrington, are all doubtful.

The weather forecast is of fine weather – but possible thunder – tomorrow.

## INDIANS UP AGAINST IT
### JUNE 3–9

IN the second round of the week, Kent held out to draw with Middlesex who had taken a long first innings lead; Michael Buss scored the fastest hundred of the season (in 103 minutes, against Warwickshire); Peter Willey, the 17-year-old Northants batsman, scored his first 50 in first-class cricket – he is one of the most promising young players of recent years.

The Test match, thus far, has been a tragic affair. As so often happens, the luck was against the weaker side from the start. Pataudi lost the toss on a cold day with an easy wicket; by middle afternoon one of his opening bowlers, Surti, and his stock spinner, Bedi, were off the field injured; and his fielders missed two catches and a run out. Boycott, out of form and practice, took the opportunity to grind through the first day for 106 not out: on Friday he went on, at greater pace, to 246 not out, beating Hammond's 217 of 1936 as the highest

Peter Willey establishing himself as a Northants regular.

score in England-India Tests: but it was only statistically a major innings. D'Oliveira made his first Test century and Barrington a spritely 93 against this sorry attack. Nine Indians – all but the wicket-keeper, Engineer, and Borde, whose damaged shoulder does not allow him to bowl – entered the lists as bowlers and the three surviving regulars, Chandrasekhar, Prasanna and Guha, all were hit for over a hundred runs. Close declared at 550 for four wickets and his bowlers of all types proceeded to plague the Indian batsmen who could not distinguish between Illingworth's off break and the ball which floated on towards the slips.

## PATAUDI LEADS FIGHT BACK
### JUNE 10–16

NOTHING in cricket for years has been quite so dramatic or so unexpected as the Indian revival in the First Test. On Friday night, at 86 for six wickets, they were an apparently beaten and, we might assume, dispirited, side. On Saturday morning, however, Pataudi proceeded to play an innings of firm command. There was no extravagance about it; only a quiet

certainty. It is said – and it seems likely – that he had indulged some plain speaking to his team during the previous evening. Whatever the reason, they rallied to him. The injured Surti and Bedi appeared with runners and, though India followed on 386 behind, they were a changed team when they did so. Surti even came in first – again with a runner – and, though he was soon out, Wadekar (91) who had barely made a convincing stroke hitherto on the tour blossomed beside Engineer (87) in a stand of 168 for the second wicket. Borde (33) proved stubborn, if not at his best; Hanumant Singh (73) was lively and confident. But again Pataudi was the dominating figure and in an innings of precise judgment, positive strokes and, above all, character, he made 148: again, as in the first innings, he was out playing an attacking stroke in an attempt to make quick runs before the tail collapsed around him. The Indian total was 475. India indeed, had the better of the last three days but the match had, in fact, been settled on Friday afternoon when their first innings crumpled, and England needed only 125 to win. In face of some good spin bowling by Chandrasekhar and Prasanna as the pitch, at last, began to crumble, they made a jittery,

Bedi is lbw to Hobbs. There seems little doubt on the faces of Close, Barrington, D'Oliveira and wicket-keeper Murray.

### ENGLAND

| First Innings | | Second Innings | |
|---|---|---|---|
| G. Boycott not out .. .. .. 246 | | | |
| J. H. Edrich c Engineer b Surti .. .. 1 | | c Wadekar | |
| | | b Chandrasekhar | 22 |
| K. F. Barrington run out .. .. 93 | | c Engineer | |
| | | b Chandrasekhar | 46 |
| T. W. Graveney c sub b Chandrasekhar 59 | | b Chandrasekhar .. | 14 |
| B. L. D'Oliveira c sub b Chandrasekhar 109 | | not out .. .. .. | 24 |
| *D. B. Close not out .. .. .. 22 | | | |
| †J. T. Murray .. .. .. .. – | | c sub, b Prasanna .. | 4 |
| R. Illingworth .. .. .. .. – | | not out .. .. | 12 |
| Extras (b 8, lb 12) .. .. 20 | | Extras (b 3, lb 1) .. | 4 |
| Total (4 wkts. dec.) .. .. 550 | | Total (4 wkts) .. | 126 |

BOWLING: Guha 43—10—105—0; Surti 11—2—25—1; Chandrasekhar 45—9—121—2; Bedi 15—8—32—0; Prasanna 59—8—187—0; Pataudi 4—1—13—0; Wadekar 1—0—9—0; Singh 3—0—27—0; Saxena 2—0—11—0. *Second Innings:* Guha 5—0—10—0; Wadekar 2—0—8—0; Prasanna 21.3—5—54—1; Chandrasekhar 19—8—50—3.

### INDIA

| First Innings | | Second Innings | |
|---|---|---|---|
| †F. M. Engineer c and b Illingworth .. 42 | | c and b Close .. .. | 87 |
| R. Saxena b D'Oliveira .. .. 9 | | b Snow .. .. .. | 16 |
| A. L. Wadekar run out .. .. 0 | | c Close b Illingworth .. | 91 |
| C. G. Borde b Snow .. .. 8 | | b Illingworth .. .. | 33 |
| Hanumant Singh c D'Oliveira | | c D'Oliveira | |
| b Illingworth .. .. .. 9 | | b Illingworth .. | 73 |
| *Nawab of Pataudi c Barrington | | | |
| b Hobbs .. .. .. 64 | | b Illingworth .. | 148 |
| E. A. S. Prasanna c Murray | | | |
| b Illingworth .. .. .. 0 | | lbw, b Close .. .. | 19 |
| S. Guha b Snow .. .. .. 4 | | b Higgs .. .. | 1 |
| R. F. Surti c and b Hobbs .. 22 | | c Murray b Illingworth .. | 5 |
| B. S. Bedi lbw b Hobbs .. .. 0 | | c Snow b Hobbs .. | 14 |
| B. S. Chandrasekhar not out .. 0 | | not out .. .. .. | 0 |
| Extras (lb 6) .. .. .. 6 | | Extras (b 10, lb 13) .. | 23 |
| Total .. .. .. .. 164 | | Total .. .. .. | 510 |

BOWLING: Snow 17—7—34—2; Higgs 14—8—19—0; D'Oliveira 9—4—29—1; Hobbs 22.2—9—45—3; Iillingworth 22—11—31—3; Close 3—3—0—0. *Second Innings:* Snow 41—10—108—2; Higgs 24—3—71—1; D'Oliveira 11—5—22—0; Illingworth 58—26—100—4; Hobbs 45.2—13—100—1; Barrington 9—1—38—0; Close 21—5—48—2.

inglorious affair of it and, with the benefit of some dropped catches – the Indian close fielding is not good enough – they came home, with no dignity, by six wickets.

In scorching, uninterrupted sunshine – how easy to forget to be grateful when we have it – the quarter finals of the Gillette Cup produced exciting cricket and large crowds. At the Oval, Alan Dixon, of Kent, with the best bowling figures in the history of the competition – seven for 15 – effectively beat Surrey. Lancashire, in a match which should hearten them after too long in depression, beat Yorkshire by four runs in the last over. Lever – four wickets and an innings of 20 – was made Man of the Match, but it was a *team* win. Yorkshire were without Close, who developed eye trouble during the Test: a colt, C. Old, replaced him and took four wickets.

Somerset, who have warmed to knock-out cricket, beat Northants by 36 runs: here the old, but not elderly, Bill Alley was Man of the Match with an innings of 30 and the remarkable – and, in knock-out cricket, match-winning – figures of 12 overs, 6 maidens, 8 runs, 2 wickets.

## BOYCOTT LOSES HIS TEST PLACE
### JUNE 17–23

A week of sunshine and significant activity in the County Championship ended on Friday with thunderstorms over much of the country and India, in the Test at Lord's, in a position which, but for their amazing recovery at Headingley, could only be called hopeless.

The news buzzed round another series of good and lively Sunday crowds that the selectors had dropped Boycott – presumably as corrective treatment for his

### LORD'S TEST MATCH

# BOYCOTT MADE TO PAY PENALTY

## Barrington as opener

### By JOHN WOODCOCK, Cricket Correspondent

slow scoring at Leeds – and that Barrington would open the innings with Edrich; Amiss, the heaviest scorer of the season, took the vacant batting position and Higgs, England's only regular player through the 1966 series with West Indies, had lost his place to David Brown of Warwickshire.

*Interesting to peruse what might have happened if Amiss had been tried as an opener at this stage of his career. It was very much the making of him later on.*

Boycott, as we should expect of him, marked the loss of his Test place with an innings of 220 not out against Northants, for whom Milburn, another of the five serious candidates to open the England innings, made 61 in their first innings and, when they collapsed for 99 in the second, an even more impressive 63.

In the Test India won the toss and batted first on a Lord's wicket livelier in pace and bounce than that at Headingley: they were put out by Snow – who bowled better and faster than his three for 49 might argue – and Brown, for 152. Edrich, out for 12 and unlikely to have another innings in the match, must now contemplate the wide and varied competition for his place. Barrington batted competently until he was completely beaten by Chandrasekhar – an unlucky bowler – playing with the care of one only three short of his first century in a Lord's Test. Graveney batted stylishly but at an easy rate and England, three wickets down, were exactly a hundred in front when the rain came at three o'clock: strong advantage if the weather has affected the wicket, sound foundation for a large score if it has not.

## INDIA LOSE THE RUBBER AND PAKISTAN SHOW THEIR PACES
### JUNE 24–30

THE Indians did not repeat their recovery of Headingley, and, when they lost the Second Test by an innings and 124, they lost the rubber with it. Their ultimate collapse stemmed from their inability to play Illingworth's off-breaks on a wicket which proffered some turn for spin, but was never truly difficult. Kunderan played an innings of sensible resistance and only he played the off-break as English batsmen have learnt to do, in the shadow of the front pad.

The Pakistanis were bound to be compared with the
Indians, and, on the evidence of their opening
first-class match – against Essex – they bat more
responsibly and have bowlers of some pace as India
have not. In their opening burst, at the end of the first
day, Majid – son of Jahangir Khan of Cambridge
University and India – and Salim took the wickets of the
first three Essex batsmen at the expense of only five
wides. They did not continue so spectacularly: their
fielding was not above criticism and in the end they
were content with a draw.

In the Championship Barry Dudleston, a
twenty-one-year-old from Cheshire, who was tried for
Lancashire Second XI, scored a century in only his
third Championship match for Leicestershire who,
however, lost on the first innings to Somerset.

Matches now are being finished in fair June weather
but the atrocious May is reflected in the figures – only
Eric Russell and Dennis Amiss have so far scored a
thousand runs.

Don Kenyon, at his best only a little short of the
highest level as an opening batsman, has announced
that he will retire from first-class cricket at the end of
this season. It is not, presumably, purely coincidental
that Worcester have said they hope to take the Indian
wicket-keeper batsman, Engineer, on to their staff.

Don Kenyon at the end of
a distinguished career.

*A hope soon dashed by Lancashire who had more with
which to entice that sparkling wicket-keeper and
batsman.*

## SUNDAY HOURS ENCOURAGE
## DULL PLAY
### JULY 1–7

IT was sad that the first Sunday of county cricket at
Lord's should have come in a match – Middlesex v.
Hampshire – which proved desperately unsatisfactory.
In three days interrupted only by a stoppage of a quarter
hour for bad light, the two sides failed even to reach a
decision on the first innings.

A disappointing aspect of Sunday play, and one
which requires urgent attention, is that the spectators
are often being offered poorer entertainment than that of
other days. These Sunday attendances, including many
new, or reclaimed, spectators *must* be kept if county
cricket is to survive. They will not be kept, however, if
they see only slow batting. That, however, is likely, for
two reasons, the first is the new scoring system which
persuades many sides to play for the six points of first
innings lead only. The second is the fact that the 2 p.m.
to 7 p.m. "day," with half an hour for tea, gives only
four-and-a-half hours of play, a significant difference
from the normal six hours in several ways. The players
themselves seem to feel that it is not long enough for
them to change the balance of the match: and certainly
it is short enough for the fielding side to keep their
faster bowlers relatively fresh, so that there is little
chance of the fast scoring which might occur towards
the end of six hours when the main bowlers are – or, as
the batting side might say, *have been* – tired.

*This makes interesting reading at a time when the
TCCB are again thinking of Championship – as
opposed to limited-overs – cricket on Sundays. (The Palmer
report of 1986 suggested the reduction of the John Player
League and the introduction of some four-day
Championship games.)*

The Pakistanis played Middlesex on yet another
perfect – too perfect – slow wicket at Lord's. In the first
innings of the touring side, Latchman, the little
Jamaican leg-spinner, achieved the best figures of his
career, seven for 91. Then Eric Russell and Michael
Harris, with an opening partnership of 312, broke the
Middlesex record for the first wicket, of 310, set by Syd
Brown and Jack Robertson in the county's rich year of

1947. At the last the Pakistanis had no difficulty in drawing the match: Majid, scored his second century of the tour – he is full of runs and confidence – and Burki his first. The Pakistanis are, of course, automatically compared with Pataudi's Indians; and in batting they seem sounder in defensive technique. The Lord's pitch, however, provided a searching examination of their bowling. Certainly they have several bowlers faster than any in the Indian side but they are not truly fast and the gradations of fast medium are not significant at Test level. More important, their spin bowling, in the Middlesex match, included no one so dangerous as Chandrasekhar, so steady as Bedi or who spun as much as Prasanna. They may be grateful for the availability of the two leg-spinners, Mushtaq Mohammad of Northants and Intikhab Alam who is a club professional in Scotland, and Nasim, slow left-arm, for Tests.

Leicestershire had another turning wicket for their match with Yorkshire. They have made great improvements in playing strength, facilities for staff and spectators and in general atmosphere since they at length acquired the Grace Road ground last year. But these explosively dusty wickets will give rise to complaints from most of their opponents – certainly from those who lose. Yorkshire are always tough opponents on a bad wicket, masters of finger spin and, on the batting side, of playing it. Illingworth, as successful as any player in the country this season, took six for 52 and five for 27 and scored 60.

*I wonder if it was during this match that Leicestershire's shrewd manager, Mike Turner, began to see Ray Illingworth as the ideal successor to Tony Lock?*

Despite Lock's immense efforts – he caught four and bowled four of the first eight Yorkshire batsmen – Yorkshire won by an innings and are back in the lead in the Championship with Leicestershire second, then Kent, Sussex and Middlesex.

Bob Barber has told the selectors that he is unlikely to be available for the West Indies tour this winter. The selectors, for their part, have issued a writ for libel against Michael Parkinson who described them as "palsied twits". Never a dull moment.

## INDIANS WEAKENED BEYOND RECOVERY
### JULY 8–14

ANOTHER week of sun, interrupted only by late thunder. At the end of it, India, at Edgbaston, stand on the brink of their third Test defeat of the series: indeed, had Close enforced the follow-on today, they might well have been beaten by now. Their ill luck in the matter of injuries has been quite grotesque. Sardesai, the opening batsman, has returned to India with a broken finger and Surti – a casualty in the pre-Test nets – and Guha were unfit for this match while Prasanna has played with a fractured finger on the left hand. England batted no more than usefully on a wicket with some pace, life and turn. Despite a bright start by a – chastened? – Boycott, and Milburn, and a bustling 75 by Barrington, the middle batsmen were troubled by the Indian spin and at 191 for eight England were having the worst of the first day when Murray, with a healthily robust approach, and aided by Snow and Hobbs, carried them to 298. The Indian first innings reached nine for no wicket on the first evening. It was over by lunch on the second day. Brown and Snow made the first inroads: Hobbs and Illingworth completed the operation: only Engineer – 23 – scored more than twenty, though Hanumant Singh made some crisp strokes and Venkataraghavan enlivened the last few minutes. To the indignation of some, Close did not enforce the follow-on. His early batsmen batted semi-seriously and only the fifth wicket stand of 78

The Queen, guided by the Nawab of Pataudi, meets the injured Sardesai who nevertheless offers his heavily strapped hand.

between a somewhat subdued Amiss and Close himself hoisted the England total to 203. That, however, set India 410 to win, a total which must be far beyond their powers.

Hampshire and Northants took all but one hour and a half of their three day match to settle the issue of first-innings lead: Glamorgan and Notts spent 16½ hours over the same matter. John Edrich marked his replacement by Milburn with innings of 236 not out, 19, 90 and 62 in the week. Basharat Hassan, the 23-year-old Kenyan now with Notts, scored the fastest hundred thus far in the season: aided by some "gift" overs by Glamorgan's non-bowlers he made it in 98 minutes.

## SUPERB GILLETTE SEMI-FINAL AND 8 FOR 25 BY GREIG
### JULY 15–21

THIS week has seen English cricket at its peak and at the bottom of the pit. A superbly contested Gillette Cup semi-final between Kent and Sussex at Canterbury drew, and delighted, a crowd of over 16,000. But over the previous weekend, the Championship match between Kent and Hampshire at Southampton did not reach a decision on the first innings until ten minutes to six on the third day.

In the fine weather that has followed that ghastly May, more than half the first-class matches played have ended in draws. Billy Griffith, in an interview with J. L. Manning, described this cricket as "unintelligible." The short day on Sunday and the new first innings points allocation are ingredients of the situation. But, above all, it seems that the players cannot see the wood for the trees. In fact they are pricing themselves out of business.

Their situation might be more defensible but for the magnificence of the play at Canterbury on Wednesday. Kent batted first on a hard, true wicket and lost Denness at three – the kind of situation which so often produces stalemate in Championship matches. But Shepherd (77) met the crisis with gay attacking strokes; Luckhurst (78), acting as anchor-man, nevertheless scored steadily, and Cowdrey (78) batted with a felicity, ease and certainty such as even he has rarely shown before; indeed, no one on the ground could recall a

better innings from him. At one point he took 31 from three consecutive overs of John Snow and forced Parks to take him off. In face of a total of 293, Sussex batted with too great anxiety, one eye on the clock, another on their wickets; they matched the Kent scoring rate for a considerable period but no batsman played a major innings and, despite some characteristically busy runs from Suttle, shrewd aggression by Parks and some big hits by Greig, they were beaten by 118 runs. A day of 468 runs, fifteen wickets, some superb ground fielding and intelligent bowling was enough to please the most captious spectator.

In the other semi-final, a rainstorm at Old Trafford delayed the decision between Lancashire and Somerset until the second day. Somerset had made 100 for two before the downpour and that proved a winning advantage on the rain-affected wicket where Ken Palmer – declared Man of the Match – and Bill Alley – a master of this kind of play – bowled out Lancashire for 110. The coachload of Somerset supporters who set off for the match with forty gallons of cider had much to celebrate. A minor public triumph occurred on the first day when, after a shower, it was decided to restart play at three o'clock: but the slow hand-clap from a crowd of 15,000 brought the players out a quarter of an hour earlier.

Tony Greig of Sussex took eight for 25 against Gloucestershire, the best bowling performance of his career: he and Euros Lewis were given their county caps. Less happily, Surrey batsman Mick Willett has announced his retirement because of complications following his cartilage operation; a cheerful cricketer and a useful batsman who liked to get on with the game, he made the decision reluctantly and he will have the sympathy of everyone who understands how the best kind of cricketers feel about the game.

## BARRINGTON'S FIRST TEST CENTURY AT LORD'S
### JULY 22–28

THE Pakistanis have taken some credit, if not a strong position, in the Test. After only one win so far on tour, they brought in Ibadulla from Warwickshire, Mushtaq Mohammad from Northants and Intikhab Alam and Nasim-ul-Ghani who are both league professionals

County Championship (as at July 18)

| | | P | Pts |
|---|---|---|---|
| **1** | Yorkshire | 16 | 104 |
| **2** | Kent | 17 | 100 |
| **3** | Leicestershire | 18 | 96 |
| **4** | Sussex | 17 | 86 |

over here. But, apart from Mushtaq's three tail-end wickets, members of the touring party have so far been most successful. Salim and Asif, the opening bowlers, had a magnificent first spell and were extremely unfortunate to take only the wicket of Milburn. Russell, in place of Boycott who withdrew on the death of his father, played a pleasant innings and then Barrington – with his first Test century at Lord's – and Graveney put together a solid stand of 201, only for Salim and Asif to cut into the batting on the second morning so sharply that the last eight wickets went down for 86, 59 of which were scored by D'Oliveira. Then, however, Higgs, who took three wickets, and John Snow who bowled as fast and as well as he has ever done and took none, showed the early Pakistan batting to be both tentative and unenterprising. Still, however, Hanif remains not out, having made batting seem a simple, if contemplative, exercise. His is a team of much talent; he used eight bowlers; if Pakistan tradition is maintained the tail may be stronger than most.

Barrington, having made 155 against Yorkshire, bowled his leg-breaks valuably in their first innings – they are traditionally vulnerable to wrist spin – and Pocock bowled them out in the second. Barrington chugged on accumulating runs down the week and at its end entered the small group of men who have scored more than 6,000 runs in Test cricket: Hammond, Bradman, Hutton, Cowdrey and Harvey are the others.

Hanif Mohammad congratulates Ken Barrington on becoming only the sixth cricketer to reach 6000 runs in Test cricket.

## *RESISTANCE FROM PAKISTAN*
### *JULY 29–AUGUST 4*

THE most significant aspect of the week's cricket has been the tough resistance which gave Pakistan at one point a strong position, and, eventually, a comfortable draw, in the Lord's Test. The chief individual performance was Hanif's innings of 187, made slowly but never ponderously: with masterly assessment and economy of movement he concentrated upon occupation, leaving his partners to make the attacking strokes; and Asif did so pleasingly in their eighth wicket stand of 130.

In the Championship, Kent, in their one match of the week beat Sussex by an innings and 136: Underwood took 14 wickets for 82 – on, be it noted, a Sussex wicket – and became easily the first bowler of the season to a

hundred wickets. Leicester took a first innings lead from Warwickshire at the start of the week and, at the end, after being behind Derbyshire on the first innings, beat them by five wickets: Lock took ten for 79 in the match and it is reported that he has been asked whether he is available, if selected, for the West Indies tour.

## *GODFREY EVANS RETURNS AND A WET START FOR THE TEST*
### *AUGUST 5–11*

A week of important Championship matches, of six changes in the England team for the second match with Pakistan, a great hitting innings and a generally busy atmosphere ended in torrential storms and a disappointing beginning to the Test.

A sad note was struck at the start with news of the death of Peter Smith, of Essex, while he was on holiday in France; he was 58. A lively cricketer, he genuinely spun the leg-break and googly – even if his length was not always accurate – was a forthright batsman, who played four times for England, and an amusing, sociable companion. In 1947 at Chesterfield, because he had been ill, he went in last, but then proceeded to make a record score for a number 11 batsman – 163 – and to put on 218 for the last wicket with Frank Vigar against the conspicuously hostile Derbyshire bowling.

The selectors, as had been foreseen, punished Milburn by dropping him, did not forgive Murray's lapses nor Hobbs's lack of wickets, rested Snow – who is genuinely tired – and Illingworth and decided not to persevere with Russell. In their places they recalled

Three men of Kent put in some slip practice before the Oval Test. Left to right: Alan Knott, Derek Underwood and Colin Cowdrey.

Boycott, Cowdrey, whose class is such that it seems grotesque ever to leave him out, Underwood, top of the bowling averages and Titmus, and, for the first time, picked Knott of Kent and Arnold of Surrey.

This has been a bad Canterbury week for Kent – apart from the fact that some 39,500 people paid £6,082 for admission on the six days, a record for Canterbury and alone a sign of the health of cricket in a county which, even in its poorer years, has always been able to command generous support.

On the playing side, they had no doubt hoped to strengthen their attempt on the Championship in matches with their chief competitors, Leicestershire and Yorkshire. Leicestershire, however, grimly took first innings points (Lock six for 54) and refused to hazard them by a practicable declaration on the last day. In the match against Yorkshire – and there were some mutterings in Kent that Cowdrey, Knott and Underwood were summoned for the Test and Illingworth was not – Godfrey Evans returned, to take Knott's place. Luckhurst's hand was broken by a short ball from Trueman, but crucially, Kent dropped catches and, losing heart, collapsed in their second innings and were well beaten. A bare two points from the two matches cost them much of their hopes for the Championship.

At Swansea, Majid Jehangir made the fastest century of the season – in 61 minutes – against Glamorgan's regular bowlers: at one point he hit five 6s in a single over and, altogether, 13 in his innings, a record for English cricket not exceeded even by Jessop. John Savage, formerly of Leicestershire and now Lancashire, had the remarkable analysis of five wickets for one run against Hampshire who were bowled out for 39 and 148 and beaten by an innings. Tom Cartwright of Warwickshire had the best match figures of his life – 15 for 89 – against Glamorgan. A cloudburst which flooded the Worcester ground almost certainly cost Notts their first win of the season: Worcestershire with four second innings wickets left, still needed 11 runs to avoid an innings defeat.

The Test match, too, suffered from storms: Trent Bridge was spectacularly flooded on Thursday afternoon but the ground staff and the Fire Brigade pumped off 240 tons of water so that, surprisingly, play was resumed on Friday morning. Pakistan won the toss and went in on a perfect Trent Bridge wicket but they batted

Return of the old master – Godfrey Evans catches Illingworth off Dixon during his first county match for eight years.

indifferently. Higgs, Arnold and D'Oliveira bowled steadily in an atmosphere which encouraged swing, and they were put out for 140. Rain and bad light shortened the second day, when England made a slow way to 119 for four – Barrington 34 in 160 minutes.

## A GO-SLOW BARRINGTON AND TIME-WASTING BY YORKSHIRE
### AUGUST 12–18

THIS has been a thoroughly depressing week for cricket and cricketers. At the beginning the Test, its attendance severely affected by bad weather, went sadly slowly and, at the end, there was trouble at Edgbaston which seems to have been something more than a storm in a teacup.

In the Test Pakistan had batted first and made 140; England slid down to 92 for four and were lifted to 252 for eight largely by Barrington who scored 109 in almost seven hours; deadly slow going, though it is worth noting that his colleagues went no faster and scored less. It was not an entertaining innings to set before the Saturday crowd at Trent Bridge where the Notts club has not found life easy in the last few years, but, after Monday was rained off, it proved decisive. A letter defending – indeed, commending Barrington's innings and attacking his many critics – appeared in the press above the name of none less than Percy George Fender who in 1920, for Surrey against Northants, scored the fastest century recorded in first-class cricket – in 35 minutes.

*Typical of Fender to support the man under fire and to disagree with the conventional thinking.*

Rain had leaked, or seeped under the covers and, as the pitch dried, Underwood – five for 52 – systematically cut down Pakistan to 114 and a ten wickets defeat. Only two of their batsmen made more than six in the second innings: Intikhab Alam, with 16, and Saeed who made a fine 68, compounded of neat defence and fine, full, free attacking strokes. The outstanding English success of the match was Alan Knott, the Kent wicket-keeper. It is long since a cricketer of 21 stepped by unquestionable right into an England place, for he is not "number two" to any

County Championship
(as at August 15)

|   | | P | Pts |
|---|---|---|---|
| **1** Yorkshire | | 25 | 138 |
| **2** Kent | | 23 | 134 |
| **3** Leicestershire | | 24 | 134 |
| **4** Surrey | | 24 | 122 |

wicket-keeper in the country. It was not merely that he held seven catches and did not allow a bye in either innings, but his whole manner and style were so impressive and one attempt at stumping – one-handed from a ball going down on the leg side – was as adroit as anything ever done by a wicket-keeper.

The affair of Yorkshire allegedly wasting time in their match against Warwickshire at Edgbaston has no bright points. They were twice bowled out – by Cartwright, Brown and the left-arm, fast-medium Cook – for 238 and 145 so that Warwickshire needed 142 in 102 minutes to win. In that period Yorkshire bowled only 24 overs; rain fell during play and it was apparently necessary often to dry the ball, but the fact that only two overs were delivered in the last quarter hour seems to put Yorkshire in an indefensible position. At the start of that period Warwickshire needed 24 runs: they failed to win by nine. Fortunately Charles Elliott was one of the umpires and when his, his colleague Laurie Gray's, and the captains' reports reach Lord's, no doubt some firm judgment will be made. It is, though, unfortunate, that England's captain should be involved.

Lancashire, who beat Northants, are slowly growing up as a team. Shuttleworth has as good an action as any young pace bowler in the country; Wood is maturing steadily and determinedly; Atkinson is finding his feet and Pilling effectively won the match against Northants. Somewhat puzzlingly, however, they have decided not to re-engage David Green, a strong character-batsman who two years ago performed the unique feat of scoring over 2,000 runs in the season without a century.

## THE CLOSE AFFAIR — THE BUZZ OF TALK PERSISTS
### AUGUST 19–25

ALL this week the cricket "circus" – to use Brian Sellers's term – and the sporting press have been deeply immersed in the matter of Brian Close and the allegations of time-wasting in Yorkshire's match with Warwickshire. Close was summoned to a meeting of the Counties' Executive Committee at Lord's on Wednesday, where a unanimous decision was reached that "The Yorkshire team had used delaying tactics during the second Warwickshire innings, and that these tactics constituted unfair play and were against the best interest of the game. Furthermore the committee held the captain, Brian Close, entirely responsible for these tactics. They have therefore severely censured him and this decision will be conveyed to the Yorkshire County Cricket Club."

The announcement of the captain and team to tour the West Indies was deferred from Thursday until next Wednesday; and the Yorkshire Committee meets on Monday. Conjecture and argument on the subject have produced an almost unbroken buzz for days. On the face of it, MCC probably would find it difficult to administer such an unprecedented censure, *and* award the England captaincy on tour, to the same man in the same week. The question will soon be resolved.

Meanwhile, Close has captained England in the third Pakistan Test with no little acumen. Winning the toss he sent Pakistan to bat on an unusually hard, fast and green Oval wicket. First Higgs and then Arnold – five for 58 – dealt with the Pakistani batting, delayed only by Mushtaq who played a shrewd, skilful – and quite uncharacteristically dour – innings of 66. Boycott was unwell – pursued by the virus that has been worrying the Yorkshire side for the past week – and Close opened the England innings in his place with Cowdrey. Asif and Salim gave the early England batting a hard time of it, making the ball move off the seam and often bounce quickly. But again Barrington made a century – he has made a hundred in each Test of this series with Pakistan – and Graveney played with admirable style for 77 so that, by tonight, England, with 257 for three, are 41 ahead with seven first innings wickets in hand.

In one of the first matches to be played in the new Cricketer Cup, Eton Ramblers batsman Henry Blofeld turns a ball down the legside during his innings of 95 against Old Westminsters.

Last Sunday the selectors named the same twelve for the Oval as had been called to Trent Bridge. On the same day Repton Pilgrims, captained by Donald Carr, beat Radley Rangers – despite Dexter's 80 not out – to win the first final of The Cricketer Cup.

Much other news which would have attracted attention in an ordinary week was overshadowed by the Close affair. Mike Smith announced that he will retire from cricket to take up a business appointment at the end of the season: he had still much to offer to cricket. Dick Richardson, of Worcester, too, announced that this will be his last season: he is only 32 and, coinciding with the retirement of Don Kenyon, Jack Flavell and Jim Standen, this faces Worcestershire – who have again finished the summer strongly – with weighty problems.

At Eastbourne, against Sussex, Colin Milburn scored the fastest Championship century of the summer – in 78 minutes – and Northants won by ten wickets. The Counties' Adjudication Committee announced that it "was not satisfied with the basic action" of Malcolm Scott, the slow left-arm bowler of Northants, and barred him from bowling in county cricket for the remainder of the season. Scott, a pleasant person and keen cricketer, has said he will study the films of his action and work to correct it during the winter. Gloucestershire, whose batting has been barely held up by Arthur Milton, announce that they have recruited Sadiq – Hanif's youngest brother – the West Indian, Lloyd, and David Green, the Oxford University and Lancashire opening batsman: these are interesting cricketers who if they joined the county would do much to make good its main deficiency.

## CLOSE DEPOSED FOR WEST INDIES TOUR
### AUGUST 26–SEPTEMBER 1

THE dropping of Close from the England captaincy for the West Indies tour has dominated the week's thought and talk about cricket. The offence of time wasting according to the printed Match Regulations which are in effect part of the Laws was undoubtedly proved against Close and it seems likely that if he had admitted as much – which was the obvious thing to do – and offered an undertaking not to repeat it, the matter would have become a single, isolated, past incident. He, however, in his statements to the press has apparently taken the line that he does not recognise the regulation or its application to him: he owes no apologies, says that he was only doing his duty to Yorkshire, and that in similar circumstances he would do as much again. This is tantamount to denying the right of authority to define unfair play or to find him guilty of it. This was an impossible position for the MCC committee faced with a recommendation from the selectors that he should take the MCC team to the West Indies and it is hard to see that they could have done otherwise than reject the recommendation.

Before the news of his deposition – though after the deferment of the announcement of the team which gave a strong hint of what was to come – Close captained England to an eight wickets win against Pakistan. Barrington's third hundred of the series and a pleasing innings of 77 by Graveney, 65 by Titmus and 59, in his second Test, by Arnold, were followed up by Higgs on Saturday evening when he took three wickets in as many overs so that Pakistan began on Monday needing 198 to avoid an innings defeat, with six wickets left. On that morning, Higgs and Underwood reduced them still further to 65 for eight, at which point only three men had scored double figures. Then Asif with fine, bold, full-blooded strokes and Intikhab, playing like the competent, stable professional he is, set a new record for all Test cricket with a ninth wicket stand of 190. By now the wicket had lost its greenness and life of the first three days; Asif and Intikhab swept regally through the new ball taken by Higgs and Arnold and, so sound was their method and so assured their manner, that it seemed that they might bat on indefinitely until, a few moments before tea, Close put himself on, beat Asif through the air and had him stumped for 146, only the second century of his career.

They had ensured England had to bat again, only to make 34, but, before they got them, the elated Asif had taken the wickets of Close and Cowdrey, had Amiss dropped at slip and provided a dramatic and cheering flourish to the end of a rather one-sided series.

On Wednesday the MCC side for the West Indies was announced with Colin Cowdrey captain, F. J. Titmus vice captain, K. F. Barrington, G. Boycott, D. J. Brown, B. D'Oliveira, J. H. Edrich, T. W. Graveney, K. Higgs, R. N. S. Hobbs, I. J. Jones, A. Knott, C. Milburn, J. M. Parks, P. I. Pocock and J. A. Snow. There are few real surprises though Arnold, after five

| | | P | Pts |
|---|---|---|---|
| **1** | Kent }<br>Leicestershire } | 27 | 164 |
| **3** | Yorkshire | 26 | 162 |
| **4** | Surrey | 27 | 142 |

first innings wickets and a fifty in the Test, might feel himself unfortunate while Russell might have expected the place that went to Edrich, and Underwood that which was given to the promising Pat Pocock.

Rain ended the match between Sussex and the Rest of the World XI at Hove after 1,082 runs had been scored in less than three full days of play. Bland scored 132 not out, Kanhai 107 and Graeme Pollock 59 for the Rest, Dexter 71 and Suttle 79 for Sussex in a draw which, as intended, provided stimulating entertainment.

## CONSOLATION FOR KENT AT LORD'S
### SEPTEMBER 2–8

YORKSHIRE are County Champions – for the sixth time in the last nine years – and Kent, runners-up in the Championship, Gillette Cup winners.

*Yorkshire – County Champions, 1967. Back, left to right: P. Sharpe, G. Boycott, D. Wilson, P. Stringer, A. Nicholson, D. Padgett, J. Hampshire. Front: J. Binks, F. Trueman, B. Close (captain), R. Illingworth, K. Taylor.*

Gillette Final day has become a genuine cricket occasion, giving the end of the season a gay fillip, despite the onset of football. This year the building work at the Tavern-Clock Tower corner of Lord's restricted space but, on an all-ticket day, 18,500 spectators paid to come in and it was estimated that about 6,000 MCC members watched also. It was a pleasing day, partisan feeling tempered by good humour.

Kent won the day, in fact, before lunch. Nerves – few of the players except Cowdrey and Brown had ever before played in front of so large a crowd – probably were at the root of some loose bowling by Somerset at

the start. Denness – particularly – and Luckhurst made the most of it in a first wicket stand of 78 and Luckhurst, an industrious anchorman, continued with Shepherd to 138 before the second wicket fell. Though Somerset first tightened the game and then took six wickets for only 12 runs in early afternoon, the task ahead of them was made decisively difficult by the two young men, Knott and Ealham, who put on an extremely sensible 27 at the end.

Peter Robinson, moved up from number eight or nine to open the innings a fortnight before, after Clarkson's injury, played a firm, well-judged innings of 48 but Somerset conclusively lacked a major batsman in the middle of the order. Alley, who had bowled them back into the match by his admirable economy, never found his batting touch; and the promising stand between Barwell and Burgess ended when Barwell was unnecessarily run out. So, although the final difference was only 32 runs, Somerset were always one trick short of a winning position. Shepherd bowled gamely and thriftily despite a leg injury and Kent's outcricket was, as throughout the season, highly effective. Denness was made man of the match.

One day more of county cricket remained, the third of the match between Somerset and Lancashire at Taunton. It was a nostalgic time, as final matches always are and this saw a generous and deserved farewell from crowd and players to Colin Atkinson who is giving up the Somerset captaincy to become deputy head of Millfield School. He has been a diligent, sympathetic captain, combative while retaining his ideals.

*He is now head of Millfield, Chairman of Somerset, and still true to his ideals.*

## OVERSEAS PLAYERS ESSENTIAL
### SEPTEMBER 9–12

YORKSHIRE ended the season as they began it, by beating MCC, this time at Scarborough. Barrington finished top of the batting averages with 2,059 runs at 68.63, an average 14 higher than the next man, Amiss. Only Barrington, Milton and Edrich scored more than 2,000 runs; but, more surprisingly, only 18 bowlers took 100 wickets. Underwood was first in the bowling

*A victorious Colin Cowdrey with the Gillette Cup.*

table and Cartwright – 147 – took most wickets.

The most significant feature of the season has been the establishment of Sunday cricket, though in county matches the players did not always do enough in their four-and-a-half hours to please the crowds; sometimes the reverse. The Cavaliers' games were highly successful: their match with Middlesex drew the biggest crowd of the season at Lord's, apart from that for the Gillette Cup final – appreciably more than on any day of the two Test matches.

One of the main disappointments has been the new points-scoring system in the County Championship. By giving only eight points to a side coming from behind to win – while four go to the defeated team which led on the first innings – it virtually punishes recovery. The six points award for first innings lead, too, has led many teams into being satisfied with a draw at an all too early stage.

Many and important decisions must be taken by the counties' Advisory Committee this autumn. Among them must, surely, come a move to relax qualification conditions for overseas players to join English counties.

## County Championship Table

| | | | P | W | L | D | Tie | No 1st inns. dec. | No 1st inns. lead | Pts. |
|---|---|---|---|---|---|---|---|---|---|---|
| Points awarded | ... | ... | — | 8 | — | 2 | 4 | | 4 | — |
| Yorkshire (1) | ... | ... | 28 | 12 | 5 | 9 | 0 | 2 | 18 | 186 |
| Kent (4) | ... | ... | 28 | 11 | 3 | 12 | 0 | 2 | 16 | 176 |
| Leicestershire (8) | ... | ... | 28 | 10 | 3 | 12 | 0 | 3 | 18 | 176 |
| Surrey (7) | ... | ... | 28 | 8 | 4 | 12 | 0 | 4 | 15 | 148 |
| Worcestershire (2) | ... | ... | 28 | 6 | 6 | 16 | 0 | 0 | 13 | 132 |
| Derbyshire (9) | ... | ... | 28 | 5 | 5 | 17 | 0 | 1 | 14 | 130 |
| Middlesex (12) | ... | ... | 28 | 5 | 4 | 14 | 1 | 4 | 14 | 128 |
| Somerset (3) | ... | ... | 28 | 5 | 7 | 14 | 0 | 2 | 13 | 120 |
| Northamptonshire (5) | ... | ... | 28 | 7 | 8 | 11 | 0 | 2 | 10 | 118 |
| Warwickshire (6) | ... | ... | 28 | 5 | 4 | 15 | 0 | 4 | 11 | 118 |
| Lancashire (12) | ... | ... | 28 | 4 | 3 | 17 | 0 | 4 | 12 | 116 |
| Hampshire (11) | ... | ... | 28 | 5 | 6 | 13 | 1 | 3 | 10 | 114 |
| Sussex (10) | ... | ... | 28 | 5 | 9 | 12 | 0 | 2 | 10 | 104 |
| Glamorgan (14) | ... | ... | 28 | 4 | 7 | 15 | 0 | 2 | 9 | 100 |
| Essex (16) | ... | ... | 28 | 3 | 9 | 14 | 0 | 2 | 9 | 88 |
| Nottinghamshire (17) | ... | ... | 28 | 0 | 4 | 22 | 0 | 2 | 11 | 88 |
| Gloucestershire (15) | ... | ... | 28 | 3 | 11 | 9 | 0 | 5 | 11 | 86 |

If a man wants to be a professional cricketer he must play in England, whose season is isolated, overlapping no other, and running intensively enough to afford some fair living as overseas seasons do not. It is clear, too, that such great players as Sobers and Kanhai are wasted on Saturday appearances in local leagues. They could revitalise county cricket gates; and it is manifestly unfair to bar them from a Test series – as Gibbs may be from this winter's Tests in the West Indies – by the need to stay in a climate which chills their bones in order to qualify for a county. It should not be beyond the wit of the game's administrators to frame a series of controls which would prevent anything remotely like the soccer transfer system they fear.

*There had been cricketing controversies before the late 1960s but the "Close Affair" of 1967 and the "D'Oliveira Affair" which was to follow a year later marked the period when cricket became front-page news, too often for the wrong reasons. It has seldom been far from the forefront of the news ever since.*

*John Arlott's characteristically fair summary of the events reminds us of the extraordinary pride and obstinacy which cost Brian Close the immense honour of captaining England in the West Indies. Only, perhaps, a Yorkshireman could have dug in his toes to such an extent and only Yorkshire folk, I suspect, fully understood his refusal to apologise. To others, his reaction, although admirable in its total lack of expediency, was also unnecessarily stubborn: outside the broad acres there was general agreement that he had sinned against the spirit of cricket and that the best thing to do was to admit it and accept the legitimate prize for his successful summer as captain of victorious Yorkshire and England teams. No-one could guess then how soon and how far the fortunes of Yorkshire cricket were to fall.*

*In Close's absence, Colin Cowdrey enjoyed some of his happiest hours in the West Indies. E. M. Wellings, no respecter of any Establishment, wrote that "A team in the full sense of the word played good cricket in most testing circumstances. Neither on or off the field did they obviously put a foot wrong, despite unpleasant incidents, which might have provoked a group of players less well controlled."*

*That control was in the hands of Cowdrey and his manager, Les Ames. The provocations included poor umpiring and unruly crowds. Wellings said in Wisden that England had to play 30 per cent better than the opposition to win. Cowdrey himself, at last given the England captaincy for an entire campaign, engendered a fine team cohesion and increased the assertiveness of his own cricket, making 534 Test runs at an average of 66. Four of the Tests were drawn but England won the fourth at Port of Spain after a generous declaration by Gary Sobers, then held on for an exciting draw against a rampant Lance Gibbs on the sixth day of the final game at Georgetown.*

# ⊹ 1968 ⊹

### *ALRESFORD: APRIL 2*

IT is not merely the annual optimism of one who likes cricket and sees little wrong with it that makes me confident of a better summer's cricket in 1968 than in 1967, when that terrible May of rain, two one-sided Test series and some rather depressing Sunday play in the Championship tended to disenchant.

An Australian year always produces history; this time, too, Bill Lawry brings with him a side of many young players, virtually unknown in England, but of quite exciting possibilities. England will face them with the confidence of a side which has returned as winners of a series in the West Indies.

For once, however, an Australian team is not completely certain to overshadow the domestic season. Last year showed a group of counties to be of roughly equal quality on the heels of Yorkshire: Surrey, for instance, after an atrocious start, had a fine record through July and August: Kent came within a stride or two of winning and Leicestershire surprised, surely, even themselves and finished a strong third. Now, however, a dozen counties have availed themselves of the new regulations to engage overseas players who become instantly available for Championship play. It is important not only that these men, chosen in most cases to make good their sides' known weaknesses, are better than the players they will replace, but also that they are, almost without exception, entertaining cricketers, stroke-making batsmen, fast bowlers or wrist-spin bowlers: they must, therefore, add to the general gaiety of the domestic game.

We have, too, a new points-scoring system for the Championship – by my reckoning the twenty-ninth system since the competition began, but that could be a considerable under-estimate. It should provide interest and, once it has come under the forensic study of the county captains, it could produce some actions and yield some results – which the progenitors of the system never intended.

*The same was true, perhaps, of the influx of overseas players. Within a few years they were to be blamed for taking the prime places in county sides to the detriment of England's Test team.*

## AN EARLY CENTURY FOR KANHAI
### *APRIL 27–MAY 3*

THE start of the cricket season was, as usual, the signal for a spell of summer weather to dissolve into rain. Nevertheless there has been enough play this week to show striking evidence of the effect of two of the new pieces of legislation. Garfield Sobers, engaged on terms which for any other cricketer in the world might be regarded as extravagant, as captain, seam-bowler, finger-spinner, wrist-spinner, batsman and close fieldsman for Nottinghamshire, led his side into their first Gillette Cup tie of the season – against Lancashire.

Gary Sobers makes his debut for Nottinghamshire against Lancashire. Engineer is the batsman and Halfyard, Hill and Murray the attentive fielders.

He took three good wickets for 28 and, though five of his batsmen failed to reach double figures, he – straight from the sunshine and hard pitches of the Caribbean – batted through darkness and rain to make 75 out of a total of 169 for seven and win the match by three wickets. Notts must already feel that their money is well spent. The only question is whether any man can play to this standard for six days a week – sometimes seven for, on Sunday, he effectively won the Cavaliers' match against Cambridge University Past and Present.

Rohan Kanhai, specially registered for Warwickshire, scored a century against Cambridge

Rohan Kanhai – an early success for Warwickshire.

University. Few of the other new overseas players have yet had the chance to show their quality, but the point has been made.

In the first Championship match to be started this season – Sussex v. Hampshire at Hove – Hampshire bowled out Sussex for 140, well within the statutory 85 overs and, thus, took five bonus points (at a rate of one point per two wickets). Then, when they, in their turn, had reached 135 for nine, having nothing to gain from first innings lead and little hope of reaching 175 for a bonus batting point, Marshall declared – leaving Sussex at a disadvantage by one point. It was the first manipulation of the new points-scoring system. The match was drawn after some impressive and enterprising batting by several young men – Peter Graves and, in the end, Tony Greig of Sussex; Keith Wheatley, Richard Gilliat and the newly registered batsman from Natal, Barry Richards, for Hampshire.

The Australians have practised hard in the indoor nets at Lord's and Bill Lawry has made a very funny speech indeed at the Cricket Writers' Club dinner to the Australians. Tomorrow looks a busy day: the Australians will make an appearance at Arundel but they will not draw bat from bag with serious purpose until Wednesday at Worcester.

Barry Richards – a new acquisition for Hampshire.

## AUSTRALIANS WASHED OUT
### MAY 4–10

THIS week has borne an ominous resemblance to the beginning of last season. In almost incessant rain the traditional opening tour-fixture was completely washed out: so, for the first time in any Australian match against a county since their tours began, and for the first time in any of Worcestershire's matches with any touring side, not a ball was bowled. The Australians arrived here on April 26 and since then they have had three and a half days in the nets and half a day at Arundel on turf. So we still await our first sight of the promised batting delights of their young men.

In the second half of the week, no match was completed though, at Taunton, Somerset who declared their first innings with three wickets down and Yorkshire who declared at 0 for 0 achieved one bonus point – to Yorkshire – between them, though both sides, strictly speaking, "batted" twice. Speculation on the

possible forms of manipulation of the new points-scoring system is rife in the dressing-rooms: we may yet be amazed at the ideas which dawn upon the county captains.

Bill Lawry leads his Australians out for their traditional opening fixture at Arundel.

## HALFYARD'S DREAMS COME TO PASS
### MAY 11–17

THE main news in another miserably wet and cold week was made by David Halfyard, the former member of the Surrey staff, and Kent player. A leg injury sustained in 1962 put him out of cricket for the next season and, after a brave attempt to play again in two matches of 1964, he retired from active cricket and last year became a first-class umpire. But he could not accept the idea of giving up playing and, by diligent practice, he recaptured enough of his old ability with medium paced cut and swing to convince Notts that he was worth signing. Last Wednesday he took the wickets of Prideaux, Steele, Reynolds, Johnson and Durose – five for 38. He must be as happy as he was determined.

So far there have been twenty-five Championship fixtures and only five have reached a conclusion. More serious to all but the most partisan is the fact that the

Australians have had only 14 hours 50 minutes of play from a scheduled 54 hours in their first three matches. For their young men new to England this is extremely frustrating and the anxiety of some of the bowlers will be increased by having followed through so close to the line of wicket as to incur the disapproval of umpires. A few days of warm dry weather would solve many problems for them: nothing else can do so.

## MCC BATTING FAILS AT LORD'S
### MAY 18–24

THE match of the week, MCC v. Australians, lost its first day, all reasonable hope of a result and potentially one of the highest gates of the season, apart from Tests, to rain. When it began, in bitterly cold weather on Monday, Lawry batted with mature command: he was most severe on Underwood but none of the MCC bowlers gave him any apparent trouble until Jones bowled him off the inside edge. Cowper made a competent 53, partly practice and acclimatisation, but also an indication of his power. Sheahan batted with calm style and assurance: upstanding and correct, he hit the ball sweetly off the back foot. Chappell played a determined innings of late adjustment but Redpath was patently ill at ease. Inverarity never settled and Walters, whose anxiety is beginning to show through, scored only seven. Jones and Underwood took four wickets each without doing anything remarkable.

The Australians went on to Northampton where Milburn kept himself among the runners for a Test place with an innings of 90 with 15 fours but Prideaux, whose early season form had convinced some of his opponents that he was now ready for an England cap, made only 4 and 26.

Another of the new overseas players, Procter of Gloucestershire, is showing his value: he scored a century against Hampshire at Bristol and then bowled with immense stamina and at good pace.

Brian Close announced that Trueman would be left out of the Yorkshire team against Warwickshire on the grounds that he was not fully fit. Trueman now is 37: few men have bowled fast at that age; perhaps he has reached a stage at which he should take stock of his resources, ambitions and reasonable possiblities for the future.

Meanwhile, his Lancashire opponent and England partner, Brian Statham, who had said he would gradually drop out of first-class cricket, has changed his mind and will retire from the game after the August match with Yorkshire. Today he took six for 48 against Middlesex who saved the game when Hooker and Herman held out for the last wicket.

At the beginning of the week MCC announced that its government-by-invitation of English cricket would end with the first meeting, next October, of what, out of respect for tradition and the club's services to the game, will be called The MCC Council but which will be composed of a Test and First Class cricket committee, the National Cricket Association, representing all the non-first-class departments of the game and only a minority of MCC nominees.

## SELECTORS NAME FOURTEEN FOR OLD TRAFFORD
### MAY 25–31

THE selectors announced they had called these players to Old Trafford:
M. C. Cowdrey (Kent) captain, D. L. Amiss (Warwickshire), K. F. Barrington (Surrey), G. Boycott (Yorkshire), D. J. Brown (Warwickshire), T. W. Cartwright (Warwickshire), J. H. Edrich (Surrey), T. W. Graveney (Worcestershire), K. Higgs (Lancashire), A. P. E. Knott (Kent), B. L. D'Oliveira (Worcestershire), P. I. Pocock (Surrey), J. A. Snow (Sussex), D. L. Underwood (Kent).

The nomination of fourteen men thus far in advance

Colin Milburn bursting with aggression.

Mike Procter – good value for Gloucestershire.

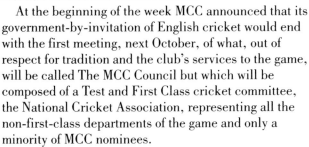

Brian Statham during his last season.

Words of advice from Bill Lawry for Ashley Mallett during practice at Lord's before the First Test.

is, within my memory, unique. The Chairman of Selectors, Douglas Insole, said it was made to cover every eventuality of fitness and weather, and that it will not be the practice throughout the series. The side was announced on Friday instead of Sunday, we are told, because this is a Bank Holiday weekend – which seems odd reasoning unless the selectors are all going away for a holiday. The players will meet at Manchester on Tuesday evening instead of Wednesday as they have done since Thursday starts began. A team conference, perhaps; the creation of an England cadre after the fashion of the England soccer team? Cowdrey has a strong belief in team atmosphere which certainly contributes to the morale of touring sides.

## WONDERFUL START FOR AUSSIES IN TEST
### JUNE 1–7

THE week began on a sad note for cricketers with the death of A. A. Thomson, which took place, poignantly enough, during the Yorkshire-Lancashire match, of which he lately wrote the history. "A. A. T." made his first reputation as a novelist of friendly and humorous touch whose theme often was of Yorkshire life. Then, in 1953, he published his first cricket book, *Cricket My Pleasure* (no title could have expressed his attitude more exactly) and he went on to write a dozen more books on the game, all of which reflected his delight in the game, in the character of its players, its tradition and anecdotes.

In the Old Trafford Test Australia hold the initiative. They won the toss and batted first on an easy wicket which the local experts think may eventually take spin. Lawry, in an innings of considerable technical, tactical and temperamental quality, steadied the side past the loss of Redpath and Cowper at 27. The young men, Sheahan, Walters and Chappell all came off: the first two made their highest scores of the tour and Chappell his highest but one, and at 319 for four they had scored at well over the usual Test match rate and stood only little short of a position of command. Today, in bleak windy weather, England held their own. Chappell was run out in a muddle with Sheahan and then Snow – who made the initial breakthrough – Higgs and D'Oliveira brought about complete collapse: the last six wickets

fell for only 38 more runs and England were batting by lunch time. In poor light and interrupted by rain, Boycott and Edrich went cautiously to 60 off 43 overs, bowled largely by McKenzie, Hawke and Connolly.

## D'OLIVEIRA CANNOT SAVE ENGLAND
### JUNE 8–14

IN the first week of true summer, Australia won the First Test, an advantage which England have never reversed to win in the matches between the two countries in England during this century. It was all well and efficiently, even gallantly, done. England's slow start on Friday became, in perspective, a mighty affair when, on a pitch never quite trustworthy after the first day, but never truly difficult, they were put out for 165.

Monday was the day of complete disaster: they had been behind but not without hope on Saturday night.

John Snow during his undefeated innings of 18 which saved England from the follow-on in the First Test. Barry Jarman is the wicket-keeper with Ian Chappell at slip.

County Championship (as at June 5)

| | P | Pts |
|---|---|---|
| **1** Yorkshire | 8 | 69 |
| **2** Kent | 7 | 51 |
| **3** Derbyshire | 7 | 41 |
| **4** Surrey | 5 | 39 |

That situation was reached on Monday when Cowper (37) batted usefully, Walters (86) suddenly emerged from his former anxiety to look, at last in England, a world-class batsman and Jarman hit sensibly in a total of 220. Pocock, on a pitch where the ball turned slowly, had six wickets for 79.

England were thus set 413 to win – more than has ever been made in the fourth innings to win a Test match – and had 550 minutes remaining for the operation. They – at least Boycott and Cowdrey – made such an aggressive start as to declare that they thought the task within their compass; but McKenzie, on a pitch by no means to his liking, took both those crucial wickets – Boycott's with a poor ball, Cowdrey's with a superb one – and England, 152 for five that night, were never again in the hunt. Some self-respect was regained next morning when Barber went on to 46 and D'Oliveira, even more impressively, to 87 not out, mostly in the boundary hits which punctuated placid defence.

## THUNDER FROM HEAVEN — AND FROM MILBURN
### JUNE 15–21

COLIN Milburn gave England's cricket a new, attractive face today, in the second day of the Second Test at Lord's – the two-hundredth match

### Second Test—Second Day

# MILBURN DEMOLISHES AUSTRALIAN ATTACK

---

## ENGLAND FAIL TO TAKE FULL ADVANTAGE

*England took their first innings score to 314 for five.*

### By E. W. SWANTON

LORD'S, Friday.

COLIN MILBURN this morning played, I think, the ¹ ˉ˙ innings for England in a Test at 's famous 70 aga˙

ˉˢ ᵃ⁷⁰

between England and Australia. On Thursday England, from their summoned thirteen players, left out D'Oliveira and Pocock (ironically, their most successful batsman and bowler at Old Trafford) and played Knight – replacing Cartwright, who has a damaged knee – Underwood, Milburn, Brown and Barrington. Then Cowdrey won the toss. England, of course, batted, on a wicket initially mild, and lost Edrich at ten, a few minutes before a thunder shower which stopped play. The rain so enlivened the pitch that Milburn – coming in somewhat surprisingly ahead of Cowdrey – and Boycott needed plenty of experience and courage to survive against the bowling of McKenzie, Hawke, Connolly and Walters to 53 for one and the first ball after lunch. Then a spectacular thunderstorm broke over the ground: it lasted only seven minutes and, at the end, Lord's looked like a winter snow scene. The hail thawed as fast as it had fallen and streams flowed across the pitch and down the historic slope to the Tavern – now replaced by the new and attractive Tavern stand. A second storm flooded the pitch before play was abandoned.

Today Milburn went on to play a heart-warming innings of simple power which argued convincingly that he should never again in his active cricket life be left out of an England team. He may not often be able to bat so magnificently: no one else now in sight could do so at all. He hit Cowper high into the grandstand for six and, sweeping Boycott – a most intelligent and reliable foil – along with him, he took the initiative from the Australian bowlers. There was no sign of his old, self-destroying taking of risks: he defended sensibly against the good ball. But once or twice in every over he found the ball to hit and he struck it cleanly and far. He and Boycott were past the hundred and moving at a run a minute when Lawry, as his last card, brought on Gleeson. He did not bowl a bad ball until he sent a long hop to Milburn who hooked it high to mid-wicket where it fell into the hands of Walters a bare couple of yards inside the boundary. Milburn had made 83: but his innings did not need the statistical distinction of three figures to be recognised as great. The cricket was never the same after he went. Boycott (49), Cowdrey (45) – both out to McKenzie – and Barrington (61, retired hurt) could not maintain the same dominance but they profited by it to lead England to the comparative

Boycott and Edrich open the England innings at Lord's.

prosperity of 314 for five by this evening.

In the county matches of the first half of the week, Lancashire, who beat Middlesex, and Gloucestershire, victorious by 112 runs over Warwickshire, both had their first Championship wins of the season; Notts (without Sobers, injured) beat Derbyshire, and Yorkshire, Hampshire and Kent also won.

In the second half, Yorkshire and Derbyshire both won in two days; Hampshire and Somerset in three. At Basingstoke, Hemmings, a nineteen-year-old medium-pace bowler playing his first match for Warwickshire, took the first six Hampshire wickets. Barry Richards, the South African who has taken Marshall's place as opening batsman for Hampshire, survived and scored the century which was the foundation of a win confirmed by Cottam (seven for 61 in the second innings).

## RAIN DEFEATS ENGLAND AT LORD'S
### JUNE 22–28

SATURDAY – and Lord's Test Saturday is for many the peak of the English season – was a misery of drizzle in which thirteen-and-a-half overs were bowled in three separate periods. Cowdrey declared before play on Monday and Brown, Snow and Knight harried the Australian batting with seam bowling of quite admirable length and line. Only two Australians, Walters – who played some fluent strokes – and Gleeson, who was bold, reached double figures. The English fielding was uniformly good, some superb catches were taken, and Australia, all out 76, followed on. Lawry and Redpath made a cautious 50 without losing a wicket on Monday evening and all seemed set for an immense tussle on Tuesday only for the rain to move in on the morning and prevent any play until only two hours 25 minutes remained. Redpath, Lawry and Cowper saw Australia to safety.

For some weeks now there have been rumours of dissension and impending trouble in the Yorkshire team. Close has been out of action with a persistent knee injury and Nicholson with a damaged hamstring. Trueman has captained the team with some success. The official attitude is, apparently, that there is no trouble except that invented or exaggerated by the Press

from casual remarks or jokes. If success counts, as it usually does in sport, there should be no major rifts in a team which has won the Championship in the past two seasons and leads the present table.

It would not be strange, however, if the Yorkshire committee decided that their team, though efficient, is ageing to a point where young men, natural replacements for established players, are being asked to wait too long for their caps. Yorkshire have at the moment twelve capped players – who have been capped, on average, for ten years. Meanwhile Balderstone, Old, Stringer, Cope and Leadbeater have been blooded and are stamping out time in the Second XI or the clubs. It would be surprising if there were wholesale sackings but it is likely that the Yorkshire committee would be relieved if some of the older players saw fit to move on to another county or to League cricket for longer careers.

## YORKSHIRE HUMBLE THE AUSTRALIANS
### JUNE 29–JULY 5

THE outstanding event in a week of humid heat and thunder was Yorkshire's win over the Australians by

### YORKSHIRE

| | | |
|---|---|---|
| G. Boycott, c Taber, b Chappell | | 86 |
| P. J. Sharpe, c Lawry, b Gleeson | | 47 |
| D. E. V. Padgett, st Taber, b Gleeson | | 56 |
| J. H. Hampshire, c Lawry, b Gleeson | | 33 |
| K. Taylor, c Taber, b McKenzie | | 24 |
| R. Illingworth, not out | | 69 |
| †J. G. Binks, c Taber, b McKenzie | | 0 |
| R. A. Hutton, c Walters, b McKenzie | | 2 |
| *F. S. Trueman, c Sheahan, b Gleeson | | 13 |
| D. Wilson, c Redpath, b McKenzie | | 0 |
| P. Stringer, not out | | 12 |
| Extras (lb 6, w 1, nb 6) | | 13 |
| | | |
| Total (9 wkts. dec.) | | 355 |

BOWLING: McKenzie 27—7—73—4; Renneberg 19—2—58—0; Connolly 32—16—49—0; Gleeson 47—12—123—4; Chappell 6—0—33—1; Walters 7—5—6—0.

### AUSTRALIANS

| | First Innings | | Second Innings | |
|---|---|---|---|---|
| *W. M. Lawry, c Trueman, b Illingworth | 58 | b Hutton | | 0 |
| I. R. Redpath, c Binks, b Trueman | 12 | lbw, b Hutton | | 12 |
| K. D. Walters, c Trueman, b Hutton | 4 | c Illingworth, b Trueman | | 62 |
| A. P. Sheahan, c Trueman, b Hutton | 10 | b Trueman | | 17 |
| I. M. Chappell, run out | 18 | c Hutton, b Illingworth | | 26 |
| R. J. Inverarity, c Stringer, b Illingworth | 2 | lbw, b Illingworth | | 1 |
| †H. B. Taber, b Illingworth | 9 | st Binks, b Illingworth | | 0 |
| G. D. McKenzie, c Hutton, b Illingworth | 6 | c Binks, b Trueman | | 0 |
| J. W. Gleeson, b Trueman | 4 | b Illingworth | | 12 |
| A. N. Connolly, b Trueman | 20 | run out | | 0 |
| D. A. Renneberg, not out | 0 | not out | | 4 |
| Extras (b 2, w 1, nb 2) | 5 | Extras (lb 2, w 1, nb 1) | | 4 |
| | | | | |
| Total | 148 | Total | | 138 |

BOWLING: Trueman 10.2—22—3—3; Hutton 12—3—37—2; Stringer 4—2—6—0; Illingworth 17—3—44—4; Wilson 9—1—20—0; Taylor 1—0—4—0. *Second Innings:* Trueman 19—4—51—3; Hutton 12—5—35—2; Illingworth 22—12—23—4; Wilson 13.1—7—25—0; Boycott 1—1—0—0.

County Championship
(as at July 3)

| | P | Pts |
|---|---|---|
| **1** Yorkshire | 13 | 123 |
| **2** Derbyshire | 14 | 106 |
| **3** Kent | 13 | 101 |
| **4** Hampshire | 14 | 101 |

an innings and 69 runs, an unheard of performance which left all Yorkshire – and Yorkshiremen all over the world – in a state of euphoric self-satisfaction intolerable to followers of other counties. It was well done. In the absence of Close, in a debilitating atmosphere of steam heat, smoke and mist, and on a wicket which was never fast or difficult, Trueman captained Yorkshire to a highly professional team victory. A steady opening stand by Boycott and Sharpe, good support from Padgett, Hampshire and Illingworth took Yorkshire to 355 for nine. Then in each Australian innings, Richard Hutton and Trueman made the early breaks and Illingworth, baffling the younger Australian batsmen by his variations on the dual themes of off-spin and slow out-float, worked down the batting.

At half past three on Tuesday they completed the operation and the crowd, compensating for its meagre numbers by its enthusiasm, swept to the pavilion and then, typically Yorkshire, made a ritual pilgrimage to stare at the wicket before going home deep in happiness and reminiscence.

Over the same weekend, Derbyshire – unspectacularly one of the two most improved county sides of the season – Middlesex, Kent and Hampshire all won their Championship matches. In the Gillette Cup quarter-finals on Wednesday, Gloucestershire, Middlesex, Warwickshire and Sussex – the last two for the fourth time – came through to the semi-finals.

Yorkshire (13 matches, 123 points), Derbyshire (14 matches, 106 points), Kent (13 matches, 101 points), Hampshire (14 matches, 101 points) and Notts (13 matches, 94 points) lead the County Championship.

## ENGLAND START SOUNDLY AT EDGBASTON
### JULY 6–12

D AMN the weather. Storms of amazing violence for any time of any year took the first day of the Third Test and virtually ruined the second half of the week in the Championship. So today England and Australia began in effect a four day Test match and England at once met the increased urgency by leaving out Keith Fletcher and playing five main bowlers of a variety planned to meet any turn of wicket or weather – Brown, Snow, Knight, Illingworth and Underwood. England's

short batting demanded a safe start and Boycott and Edrich carefully provided it – 80 by a quarter to three when Boycott was out. Edrich went grimly on to 88 but Cowdrey, taking risks, giving a couple of half-chances and playing some memorable strokes increased the scoring rate. He pulled a muscle in taking a quick single and had to have a runner but with Graveney, who was in much greater confidence than previously in the series, he lifted England to 258 for three.

In the first half of the week the University match started brightly when Goldstein – since appointed captain of Oxford for a second year in 1969 and undoubtedly the best player at either University – scored a belligerently fast 158. Knight (69), Cosh (59)

The Cambridge team at Lord's.
Back, left to right: C.E.M. Ponniah, J.F. Fitzgerald, E.D.C. Haywood, R.D.V. Knight, A.M. Jorden, P.G. Carling. Front: D.L. Hays, D.L. Acfield, G.A. Cottrell, D.W. Norris, N.J. Cosh.

and Haywood (62) saved Cambridge from following on and Cosh and Jorden played them to safety in the second innings, and made a draw.

The MCC committee issued a statement concerning the bowling action of G. A. Cope, the 21-year-old Yorkshire off-spinner. In their opinion his delivery shows a slight straightening of the bowling arm immediately before delivery; but they feel it can be easily corrected.

*After many further high and low points, Cope's errant elbow was eventually to curtail his career, though he still plays Minor County cricket.*

## THE WOEFUL WEATHER WINS AGAIN
### JULY 13–19

I T may be monotonous to read during the coming winter, but not so infuriatingly monotonous as it is to go on writing week after week, that the weather has ruined cricket. The fact is that, having taken the entire first day of the Third Test match last week it has washed away most of the fifth day this week, and everyone feels thwarted – except, perhaps, the Australians, who make semi-shamefaced jokes about it.

On Saturday, Cowdrey duly came to his century, remarkably appropriate in his hundredth Test match: Graveney just missed his and, if the late batting – except a last wicket partnership by Snow and Underwood – seemed to lack purpose, 409 was a healthily safe total. Lawry was hit on the hand in the first over of the Australian innings and went off with what proved to be a fissure fracture of the little finger and took no further part in the match. Australia came to 109 for one on Saturday evening and went on into Monday morning. Cowper was out at 121, Chappell at 171 and then, as Underwood and Illingworth found some turn in the pitch, Sheahan went at 176. Walters and Taber batted steadily enough, past the possibility of Australia following on, and into the afternoon when, in an amazing collapse, five wickets went down to the spinners for nine runs in half an hour and Australia, all out for 222, were 187 behind on the first innings. England, in high spirits, batted again and looked for quick runs. McKenzie, acting as Australia's captain in place of Lawry, bowled a huge spell to contain them but Boycott, Edrich and Graveney contrived to build up to 142 for three before Graveney, deputising for Cowdrey, declared to set Australia 330 to win with twelve minutes batting on Monday night and all day Tuesday beyond: it was an immensely confident declaration. Cowper and Redpath began the innings and on Tuesday morning, with the score at 44, Redpath was once more lbw to Snow. Chappell again came in early and he and Cowper batted assuredly, scoring at a good rate against the faster bowlers. But they had fallen on to the defensive against the spin bowlers – and Cowper had not scored for half an hour – when, at half past twelve rain which had long been in the air grew heavier, the players came off the field and never went back. So in a second Test, rain prevented a finish.

Jim Parks has given up the captaincy of Sussex which he says has affected his cricket and his health. Any wicket-keeper-batsman-captain is subject to complicated cross-tugs of stress; and in addition Parks

Mike Griffith, the new Sussex captain.

has defended and lost an England place, and has been completely out of form as a batsman. Mike Griffith has been appointed to replace Parks for the remainder of the season, after which he and the Sussex committee can review the situation.

The English selectors at their meeting this weekend, to pick the team for next Thursday's Test at Headingley, face an unprecedented string of problems. Jones and Cartwright have never been available; Milburn's injury will keep him out of cricket for at least another ten days; Boycott is unavailable; Cowdrey, whose hamstring injury became serious at Edgbaston, must be unlikely to play; and now it is said that Graveney's fitness is doubtful. So Dexter, who has played only one first-class

Colin Cowdrey confined to a chair in the dressing-room during the Edgbaston Test.

match since 1966, has been asked if he is available for the Test, has said he is, and will play for Sussex against Kent at Hastings tomorrow – not the opposition or the pitch that a man would choose for his return to competitive three-day cricket after two years. It is much for the selectors to ask of Dexter or for him to ask of himself. To come from Sunday afternoon play by way of one county match to a five-day Test against Australia which England must win to have a chance of taking the Ashes is a story-book situation. In some ways Dexter is a story-book character, but this, surely is beyond even him.

## DEXTER RETURNS IN THE GRAND MANNER
### JULY 20–26

TWO items of news struggle for first mention: the entire week has been one of fine weather – surely the first such in this benighted season – and Dexter did it. The weather passed almost without comment but Dexter was the talk of the country when, in his first competitive match at first-class level since 1966, he made 203 not out, the highest score of his career, against Kent. Moreover he came in with the score at six for two, lived on past 27 for four and made his runs without a mistake.

🏃 *Storybook stuff, indeed. Derek Underwood had seldom been treated with such disrespect. It was, in fact, Dexter's highest score for Sussex – he had made 205 for England against Pakistan.*

Of course the performance put him into the team for the Fourth Test: he was the one man who could not be left out. The selectors nominated thirteen players. Boycott, Milburn, Cartwright and Jones were ruled out of selection. Prideaux and Fletcher, neither of whom had ever played for England, were named; and, when Graveney became doubtful because of a cut hand, the match between Essex and Yorkshire was stopped by public address system a moment before the first ball would have been bowled and Sharpe, who would have received it, was pulled out of the match and sent to Headingley as a standby. In the event he was not needed. Cowdrey was not fit, Graveney was, and took on the captaincy; Prideaux and Fletcher both came in and Knight – the third major seam bowler – was left out. Lawry could not play for Australia; Jarman, recovered from his injury, became captain and Inverarity played as opening batsman with Cowper, Redpath dropping to number three in the batting.

Jarman won the toss and Australia batted on an easy wicket which had been completely under water a week before and could, the experts asserted, never be fast, though it might have a little turn for the spinners. Apart from Cowper who, charged with Lawry's responsibility as anchor-man, scored five in the two hours to lunch, and Chappell, not one of the Australians looked secure. Redpath, previously over-defensive and almost strokeless in Tests, obviously had been told to pursue the stroke-making method he has found so profitable in county matches; and he made 92 in a quite staggering mixture of bold, handsome strokes and complete misses.

Today Australia went on to 315, largely through

Keith Fletcher – Test debut at Headingley.

Chappell's game and watchful 65, made determinedly in 220 minutes with only two fours. Underwood mopped up the innings and finished with four for 41; Snow who bowled as well as at any time in the series, three for 98.

Edrich and Prideaux began the English innings with the highest opening partnership for either side this summer. They made four off the single over before lunch; reached 82 by tea and then afterwards, for three-quarters of an hour, they controlled the game. Edrich remained grimly competent, playing within his self-recognised limits, disposing efficiently of the bad ball. Meanwhile Prideaux, remarkably for a man in his first Test, set out to take command of the game. His 64 was even more impressive for its manner than its extent and he must surely be on the boat for South Africa. No sooner was he gone than Edrich reached for a short ball from McKenzie and was taken at the wicket. McKenzie, as if roused by the sight of Dexter, suddenly found new pace and though Dexter played carefully and correctly, eventually a short ball proved fast enough to take the inside edge and run into the stumps. Three wickets had gone down for 18 runs and Graveney and Barrington were quite content to steady the innings and leave its rebuilding until tomorrow.

## AUSTRALIAN STEM THE RUNS AND HOLD THE ASHES
### JULY 27–AUGUST 2

AUSTRALIA drew the Fourth Test match and retained The Ashes: that comprises the outstanding historic event of another rain-bedevilled season, but the rain had nothing to do with this particular result. Australia deserved to achieve this negative triumph – by avoiding defeat – because their batsmen fought out the decisive third innings of the match resolutely and capably. On the other side England missed chances – their number put varyingly between eight and twelve; if even three simple ones had been held they would have been left with 80 fewer runs to make and two hours more to make them than the eventual 326 in 295 minutes. The English first innings lost its momentum of Friday, and Saturday, for all Graveney's efforts, was desperately slow going until Underwood and Brown mocked the earlier care with a stand of 61 in 51 minutes. Fifty minutes were lost on Monday to rain and bad light but, crucially, Australia carried their score from the 92 for two wickets of Saturday to 283 for six, gradually squeezing out England's remaining hopes. Again on the last morning McKenzie was dropped and more of England's scanty time was lost. Edrich, Dexter, Graveney and Barrington all did their skilful utmost to force the pace but they were kept in check by Connolly – who bowled from a quarter to one until five past five in a spell of 31 overs – and McKenzie.

## GLAMORGAN'S WEEKEND OF GLORY
### AUGUST 3–9

IN a weekend of blazing sunshine in Wales – though not in southern England – Glamorgan beat the Australians. It was a national affair: as one Glamorgan player put it – "We have won the fifth Test: now can England win the sixth?" Glamorgan now are in a winning mood: it was impressive too, that of the five outstanding individual performances, four – excluding Alan Jones's well-made 99 – were by uncapped players, Bryan Davis and Majid Jahangir as batsmen, Malcolm Nash and Brian Lewis as bowlers.

The Yorkshire-Lancashire match, Ken Higgs's benefit and Brian Statham's last appearance, with Yorkshire leading the table and Lancashire's young players showing fight and fire, drew nostalgically large crowds. Statham took six for 34 in the first Yorkshire innings. It was a fine curtain; there have been few better fast bowlers and no nicer person in the game. Yorkshire in the end were content to draw. Meanwhile Kent were beaten by Notts – Sobers seven for 69 and four for 87, 17 and 105 not out – so Yorkshire's lead was not affected.

There were no Championship matches in the second part of the week, which had been allocated to the Gillette Cup semi-finals: but, because of the unending rain, not a ball could be bowled in the Middlesex-Warwickshire tie and that between Sussex and Gloucestershire took three days to decide. Sussex, batting on Wednesday, lost three wickets for 34 before Dexter played a controlled and imposing innings and Greig joined him in an attractive stand of 84. Parks and Cooper added crucial runs for the seventh wicket on Friday and the Gloucestershire batting simply never

found momentum. Sussex are highly experienced in this kind of play, and now go to the final for the third time in six years.

## PARFITT GETS CAPTAINCY OF MIDDLESEX
### AUGUST 10–16

IN the weekend matches all but three reached a conclusion but in the second half only one – in which Yorkshire beat Somerset by an innings and 29 runs – was finished. Even Lancashire – where, unusually if not freakishly, there had been sunshine while the rest of the country was water-logged – now suffered its share of the worst summer any cricketer can remember: in any case, few of them *want* to remember it.

After Middlesex had lost to Yorkshire on Monday it was announced that Fred Titmus had given up the captaincy of Middlesex and had been succeeded by Peter Parfitt.

On Tuesday it was possible to play the deferred Gillette Cup semi-final between Warwickshire who won by three wickets, and Middlesex. So Warwickshire, like their opponents, Sussex, go to the final for the third time.

Colin Cowdrey was offered and was "delighted and honoured to accept" the captaincy of MCC in South Africa a few hours after he had scored a smooth and often handsome century against Surrey in his first innings since he damaged his leg in the Third Test. South Africa were, he thought, the toughest problem for England at the present time but he believed that, with all players fit, England could beat them.

## EDRICH GIVES ENGLAND A SOLID START
### AUGUST 17–23

A week that began with most of the Saturday fixtures washed out, ended with England building a huge total in almost tropical heat in the Fifth Test at The Oval. It has been announced from Lord's that the new Sunday league has found a sponsor; that the International Cavaliers' matches are to be excluded from television. At Bradford a letter from Ray Illingworth was made public: he has asked Yorkshire for his release so that he may obtain elsewhere the security of a long contract which his county will not give him.

England, with Boycott, Jones, Cartwright and Prideaux unfit, brought in D'Oliveira – dropped since the First Test – and Milburn and retained Dexter. Cowper's fractured thumb kept him out of the Australian team but Lawry came back and the young off-spinner, Mallett, came in for his first Test, Cowdrey won the toss and England batted on a slow, true wicket. The more exciting early batsmen – Milburn, Dexter and Cowdrey – were out for 45 between them; but John Edrich, the artisan, stayed and with first Graveney (66) and then D'Oliveira, built up an innings of 164 which carries him to within 25 of Compton's record 562 for an English batsman in an Australian series at home. Today D'Oliveira made a realistic 158.

The decisions, first not to include the Cavaliers in the Sunday league and then to rule that their matches cannot be televised will be seen by many of the public as an unnecessary deprivation and by others as an extremely harsh rebuff to Rothmans who subsidised the team and who have been the most generous sponsors English cricket has ever had.

It is assumed that Yorkshire will adopt their usual attitude of not attempting to keep a discontented player and that Illingworth, now at the height of his maturity as an off-break bowler, will join another county. Notts would find him immensely useful: so would Northants or Somerset.

*Illingworth may already have known his destination, but, if so, it was a well-kept secret. His decision to leave Yorkshire was to transform his career.*

## ENGLAND'S DRAMATIC VICTORY . . . AND THE AFTERMATH
### AUGUST 24–30

AFTER England's massive 494 in the first innings of the Test, Lawry batted all day on Saturday for 135 not out with little assistance from anyone except Redpath, the only other Australian batsman to make more than 14 in their score of 264 for 7. Snow, Brown and Illingworth shared the wickets and the England fielding was happier than on some other days. Monday saw the match begin to burn. Lawry was out early and Australia still needed 26 to avoid the possibility of following on. But, though Cowdrey exerted maximum pressure, Mallett batted so soundly and correctly, and had such faithful support from Gleeson and Connolly that the last two wickets endured until after lunch and took the total to 324. England had little time to spare and set out for quick runs; but Connolly and Mallett, bowling to restrictive fields most magnificently manned, kept them to a run a minute and bowled them out for 181. So Australia needed 352 to win and had a maximum of six hours thirty-five minutes in which to make them.

Tuesday proved a day of excitement, seeming frustration and eventual high drama. Mounting an uncompromising attack, ridding themselves of Chappell early in the morning and chipping out Walters and Sheahan, by a moment or two before lunch, England were moving in on the Australian tail with only Inverarity of the recognised batsmen remaining and the score 86 for five, when a huge thunderstorm broke over The Oval.

Within an hour there were pools all over the ground and although the run-ups were covered, the wicket was soaked. The ground staff were assisted by an amazing number of volunteers – at least 50 of them – from the crowd and their efforts were so successful that it proved possible to restart play at a quarter to five – with an hour and a quarter left. Cowdrey set such fields as surely have never been seen in first-class cricket before: for Underwood he had ten men within four or five yards of the bat; for Illingworth, nine. No two consecutive overs of the first five from the pavilion end were bowled by the same man but the pitch was placid and slow: the ball came easily on to the bat and Inverarity and Jarman had survived with little trouble for 40 of the 75 minutes minutes when Jarman left alone a ball from D'Oliveira which flicked out the off bail. At once Cowdrey whisked away D'Oliveira and brought back Underwood. Perhaps the ball from which Mallett was caught at short leg stopped and stood up but nothing else happened which should have beaten a correct defensive stroke. Underwood, however, plugged on with Illingworth at the other end. McKenzie's forward defensive push was an inch or two off the ground and Brown, at silly mid-on, scooped it up.

County Championship
(as at August 27)

| | P | Pts |
|---|---|---|
| **1** Yorkshire | 27 | 255 |
| **2** Glamorgan | 25 | 224 |
| **3** Kent | 25 | 213 |
| **4** Nottinghamshire | 26 | 201 |

Underwood claims his fifth wicket and Australia are on the brink of defeat with the England side crowded around the bat. Left to right: Illingworth, Graveney, Edrich, Dexter, Cowdrey, Knott, Brown, Snow, Milburn and D'Oliveira. McKenzie is the victim and Inverarity the non-striker.

Gleeson stayed a quarter of an hour with Inverarity before he was bowled by a ball from Underwood to which he offered no stroke. Ten minutes left and Connolly pushed and ran dutifully. Five minutes left and Underwood barely straightened the ball, Inverarity, who had promised and deserved to carry his bat, was lbw, and England had won the Fifth Test by 226 runs. So the rubber was tied and some of the disappointments of Lord's and Edgbaston made good.

## ENGLAND

| First Innings | | Second Innings | |
|---|---|---|---|
| J. H. Edrich, b Chappell | 164 | c Lawry, b Mallett | 17 |
| C. Milburn, b Connolly | 8 | c Lawry, b Connolly | 18 |
| E. R. Dexter, b Gleeson | 21 | b Connolly | 28 |
| *M. C. Cowdrey, lbw, b Mallett | 16 | b Mallett | 35 |
| T. W. Graveney, c Redpath, b McKenzie | 63 | run out | 12 |
| B. L. D'Oliveira, c. Inverarity, b Mallett | 158 | c Gleeson, b Connolly | 9 |
| †A. P. E. Knott, c Jarman, b Mallett | 28 | run out | 34 |
| R. Illingworth, lbw, b Connolly | 8 | b Gleeson | 10 |
| J. A. Snow, run out | 4 | c Sheahan, b Gleeson | 13 |
| D. L. Underwood, not out | 9 | not out | 1 |
| D. J. Brown, c Sheahan, b Gleeson | 2 | b Connolly | 1 |
| Extras (b 1, lb 11, w 1) | 13 | Extras (lb 3) | 3 |
| Total | 494 | Total | 181 |

BOWLING: McKenzie 40—8—87—1; Connolly 57—12—127—2; Walters 6—2—17—0; Gleeson 41.2—8—109—2; Mallett 36—11—87—3; Chappell 21—5—54—1. *Second Innings* McKenzie 4—0—14—0; Connolly 22.4—2—65—4; Mallett 25—4—77—2; Gleeson 7—2—22—2.

## AUSTRALIA

| First Innings | | Second Innings | |
|---|---|---|---|
| *W. M. Lawry, c Knott, b Snow | 133 | c Milburn, b Brown | 4 |
| R. J. Inverarity, c Milburn, b Snow | 1 | lbw, b Underwood | 56 |
| I. R. Redpath, c Cowdrey, b Snow | 67 | lbw, b Underwood | 8 |
| I. M. Chappell, c Knott, b Brown | 10 | lbw, b Underwood | 2 |
| K. D. Walters, c Knott, b Brown | 5 | c Knott, b Underwood | 1 |
| A. P. Sheahan, b Illingworth | 14 | c Snow, b Illingworth | 24 |
| †B. N. Jarman, st Knott, b Illingworth | 0 | b D'Oliveira | 21 |
| G. D. McKenzie, b Brown | 12 | c Brown, b Underwood | 0 |
| A. A. Mallett, not out | 43 | c Brown, b Underwood | 0 |
| J. W. Gleeson, c Dexter, b Underwood | 19 | b Underwood | 5 |
| A. N. Connolly, b Underwood | 3 | not out | 0 |
| Extras (b 4, lb 7, nb 4) | 15 | Extras (lb 4) | 4 |
| Total | 324 | Total | 125 |

BOWLING: Snow 35—12—67—3; Brown 22—5—63—3; Illingworth 48—15—87—2; Underwood 54.3—21—89—2; D'Oliveira 4—2—3—0. *Second Innings:* Snow 11—5—22—0; Brown 8—3—19—1; Underwood 31.3—19—50—7; Illingworth 28—18—29—1; D'Oliveira 5—4—1—1.

*Yes, this was one series in which the better side did not win. England certainly had more than a fair share of bad luck.*

On the day after the Test ended, MCC announced the team to tour South Africa, the choice of the selectors, endorsed by the club's Committee. It consisted of 15 names: M. C. Cowdrey (Kent) captain, T. W. Graveney (Worcestershire) vice-captain, K. F. Barrington (Surrey), G. Boycott (Yorkshire), D. J. Brown (Warwickshire), T. W. Cartwright (Warwickshire), R. M. H. Cottam (Hampshire), J. H. Edrich (Surrey), K. W. R. Fletcher (Essex), A. P. E. Knott (Kent), J. T. Murray (Middlesex), P. I. Pocock (Surrey), R. M. Prideaux (Northants), J. A. Snow (Sussex), D. L. Underwood (Kent): the sixteenth player will be I. J. Jones of Glamorgan if he proves to be fully fit after an elbow injury.

The omission of D'Oliveira aroused violent controversy. Mr. S. C. Griffith, Secretary of MCC, announced that there had been no question of political pressure or even of consultation with the South African Cricket Association. The selection had been made solely on cricketing grounds. There is no reason to doubt his word: the selectors are honourable men. Their naïveté, however, is staggering. What was the rest of the world to think when a man who on Tuesday, as one of England's best eleven, scored 158 and took the crucial wicket in the only Test of the series which England won, was not included in their best sixteen a day later? It is difficult to think of any step ever taken by the cricket "establishment" more calculated to mar its image.

## SOBERS DOES THE IMPOSSIBLE AND A FAST BOWLER EMERGES
### AUGUST 31–SEPTEMBER 6

ON Saturday, at Swansea, Garfield Sobers, playing for Notts against Glamorgan, hit Malcolm Nash — left arm, near-medium — for six sixes in an over. The fifth stroke was caught by Roger Davis, who then fell over the boundary line and, after a consultation between the umpires, it was declared a six. So this most talented and remarkable cricketer has imprinted yet another mark on the game, this latest effort being, moreover, statistically ineradicable.

As a result of that match, in which Glamorgan lost to Notts, Yorkshire became Champions – their third "hat-trick" of wins – and Glamorgan were overtaken in the table by Kent, who beat Northants through the batting of Shepherd (170), Dixon, Knott, Ealham and Cowdrey and the bowling of Shepherd, Underwood and Dixon.

In the drawn match between Hampshire and Derbyshire at Derby, Alan Ward, who took five wickets in Hampshire's first innings and three in their second, emerged as the outstanding young player of the season. He is unquestionably the fastest bowler in England, almost certainly in the world. Twenty-one years old, six-foot-four tall, he comes from Dronfield in northern Derbyshire, near the Yorkshire boundary, and he bowls from a high, smooth action and makes the ball move and bounce. He is willing to learn and if his physique, which is not yet robust, stands up to the strain of county cricket, he should soon be England's first choice as a pace bowler.

The Australians ended their tour at Lord's by beating a Rest of the World XI sadly out of match-training. These 1968 Australians have been successful in retaining The Ashes, but not an impressive team; as personally charming and cheerful as any England has ever received, technically they have fallen below their promise and their hopes. Thus, only two of them have been engaged by English counties, many of whom had waited in expectation of great gains: McKenzie will join Leicestershire and Connolly, after negotiations with Surrey, goes to Middlesex.

Four counties, Glamorgan, Notts, Hampshire and Lancashire, have all made considerable advances. The first three have all benefited considerably from the additional power provided by their specially registered overseas players, Majid, Sobers and Richards. It is, too, one of the most dramatic facets of the county season that Sobers has fired the remainder of the Notts side to greater confidence and achievement. Lancashire have had the services of Engineer, whose general approach has been heartening, even if he has not proved a heavy scorer. But they will attribute much of their improvement to the lively and optimistic captaincy of Bond who, by his forthright approach, and with the enthusiastic support of some young, though not great,

players has cleared many of the fogs which have overlain the county's cricket for too many years past.

The degree of public protest against the omission of D'Oliveira from the MCC side for South Africa continues to grow: so does the conviction that MCC, when they left him out, set afoot forces they did not fully understand.

## THE FINAL VERDICT – AN UNHAPPY SEASON
### SEPTEMBER 7–13

THE last week began with the closest of all the Gillette Finals, played between the two counties most experienced in this competition, for both Sussex and Warwickshire were taking part in the final for the third time.

Sussex won the toss, batted on as good a wicket as could be wished and made the slow but safe start which is a deliberate item of their strategy, in which Oakman – playing in his last match for Sussex – and Michael Buss put on 54. Then Ibadulla, a valuable bowler in these matches, took three wickets, Suttle was unnecessarily run out and Sussex had subsided to 85 for four. They were lifted by a stand of 78 between Greig and Parks, who hit handsomely and shrewdly, and then by some late swings from Cooper and Griffith which took them

THE GILLETTE CRICKET CUP FINAL
**SUSSEX v WARWICKSHIRE**
AT LORD'S

OFFICIAL SOUVENIR PROGRAMME 2/6

SATURDAY 7th SEPTEMBER 1968

Warwickshire captain and Man of the Match, Alan Smith is chaired by (left to right) Billy Blenkiron, Lance Gibbs, David Brown and Jim Stewart.

by the end of the sixty overs, to 214 for seven wickets – a total higher than any side batting second had ever made in a Gillette final.

Barber and Kanhai, Warwickshire's two chief hopes as run-scorers, made only 18 between them; but Stewart stayed solidly to make 59, the highest score of the match, and Ibadulla a valuable 28. But when Stewart and Abberley were both out quickly, Warwickshire were 155 for six and A. C. Smith came in to join Amiss at the end of their main batting, in what seemed a losing position, for the Sussex bowling and fielding were tight and Griffith still had three overs of Snow in hand. But, while Amiss kept an end closed, Smith played an innings of utterly impressive command, heart and judgment: cutting, driving and pulling, he drove the field from the restrictive into defensive retreat and swept on to win the game with three overs to spare.

*The debate about cricketing relations with South Africa had begun in earnest. Eighteen years later, it rages still, though not with quite the same fury as in the weeks after the announcement of the England team, sine D'Oliveira. Curiously enough it is possible to see in the attitude of the MCC Committee the same policy of extreme honesty and total avoidance of expediency which had cost Brian Close the captaincy a year before. Had the selectors this time chosen D'Oliveira they would have been spared the bitter calumny which later broke about their ears.*

*It had already been established by MCC that the team to tour South Africa would be chosen on merit. S. C. Griffith, the Secretary, had made this clear to the South African Cricket Association on a visit to South Africa in 1967 and in January of the same year the Minister for Sport, Denis Howell, had repeated the policy in the House of Commons. In April the same year the South African Prime Minister, Mr John Vorster, speaking in the House of Assembly in Cape Town, said that visiting teams of mixed race would be able to tour the country if they were teams from nations with which South Africa had traditional sporting ties and "if no political capital was made out of the situation". But MCC were unable to get from the SACA during 1968 an unequivocal declaration that, if selected, D'Oliveira would be acceptable.*

*Even now it is hard to decide how likely the selection committee would have been to leave out any man who had scored 158 not out in a memorable Test victory against Australia even though they honestly felt that he would not be a suitable choice for a tour of South Africa. D'Oliveira had been disappointing in West Indies the previous winter and would not have been likely to take many wickets in South African conditions. Moreover his batting form might have been affected by worries about possible off-the-field demonstrations and racial embarrassments.*

*The uproar from those who felt that his omission was mere expediency, however, was increased when he was named as replacement for Tom Cartwright, who withdrew through injury. The chairman of selectors, Doug Insole, had given as the reason for D'Oliveira's omission the fact that he would not bowl effectively in South Africa. Now he was named to replace an all-rounder who was primarily a bowler. In fact, the decision was less illogical than it seemed because for various reasons Barry Knight and Ray Illingworth were unavailable to tour.*

*The South African Prime Minister, in a crudely worded speech, immediately made it clear that D'Oliveira would not be welcomed and MCC called off the tour.*

*In December, at a special general meeting of MCC in London, attended by over 1,000 members, the Committee survived a resolution that they had mishandled affairs and a suggestion was defeated that there should be no further tours to or from South Africa until evidence of progress towards non-racial cricket in South Africa could be given. But the suggestion was eventually put into practice and there have been no further tours, despite intensive efforts by South Africa's white cricketing authorities to open their doors to all races. MCC undertook an alternative tour to Ceylon and Pakistan. Ceylon showed the strength which was ultimately to lead to Test status by drawing their three-day match comfortably, but the Cowdrey/Amiss combination had a much less happy time in Pakistan than they had in West Indies the year before. The visit, constantly threatened by disorder, was finally abandoned in the middle of a Test match after a dangerous riot. D'Oliveira played in all three Tests, making a superb 114 not out at Dacca, though he bowled only occasionally.*

# — 1969 —

### ALRESFORD: APRIL 25

THIS is a year of high, but reasonable, hope for English cricket. The new Sunday League appears by far the best of all the ideas put up in recent years to draw back the lost spectators and to create and hold a fresh generation of followers. Thus over-limit cricket may subsidise the three-day game which is the foundation of Test performance.

The West Indian touring side represents their attempt to replace a generation which stood at the top of world cricket. They have always had the ability to surprise us with young men who come out of obscurity to Test eminence at a single stride.

Their short tour will be followed by one of the New Zealanders, fresh from beating the West Indies for the first time: they are the friendliest of tourists and they have built up their cricket steadily.

## PLAYER'S LEAGUE STARTS BRIGHTLY
### APRIL 26–MAY 2

THE Sunday League made a bright start. There were some close results and some fine cricket. Crowds were not huge but they were good for April; and the play itself should have proved an effective advertisement for future games.

MCC beat Yorkshire in the traditional opening match at Lord's. It was a game of three declarations, decided by a stand in which Milburn and Greig put on 95 in 49 minutes for the third wicket – a magnificent aperitif for the season, served in bright sunshine but to sadly small crowds.

## ALL-ROUND ABILITY PAYS FOR ESSEX
### MAY 3–9

THE Sunday League continues to entertain and to flourish. For Essex, who made a remarkable 265 off their 40 overs against Lancashire, Boyce scored 50 in 23 minutes. With their strength in seam bowling

(though both East and Hobbs took wickets against Lancashire) and a round half dozen of forcing batsmen, Essex have emerged as tough competitors in this type of cricket.

The West Indians lost three days and several hours out of their week's cricket and, to add to their troubles, Sobers is ill with influenza. In their limited opportunities, Shillingford and Holder bowled usefully at Worcester, and Camacho and Davis showed much resource, for batsmen without previous experience of English conditions, in their innings against Lancashire.

Ray East – taking wickets in one-day cricket.

## THE WEST INDIANS BROOD AS THE RAINS COME DOWN
### MAY 10–16

MORE cruel weather has emphasised the wisdom – this year, at least – of reducing the number of early-season Championship matches. Ten have been played so far and not one has reached a positive result. Middlesex are top of the table with 12 bonus points. Meanwhile the West Indies have lost six full days from fifteen and many odd hours besides.

In the Championship, Peter Lever of Lancashire did the hat-trick against Notts, and Illingworth, for his new county, Leicestershire, took seven Warwickshire wickets for 27 – at one juncture he had seven for 13. Leicestershire's batting callapsed in turn before McVicker, the leanly built, medium-fast bowler whom Warwickshire shrewdly registered from Lincolnshire. Woolmer, a new young seam bowler of Kent, had figures of seven for 47 against Sussex in an exciting draw at Canterbury: Kent needed seven to win with their last two batsmen together, when the game ended.

## MILBURN LOSES HIS LEFT EYE
### MAY 17–23

AS I settle to type this week's entry, before play begins in the Roses Match at Old Trafford, I have been told that Colin Milburn is to lose his left eye after a car smash last night. This is a savage irony. To leave this man – of such gaiety in approach, such simple might in batting, such sensitivity of timing, such gallantry of decision – without the eye that informed his play, is like hamstringing a great racehorse. On

**Trent Bridge**
England v. New Zealand,
Fourth Test Match,
August 1983.

**Lord's**
India v. West Indies,
World Cup Final,
June 1983.

**Headingley**
England v. Australia,
First Test Match,
June 1985.

**Old Trafford**
England v. Australia,
Fourth Test Match,
August 1985.

**The Oval**
England v. New Zealand,
World Cup, June 1983.

**Edgbaston**
England v. Australia,
Fourth Test Match,
August 1981.

Thursday we dined together: he was well content. After his splendid season in Australia and his century in the Karachi Test, his hundred in his first Championship match of the season – against Leicestershire last weekend – when he made 158 in the course of 77 overs with five sixes and seventeen fours, all promised a happy and successful season. Now this has happened: and it is difficult, if not impossible, to write about it objectively. Hope, cornered, turns to thoughts of eye-grafts, of Pataudi continuing to make runs – but with a partly-sighted, not a lost, eye – of Nupen and William Clarke. The fact remains that, if Colin Milburn bats to his old standard with one eye, he will be unique among games players.

🏃 *Alas, he was not, bravely though he tried to continue his career later.*

In the second round of three-day matches, the West Indians lost for the first time on their tour – by 65 runs to Northants. The match was eventually decided by a spell in which Crump took four wickets – including that of Sobers – for nine runs: previously Prideaux, Mushtaq – twice – and Milburn had batted well for the county, Butcher – twice – Foster, Camacho and Davis for the West Indies. Shillingford bowled at lively fast medium for good figures in both innings of Northants.

## . . . AND THE OTHER COLIN GOES TO HOSPITAL
### MAY 24–30

Colin Cowdrey exercises his damaged Achilles tendon.

AS the second visitation of ill luck which so often follows a first, it was announced last Sunday – the day after Colin Milburn lost his left eye – that Colin Cowdrey had suffered a ruptured Achilles tendon during the match between Kent and Glamorgan, which established his county at the top of the Sunday League table with their four matches all won. He has undergone an operation but he can barely hope to play until the end of the season. So, by comparison with their predecessors' choice of last August, the new selectors cannot call upon Cowdrey, Milburn, Barrington or Dexter (who has declared his availability for the "banned" Cavaliers team in televised Sunday matches).

## . . . SO ILLINGWORTH ASCENDS THE VACANT THRONE
### MAY 31–JUNE 6

Ray Illingworth, the new England captain.

THE outstanding event of the week has been the nomination of Ray Illingworth to captain England in the First Test against the West Indies. The announcement was deferred until the end of the MCC v. West Indians match and beyond: but it seems a good choice. Illingworth's experience as an appointed captain in first-class cricket consisted of seven matches for Leicestershire when he was appointed: and it is ironic that, if he had not differed with the Yorkshire committee last season and left them because they would not give him a three-year contract, he could hardly have entered the selectors' minds as the England captain.

The MCC v. West Indians match gave the selectors little positive information. Edrich (125 and 77 not out), especially, and Boycott batted well but the three batsmen on trial – Prideaux, Fletcher and Hampshire – all failed; and the bowling was not convincing when Sobers attacked it, which he did quite brilliantly on Monday afternoon. He did not bat against Somerset when the West Indians made 422 for four and 228 for three (with centuries by Lloyd, Carew and Davis and innings of 51 not out and 87 not out by Foster); but he took three for 11 in the first Somerset innings, two for 49 in the second and the West Indians won their first first-class match of the tour. Now they may feel that the weather has ceased to torment them, for it has been a week of clear skies.

Younis Ahmed, the Pakistani left hander, is first in the batting averages: then come the West Indian Charles Davis, Mushtaq, Luckhurst (batting capably and enterprisingly) and Edrich. Second to Illingworth in the bowling table is Norman McVicker, then come Snow, Cartwright, Underwood and Ward.

## EDRICH AND BOYCOTT BUILD A FIRM BASE
### JUNE 7–13

TONIGHT, surprisingly after only two days' play in the First Test match, England stand in what could be called a winning position if Garfield Sobers were not on the other side. This has been an important match for

Lancashire; Test gate receipts at Old Trafford have been so poor in recent years – through small attendances on fine days as much as through bad weather – that the ground's future as a Test venue was clearly in hazard. In bright sun there have been two ten-thousand gates – both including members – and something appreciably better than that will be necessary tomorrow to fend off the competition of Trent Bridge and Edgbaston.

England batted solidly. Edrich, who is in full flow, was the more purposeful member of the first century partnership he and Boycott have made for England in a home Test match. When he was run out, the entire innings lost impetus. Graveney made his highest score in a Test at Old Trafford, which has never been a profitable ground for him. He has scored 119 centuries but never one there. He is not in form and, by his own fluent standards, he ground along. Boycott did not hurry: he was mainly and soundly defensive but his runs came through finely wrought strokes, cover drives, hooks and some cuts of infinite delicacy. Once England had built up a total of 413 they were in a position to attack, and after tea today Snow and Brown shot away the main body of the West Indian innings, leaving them with only Lloyd and Shepherd of their recognised batting at 104 for six – 309 behind.

Wicket-keeper Jackie Hendriks celebrates John Shepherd's first success in Test cricket but Boycott had already scored 128.

## ENGLAND WIN AT OLD TRAFFORD BUT GRAVENEY FALLS FROM GRACE
### JUNE 14–20

IN the Test, West Indies never recovered from their failure to take catches and a spectacular and entertaining, but illjudged, first innings. When they followed on, Carew, Fredericks, Butcher and Sobers batted well but none of them could produce the truly long innings needed to turn the course of the game. Illingworth and Underwood were subtle and economical while the faster bowlers were rested, and it could be said that every member of the team justified his choice. Sharpe, the only batsman to fail as a batsman, took two fine slip catches. One, which probably no other player in the match could have taken, broke the important opening stand of the second West Indian innings, while the other dismissed Sobers.

Most people would have expected the same team to

be chosen for Lord's on Thursday as a reward and vote of confidence. That, however, was rendered impossible by yesterday's decision of the Disciplinary Committee of the Test and County Cricket Board. The facts of the matter have never been in dispute: Tom Graveney twice asked permission to play in a match for his benefit fund at Luton on the Sunday of the Test match weekend. Both before he was chosen for Old Trafford and during the match he was forbidden to do so. Nevertheless he went to Luton, took part in the game and, apparently, received a fee of £1,000 from a Mr. A. T. Hunt. The Disciplinary Committee was hastily convened so that its findings could be announced before the Test team was chosen. The decision means that Graveney is not available for the two Tests – those remaining in the West Indies rubber – for which England positively need him.

*This was the end of Graveney's Test career – and a sad, unnecessary end it was.*

On the last – Tuesday – afternoon of the match between Hampshire and Glamorgan it was raining steadily and the Hampshire team, apparently under the impression that the game had been abandoned, left the ground. At about five o'clock the umpires, Peter Wight and a former Hampshire player, Lloyd Budd, decided the pitch was fit for play; they took the field and so did the Glamorgan team, and after the statutory two minutes Glamorgan claimed the game by default. They seem entitled to do so, but the decision has been referred to Lord's.

The outstanding performance in last Sunday's League matches was Somerset's win over Surrey by nine wickets. Gregory Chappell, the young South Australian, scored 128 out of 175 – and had the wisdom to do it on television.

Greg Chappell – first taste of English conditions with Somerset.

## DAVIS MAKES FIRST TEST CENTURY AND ENGLAND WOBBLE
### JUNE 21–27

AS those who know modern Test cricket would assume, England, a match ahead, left out a bowler in favour of a batsman. Underwood – of all people – Ward and Denness, summoned as standby when Edrich

County Championship
(as at June 20)

|   |                  | P | Pts |
|---|------------------|---|-----|
| 1 | Surrey           | 9 | 69  |
| 2 | Warwickshire     | 8 | 61  |
| 3 | Gloucestershire  | 7 | 56  |
| 4 | Nottinghamshire  | 8 | 52  |

became doubtful through bruising, were the men omitted: so Parfitt took Graveney's place and Hampshire became the "extra" batsman. West Indies, committed to attack, left out a batsman – Foster – and brought in an extra fast bowler in Shillingford. Sobers won the toss; Fredericks and Camacho made a good start – 106, a new first wicket record for West Indies in a Test in England – but Butcher was soon gone and Sobers tragically run out so that their 246 for four at the end of the first day was less secure than it looked, for there was little to come before a long and inexperienced tail. On Friday, however, when Lloyd was again out to a short fast ball, Davis, who slowly but surely made his first Test century, and Shepherd took them to 324, and the last few batsmen, given a lively cue by Gibbs, put on another 56; 380 represented security.

If the West Indian batting had been over-deliberate, England's beginning was slower still: Edrich and Boycott made 19 in the hour before Edrich flicked Holder ankle high to backward short-leg. Soon Sobers, who had opened with four overs at the cost of a single boundary, came back and Parfitt, who never looked as if he relished batting, was caught at gully off a ball that nipped at a passive bat. Next he had D'Oliveira taken at slip: at the other end Boycott edged Shepherd to the new wicket-keeper, Findlay; so England had lost three wickets for no runs in 13 balls and were 37 for four. Hampshire – Sobers's particular target – and Sharpe held on in acute discomfort to the end of the day's play, but the Lord's Saturday crowd can expect little adventure from the England batsmen tomorrow.

At Bristol, Michael Procter, who has had much to do with the rise of Gloucestershire, hit his Natal team-mate and travelling companion, Richards of Hampshire, with a bouncer and sent him to hospital. Colin Milburn is broadcasting about the Tests on television and writing about them in the press: thus does the game remember its heroes.

Colin Milburn in action as commentator.

## HAMPSHIRE BIDS FOR A PLACE WITH THE IMMORTALS
### JUNE 28–JULY 4

THIS has been a week of delights and surprises in blazing sunshine. The Test match revived to a level of gallantry which seemed unlikely last Friday night:

Lord's ground was full and the crowd had a day of enjoyment. England had fallen to 61 for five and fears of following on when John Hampshire proceeded to score a century in his first Test innings – the first Englishman to do so at Lord's. He had his early anxieties but gradually he overcame them, signalled his defiance with a superb cover drive off Sobers and swung on to 107.

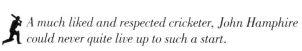
*A much liked and respected cricketer, John Hamphire could never quite live up to such a start.*

The second West Indian innings included a useful start by Camacho and Fredericks and two fine stroke-making innings by Lloyd and – although he batted with a runner – Sobers. Sobers, in his keenness for a win, declared – setting England 332 to win in five hours – and kept the match open to the last: but England spent too long making sure they did not lose and had not enough time left to win. Boycott scored a steady century but Sharpe's clear minded and bold innings of 86 had more bearing on the possibility of winning. England with three wickets in hand were 37 runs short when play ended with the last available over left unbowled.

At Southampton, Richard Gilliat scored 223 not out against Warwickshire at a run a minute and Hampshire – 426 for five from 83 overs – took a record eleven bonus points for batting. As everyone insists on pointing out, Gilliat has batted quite magnificently ever since he was hit on the head in the Essex match at Ilford on June 11. The day afterwards he scored the fastest hundred of the season and has made centuries in four of his past five matches. A left-handed bat who was at Charterhouse and captained Oxford, he is essentially a true wicket player with considerable hitting power.

David Allen, acting captain of Gloucestershire, had the best analysis of his career – eight for 34 – in the innings defeat of Sussex which set Gloucestershire 26 points ahead of Glamorgan at the top of the County Championship.

West Indies, with six of their Test team playing, were put out for 25 by Ireland on the ground at Sion Mills in Tyrone: at one point they were 12 for nine but fast bowler Grayson Shillingford became top scorer with nine. O'Riordan took four for 18, Goodwin five for six

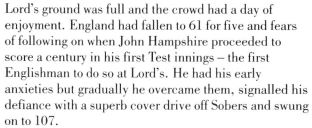
John Hampshire – a century in his first Test.

## SEVENTEENTH MATCH v. IRELAND
### WEST INDIES

| First Innings | | Second Innings | |
|---|---|---|---|
| S. G. Camacho, c Dineen, b Goodwin | 1 | c Dineen, b Goodwin | 1 |
| M. C. Carew, c Hughes, b O'Riordan | 0 | c Pigot, b Duffy | 25 |
| M. L. Foster, run out | 2 | c Pigot, b Goodwin | 0 |
| *B. F. Butcher, c Duffy, b O'Riordan | 2 | c Waters, b Duffy | 50 |
| C. H. Lloyd, c Waters, b Goodwin | 1 | not out | 0 |
| C. L. Walcott, c Anderson, b O'Riordan | 6 | not out | 0 |
| J. N. Shepherd, c Duffy, b Goodwin | 0 | | |
| †M. Findlay, c Waters, b Goodwin | 0 | | |
| G. Shillingford, not out | 9 | | |
| M. P. Roberts, c Colhoun, b O'Riordan | 0 | | |
| P. Blair, b Goodwin | 3 | | |
| Extras (b 1) | 1 | Extras (lb 2) | 2 |
| Total | 25 | Total (4 wkts.) | 78 |

FALL OF WICKETS: 1—1, 2—1, 3—3, 4—6, 5—6, 6—8, 7—12, 8—12, 9—12. *Second Innings*: 1—1, 2—2, 3—73, 4—78.
BOWLING: O'Riordan 13—8—18—4; Goodwin 12.3—8—6—5. *Second Innings*: O'Riordan 6—1—21—0; Goodwin 2—1—1—2; Hughes 7—4—10—0; Duffy 12—8—12—2; Anderson 7—1—32—0.

### IRELAND

| | |
|---|---|
| R. Waters, c Findlay, b Blair | 2 |
| D. M. Pigot, c Camacho, b Shillingford | 37 |
| M. Reith, lbw, b Shepherd | 10 |
| J. Harrison, lbw, b Shepherd | 0 |
| I. Anderson, c Shepherd, b Roberts | 7 |
| P. J. Dineen, b Shepherd | 0 |
| A. J. O'Riordan, c & b Carew | 35 |
| G. A. Duffy, not out | 15 |
| L. P. Hughes, c sub, b Carew | 13 |
| Extras (lb 2, nb 4) | 6 |
| Total (8 wkts. dec.) | 125 |

*D. E. Goodwin and †O. D. Colhoun did not bat.

FALL OF WICKETS: 1—19, 2—30, 3—34, 4—51, 5—55, 6—69. 7—103, 8—125.
BOWLING: Blair 8—4—14—1; Shillingford 7—2—19—1; Shepherd 13—4—20—3; Roberts 16—3—43—1; Carew 3.2—0—23—2.

and Ireland won by nine wickets.

*This was at once a freak and a genuine result. It proves the cliché that anything really can happen between two sides of eleven people!*

The New Zealanders have loosened up in friendly fashion at Eastbourne and Glasgow, and more searchingly at Bradford; as usual they are a cheerful side.

## MEDIUM-PACERS TAKE CHARGE AT HEADINGLEY
### JULY 5–11

THERE had been no sunshine to dry out the Headingley pitch to its usual state of perfection for batsmen and the medium-pace bowlers, notably Shepherd, Holder, Sobers and Knight, have made the ball move awkwardly off the seam and, with the aid of a strong cross wind, through the air.

Illingworth won the toss and gave England first innings but only Edrich, D'Oliveira and Knott batted with any important effect in a total of 223. Holder's four

for 48 was his best Test analysis. The West Indian batting, apart from Butcher, briefly Sobers and, later, Lloyd and, surprisingly, Holder, was never convincing. Knight in a spell of eighteen overs took their first four wickets; Shepherd who has a back injury could not bat; Snow and Brown cut off the loose ends, and England came out with a first innings lead of 62. When they batted a second time the second ball from Sobers was an outswinger which Boycott touched and Findlay caught. Boycott now has suffered four "ducks" in Test cricket – three of them at the hands of Sobers. England are 75 in front but it could yet prove that batting is easiest in the fourth innings.

*He has always been vulnerable to left-arm, over-the-wicket bowlers. Not just Sobers but also Lever, Solkar, Gilmour, etc.*

A shallow trench was dug across the square in the Parks at Oxford before the match between the University and Wilfred Isaacs's XI from South Africa: it was repaired in time for play to take place when there was an orderly anti-apartheid demonstration. Graeme Pollock, playing for Isaacs's XI, was dropped by Fred Goldstein, the Oxford captain, before he had scored and went on to make 231 not out.

## ENGLAND CLINCH THE RUBBER
### JULY 12–18

IN a week of intense heat, England have taken the Test rubber with West Indies by two to nothing; Gloucestershire have opened up a huge lead in the County Championship; and the New Zealanders have begun to find their feet.

On Saturday Sobers, in a magnificent sustained spell of bowling, took five English wickets for 36 in a score of 214 for nine. West Indies eventually needed 303 to win with most of Monday and all Tuesday to make them. After Fredericks was out early, Camacho, in a controlled innings, Davis, who grew from discomfort to confidence, and Butcher, shrewd in what may have been his last Test, brought them to 219 with only three wickets down.

Then, however, four changes of bowling by Illingworth brought England four wickets – including that of Sobers, driving with his head up – in the course of five overs.

This was not a strong West Indies side; everyone knew that before the tour started. The disappointment is that, apart from the advance of Camacho and Fredericks as batsmen, virtually nothing has been gained: none of the young players has stepped up to Test class. England are in little better situation: their successes have all been cricketers of known quality with the exception of Hampshire, who has yet to show consistency.

The New Zealanders batted enterprisingly when a declaration by Parfitt gave them a chance to beat Middlesex at Lord's. On Thursday evening Dowling, in a speech at dinner given to his team at Lord's, asked for a series of positive cricket, and declared that the New Zealanders would attack. It is not certain that the New Zealanders – or for that matter, England – have players great enough to play attacking cricket in face of modern tight bowling techniques, restrictive field settings and attritional batting on good pitches. Nevertheless, yesterday the New Zealanders went determinedly and sensibly for their objective and, if Taylor had not been unnecessarily run out, they might have won. On Thursday they begin the First Test on the same ground.

## NEW ZEALAND START WELL AND GLAMORGAN BEAT GLOUCESTER
### JULY 19–25

ENGLISH groundsmen, from long experience, construct wickets on the assumption that there will be some rain during most matches. So a long, hot, dry period such as the last fortnight produces parched wickets like the one on which the Lord's Test match is being played. England played Ward and Fletcher for Snow and Hampshire of the team at Leeds. When Illingworth won the toss he hesitated about batting and, surely enough, England lost their first five wickets to the three New Zealand seam bowlers – Motz, Hadlee and Taylor – for 53. D'Oliveira, Illingworth and Knight rebuilt the innings in the afternoon, when Howarth, slow left-arm, took his first wickets, but surely by no means his last, in Test cricket.

England were put out for 190, but on Friday, although Dowling and Congdon put on 62 for the second

wicket, uncompromising out-cricket, especially the bowling of Illingworth, Underwood and Ward, gave England a lead of 21 on the first innings. After Boycott had taken half-an-hour to avoid his third consecutive "duck" in Test matches, he and Edrich doubled the lead, but England are still not in command. New Zealand are inexperienced but immensely keen and their bowling has edge.

In the County Championship, Glamorgan, who have not been beaten this season, ended Gloucestershire's sequence of seven wins and, in the week, scored 39 points to Gloucestershire's seven. So Gloucestershire are now only 18 ahead of Glamorgan who have played two fewer matches. The award of ten points to Glamorgan for staying on when Hampshire left the ground at Bournemouth has been confirmed by the Test and County Cricket Board: but Hampshire have appealed against the decision.

## ENGLAND GO ONE UP
### JULY 26–AUGUST 1

ENGLAND, in their second innings, went grimly about making certain that there was no such early collapse as in the first. Boycott made a riskless 47, Edrich a firm, rounded 115, and Sharpe a shrewd 46. Knight in the latter stages played some lively strokes.

Eventually New Zealand were set 362 runs to win. Against Underwood (seven for 32) on a pitch of uneven bounce they never looked like making the runs though Turner hung on doggedly to become the first New

Glenn Turner shows the defence that enabled him to carry his bat through the New Zealand second innings at Lord's.

Zealander to carry his bat through a completed Test innings: they lost by 230 runs.

Brian Langford, the Somerset captain and off-break bowler, performed the ultimate in the Sunday League when he bowled his statutory maximum of eight overs for no runs.

| County Championship (as at July 31) | | |
| --- | --- | --- |
| | P | Pts |
| **1** Gloucestershire | 17 | 169 |
| **2** Glamorgan | 15 | 153 |
| **3** Surrey | 16 | 136 |
| **4** Hampshire | 16 | 129 |

There was an important development on the Glamorgan-Hampshire fixture at Bournemouth in which the umpires awarded the match to Glamorgan after the Hampshire players had left the ground. Their decision was upheld by Messrs Griffith and Insole; but, when Hampshire appealed against their ruling, an emergency executive committee of the MCC Council called witnesses, "heard all the evidence" and decided as follows:

"In the event, the umpires acted correctly in accordance with the rules of cricket, but in the context of the County Championship . . . the match should be recorded as a draw, with each side retaining (bonus) points gained in the first innings."

Since Hampshire were having the better of the match and it seems that there was, in the words of the committee, "a lack of communication between the umpires and captains" it was perhaps a just conclusion to an unusual and rather funny occurrence. The judgment means that the position at the top of the Championship table now is – Gloucestershire 17 matches, 169 points: Glamorgan 15 matches, 143 points: Surrey 16 matches 136 points: Hampshire 16 matches, 129 points.

Harold Rhodes of Derbyshire has announced that he will retire from first-class cricket at the end of this season. He has prepared a career for himself outside the game and is considering offers to play in the Lancashire League. His action has been officially cleared.

Sussex, disturbed by their defeat in the Gillette Cup, have decided to drop Ken Suttle from their team to play Surrey tomorrow: thus ends the record run of 423 consecutive County Championship matches by the little man who in every department of the game has served Sussex well: he is forty now but says he has no intention of retiring.

Ken Suttle – left out by Sussex.

## EDRICH AND SHARPE HAVE FUN IN THE SUN
### AUGUST 2–8

TRENT Bridge produced a perfect wicket for the Second Test but New Zealand, batting first, did not use it as well as they should have done. One batsman after another got in, found his feet and then, when he should have built an innings, was trapped by the sheer professionalism of the England bowling. Hastings batted soundly and with some distinction, and Hadlee looked much better than a number eight. Ward took four wickets, and Snow bowled well with no tangible result. When England batted for a quarter hour before lunch on Friday, Boycott, who had not scored, went to hook Motz, missed, the ball hit his body and, as he turned it fell on to his wicket. So he had to sit nursing his duck while Edrich (117 not out) and Sharpe (103 not out) put on 223 in a still unfinished second wicket stand. Edrich grows a better batsman every day: his command and placing have reached a high peak, his courage and concentration are still unwavering and he has an insatiable run-hunger. Sharpe moved pleasantly until he reached 98, where he hung for almost half an hour before he completed his first Test century. England now are in a position to conduct one of their steam-roller operations.

In the first round of Championship matches, Yorkshire and Lancashire played a quite amazing draw. Lancashire, who had seemed safe at 150 for two, fell to 160 for eight. Then Bond (almost two and a half hours for 17), Simmons (73 minutes for 0) and Higgs held on until Yorkshire had to score 65 from the 19 overs allocated to the last 55 minutes. They began the last over – bowled by Higgs – at 64 for three, needing one run to win; they ended it 64 for six – Leadbeater, Wilson and Hutton were all put out by Higgs – and Lancashire had avoided defeat.

## GLAMORGAN TROUNCE GLOUCESTERSHIRE AGAIN
### AUGUST 9–15

TRENT Bridge had the ill luck, after such a long spell of fine weather, virtually to lose their Test match Saturday to rain; twenty minutes' play only was possible and the anticipated large attendance never materialised. On Monday, England moved to a lead of 157 before Illingworth declared and New Zealand scored 37 for no wicket. On Tuesday, there was less than an hour's play and at the end of it New Zealand were 66 for one.

In the week-end round of Championship matches, Gloucestershire, after much loss of time to rain, took

Phil Sharpe and John Edrich about to continue their assault on the New Zealand bowling at Trent Bridge.

A wet Saturday at Trent Bridge. Left to right: Howarth, Turner, Collinge and Taylor kill time in the dressing-room.

the last seven Worcestershire wickets for 33 runs in three-quarters of an hour at Cheltenham and won by an innings and 57 runs, through the bowling of Brown, Procter and, at the end, Allen and Mortimore, plus the batting of Green, Milton and Pullar.

On Wednesday, Glamorgan went to the Cheltenham Festival for their important match with Gloucestershire and took it in their stride. First they bowled Gloucestershire out on a slow wet pitch for 73 (Nash six for 31) to take five bonus points for bowling, and then made 198 for four (Majid a brilliant 69) by the close. On Thursday, they went on to 285 and five bonus points for batting, and then put out a disheartened Gloucestershire for 160 and won by an innings and 50 runs.

In the Sunday League, Lancashire beat Leicestershire – rather too easily – while Essex lost to Surrey in a low-scoring match; so now Lancashire lead by eight points with only three matches to play. Surrey and Hampshire both won and, with Kent, retain an outside chance, but Lancashire should now hold their position.

Last Sunday, Colin Cowdrey played cricket for the first time since his Achilles tendon injury – against an England women's team for Alan Dixon's benefit. He played in another benefit match on Wednesday: he did not field because he still feels some tenderness in the ankle, and when he batted he was caught at slip for five.

Tom Graveney confirmed that he was considering a "tempting" offer of a coaching appointment with the Queensland Association. He commented that he hoped to stay at least a couple of seasons with Worcestershire who, he thought, had a Championship team in the making.

*He went to Queensland eventually and duly stayed on for one more season for Worcestershire, who had won the title in 1964 and 1965, but were not to do so again until 1974.*

## RAIN FAVOURS UNDERWOOD AND ENGLISH BATSMEN
### AUGUST 16–23

ONCE more New Zealand had little luck. They won the toss and batted first, only for the wicket to be so affected by rain after their innings began that Underwood found sufficient assistance to take four wickets for 25. In the event, England, taking second innings, had the better of the pitch. Against some tight New Zealand fielding, Boycott and Edrich went steadily to 88 before Boycott played across a quite ordinary ball from Cunis. Denness, in his first Test, never settled: he scored two in three quarters of an hour; and soon after he was out, Edrich, who was batting as if for a century, was beaten through the air by Howarth and remarkably well caught by Cunis, diving at cover point. A lively stand by Sharpe and Knott carried England eventually to 174 for five, 24 in front, but a pronounced tail means that their eventual lead could be small.

## LANCASHIRE WIN THE SUNDAY LEAGUE . . .
### AUGUST 23–29

A last wicket stand between Ward and Snow took England to a first innings lead of 92 in the Test match. Turner, Dowling, Congdon, and, notably, Hastings, put on a front of resistance for New Zealand but Ward and Underwood worked their way through their batting on Monday and Boycott was out for eight that evening. On Tuesday, Sharpe and Denness, with some lack of haste despite the threat of rain, saw England home by eight wickets.

The New Zealanders have been, as ever, charming visitors; they enjoy their cricket, learn from these tours and plough back their experience into the cricket of their own country. At Test level, however, they are relatively unsophisticated and Australia, who are in the best position to help them, have been sadly and pointedly uninterested. Of this team, Hastings could

County Championship (as at August 13)

| | | P | Pts |
|---|---|---|---|
| 1 | Gloucestershire | 19 | 189 |
| 2 | Hampshire | 19 | 166 |
| 3 | Surrey | 18 | 166 |
| 4 | Glamorgan | 17 | 165 |

Tony Lush, Old Brightonian captain of The Cricketer Cup winning side which also included his brother, Peter, later to become a leading cricket administrator.

develop as a batsman and Howarth as a slow left-arm bowler by a season or two in English county cricket. Wadsworth is a much-improved wicket-keeper and Milburn an unlucky one: if he were as good a batsman or bowler as he is a wicket-keeper, he would have played in all the Tests instead of none.

🏏 *This was why there was so much rejoicing when New Zealand defeated Australia in an "away" series for the first time in 1985–86.*

Lancashire beat Warwickshire by 51 runs at Nuneaton and won the Sunday League because Hampshire lost by 42 runs to Essex: no other county can now equal Lancashire's 49 points. Lancashire made 204 for five – Clive Lloyd, 59, Sullivan 60 not out – and fine fielding, and wickets shared between six bowlers, put out Warwickshire for 153. Hampshire, needing 196 to win, made 93 for the first wicket but lost their last seven wickets for 12 runs to Lever and Turner. The second and third places could go to Essex, Hampshire or Surrey.

Two of our seasoned professionals – Terry Spencer and Maurice Hallam of Leicester – have decided to retire at the end of the season: they will be missed both for their skills and their pleasant personalities.

## . . . GLAMORGAN TRIUMPH AT SOPHIA GARDENS . . .
### AUGUST 30–SEPTEMBER 5

GLAMORGAN won the County Championship today when they beat Worcestershire by 147 runs before a huge and splendidly triumphant crowd at Sophia Gardens, Cardiff. They had seemed certain to win the title and during their brief period at the top of the table they barely had time to come under great pressure or to lose their gay self-confidence. They have not been beaten this season.

It was appropriate that, in the conclusive game, Majid Jahangir made a brilliant century and Don Shepherd took the two-thousandth wicket of his career. In their match of the previous weekend, Glamorgan and Essex both declared and Glamorgan won by one run when Lever ran himself out going for a second run from the last possible ball of the match. Some supporters of

Glamorgan – the first undefeated County Champions since 1930. Back, left to right: Eifion Jones, Bryan Davis, Malcolm Nash, Lawrence Williams, Roger Davis, Majid Jahangir. Front: Tony Cordle, Peter Walker, Tony Lewis, Don Shepherd, Alan Jones.

other counties have suggested that the first Essex declaration, made when they were in a position of considerable strength, was unduly generous and that the final run out was sacrificial. They point, too, to the fact that Essex won by one run in their intervening match in the Sunday League where success was more important to Essex. In Glamorgan's two Championship matches, Walker batted valuably and Cordle, Nash, Shepherd and Wheatley were the most effective bowlers.

## . . . AND YORKSHIRE FIND CONSOLATION AT LORD'S
### SEPTEMBER 6–12

IN a week when the weather began to break up, Yorkshire won the Gillette Cup and Hampshire made certain of being runners-up in the Player's Sunday League.

Yorkshire's team strength was first threatened when John Hampshire contracted tonsillitis. He recovered in time but Boycott, struck on the hand by John Snow in the preceding county match, was unable to play: he has a broken finger to end the unluckiest season of his career. Experimenting with contact lenses, he has had some disappointing innings but he has made no excuses and, on his days, he has looked as good a batsman as ever.

On form Derbyshire could hardly expect to win the Gillette Cup but, in the absence of Boycott and with the inexperienced and uncapped Leadbeater and Woodford opening the innings, there was the possibility that Yorkshire, like Sussex in the semi-final, might prove

THE GILLETTE CRICKET CUP FINAL
**DERBYSHIRE v YORKSHIRE**
AT LORD'S

OFFICIAL SOUVENIR PROGRAMME 2/6

SATURDAY 6th. SEPTEMBER 1969

Brian Close with his winning Yorkshire team after the Gillette Cup Final.

crucially vulnerable to the Derbyshire fast bowlers. No doubt with that in mind, and hoping for some greenness in the wicket with an early – quarter to eleven – start, Morgan put Yorkshire in to bat when he won the toss. On only one other occasion has a side been put in in a Gillette Cup final and that was Yorkshire in 1965 when Boycott made 146 – still a record for the competition – and Surrey were virtually beaten by lunch time.

It was a long losing battle for Derbyshire after Yorkshire's good start in the morning against Ward and Rhodes, aided by three dropped catches, a shrewd innings by Leadbeater and 37 runs in 36 balls by Close.

## CONCLUSION: A SUNNY AND INTERESTING SEASON
### SEPTEMBER 13–17

THE first *Cricketer* National Club Knockout was won by Hampstead, who beat Pocklington Pixies by fourteen runs, a finish which might have been even closer but that Pocklington were handicapped by having to bat in bad light. Mid-September evenings, as the county players found this week, simply do not grant enough light for cricket. The competition, which drew 256 entrants, has aroused considerable interest among club cricketers.

*It was set up jointly by* The Cricketer *and the Midlands-based entrepreneur and cricketing globe-trotter, Derrick Robins. The final in that first year was at Edgbaston: now it is at Lord's.*

The outstanding event of the summer has been the success of the Sunday League. It, and the Gillette Cup, maintained healthy interest in the cricket of several counties – notably Yorkshire, Derbyshire, Lancashire and Essex – who were well out of the Championship running and who could hardly have expected to retain support in opposition to football without this extra-mural success.

The Sunday League, the attitude of the freshly registered overseas players and, perhaps, bonus points, seem to have combined to produce enterprising play. The outstanding figures in this direction have been recent importations – Sobers, of course, but also Majid Jahangir, Ackerman. Engineer, Younis Ahmed, Chappell, Richards, Irvine, Boyce, Bryan Davis; and next to them is another group of overseas players – Mushtaq Mohammad, Greig, Marshall and the young Middlesex Rhodesian, Featherstone. There might seem room for British self-consciousness but that, in such young men as Graves, Roope, Gilliat, Lewis, Ealham, Johnson and Hemsley, may be distinguished a rising generation of English stroke-makers.

It has, too, been a notable season for fast bowling, with the emergence of Ward and Old to give England a choice of bowlers of pace. On the other hand Underwood, still only 24, has taken a hundred wickets in a season for the sixth time: his maturity is amazing and his ultimate figures could be staggering.

*The gradually increasing amount of limited-overs cricket prevented the figures challenging the likes of Wilfred Rhodes, but, in 1986, he is still going deadly strong!*

Basil D'Oliveira, with his nine-year-old son Damian, after receiving his OBE for services to cricket.

## FINAL CHAMPIONSHIP TABLE

|  |  | P. | W. | L. | D. | Bonus Bt. | Bonus Bw. | Pts. |
|---|---|---|---|---|---|---|---|---|
| 1 | Glamorgan (3) | 24 | 11 | 0 | 13 | 67 | 73 | 250 |
| 2 | Glos (16) | 24 | 10 | 6 | 8 | 26 | 93 | 219 |
| 3 | Surrey (15) | 24 | 7 | 1 | 16 | 64 | 76 | 210 |
| 4 | Warwicks (11) | 24 | 7 | 3 | 14 | 41 | 89 | 205 |
| 5 | Hampshire (5) | 24 | 6 | 7 | 11 | 56 | 87 | 203 |
| 6 | Essex (14) | 24 | 6 | 6 | 12 | 44 | 85 | 189 |
| 7 | Sussex (17) | 24 | 5 | 8 | 11 | 47 | 88 | 185 |
| 8 | Notts (4) | 24 | 6 | 2 | 16 | 49 | 75 | 184 |
| 9 | Northants (13) | 24 | 5 | 7 | 12 | 47 | 66 | 163 |
| 10 | Kent (2) | 24 | 4 | 6 | 14 | 35 | 76 | 151 |
| 11 | Middlesex (10) | 24 | 3 | 7 | 14 | 40 | 76 | 146 |
| 12 | Worcs (7) | 24 | 5 | 7 | 12* | 30 | 62 | 142 |
|  | Yorkshire (1) | 24 | 3 | 6 | 15 | 30 | 77 | 142 |
| 14 | Leics (9) | 24 | 4 | 7 | 13 | 26 | 64 | 130 |
| 15 | Lancashire (6) | 24 | 2 | 1 | 21 | 39 | 67 | 126 |
| 16 | Derbyshire (8) | 24 | 3 | 5 | 16* | 20 | 69 | 119 |
| 17 | Somerset (12) | 24 | 1 | 9 | 14 | 17 | 69 | 96 |

Figures in brackets indicate 1968 positions.

Warwickshire and Yorkshire totals include five points in drawn matches where the scores finished level and they were batting.

* Drawn game totals for Worcestershire and Derbyshire include one match abandoned without a ball being bowled.

## FIRST-CLASS AVERAGES, 1969

### BATTING
(Qualifications: 8 innings, average 10.00)

|  | I. | N.O. | R. | H.S. | Av. |
|---|---|---|---|---|---|
| J. H. Edrich | 39 | 7 | 2238 | 181 | 69.93 |
| E. J. O. Hemsley | 16 | 5 | 676 | 138* | 61.45 |
| Mushtaq Mohammed | 40 | 9 | 1831 | 156* | 59.06 |
| B. A. Richards | 31 | 6 | 1440 | 155 | 57.60 |
| C. H. Lloyd | 36 | 6 | 1458 | 201* | 48.60 |
| B. W. Luckhurst | 44 | 4 | 1914 | 169 | 47.85 |
| Younis Ahmed | 46 | 9 | 1760 | 127* | 47.56 |
| M. J. Stewart | 37 | 7 | 1317 | 105 | 43.90 |
| C. Milburn | 8 | 0 | 341 | 158 | 42.62 |
| G. S. Sobers | 26 | 2 | 1023 | 104 | 42.62 |
| J. B. Bolus | 43 | 5 | 1603 | 147 | 42.18 |
| R. B. Kanhai | 29 | 4 | 1044 | 173 | 41.76 |
| M. H. Page | 30 | 4 | 1037 | 162 | 39.88 |
| Majid Jahangir | 40 | 1 | 1547 | 156 | 39.66 |
| R. M. C. Gilliat | 38 | 3 | 1386 | 223* | 39.60 |

### BOWLING
(Qualification: 10 wickets in 10 innings)

|  | O. | M. | R. | W. | Av. |
|---|---|---|---|---|---|
| A. Ward | 482.5 | 135 | 1023 | 69 | 14.82 |
| M. J. Procter | 639.3 | 160 | 1623 | 108 | 15.02 |
| D. L. Underwood | 808.3 | 355 | 1561 | 101 | 15.45 |
| T. W. Cartwright | 880.5 | 372 | 1748 | 108 | 16.18 |
| D. Wilson | 964.1 | 384 | 1772 | 102 | 17.37 |
| D. N. F. Slade | 393.1 | 156 | 734 | 42 | 17.47 |
| H. J. Rhodes | 499.3 | 138 | 1156 | 64 | 18.06 |
| J. N. Graham | 726 | 218 | 1460 | 79 | 18.48 |
| C. M. Old | 433 | 98 | 1061 | 57 | 18.61 |
| R. Illingworth | 599.1 | 206 | 1186 | 62 | 19.12 |
| D. W. White | 696.3 | 157 | 1775 | 92 | 19.29 |
| S. Turner | 201.1 | 52 | 428 | 22 | 19.45 |
| M. Nash | 659.1 | 190 | 1560 | 80 | 19.50 |
| Majid Jahangir | 154 | 40 | 298 | 15 | 19.86 |
| J. A. Snow | 680.1 | 164 | 1740 | 87 | 20.00 |
| N. M. McVicker | 518.1 | 125 | 1484 | 74 | 20.05 |

There was no MCC tour involving Test matches in 1969-70, a welcome break in the increasingly busy schedule of international matches, although in these pre-World Series cricket days, a winter off was still not considered a freak. Some of England's leading players did have experience overseas, however, an MCC side under A. R. Lewis making a tour of the Far East (they were due also to go to East Africa but for the first of many times, political objections to the forthcoming South African tour of England prevented their doing so) and a strong side touring the Caribbean under the banner of the Duke of Norfolk, with E. W. Swanton as Major Domo.

An unusual feature, in modern times at least, of the MCC tour was that the team was accompanied by its own umpire, Syd Buller, then widely respected as the best in the world. The opening match in Colombo against Ceylon was won by 173 runs, despite the loss of Geoff Boycott to the second ball of the match. On this tour,

although Boycott inevitably finished as the team's leading scorer, with hundreds at Singapore, Ipoh and Bangkok, the Glamorgan opener Alan Jones did almost as well and was reckoned by his team-mates to be very much in the same high class as the Yorkshire champion. Jones was deeply unfortunate to play in only one unofficial Test match for England the following summer. Of the remainder of Lewis's team, only another Welshman, Don Shepherd, the Oxford and Hampshire captain Richard Gilliat, and the Warwickshire seamer Bill Blenkiron did not win an England cap. In a month's cricket the team was unbeaten and all but one of the nine matches was won.

The Duke of Norfolk's side, in the Caribbean at the same time, were led by Colin Cowdrey and also had an accompanying umpire, Charlie Elliott. Five of their nine fixtures were won, only two lost. Their most successful bowler, by far, was the leg-spinner Robin Hobbs. In the team was a young South African who had come to make his cricketing fortune in the land of his Scottish father, Tony Greig. Did he look with special interest at the scores of the simultaneous Test series in South Africa, in which Bill Lawry's Australians were receiving a rare hiding? It would only have been natural had he done so, because for whatever reasons he had chosen to play for Sussex, he was on the verge of a glittering Test career whilst the South African team he was not at that stage good enough to join were enjoying not only one of the greatest but also the most short-lived triumphs in Test history. It was as if a brilliant Opera Company had given one last superb performance before the crashing of their coach on the way to the next venue: the stars never performed together again.

Amongst those playing their last Test matches in this series were Graeme Pollock and Barry Richards, who each scored more than 500 runs in only seven innings, Eddie Barlow, who made two Test hundreds and took 11 wickets, and Mike Procter, who took 26 wickets at 13 each, apart from his 209 runs at 34, and who completely outbowled the great Graeme McKenzie. The latter, like all the Australian team, was tired out after a tour of India, but these performances were to be looked back upon by many a nostalgic eye through the long winter of political discontent which lay ahead, nipping those cricketing flowers from South Africa in early bud and blighting all their successors, perhaps for ever.

# — 1970 —

"STOP the 70 Tour" – the anti-apartheid campaign which aims to prevent or disrupt the visit of the South African side to this country – has enmeshed English cricket in a political net. Each twist the Cricket Council has made to free itself, making decisions based solely on the eternal maxim "in the best interests of cricket", has brought a deeper entanglement. The South Africans are coming, but cricket played on barricaded grounds, with barbed wire, a massive police force, the smuggling of teams to and from hotels, and a multitude of practical defences against demonstration and disruption – a macabre prospect, 1970.

But now let's face the practical job of sorting out the

new lbw law to the best advantage. See those umpires resplendent in new uniform (hats by Dunn, of course). See Tom Cartwright in Somerset colours, with Maurice Hill; Majid at Cambridge; Sarfraz beginning with Northants, and Colin Cowdrey setting out on the road to recovery, back in the Kent team after missing a large slice of last season through the Achilles tendon injury.

## THE CLOUDS GATHER
### APRIL 25–MAY 1

THE threats of the Hain group – "Stop the 70 Tour" – become more menacing and suggest that the possibility of getting one peaceful hour's cricket against the South Africans is remote. But if so the demonstrators must certainly infringe on the rights of the British citizen, who is legally entitled to see the tour without interruption from anyone. It is becoming a matter of law and order, and its acceptance as high political drama was made clear this week when Mr

Harold Wilson, Mr Heath, and Mr Thorpe appeared on television to answer the pertinent questions.

The Prime Minister fervently appealed to the Cricket Council to stop the tour. He pointed to the risk of African countries withdrawing from the Commonwealth Games. Mr Heath disagreed with this thinking. It is just and lawful that the South African tour should continue. Contact with them will prove a more effective weapon against apartheid than isolation.

*This threat of disruption to other sports has frequently been raised, but rarely, if ever, carried out.*

A motion at the Oxford Union that "this House would disrupt the South African cricket tour" was defeated by nine votes – 400 to 391. Wilfred Wooller and Peter Hain were, as ever, the chief protagonists.

Wilfred Wooller (far left) and Peter Hain, spokesmen for the two sides in the debate.

Well, midst all this, Sir Edward Boyle and the Bishop of Woolwich are pressing a more reasoned and articulate case for the cancelling of the tour, under the banner of the Fair Cricket Campaign. The damage to community relations and the effect on other sports are their concern. Meanwhile the Cricket Council have sought advice from every possible quarter, and remain unshakeable in their conviction – the tour must go on.

But somehow the imagination was most fired by the return of Bill Edrich to Lord's. Thirty-two years ago a Test player, he now batted against Middlesex for Norfolk, and like the story book, reincarnated the defiant jaw, struck 22 runs off six balls from Jones, and spread a glow of satisfaction through the cricket world. Heroes should always remain heroes, and Bill Edrich did not let us down. The millions like me who were weaned on talk of Edrich and Compton smiled quietly. We knew he would make them fight.

It is a little early to assess the new lbw law, but some of the bowlers' appealing has reached the heights of optimism when the batsman offers no stroke outside the off-stump. Bowlers seem to think a rag-and-bone man's voice will aid the cause. What noisy people. But that's a batsman's view, and very biased!

### POLITICS AND SOME STURDY BLOWS BY NASH
#### MAY 2–8

IT was a peculiar feeling, playing for Glamorgan at Lord's on Wednesday. On a rather dark evening the cricket meandered peacefully to a quiet close, no applause, no noisy tavern or excited members. But there *was* noise, a lot of it, and nothing to do with the cricket being played.

The Long Room rocked with debate of the South African tour decision. Members crammed in to support or defend. The bellowings of disapproval could be heard all over St. John's Wood. Certainly the Middlesex and Glamorgan players realised that the playing of the game is of secondary importance in the cricket world at the moment.

Wilfred Wooller continues to be the most public supporter of MCC and the Cricket Council. Peter Hain is the youthful rebel rouser. Neither communicate successfully to the other's age group or generation. The temperature of demonstration is rising. Time will tell.

Cricket came second, perhaps, but it has been lively enough. The first John Player League matches brought the usual high tension dramas.

The performance of the day came from my colleague, Malcolm Nash, who struck 54 off 33 balls, including five sixes, against Kent. He came in when Glamorgan were 57 for seven and when on TV the foreboding voice of Jim Laker was predicting no contest. Glamorgan narrowly won an exciting match. The BBC prize of £250 to the scorer of the fastest 50 is likely to stay with Nash until the batsmen really warm up.

Sir Cyril Hawker was chosen as successor to Maurice Allom as President of MCC. The President is the ex-officio Chairman of the Cricket Council, which, as current events testify, is a position of responsibility and importance. Sir Cyril, 70 in July, is Chairman of Standard Bank, and his business connections on a world-wide scale suggest his obvious suitability for the busy office.

### MOVES TO ISOLATE SOUTH AFRICA
#### MAY 9–15

THE whole country is now embroiled in the South African affair, not just the cricketing fraternity. On Thursday, the Commons held an emergency debate.

Apart from the rights and wrongs of inviting South Africa in the first place, discussion seems to have settled on the responsibility for calling it off, Government or Cricket Council. The Council certainly stand firm behind their resolution to keep going and play. As for the main political parties, they both have an eye on the impending general election. The Labour Government believe that the Cricket Council should cancel the tour. The Conservatives say that it is the onus of the Government.

I believe that even the honest cricket supporter, who looked forward to seeing one of the greatest cricketing sides in action in England is now having moments of grave doubt. The Commons debate ended with Denis Howell, MP, Minister of Sport, announcing the Sports Council's resolution to withdraw South Africa's invitation because of the harmful repercussions on sport, especially multi-racial sport. No vote was taken at the debate, but point was given to Mr Howell's announcement on Friday, when the International Olympic Committee withdrew recognition of the South African National Olympic Committee. South Africa's isolation in world sport took a leap forward.

Tom Graveney looks likely to sign a three-year contract with Queensland and take his family with him to Australia. Apparently his last Championship innings at Lord's (not of the season), this week against Middlesex, was as magnificent as he has ever played: 36 not out, not many, but full of his inimitable, mellow skill. "Graveney plays the old strokes" was a newspaper heading. No finer sight imaginable.

## Poll verdict: Test tour should go on

**By Daily Mail Reporter**

MORE THAN half the people in Britain think the South African cricket tour should still go ahead this summer. This is rev---
Natic

## HAIN CELEBRATES AND LANCASHIRE ARE CONFIDENT
### MAY 16–22

ON the evening of May 22, the death knell sounded for the South African tour. The unsavoury mix of sport and politics, months ago just an academic talking point, has this week dominated the nation's conscience and gossip, and it has all ended with the Cricket Council withdrawing South Africa's invitation at the request of the Government.

Earlier in the week the Council met and announced that nothing had altered their thinking and that the tour was on. But then Mr James Callaghan, on the Government's behalf, wrote the official request and the Council "found no alternative".

The obsequies were brief. The ending was terse. The giant balloon fell quickly flat, and the talk is now of a substitute Test series in England this year.

Poor Arthur Milton broke his arm, fending off a delivery from Alan Ward and is likely to be out for four weeks. The inimitable Garfield Sobers scored two hundreds in the game against Surrey, and still Surrey snatched the victory. 160 and 103 not out is a fair contribution to a three-day match.

Top of the national batting averages is Roy Marshall (ave. 91 decimals omitted), second is Clive Lloyd (ave. 84). Don Shepherd of Glamorgan heads the bowling with 36 wickets at 15. He has bowled 332 overs already. An interesting comparison is Derek Underwood who has bowled a mere 173.

In front of 11,000 devotees of the Sunday League Champions, Lancashire thrust aside the challenge from Northants, Harry Pilling 79, Clive Lloyd 46. By all reports this was a fine display of remarkable stroke play. A lot has been talked of mathematics and slide rule cricket on a Sunday, but Lancashire have an asset greater than a head for figures: that is, confidence. The bad ball goes for four, the quick single is never missed, fielding sides are put under pressure, and the whole performance gathers momentum week by week with success. Failure to succeed at the Sunday game persuades a side to rush headlong for a big score or graft carefully for a respectable one. The complexities of the game dominate performance. Watching Lancashire play at their best, I see no complexities in the short game.

They just bowl and field as tight as possible, then smash the ball around the park. Their turn to struggle will obviously come, but at present they are the captain's dream. "Play all your shots but don't take any chances," is the famous command.

## INTIKHAB'S WEEK
### MAY 23–29

THE acrimony of the past weeks has gone. Most people agreed that a Rest of the World side should take on England in five Tests. Most people wished the tournament to be given status and true competitive spice by inviting players from all over the world, not just a mix of those currently playing in England, and by awarding England caps to the home side. So it has been decided.

*Whether the matches were official Tests or not has long been a matter for bitter dispute amongst statisticians. The decision, eventually, was that they were not official, but those who played knew how much harder a series it was to play in than many which have gone down in official Test records.*

Glamorgan's model opening batsman, Alan Jones, raised a flutter of speculation when he began the week with a century against Worcestershire and had three innings to play and 193 runs to score to become the first player for 32 years to make the 1,000-run target before the end of May. Not to be, but a notable performance.

Perhaps it was rather Intikhab's week. His five for 29 helped Surrey to an exciting win by 10 runs over Hampshire at Bournemouth, though a classic 121 by Roy Marshall and a flailing 73 by Castell all but took the result the other way. Intikhab then went to Lord's and against Middlesex captured eight for 74 in the first innings and scored 106 and 34. Peter Parfitt's second innings score of 133 thwarted Surrey victory hopes here.

In the first part of the week, Lancashire batted on into the second day of their Roses match at Headingley, reaching 381. Lever and Shuttleworth then rushed out the Yorkshiremen for 121. Following on, Boycott and Hutton provided most opposition, but even without Shuttleworth who was injured, Lancashire bowled

Yorkshire out and easily got the required 22 for their first Roses win in 10 years.

To rub salt into the Tykes' wounds, it was Yorkshireman Barry Wood who compiled an important century on the first day for Lancashire. He follows in the footsteps of Albert Ward who thus treated his native county in the Roses match in 1892 and also Phil King in 1946.

## BOWLERS PRAY FOR RAIN AND REST OF THE WORLD CHOSEN
### MAY 30–JUNE 5

WILL it never rain in England again, the bowlers groan! The week's cricket has been conducted with much incident and excitement under an azure sky. The grounds are hard, and ring out like hollow concrete under the fielders' chase.

Colin Milburn went to the nets at Northampton, and the cricketing world wished him well. He held out little hope of batting with adequate vision, but owed himself the effort of trying – the first attempt to play since the car accident which took away his eye last May. He was surprised by the reasonable sight he got of the ball and thinks he will try again.

After many amateur selectors and professional critics had their game of selecting the Rest of the World team for the First Test at Lord's, Messrs F. R. Brown, Ames and Sobers, the captain, produced the official choice, and no more formidable line-up of batsmen, or at least stroke-making batsmen, could be imagined. B. A. Richards, E. J. Barlow, F. M. Engineer, L. R. Gibbs, Intikhab Alam, R. B. Kanhai, C. H. Lloyd, G. D. McKenzie, R. G. Pollock, M. J. Procter, G. Sobers (capt.) and the twelfth man Mushtaq Mohammad. County players feel that there could be "an awful lot of stick flying around" for our bowlers, but no-one would really worry too much about batting against them. Time will tell, but I agree. England bowlers, stand up and be recognised!

Ray Illingworth is one, because he has been announced as captain for the First Test. Colin Cowdrey's lack of runs debars him, but his Gillette Cup innings of 83 not out on Saturday against Worcestershire proclaimed his classic presence.

Kent beat Cambridge University in an even game which was a credit to the University. Majid apparently has students hurrying from their colleges at lunchtime if news reaches them that he is not out at lunch. His reputation blossomed with a magnificent 159. Bowling to Majid at Fenner's in this dry spell is considered by even the best county bowlers an expendable experience!

## ALAN WARD STRIKES
### JUNE 6–12

SUSSEX had little joy following their elevation to the top of the County Championship table. Derbyshire struck them down uncompromisingly, beating them at Buxton in the week-end Championship match and flattening them in the John Player League at Derby. Chief executioner was Alan Ward, who took 10 wickets at Buxton and on Sunday captured four early wickets in four balls.

His was the performance of the week, but not far behind was Barry Richards, who played an extraordinary innings of 155 not out in Hampshire's 215 for two against Yorkshire at Sheffield, and Harry Pilling – 401 runs in two matches for Lancashire.

## VIRTUOSO SOBERS
### JUNE 13–19

I suppose the event, or non-event, of the week was the start of the First Test between England and The Rest of the World. The "event" was the most magnificent innings by Garfield Sobers, who, having personally bowled out England for 127, then proceeded to follow

The England team for the first match against The Rest of the World. Back, left to right: A. Jones, B. Luckhurst, D. Underwood, A. Ward, K. Shuttleworth, M. Denness. Front: B. D'Oliveira, J. Snow, R. Illingworth, P. Sharpe, A. Knott. Sadly Alan Jones's only appearance for England was to be removed from the records when the series was later ruled to be "unofficial".

Barlow's fine century with a treat of sustained magic, to the extent of 183 runs in four and three-quarter hours.

The "non-event" was England's batting – Edrich withdrew through injury to his finger – and the only batsmen emerging from a rather pained experience with a ticket for the Second Test certainly booked seem to be Luckhurst, D'Oliveira and Illingworth, who has nobly compiled 63 in the first innings and 36 not out in the second. Alan Ward's bowling gave rise to most optimism when one considers Australia, or even getting out of the series "in one piece". Ward took four for 121 in 33 overs in the Rest of the World's mammoth innings of 546. England have so far replied with 127 and 228 for five.

The accolade goes unquestionably to Sobers. It is fascinating now to recall the balderdash that was talked and written about him the summer before. A "retarding of the reflexes", someone said; "the edge has gone", "he has played too much in one lifetime". This deed of virtuosity at Lord's held the purist enthralled, and even the stuffy statistician could rejoice in the trivia – only a dozen men in the history of Test cricket have taken five wickets or more in an innings and made 100 in the same match. Sobers, including this performance, has done it three times. When he bowled out Sharpe, he became the second player in Test history to take 200 wickets and score 2,000 runs. Well, that just about keeps everyone happy!

John Mortimore made his first appearance of the season this week, now fully recovered from the breaking of a collar bone sustained in a football match before the season started. A return also for Maurice Hallam, out of retirement just for one match, against Warwickshire at Nuneaton. Rohan Kanhai this week became the first player to score 1,000 runs. My unfortunate colleague Alan Jones, who had made such a brilliant assault on the "1,000 in May" target, ran into unjury, ill-luck and a moment of indifferent form, just as the month ended and his first Test match came along. He deserves another chance.

## *ENGLAND IN RUINS*
### *JUNE 20–26*

O N Monday, the fourth day of the First Test, England went under by an innings and 80 runs to the Rest of the World. Ray Illingworth fought it out with characteristic determination and took his personal score to 94. But Intikhab, who had modest figures for most of England's second innings, mopped up the tail and came off with six for 113 in 54 overs. Genuine pace or leg spin – tail enders often play one or the other with reasonable skill, but rarely do they manage to survive both.

**FIRST TEST**
Played at Lord's June 17, 19, 20, 22, 23
**Rest of the World beat England by an innings and 80 runs**

**England**

| First Innings | | Second Innings | |
|---|---|---|---|
| A Jones c Engineer b Procter | 5 | c Engineer b Procter | 0 |
| B W Luckhurst c Richards b Sobers | 1 | c Engineer b Intikhab | 67 |
| M H Denness c Barlow b McKenzie | 13 | c Sobers b Intikhab | 24 |
| B L D'Oliveira c Engineer b Sobers | 0 | c Lloyd b Intikhab | 78 |
| P J Sharpe c Barlow b Sobers | 4 | b Sobers | 2 |
| R Illingworth c Engineer b Sobers | 63 | c Barlow b Sobers | 94 |
| A P E Knott c Kanhai b Sobers | 2 | lbw b Gibbs | 39 |
| J A Snow c Engineer b Sobers | 2 | b Intikhab | 10 |
| D L Underwood c Lloyd b Barlow | 19 | c Kanhai b Intikhab | 7 |
| A Ward c Sobers b McKenzie | 11 | st Engineer b Intikhab | 0 |
| K Shuttleworth not out | 1 | not out | 0 |
| Extras (lb 5, nb 1) | 6 | Extras (b 4, lb 8, nb 6) | 18 |
| **Total** | **127** | **Total** | **339** |

**Fall of wkts:** 1st Innings: 5, 17, 23, 23, 29, 31, 44, 94, 125, 127.
2nd Innings: 0, 39, 140, 148, 196, 313, 323, 334, 338, 339.
**Bowling:** 1st Innings: McKenzie 16.1-3-43-2; Procter 13-6-20-1; Sobers 20-11-21-6; Barlow 4-0-26-1; Intikhab 2-0-11-0.
2nd Innings: McKenzie 15-8-25-0; Procter 15-4-36-1; Sobers 31-13-43-2; Barlow 7-2-10-0; Intikhab 54-24-113-6; Gibbs 51-17-91-1; Lloyd 1-0-3-0.

**Rest of the World**

| First Innings | |
|---|---|
| B A Richards c Sharpe b Ward | 35 |
| E J Barlow c Underwood b Illingworth | 119 |
| R B Kanhai c Knott b D'Oliveira | 21 |
| R G Pollock b Underwood | 55 |
| C H Lloyd b Ward | 20 |
| G S Sobers c Underwood b Snow | 183 |
| F M Engineer b Ward | 2 |
| Intikhab Alam b Ward | 61 |
| M J Procter b Snow | 26 |
| G D McKenzie c Snow b Underwood | 0 |
| L R Gibbs not out | 2 |
| Extras (b 10, lb 5, nb 7) | 22 |
| **Total** | **546** |

**Fall of wkts:** 69, 106, 237, 237, 293, 298, 496, 537, 544, 546.
**Bowling:** Snow 27-7-109-2; Ward 33-4-121-4; Shuttleworth 21-2-85-0; D'Oliveira 18-5-45-1; Underwood 25.5-8-81-2; Illingworth 30-8-83-1.

So Gary Sobers accepted the £2,000 win money from Guinness; the Rest of the World selectors simply adjusted their 12th man position, Younis replacing Mushtaq, and England's selectors rushed back to the committee rooms.

From the start it always seemed that England's fairly inexperienced batting would suffer all the nerves and tension of representing their country, and of trying to prove their worth, or at least potential, for Australia. On the other hand the hired stars had no nationalistic palpitations thundering under their shirts. They could play relaxed, yet still concentrating, such was the honour of playing for a World team, and such was the handsome prize money. Talent apart, the psychological dice were heavily loaded against England.

The remedy was put forward later in the week by the

selectors, who replaced Jones, Denness, Sharpe and Shuttleworth with Edrich, Fletcher, Amiss, Cowdrey and Greig. The team is to be chosen from 12.

Lancashire's Frank Hayes made a name for himself again in his second Championship match. He was stumped off Peter Sainsbury, dancing down the wicket with his score at 99, in the penultimate over of the game. Quite superb stroke-play, by every account.

Sussex's Championship chances halted when they limped out of a game with Northants, conceding defeat. Parks, bruised foot, and M. A. Buss, pulled muscle, were unable to bat in the second innings, which Brian Crump ripped open with figures of five for 48.

Lancashire have caught Derbyshire in the John Player League. Somerset persisted with their good form in this competition by beating Derbyshire. Lancashire overcame Hants, while Sussex got their first Sunday win of the season, over Northants. Ken Suttle took four for 24.

Two well-known and well-loved cricketers died this week. B. H. "Bev" Lyon, the former captain of Gloucestershire, whose dynamic captaincy and personal example on the field led his county to their best years since W. G. Grace, from 1929-34. Also A. F. "Bert" Wensley of Sussex. He played consistently from 1922-36. He was 72.

## *ILLINGWORTH AGAIN TO THE RESCUE*
### *JUNE 27–JULY 3*

THE Second Test began at Nottingham on Thursday and everyone recognised the implications and ramifications should England fail to get into the game and be overrun as they were at Lord's. Failure by the new batsmen, Fletcher and Cowdrey (Amiss was made 12th man), would mean an even more frantic search for men in form, or perhaps more patience in waiting for Cowdrey to strike form, and then, a second rout would deprive the already underpopulated Test arena of spectators through the series.

As it turned out, Tony Greig, making his debut, enjoyed success with the ball to the extent of dismissing Richards, Sobers, Engineer and Kanhai for a mere 59 runs in 18 overs. Basil D'Oliveira also made most of the chill, damp and blustery conditions in trapping Barlow,

Pollock, Intikhab and Gibbs for 43 in 17.4 overs. David Brown replaced Alan Ward who has injured an ankle, and he helped with the tail, getting rid of Procter and McKenzie. So a Rest of the World total of 276 is modest compared with their many talents. Clive Lloyd, severely dealing with the bad ball, especially on his legs, held the innings together with an undefeated 114.

But England failed on Friday. They scored 279, led by three, but lost the chance of gaining a telling initiative. Edrich and Luckhurst put on 78 for the first wicket, but it was Illingworth again who saved the effort after Cowdrey and Fletcher had failed, with a fighting knock of 97. Barlow with five for 66 caused most damage. At the moment everyone wishes England to make a close contest of the match. The interest aroused by the conception of the series is mild. An England landslide to two defeats would just about extinguish it.

Leicestershire are reported to be seeking the services of the Sydney-born batsman Bruce Neil, 23. Bramall Lane was visited by Bert Lock and will be reseeded. The only other titbit which brought a smile from many but a grimace from all who faced them, is that Les Jackson and Cliff Gladwin are to pair up again in an MCC side to play Derbyshire in a Sunday League rule game. Rush for a thigh pad and put a towel down the inside of the right leg! The two former heroes may not possess the venom which made them so respected by all batsmen, but they can smile, satisfied to see the elixir of Derbyshire fast bowling has been safely passed down the years – Copson, Gladwin, Jackson L., Jackson B., Rhodes, and now to Alan Ward. They say young Hendrick has promise too. Yes, Derbyshire is definitely thigh-pad country.

 *Who, one might still ask, was Bruce Neil?!*

## *ENGLAND ON TOP OF THE WORLD*
### *JULY 4–10*

AN hour before lunch on the last day of the Second Test match at Trent Bridge, England won a commendable victory over the Rest of the World. The margin was eight wickets, convincing enough – and runs came from the "probationers", Luckhurst 113 not out, Cowdrey 64 and Fletcher 69 not out.

Colin Cowdrey rarely features in the class of the

County Championship (as at July 1)

|   |   | P | Pt |
|---|---|---|---|
| **1** Surrey | | 12 | 12 |
| **2** Northamptonshire | | 13 | 12 |
| **3** Sussex | | 13 | 12 |
| **4** Lancashire | | 11 | 11 |

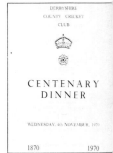

DERBYSHIRE
COUNTY CRICKET
CLUB

CENTENARY
DINNER

WEDNESDAY, 4th NOVEMBER, 1970

1870          1970

hopefuls, but he has been desperately short of runs for Kent so far this season. His pedigree is irrefutable, but one feared that the time would come when the selectors could wait no longer for performances to match it. Many professional cricketers will take delight in the success of Keith Fletcher. He played wonderfully well for his 50, out-scoring Luckhurst and bringing into the Test arena many of the attractive and telling strokes which have persuaded county sides of his extensive talents.

The reaction to the defeat by the Rest of the World selectors was to replace Graham McKenzie by Peter Pollock and Farouk Engineer by Deryck Murray. Murray has played no cricket of substance for some time and is a surprise inclusion.

Freddie Trueman offered to come back and bowl for Yorkshire if required, so it was announced early in the week. The offer was turned down by Yorkshire within a few days – a very correct decision. Yorkshire are right to accept their bad times and build for the future. It is unwise to compromise with senior players passed their best, just to edge respectability in the table. Yet Fred would, of course, always be a fine bowler, and a wicket-taker too.

The Nawab of Pataudi is back, and he is to play for Sussex immediately. Sussex maintain their efforts at the top of the County Championship table. This week they lie joint second with Glamorgan and Northants. Surrey are leading while Lancashire look ominously placed at sixth place with three games in hand.

## LANCASHIRE RIDE HIGH
### JULY 11–17

A week of high action, Test and county, and a meeting of the International Cricket Conference to debate the experimental lbw law, and also the possibility of abolishing the leg-bye.

First to the Test. Illingworth is the elected captain of England for this Third Test, but with the announcement of the Australian tour captaincy so imminent, much discussion has rested on the comparative merits of Illingworth and Cowdrey.

By Friday night, the time of writing, Cowdrey has picked up a nought – lbw b Sobers; England were bowled out mainly by Procter (five for 46) for 294, and the Rest, in threatening fashion, have compiled 296 for

four. Richards 47, Pollock 40 and Kanhai 71 built the foundation. Now Sobers (not out 63) and Lloyd (not out 62), both of whom murdered the new ball attack, are set to advance the innings.

Lancashire have three Championship games in hand, and are riding high in all three competitions, Gillette, John Player League and the County Championship. Will they do a Leeds United and miss all three? I do not think so. Because they are basically a young side, I feel they will not suffer under pressure. It may sound paradoxical, but life at the top is harder to sustain by a team who have been long-time losers or narrow failures. Lancashire might just breeze in with their youthful appetite for success and take the Gillette and the League. They will find many challenges in the Championship.

The news of Alan Ward, England's fast bowler, is that his ankle injury persists. It is clearly important to get him absolutely fit and built up for the rigours of Australia this winter.

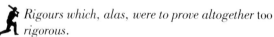 *Rigours which, alas, were to prove altogether too rigorous.*

## ILLINGWORTH CHOSEN AS TOUR CAPTAIN
### JULY 18–24

ILLINGWORTH to lead in Australia. Cowdrey offered the role to which he is painfully accustomed, that of vice-captain. This is the news of greatest moment, which at last has silenced the glut of biased journalism aimed at the destruction of the unfavoured one, rather than an appraisal of their virtues, and the closeness of the issue.

What an amazing volte-face for Ray Illingworth's career. Moving to Leicestershire to play out the remainder of his days he finds himself achieving the highest honour, knowing that he would never have skippered England had he remained with his native Yorkshire.

To my mind he is an outstanding practitioner of the game in the middle, with ball, with bat and with the mind. It was said that Colin Cowdrey was the man in possession and that Illingworth was the "caretaker". But that was scarcely the position after Illingworth had led England to a two-nil victory over the West Indies, and a two-nil victory over New Zealand, and had just levelled the Rest of the World series at one each. Illingworth has been an unqualified success; Cowdrey, too, succeeded against Australia in England and in the West Indies. Their very differing virtues became well known, and either protagonist would have been acceptable. Both would have been unlucky to come second in the race.

The Rest of the World won a five-wicket victory over England, though England's batsmen fought hard in their second effort of 409. Only Edrich and Underwood got under 20. Illingworth dismissed Lloyd and Sobers for the second time in the match, and Underwood took two wickets, Snow one.

Lancashire overpowered Somerset in the Gillette Cup semi-finals, the innings of Clive Lloyd, 43, and John Sullivan, 50, being the decisive factors. Sussex scraped home against Surrey. John Snow bowled outstandingly well, restricting Surrey to 196. Despite Sussex's efforts to give the game away by slogging too soon, it was Snow again, this time with the bat, who kept cool, struck a good off-drive off the last ball with two runs needed to win. Poor Intikhab took his eye off the ball, misfielded, and Surrey had bungled the fairly manageable exercise of laying back in the field to give the one, but stop the two. The scores ended equal, but Sussex had lost fewer wickets, eight instead of 10.

## BARLOW'S HAT-TRICK
### JULY 25–31

EDDIE Barlow, whose watchful batting and eager, bustling bowling personify resolution and competition, scythed through England's tail in the first innings of the Fourth Test at Headingley with four wickets in five balls, including the hat-trick.

It was the first Test hat-trick for 10 years, removing Knott, Old and Wilson. Illingworth followed. Indeed only M. J. C. Allom, the reigning MCC President, has ever taken four in five balls in Tests and that was in New Zealand in 1929–30.

Sobers put England in to bat, on a pitch which held some moisture and in atmosphere reasonably heavy. By lunch Sobers returned the bowling figures of 17-11-14-0. Barlow, on the other hand, had trapped

Boycott and Cowdrey for 34. Barlow finished with seven for 64, and only Fletcher 89, and Illingworth 58, resisted to great effect. For the Rest, Richards has strained his back and will not bat. Kanhai has a badly bruised thumb and will only bat if required. So Murray, the 'keeper, opened the innings and compiled 95 excellent runs. The score on Friday night is England 222, The Rest 309 for seven, Sobers ominously 75 not out.

Welcome back this week to Arthur Milton. Recovered from his broken arm, he staved off certain defeat for Gloucestershire with the fiftieth hundred of his career. Six hours 41 minutes for 149.

It was good to meet Wes Hall, who is currently managing a very successful tour for the West Indian Young Cricketers. "Schoolboy cricket has not tested us," he says. "We should have played the odd game against County Seconds."

Very impressive indeed. It suggests the West Indies will not be short of top-class Test players for long. They have one considerable skill which could upset England very soon, the art of wrist spin. There are many accurate young bowlers of this type on the islands who are not easy to read. So will testify the Duke of Norfolk's touring team, Glamorgan, who toured last April, and the English schoolboys who have had a torrid time sorting out its problems.

*Even in the Eighties the West Indies continued to produce some useful wrist-spinners – but they seldom needed to use them!*

## DEATH OF SYD BULLER
### AUGUST 1–7

ENGLAND'S heroic fight back after Barlow had virtually snuffed out their chances of beating the Rest of the World with his hat-trick, led them to the brink of a famous victory at Headingley when the World side needed a fairly modest 223 runs to win.

Sobers and Intikhab put on 115 for the sixth wicket, and this was the crucial partnership. Greig dropped a slip catch off Intikhab early on the last day – that would have made it 82 for six. The injured pair, Kanhai and Richards, were forced to bat, the former going quickly, but Richards, 21 not out, and Procter, 22 not out, kept

County Championship
(as at August 5)

| | | P | P |
|---|---|---|---|
| **1** | Surrey | 17 | 1( |
| **2** | Derbyshire | 17 | 15 |
| **3** | Lancashire | 16 | 15 |
| **4** | Glamorgan | 18 | 15 |

Syd Buller leaves the field at Edgbaston deep in conversation with Dave Halfyard and followed by Dennis Amiss and Gary Sobers. Only moments later he collapsed and died in the pavilion.

Gibbs from the crease and fended off a magnificent English rally.

The close of the week brought bitter news of the death of Syd Buller. He died at his post during the match between Warwickshire and Notts at Edgbaston. He was 60. Buller was a man of authority, yet gentleness. He was infinitely patient and generous with his time and attention. Travelling with him earlier in the year with MCC in the Far East, all these qualities he displayed, and with great dignity instructed the many devotees of the game in the law and the spirit. He was unquestionably the outstanding adjudicator of the present day.

England have selected Peter Lever and Denis Amiss for the last Test. Greig is omitted. It is Lever's first Test. This season's efforts have got him 70 first-class wickets at 19·44.

## CAPRI BEFORE COUNTY?
### AUGUST 8–14

"ILLINGWORTH again rescues England from collapse" – so read the now inevitable headlines in the national papers after the first day of the Fifth Test match at the Oval. Illingworth was not out at the close of the day with 47 runs, and the England total was 229 for five – Luckhurst, Boycott, Cowdrey, Fletcher and Amiss out. What an incredibly consistent series the England captain has had.

Graeme Pollock has at last come off. By this evening, Friday, he has scored 104 not out, in characteristic style, and G. S. Sobers remains ominously 55 not out. The Rest of the World score stands at 231 for four. England with their hands full again!

Pollock and Sobers – a partnership to remember for all those at The Oval.

But the most amazing game was that between the table leaders Derbyshire and their opponents Worcestershire. Ian Buxton, the Derbyshire captain, condemned the game to a bitter draw by delaying his declaration on the third day. This allowed Wilkins time to complete the season's third fastest 100 and so qualify for a Ford Capri car. Tom Graveney said at the close, "I'm so upset I can hardly think. It is a case of putting Ford Capri cars before the County Championship."

Did Ian Buxton really do this? It can hardly be true. There must be another story. But written just after the game I have no evidence to the contrary.

It probably was true. It was neither the first nor last time that professional cricketers had put material matters ahead of the game itself.

## THE CHAMPIONSHIP: ANYONE'S GUESS
### AUGUST 15–21

ILLINGWORTH, Cowdrey (captain and vice-captain), Boycott, D'Oliveira, Edrich, Fletcher, Hampshire and Luckhurst (batsmen), Lever, Snow, Shuttleworth and Ward (fast bowlers), Wilson and Underwood (spin bowlers), Knott and Taylor R. W. (wicket-keepers) – the chosen few for Australia, and all fairly predictable, all excellent professional players under a top-class captain.

England duly lost the Test. Kanhai 100, Lloyd 68, and Sobers 40 not out – this was enough to see off the required target of 287.

The County Championship is now anyone's guess, though Lancashire and Yorkshire remain favourites. Yorkshire have the easiest run in since Gloucestershire, Somerset (twice), and Lancashire is their programme. But anything is possible.

## KENT CHASE LANCASHIRE
### AUGUST 22–28

ONE matter is almost resolved. The John Player League table looks now certain to be headed by the holders of the title, Lancashire. At Dudley this week they beat Worcestershire by 33 runs and have 49 points with one game to play.

County Championship (as at August 21)

|   |            | P  | Pts |
|---|------------|----|-----|
| 1 | Glamorgan  | 21 | 195 |
| 2 | Derbyshire | 22 | 192 |
| 3 | Yorkshire  | 20 | 186 |
| 4 | Lancashire | 21 | 184 |
| 5 | Warwickshire | 21 | 179 |
| 6 | Surrey     | 19 | 172 |

South Africa's Mike Procter and Eddie Barlow enjoy the success of West Indian pair Clive Lloyd and Deryck Murray in dismissing Dennis Amiss in England's second innings.

Their rivals, Kent, have to win both matches against Notts and Hants, and Lancashire lose to Yorkshire if there is to be an upset. Lancashire have been the dynamic side of the season, youthful, talented and determined under pressure. I cannot see them falter, yet cricket, and the John Player League most especially, can produce the totally unexpected. We shall see.

## *LANCASHIRE – J. PLAYER CHAMPIONS; GOODBYE GRAVENEY*
### *AUGUST 29–SEPTEMBER 4*

IN a flurry of action at Folkestone, the County Championship has been decided if no freak weather or freak form strikes the matches between Lancashire and Surrey, and Kent and Surrey. For Kent have virtually captured the title in a week of wonderfully aggressive cricket.

They rushed to 283 for seven to meet the tough requirements of a Sobers declaration – Denness 90, Luckhurst 58, Asif 56 – in the first part of the week. Then they thrust aside Leicestershire with ridiculous ease, and the signs were evident that, at last, someone had hit true Championship form. Having dismissed Leicestershire for 152 with five bowling points, they smashed (the appropriate word it seems) 351 for four in 85 overs, accumulating eight batting points. The last point was reached by striking 19 from the final over. The run-getters were Denness 66, Luckhurst 44, Johnson 108, Asif 63, Shepherd 37, Ealham 30 not out. Kent proceeded to go top of the table as Glamorgan and Lancashire drew, a position of obvious safety which they have not occupied since 1913.

Glenn Turner put right the run-out of last week by beating C. F. Walters's record of nine hundreds in a season for Worcestershire. His tenth, 133 not out against Warwickshire at Worcester, contained all the aggression that he has grafted onto his tenacious defence this season. He has become a formidable player indeed, and must surely be a source of great strength to New Zealand for many years.

The all-important Roses match ended with Lancashire taking five points and Yorkshire three in a drawn match. Lancashire chose to bat on into the second day on a good wicket and killed the game. On Sunday, however, they clinched the Sunday League title. The Championship has eluded them, I think, but the Gillette Cup is available if they beat Sussex on Saturday next.

Tom Graveney played his last match in London this week. He leaves for a coaching appointment in Queensland soon, and his 82 not out took him to the highest spot for a home player in the national batting averages. He is second only to Sobers.

## *LANCASHIRE TAKE THE GILLETTE*
### *SEPTEMBER 5–11*

WITH Lord's almost full, Lancashire took their second prize of the season, beating Sussex in the Gillette Cup Final.

How this occasion has caught the public's fascination! Spectators, partial or impartial, indulge themselves in the cricket, the surprise meetings with old friends, the pint or the Pimms, whichever suits. This match began cat-like, with Lancashire's formidable opening bowlers, Lever and Shuttleworth, relishing the agility of their fielders which pinned down Greenidge and Mike Buss. The sight of Clive Lloyd loping avidly after the ball, then shortening his stride to ridiculously petite steps for such a tall man to make the pick-up and simultaneous pirouette in mid-air to send the ball flying in, flat and accurate to the top of the stumps – this was breathtaking, and rapturous applause momentarily broke the silent tension of the early hours. Barry Wood made brilliant stops in the gully. There was no Lancastrian who did not strain and succeed in the field.

There were times when Sussex were going well. The wicket was rather slowly paced. No one drove the ball straight back past the bowler all day. Yet when Jim Parks and Tony Greig were both yorked by David Hughes, looking to drive the left-armer, then Ken Suttle was run out, it seemed that Sussex, almost by accident, had got themselves a modest total.

Lancashire's batting was to bear that out. Harry Pilling, workmanlike, chanceless and eminently sensible, played an innings of great professionalism to see Lancashire home. If the game lacked the spice of brilliance, it was a fine tribute to Lancashire, and an

County Championship
(as at September 2)

|  |  | P | Pts |
|---|---|---|---|
| **1** | Glamorgan | 23 | 218 |
| **2** | Kent | 22 | 206 |
| **3** | Lancashire | 22 | 200 |
| **4** | Derbyshire } Sussex | 24 | 199 |

example for the whole country to see, of how they have mastered the short game of Sunday and Gillette cricket.

## THE SUMMER'S CHARACTER
### *SEPTEMBER 12–FINALE*

LANCASHIRE'S chance of taking 10 points off Surrey to finish runners-up in the Championship table was destroyed by rain at the Oval, and so the final placings are Kent, Glamorgan, Lancashire.

1970, on the field, made me certain that limited-over cricket has raised fielding standards to unexpected heights – not in the individual only, but right through whole teams. The lbw law has swung the game the batsman's way on good wickets but no batsman in the country played much differently from the season before.

The colour of the counties – Chris Wilkins thrashing the left-arm spinner flat over straight extra cover; Robin Hobbs floating his leg-spin higher and higher for greater reward in a fine season; the great pace and judgment of Mike Procter's inswing – the genuine wicket taker; Richards flat-footing it down the wicket to ground never before explored by British batsmen and reaching the pitch of the ball upright and absolutely balanced, then in a single swing of the open face powering the ball wide of mid-off – unforgettable; the passion Brian Luckhurst has given his game. I admired him as he fought his way to a position of ascendancy against the World's greatest players; I can recall Chris Old swooping in to run out Tony Greig at Scarborough with the most poetic piece of fielding I have ever seen; Roy Virgin, standing up, beating the ball mercilessly through the covers, a year of brilliance; I loved watching all Lancashire, in the field; Peter Marner thumping with science; John Price, perverse enough to blitz out a side with the old ball, second spell, on a flat wicket, when his fire could have been better used with the new 'un early on. But a fine season. Mushtaq's talent shining, not so much, but still dominant; Parks, majestic, holding the bat high on the handle, deadly effective on the leg side, and Griffith's scampering in that Gillette semi-final; Van Holder reaching new dimensions as a fast bowler; Mike J. K. Smith always turning in the innings that was needed; Boycott, and finally G. St A. Sobers. What a marvellous word to end on!

## CHAMPIONSHIP TABLE

| | P. | W. | L. | D. | Bt. | Bw. | Pts. |
|---|---|---|---|---|---|---|---|
| 1—Kent (10) | 24 | 9 | 5 | 10 | 70 | 77 | 237 |
| 2—Glamorgan (1) | 24 | 9 | 6 | 9 | 48 | 82 | 220 |
| 3—Lancashire (15) | 24 | 6 | 2 | 16 | 78 | 78 | 216 |
| 4—Yorkshire (13) | 24 | 8 | 5 | 11 | 49 | 86 | 215 |
| 5—Surrey (3) | 24 | 6 | 4 | 14 | 60 | 83 | 203 |
| 6—Worcestershire (12) | 24 | 7 | 1 | 16 | 46 | 84 | 200 |
| 7—Derbyshire (16) | 24 | 7 | 1 | 10 | 51 | 78 | 199 |
| Warwickshire (4) | 24 | 7 | 6 | 11 | 53 | 71 | 199 |
| 9—Sussex (7) | 24 | 5 | 7 | 12 | 62 | 87 | 199 |
| 10—Hampshire (5) | 24 | 4 | 6 | 14 | 69 | 88 | 197 |
| 11—Notts (8) | 24 | 4 | 8 | 12 | 71 | 73 | 184 |
| 12—Essex (6) | 24 | 4 | 6 | 14 | 64 | 76 | 180 |
| 13—Somerset (17) | 24 | 5 | 10 | 9 | 40 | 86 | 176 |
| 14—Northamptonshire (9) | 24 | 4 | 6 | 14 | 60 | 74 | 174 |
| 15—Leicestershire (14) | 24 | 5 | 6 | 13 | 46 | 77 | 173 |
| 16—Middlesex (11) | 24 | 5 | 5 | 14 | 47 | 69 | 166 |
| 17—Gloucestershire (2) | 24 | 3 | 8 | 13 | 56 | 80 | 166 |

*Colin Cowdrey must have taken peculiar satisfaction from Kent's late run to win the Championship, following as it did his bitter disappointment at losing the opportunity of captaining England in Australia. Injury had lost him the job originally, but Ray Illingworth's steel and shrewdness as a leader had been apparent at once and he was now to lead England to a rare success in Australia, with John Snow, John Edrich and Geoffrey Boycott as his outstanding individual players.*

*The relationship between Illingworth and the tour manager, David Clark, an MCC stalwart of the old school who put the spirit of the game above the need to win, was in sharp contrast to the harmonious partnership of Cowdrey and Les Ames in West Indies two winters before. Illingworth and Clark quarrelled openly at times, most notably over Clark's decision to agree to an extra Test match after the washout of the Third Test at Melbourne. Cowdrey found himself in the uncomfortable role of middle-man and his own form fell well below its true level on the field and with the bat, so that he never settled as one of an otherwise united team which won the six-match series (excluding the abandoned game) by two matches to nil.*

*Rightly or wrongly, the censure of certain aspects of the tour has been forgotten, in England at least, and the tour has gone down as a success and its captain as one of the best of all.*

*Illingworth and England now faced a stern challenge from India, for the other significant event in international cricket during the winter had been the first Indian success in the West Indies, based upon a phenomenal batting performance by a young man from Bombay called Sunil Gavaskar. At the age of 21 he scored 1169 first-class runs on the tour at 97·41 and in the four Tests in which he took part he made 774 runs at an average of 154·80. Another Bradman?*

# — 1971 —

"SO then cricket has a bright and a gentler side, in spite of Ashes lost or won, and yearly averages gravely scrutinized. Cricket is desecrated by futile levity, but elevated by a certain high-spirited detachment: between the extremes of indifference and over-anxiety there lies a proper mean. . . So it is with cricketers when ruffled, when embittered by disappointment, overawed by a false idea of the game's values, goaded by criticism, or puffed up by praise, that they cannot separate themselves from their pursuit. And when laughter goes out of a game it is drudgery indeed." That is how R. C. Robertson-Glasgow saw the eternal snare which forever lures the professional cricketer in his highly competitive world; the exact snare, it seems, which trapped some of the MCC players in Australia. We may talk lyrically of the Ashes regained, but this week the Cricket Council has had to censure publicly some of the acts of poor sportsmanship which discoloured the brave English effort. The Council reproaches all first-class cricketers and threatens the cancellation of a cricketer's registration should he be guilty of unsportsmanlike behaviour or sharp practice. Sad, in a way, that cricket's unwritten and envied code of conduct has had to be made an official edict rather than a matter of personal choice.

So as the cricket public chews away on all the contentious arguments brought back from Australia – Cowdrey's difficult position, Illingworth's attitude to manager David Clark, Snow's attitude to umpires and his failure to try in up-country games – let us now look forward and talk hopefully of Pakistan's visit to England during the first half of the season and India's in the second. India would seem to be the greater cricketing threat, having just won a splendid rubber in the West Indies. The country of Pakistan is torn, East against West, by a brutal civil war and for one moment this week we thought their talented cricketers were not going to arrive here. They turned up two days late.

The county game is off to a smooth start. Two men in form during the winter, Barry Richards and Brian Luckhurst, have already scored centuries, Richards against Oxford University and Luckhurst, for champion county Kent, against the MCC at Lord's. The pundits cannot separate four favourites for the County Championship, Kent, Lancashire, Surrey and Yorkshire. My thought for the season is watch Somerset with O'Keefe and Close in their ranks.

There are five new captains, Mike Brearley (Middlesex), Jim Watts (Northants), Richard Gilliat (Hampshire), Geoff Boycott (Yorkshire) and Norman Gifford (Worcestershire). Look out for Prideaux in Sussex colours! Apart from O'Keefe, overseas talent arrives in the shape of Bruce Francis, a young Sheffield Shield player come to Essex, Rhodesian Brian Davison with Leicestershire and West Indian Test opener Roy Fredericks with Glamorgan. There will be two familiar figures returning to help Sussex on Sundays, Ted Dexter and Ian Thomson.

Brian Davison – one of the season's new attractions.

## FREDERICKS MAKES HIS MARK
### MAY 1–7

FIVE hundred demonstrators chant their Bengali protests, banners waving, along the road outside the County Ground at Worcester. "Recognize Bangla Desh." "Go home, butchers." "Pakistanis play cricket in England as fathers commit genocide in Bangla Desh." Urgent messages, but very much a mini-demonstration and, it seems, the cause of the East Pakistan revolt will not attract the same volume of support as did the anti-apartheid movement.

On the field, Intikhab Alam's men ran into Glenn Turner in full flow, an uncomfortable initiation to English cricket. But Turner's 179 was repaid by Zaheer Abbas, a tall, young man, batting in spectacles, who scored a fine 110. Zaheer stands up straight to play his shots, and appears to have the timing and the wristy length to send the most accurate bowling to the boundary fence.

One more performance this week, of particular delight to me, of course, was the 145 not out scored by Glamorgan's newest player, Roy Fredericks. His left-arm wrist-spin, too, may pose a few problems around the country. It's a very quick wrist action which no one can read accurately. But there *is* a drawback, and perhaps the reason why he has a modest bowling record. It takes Roy three overs before he "drops" it somewhere near the spot. Ah well, that'll be good enough for one or two, I expect!

*Glamorgan did not make the most of their investment in Roy Fredericks.*

Freddie Brown was this week nominated President-elect of MCC – a popular choice. He is a cricketer and an administrator of the greatest enthusiasm and loyalty not averse to cracking the whip if the efforts around him need sharpening.

## GOOD NEWS FOR VILLAGE CRICKET
### MAY 8–14

PAKISTAN lost by six wickets to Northants, having drawn with Hampshire. Aftab Gul and Zaheer Abbas continue to get runs. Hylton Ackerman (105) proved their chief obstacle at Northampton. Ackerman was another who got two centuries this week, 103 against Essex was the other.

On a dangerous wicket at Sophia Gardens in Cardiff, Roy Fredericks broke an arm when he was hit by a ball bowled by Vanburn Holder, in a County Championship match. He is expected to be absent for at least a month.

John Snow is to return to the Sussex side tomorrow having missed three matches because of an injured back. Ray Illingworth has been selected to captain England in all three Tests against Pakistan – no prizes for guessing that. More interesting will be the composition of the team, now that Colin Cowdrey has struck a rich vein of form. Like Keith Fletcher and Dennis Amiss, he is one of this week's many centurions.

Finally this is a week of great impact for cricketers on the village green. A National Village Championship, sponsored by Haig, will start next season with their final at Lord's no less. So the last three Saturdays of 1972 should feature three finals at Lord's, the National Club Championship, the Gillette Cup, and the Villages! I hope the crowds turn out for the clubs and villages; they could be events of real colour. Unfortunately, there could be clashes with soccer. Last Saturday I played in a splendid day's cricket at Chelmsford, a beautiful day for watching and playing. But it was Cup Final Day at Wembley, Arsenal v. Liverpool. The Essex Secretary

welcomed 121 playing spectators. Truly we felt like a "down-and-out" music hall turn, and played like one!

## MINOR COUNTIES STOP HERE
### MAY 15–21

GILLETTE Cup time again, and this week saw the Minor Counties put to the sword, as ever. I suppose one day a freak of weather may help them steal the initiative against a professional side, but so far all moments of crisis when the respective skills are put under pressure "in the middle", are all resolved in the professionals' favour.

Colin Cowdrey is back to his most fluent form, grinding down his recent critics with persistent run-getting all around the country. No player times the ball quite like he does. Does he ever break a bat? He scarcely seems to be striking the ball, just easing it through the gaps, running it gently down to third man or fine leg, dominating with art and skill – a gentle ringmaster.

## SECOND CENTURY FOR ZAHEER
### MAY 22–28

FOR the Pakistan tourists, it was a week of build-up before the First Test. They did not fare too well against MCC at Lord's. Winning the toss they were bowled out for 190 – Peter Lever four for 28, Richard Hutton three for 52 and Alan Ward two for 41. The ball moved occasionally off the wicket and they looked vulnerable outside the off stump. Then after MCC had declared at 255 for five, they again faltered with the bat. 47 for three. Rain on the third day spared them too many blushes.

Peter Lever – early success against the tourists.

However, at Gravesend, Zaheer Abbas made his second century (138) full of fluent strokes, the ball clipped away with a high back swing. Asif Iqbal, too, took fifty off his own county. The tourists got among the wickets after rain had fallen and had Kent struggling at 156 for nine before rain returned and the game was abandoned.

Last night, Friday, England's team was announced. Firstly the selectors decided that, irrespective of a medical report, John Snow should be left out. He has been dropped by his county this week for "lack of effort". Later he was reported to have seen a specialist and to have had X-rays on an injured back.

Dennis Amiss is the only player included who did not tour Australia. Alan Ward is recalled and the line-up is: Illingworth (captain), Amiss, Boycott, Cowdrey, D'Oliveira, Edrich, Lever, Luckhurst, Shuttleworth, Underwood and Ward. 12th man is Willis.

It is of interest that Chris Balderstone, the Yorkshire all-rounder, is to move to Leicestershire on special registration. Balderstone is a nice upright striker of the ball, hitting straight and correctly through the line. A change of county could advance his career – though his professional football commitments do restrict his availability.

*He was still playing some football when he twice played for England in 1976, and he was still playing effectively for Leicestershire in 1985.*

Barry Richards has accepted an offer to play for Natal for three years, while still representing Hampshire in this country.

## A TRAGIC ACCIDENT
### MAY 29–JUNE 4

A tragic accident happened on the field of play this week – Saturday afternoon, the third over after tea, and I was crouched in the gully position as Malcolm Nash of Glamorgan bowled to Warwickshire's Neil Abberley at Sophia Gardens in Cardiff. Off the meat of the bat (without the slightest back-lift to warn the close fielders) the ball sped almost invisibly, to crack Roger Davis a lightning blow above and behind the left ear. He was crouched opposite me at short square leg – and very close. Violent grotesque convulsions and a sudden change of facial colouring warned all of us that there was immediate need for professional medical attention. Minutes later, two doctors ran on, one of whom thankfully revived Roger with mouth to mouth resuscitation, after his pulse had stopped. At the time of writing, Roger Davis's life is safe, he is in hospital and his recovery may take months.

*He was back sooner than expected and the days of close fielders wearing helmets were still some years off.*

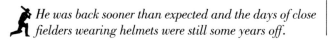
Roger Davis – a victim of the days before helmets.

News of the accident flashed round the professional cricket circuit throughout the world. It is the nearest to a fatality in the modern game and in the mind's eye everyone for a brief shattering moment lay prostrate in Roger Davis's boots just those few tiny yards from the popping crease.

If anything was calculated to stir us from depression it was a magnificent Test innings, indeed one of the very finest played in this country. Only Don Bradman (twice) Bobby Simpson and Bob Cowper (all Australians) have compiled higher individual scores than did Zaheer Abbas at Edgbaston. In nine hours of disciplined batting, full of wonderful strokes through the off-side field, Zaheer scored 274. For support he found Mushtaq (100) in quiet, workmanlike mood, and Pakistan were able to bat for the whole of the first two days for a total of 602 for 7 wickets.

Zaheer Abbas during his marathon innings at Edgbaston.

## ASIF MASOOD TAKES PAKISTAN CLOSE TO A FAMOUS VICTORY
### JUNE 5–11

THE First Test was drawn after rain had delayed the restart on Tuesday, the final day, till after 5 p.m. and bad light caused an early finish. At that time

**Pakistan**
First Innings

| | |
|---|---|
| Aftab Gul b d'Oliveira | 28 |
| Sadiq Mohammad c & b Lever | 17 |
| Zahir Abbas c Luckhurst b Illingworth | 274 |
| Mushtaq Mohammad c Cowdrey b Illingworth | 100 |
| M J Khan c Lever b Illingworth | 35 |
| Asif Iqbal not out | 104 |
| Intikhab Alam c Underwood b d'Oliveira | 9 |
| Imran Khan run out | 5 |
| Wasim Bari not out | 4 |
| Extras (b 6, lb 14, nb 12) | 32 |
| **Total** (for 7 wkts dec) | **608** |

Did not bat: Asif Masood, Pervez Sajjad.
Fall of wickets: 1-68, 2-359, 3-441, 4-456, 5-469, 6-567, 7-581.
Bowling: Ward 29-3-115-0; Lever 38-7-126-1; Shuttleworth 23-2-83-0; d'Oliveira 38-17-78-2; Underwood 41-13-102-0; Illingworth 26-5-72-3.

**England**

| First Innings | | Second Innings | |
|---|---|---|---|
| J H Edrich c Zahir b Masood | 0 | c Wasim b Masood | 15 |
| B W Luckhurst c Sadiq b Pervez | 35 | not out | 108 |
| M C Cowdrey b Masood | 16 | b Masood | 34 |
| D L Amiss b Masood | 4 | c Pervez b Masood | 22 |
| B L d'Oliveira c Mushtq b Intikhab | 73 | c Mushtaq b Iqbal | 22 |
| R Illingworth b Intikhab | 1 | c Wasim b Masood | 1 |
| A P E Knott b Masood | 116 | not out | 4 |
| P Lever c Pervez b Masood | 47 | | |
| K Shuttleworth c Imran b Pervez | 21 | | |
| D L Underwood not out | 9 | | |
| A Ward c Mushtaq b Pervez | 0 | | |
| Extras (b 16, lb 6, w 3, nb 6) | 31 | Extras (b 4, lb 5, w 6, nb 8) | 23 |
| **Total** | **353** | **Total** (for 5 wkts) | **229** |

Fall of wickets: 1-0, 2-29, 3-46, 4-112, 5-127, 6-148, 7-307, 8-324, 9-351.
Second Innings: 1-34, 2-114, 3-169, 4-218.
Bowling: Masood 34-6-111-5; Imran 23-9-36-0; Majid 4-1-8-0; Intikhab 31-13-82-2; Pervez 15.5-6-46-3; Mushtaq 13-3-39-0.
Second Innings: Masood 23.5-7-49-4; Iqbal 20-6-36-1; Imran Khan 5-0-19-0; Intikhab 20-8-52-0; Pervez 14-4-27-0; Mushtaq 8-2-23-0.
Umpires: C. S. Elliott and T. W. Spencer.

England, with five wickets standing, were still 26 behind Pakistan's first innings total.

How Intikhab's men must have been disappointed! This almost certainly would have been a famous victory if they could have separated the not out batsmen, Luckhurst and Knott, the last two capable of batting for any great length of time.

Pakistan's bowling hero was Asif Masood, a lively medium pacer who bounds into the crease and, with plenty of spring in his delivery stride, gets quite a bit of bounce the other end. He moved the ball off the seam too, and his figures read five for 111 in 34 overs in the first innings. His victims were Edrich, Cowdrey, Amiss, Knott and Lever. Then in the second innings he got four of the five, as Luckhurst (108 n.o.) led England haltingly forward to 229 for five.

It has been a rainy week and the depressing weather hit attendance at county matches. Because Worcestershire drew only £15 in admission money on Wednesday and £20.85 on Thursday, they allowed spectators in free of charge on Friday. It was cheaper than manning the turnstiles.

## HUTTON FOR ENGLAND
### JUNE 12–18

A week that began with all the drama of the Gillette Cup second round, ended depressingly with three days of rain, which has virtually destroyed the Lord's Test.

Let us begin with England's side, announced on Sunday. Cowdrey and Underwood are out; Gifford, Hutton, Price and Fletcher are included in the thirteen names. By Thursday we found that Hutton was in the side along with Gifford and Price, to the exclusion of Fletcher and Shuttleworth, who was not fit.

Perhaps I can venture a personal opinion on Richard Hutton's achievement – making this the first occasion ever that father and son have played for Yorkshire and England. I was the Cambridge captain when he went up to the University from Repton. Then, his bowling was in the minor key and his batting alone was clearly never going to earn him a ticket into the first-class game. It was therefore interesting for me to be his captain in the MCC v Pakistan game a few weeks ago when he was obviously poised for Test honours. His bowling action is still loose, leggy and rather laboured, and he would seem to be fairly low at the point of delivery. But, my word, his accuracy, on or around the off-stump has impressed every professional batsman in the country, as well as his ability to move the ball off the seam. Rather like Trevor Bailey, Hutton's attack is now based on a nagging persistence rather than an undisciplined burst

John Edrich congratulates Richard Hutton on his first wicket in Test cricket.

of pace. A slip-catcher of reasonable security and a batsman capable of taking 180 off Pakistan last week at Bradford, with the off-drive his strongest shot, his all-round talent has made him a likely successor to the Bailey, D'Oliveira type in the England side.

*Hutton was unlucky that the following winter's tour, to the Indian sub-continent, was delayed for a year. By the time it took place, Tony Greig had laid a stronger claim to the all-rounder's place.*

By Saturday, England, having won the toss, were 133 for the loss of Luckhurst, who "picked up" a superb delivery from Salim just when the wicket had found some movement and moisture on the Friday morning. Geoff Boycott is 72 not out, and Edrich not out 0. Luckhurst got 46 in a first-wicket partnership of 124.

The week also brought the resignation, for business reasons, of Reg Simpson from the Chairmanship of the Nottinghamshire Cricket Committee. Always a controversial thinker, Reg Simpson freely expressed his disappointment in the modern game, and, more than anything, was conscious of the wishes and whims of the declining spectator public. If his ideas for reform were often too radical to meet the approval of the current player, he was still an administrator who provoked careful thought.

## CLOSE PROVES HIS POINT
### *JUNE 19–25*

GREY clouds with sudden, rainy squalls put paid to the Second Test – a draw which *Wisden* alone will have noted – and then, on the county scene, created wickets for the bowlers and conclusive finishes.

I would just record two games of special interest to the professional cricketer – the ones most players turned to first of all in the morning papers at the hotel breakfast table. Both featured Yorkshire. Firstly, without Boycott and Hutton who were performing in the Test match, Yorkshire went to Taunton where Brian Close waited to prove his point in Somerset's colours. Brian believes that he can be the only cricketer to score a century against a county while he is still technically registered for that county. Patiently, head grimly over the line of delivery, Close took 102 off his former colleagues, and one could just imagine the furrowed brow, the firm-set mouth drooping at the corners in stubborn resistance. Afterwards would come the ear-to-ear beam of delight, and perhaps just the odd mention at the bar as to what Mr. Sellers could do with his band of young colts. I hope I do not malign anyone, but much of the joy of this game is the clash of persons and personalities, with success on the field the indisputable currency.

A win for Somerset then, and off Yorkshire went across the country to Colchester. Geoff Boycott has literally plundered the Essex attack for the last few seasons, and journalists now write of the Bradman touch. He has indeed had a magnificent week. 121 n.o. in the Test, and a mammoth 233 at the Garrison Ground, Colchester. Yorkshire batted through to the second day but failed to bowl out Essex twice, as they had committed themselves so to do. Again at the county players' breakfast table the comment was quickly made, "How can a side score 421 for four in their first innings and only collect two batting bonus points?" Boycott may be in his prime, but his instinct for gathering points will have to sharpen, if Yorkshire are to challenge at the top of the table.

India arrived and beat Middlesex at Lord's, while Pakistan lost to Glamorgan and offered to play an extra Test match against England. There were many administrative reasons why this could not be done, but those stressed by the TCCB were the additional burden of player losses on the county clubs, and also the uncertain financial reward of an additional Test in London.

Boycott averages 114·66 and Hutton tops the bowling, 44 wickets at 16·50. But now we can look forward to viewing that fine firm of Indian spinners, Venkataraghavan, Chandrasekhar, Prasanna and Bedi and the batting skills of Gavaskar and Sardesai. Plenty of good cricket around if only we have the weather to match it!

## DEATH OF A GREAT CRICKETER
### *JUNE 26–JULY 2*

NONE of the week's bright deeds, the effort and endeavour could put into cricket anything like as much as was taken from it by the death, on Thursday, of Sir Learie Constantine.

I have read all the obituary notices, and recognize (although I never saw him play) that Sir Learie was a happy, daring cricketer, endowed with those natural Caribbean gifts of elastic movement, lissome yet aggressive, and above all, spectacular. No one paid more vivid tribute than Michael Parkinson. "It's true that he ought to have left behind a story which told of a lot more wickets and a heap more runs. Yet Constantine's cricket was designed for the moment and not for posterity." He concludes, "Sir Learie Constantine belongs to that rare and tiny group of athletes whose deeds are not printed in record books but burned on the mind."

## LITTLE JOY FOR BOWLERS
### *JULY 3–9*

SIZZLING sunshine day after day beat down relentlessly through a heavy, thundery atmosphere. Hardness underfoot and heaviness in the air has sent players scampering for soft shoes and cool drinks.

So we spare a thought for the hard-worked bowlers. Few have found joy in this week of blinding sunshine. Let me conclude the week's report with their small role of honour. Titmus six for 92 v. Yorkshire, Holder five for 64 for Hampshire v. Sussex, Pervez six for 71 to help Pakistan beat Derbyshire and in India's win over

Leicestershire, Chandrasekhar took five for 63 and six for 64. No doubt who the weather suits most!

## *PAKISTAN'S CRUEL ILLUSION*
### *JULY 10–16*

SPORTING immortality stared the 1971 Pakistan cricketers in the face. In the Third and final Test at Headingley, pursuing a modest 230 runs to win, having bowled out England twice, they could stretch out to touch a famous victory. 184 for five and the series was theirs. Yet, at the last, the great prize was a cruel illusion. They fell prey to the hard-grafting skills of English professionalism and to the matching craft of the captain, Ray Illingworth.

The last day was one of England's few good days in the series and morally Pakistan shared the honours in three evenly fought contests. They were finally struck down by Basil D'Oliveira, who dismissed Intikhab and Sadiq, the batting hero, in the same over. The new ball was taken as the pitch worsened and Peter Lever destroyed the tail – 3·3 overs, three for 10.

Another captain attracted attention this week. Majid Khan declared the Cambridge University innings closed at tea-time on the first day of the University match (180 for seven). In a positive effort to get a result Majid then left Oxford 244 to win in three hours and twenty overs. Oxford blocked to 180 for nine and baulked the bravest bit of captaincy seen for many a year in this annual feud. Owen-Thomas made his mark on University history by scoring 146 in the Cambridge second innings. Edmonds, a tall left-arm spinner from Zambia, also seems certain to make a mark on the first-class game if he chooses. He took seven Oxford wickets for 56 in the first innings. Hamblin, four for 32 and three for 62, was Oxford's most successful cricketer.

Philippe Edmonds – making his mark in the Varsity match.

🏃 *Edmonds did choose; Owen-Thomas did not. He tried, briefly, to make a professional career with Surrey, but he was disappointing and had too many other interests to dedicate himself to cricket.*

The Indian tourists have made a splendidly successful start to their tour. By the close of the week they have beaten Warwickshire and Glamorgan, making it three wins in a row. Pakistan ended their tour with a win over Surrey and in that game their most successful batsman, Zaheer Abbas, completed his 1,500 runs for the season. Gloucestershire have signed up this fine young cricketer, and he, along with Sadiq, will greatly strengthen the batting resources of that county.

## *SNOW THE BATSMAN*
### *JULY 17–23*

AND so to the First Test match with England bowled out by India's spinners for 304. Much credit to Knott (67) and Snow (73) who retrieved nasty looking situations.

**This card does not necessarily include the fall of the last wicket**

 (5p) **LORD'S**  **GROUND** (5p)

# **ENGLAND v. INDIA**

THURS., FRI., SAT., MON. & TUES., JULY 22, 23, 24, 26 & 27, 1971    (5-day Match)

| | ENGLAND | | First Innings | | Second Innings |
|---|---|---|---|---|---|
| 1 | G. Boycott | Yorkshire | c Engineer b Abid Ali | 3 | |
| 2 | B. W. Luckhurst | Kent | c Solkar b Chandra | 30 | |
| 3 | J. H. Edrich | Surrey | c Venkat b Bedi | 18 | |
| 4 | D. L. Amiss | Warwickshire | c Engineer b Bedi | 9 | |
| 5 | B. L. D'Oliveira | Worcestershire | c Solkar b Chandra | 4 | |
| *6 | A. P. E. Knott | Kent | c Wadekar b Venkat | 67 | |
| †7 | R. Illingworth | Leicestershire | c Engineer b Bedi | 33 | |
| 8 | R. A. Hutton | Yorkshire | b Venkataraghavan | 20 | |
| 9 | J. A. Snow | Sussex | *c. Abd Ali b Chandra* | 73 | |
| 10 | N. | | | | |

The Championship table has Middlesex at the top. At the bottom are Glamorgan (not finding the taste to their liking!) and last but one, Northants. But for Northants, this week, there was a great relief against Middlesex. In beating Middlesex by seven wickets they achieved their second win of the season. Victory means that their players can now shave off their moustaches, which they decided to grow until a win arrived.

Mickey Stewart, Surrey's captain, told me after his team had beaten Glamorgan by a single run in this week's Sunday League match, that within two years he expected a major incident to flare up between opponents on the cricket field. He referred particularly to limited-overs cricket and the sharply taken singles which can send the backing-up batsman and the following-through bowler charging across each other's path. In this match at Byfleet, Geoff Arnold "mowed down" Eifion Jones. Words were passed, but there was no threatening reaction.

## GILLETTE CUP SEMI-FINALS STEAL THE SHOW

### JULY 24–30

THE First Test against India, a constantly tilting see-saw game, was finally resolved at tea-time on the last day by thick, drizzling rain. At that time England's spinners Gifford and Illingworth were turning the screw on the Indian tail – eight wickets down, the durable Solkar not out six, Bedi not out two, but 38 runs needed for victory.

Commentators, nearer to the contest than I, say justice was done, because the toss advantage went strongly in favour of Illingworth's side, and in truth England's performance was so uneven and patchy over the five days, they scarcely merited a clear-cut win.

Rather amusing, having quoted Mickey Stewart and the shoulder-charging business last week that TV audiences were treated to an example of it at Test match level. John Snow sent Gavaskar spinning when a short run had been attempted for a leg-bye. Snow was thought to have sunk his shoulder into Gavaskar's back. Gavaskar's bat went flying, Snow picked it up and discourteously threw it back at him. There followed the public knowledge that Alec Bedser, Chairman of Selectors and Billy Griffith, Secretary of MCC, instructed Snow to apologise to Gavaskar in the pavilion. The Indians, much to their credit, said the incident was forgotten, the apology accepted. I wonder if Snow will survive for the next Test?

As a comeback Snow's was reasonably successful, not surprising with bowling credentials of world-wide respect. He came out of this Test with two for 64 and one for 23. In both innings he separated the openers. But it was his batting which caught the eye. When England once more languished, Snow weighed in with an innings of 73. As I say, the toss was important. The scores ran this way, England 304, India 313, England 191, India 145 for eight. Of the twenty English wickets, 17 fell to the three spinners, Venkat, Chandra and Bedi. Norman Gifford was England's best with eight wickets in the match.

Roy Fredericks is causing a stir in Welsh cricket circles. His attacking instincts run riot from the first ball. So often he makes attacking field placings look ridiculous. Two lightning knocks of 93 and 40 put Glamorgan on the road to their first victory since May.

Leicestershire and Surrey tied a superbly fought contest at Grace Road. Hundreds here for Younis, 138 not out, and for Roope a hundred in both innings, 109 and 105 not out.

To my mind all this cricket incident, Test, County and Sunday League, which Somerset lead ahead of Essex, Worcestershire and Lancashire, made nothing like the impact on the cricket world of the Gillette Cup semi-final played between Gloucestershire and Lancashire at Old Trafford. Kent's win over Warwickshire was fought out in a minor key, Kent going into the final with the help of a fortunate toss on a wet wicket at Canterbury. Kent struck 238 in aggressive style, Luckhurst making 84. Warwickshire were rolled out on Thursday morning for 109 in 43·1 overs.

At Old Trafford the gates were closed half an hour after the start, and Gloucestershire batted first before an estimated 22,000 spectators. The huge pavilion, so often a gaunt-looking edifice surrounded by empty seats, looked truly noble, flags flying, balconies jammed.

Gloucestershire compiled 229. It scarcely seemed enough on a placid wicket and a fast outfield. And so it turned out, but not without much drama. In the field, a magnificent left-handed pick-up by Clive Lloyd at mid-wicket; the ball transferred to his right hand in a stride and the one visible stump shattered from 10 yards or so, left David Green stranded. Then tight, nagging

Jack Simmons of Lancashire traps David Shepherd to the delight of Farokh Engineer during the early stages of their dramatic Gillette Cup semi-final.

bowling by Jack Simmons, a half century of the steadier variety from Ron Nicholls, and a swashbuckling demonstration of cover driving by Mike Procter (69) set Lancashire their target.

As Lancashire made faltering progress we saw Clive Lloyd assault some fast bouncing overs from Mike Procter – a spectacular confrontation – Farouk Engineer step back onto his wicket as he hooked a short ball past mid-on, then Jack Bond deciding to continue batting in amazingly poor light. Rain had eaten time out of the day's play in the morning and eventually at 8.55 p.m., with the lights on at the nearby station and in all the pavilion rooms, David Hughes smashed an over from John Mortimore to all parts of Manchester. So, with three overs to spare, Lancashire rushed in, almost unseen, although no one had left the ground.

*Stories are still told of this amazing day's cricket. Had it not been televised, however, it might well have been forgotten – except by the participants.*

## A CAPTAIN'S NIGHTMARE
### JULY 31–AUGUST 6

BY the end of my diary week on Friday evening, England's front line batting has failed again, but the whole innings was retrieved by a splendid captain's century from Ray Illingworth (107) and a career best, 88 not out, by Peter Lever. Then in reply to our total of 386, India are 8 for no wicket.

Abid Ali looks innocuous, but is managing to wobble the ball past England's batsmen – four for 64 in 32·4 overs. Only Luckhurst (78) out of the first five, fought off his gentle seamers.

There is news that MCC will not tour India, Pakistan and Ceylon this winter. The statement of the Cricket Council reads: ". . . the best interests of cricket will be served if the proposed tour of India, Pakistan and Ceylon does not take place during the winter of 1971–72. They are, therefore, consulting with overseas cricket authorities concerned with a view to postponing the tour until the winter of 1972–73."

The Cricket Council sought Government advice before reaching their decision and, by the way, this political decision follows quickly on the International Cricket Conference ruling on South Africa – that each

Abid Ali appeals successfully for an lbw decision against Keith Fletcher during England's disastrous start to the Second Test.

country should itself settle its own policy of continuing or abstaining from sporting contact with the South African Board.

A quick mention for Somerset, my outside tip for the top. They are in heavy water at the moment but with two matches at Weston-super-Mare still to play, anything can happen. They are currently seventh with 147 points, 38 points behind the leaders with a game in hand.

Mickey Stewart this week announced he is resigning from the captaincy of Surrey, a position he has held for the last nine years, because he just cannot sleep at night. He was quoted, "lately, pressures and frustrations have built up so much that I am not enjoying the game anywhere near the way I did. I am snapping at my wife, Sheila, and my three children, and, in fact, I am sleeping no more than four hours a night. This has got to stop.

"I now find I am playing every ball, bowling every ball and fielding every ball. I think the captaincy has cost me over 600 runs a year."

Not my job to comment perhaps, but I feel more justified than most to do so. As a batting captain it is such a temptation, and so often irresistible, to try to play the exact sort of innings the team requires. It frequently tempts one outside the limits of one's own batting talents and inevitably failures result. In recent years for captains there has been only one way to educate established professionals who are tardy in the pursuit of batting bonus points and that is by selfless example – to prove that averages count for little in the team's and club's eyes.

## PRICE ROCKS INDIA; DENNESS IS DAZED
### AUGUST 7–13

GOOD old-fashioned Manchester rain, tipping remorselessly out of leaden skies, drowned England's strong chance of winning the Second Test. By Tuesday morning England had reached a position of strength through their diligent craftsmanship and superior fast bowling, as well as through India's lack of genuine pace.

Peter Lever had claimed five for 70 in India's first innings of 212. Price supported with two for 44 and

County Championship (as at August 10)

| | P | Pts |
|---|---|---|
| 1 Warwickshire | 19 | 189 |
| 2 Lancashire | 19 | 177 |
| 3 Middlesex | 19 | 175 |
| 4 Kent | 18 | 174 |

D'Oliveira with two for 40. Gavaskar continues to show promise and a class which suggests an attractive future in Test match cricket. He scored 57 and the durable Solkar 50. But England were placed firmly in a winning position by the batting of Brian Luckhurst (101), so that Illingworth could set India 420 to win, a total which has never been attained in the fourth innings of a Test match. John Price quickly rocked their remote chances by removing Mankad and Wadekar. So India faced this rainswept Tuesday with three wickets down for 65.

What of the County Championship? Plenty of shadowy prospects near the top. It is impossible to sort them out and this week produced only one result. It affected the chances of Kent, who lost to Sussex in an exciting run-chase at Eastbourne. Kent are urgently seeking the same run of form which brought them the title last season, but they are handicapped by the continuous Test match calls. With a full side all the year they would be formidable indeed.

In this match at Eastbourne they threw everything into their efforts to attain 219 off 37 overs. Luckhurst 61, Denness retired hurt 71 and Shepherd 32 put them right in touch with the formidable target but their final wicket fell with one ball remaining and only the injured Mike Denness's wicket to fall. But poor Mike lay at that very moment dazed on a dressing-room table, pads and boots off, having several stitches inserted in his nose which was bleeding internally and externally. So Sussex were winners. But let us be fair, the Sussex performance also had merit, especially a bright all-round performance by Tony Greig – 113 in his first innings and six for 42 in Kent's second.

The man who had a bumper week was Tom Cartwright. He followed his seven for 74 against Notts with an innings of 127 against Essex which, with his nine for 90 in the match, helped Somerset to an impressive victory.

A quick look back to the Sunday League shows that the titleholders, Lancashire, are well placed at the top with 40 points from 14 games, followed by Somerset, 38 from 14, and Essex, 36 from 13.

## LIFE IN THE CIRCUS
### AUGUST 14–20

LARGE crowds continue to flow into grounds on the Sunday, though I have not met a professional cricketer who truly believes forty overs to be a satisfying form of the game. Many believe it heralds the game's destruction. To my mind, the Sunday circus is the antidote or possibly the cure for cricket's cancerous financial state. So we cricketers stoically do our weekly penance under the "big top".

*Fifteen years on, more players positively enjoy the John Player League and playing before "crowds" worthy of the name. But many would still say the same as Lewis in 1971.*

Six Test matches in one home season is an overdose and the feelings of repetition has been emphasized by England's carbon-copy innings throughout both series. Early failures were bolstered to respectability by lower-order defiance. Such was the pattern on Thursday when Ray Illingworth won the toss at the Oval and chose to bat on a slow, but uncomplicated wicket.

The failures were Luckhurst, Edrich, Fletcher, D'Oliveira and Illingworth. The saviours were John Jameson with a forthright, confident innings of 82, before being run out, Alan Knott, who bustled about the crease in typical fashion, gaily sweeping Bedi, Venkat and Chandra in a splendid 90, and Richard Hutton who also found aggression paid the best dividends. His knock of 81 demonstrated his strength in the cover drive, often handsomely struck "on the up". 355 all out was, therefore, a good total and achieved with much colourful play at a fast scoring rate. What came on Friday was less colourful – grey skies and drenching rain. The series heads for an inconclusive draw?

## INDIA'S TEST WIN; SURREY NARROW GAP
### AUGUST 21–27

AJIT Wadekar's India beat Ray Illingworth's England on Tuesday afternoon at The Oval – India's first Test win in this country after 22 Test matches stretching over a period of almost 40 years.

Their endeavours over the last two days of the match write a spectacular page in Indian cricket history. They were 71 behind on the first innings, being largely restricted by Ray Illingworth's fine bowling effort – five for 70 in 34·3 overs.

Then the vast breakthrough came as Chandresekar, six for 38, Venkataraghavan, two for 44, and Bedi, one for 1, ran through England's batting for a mere 101 runs, leaving just 173 to win. It was an odd sight watching English batsmen of talent and past achievements flat-foot and prod their way around the crease. Always they seemed physically hemmed in by those waspish, close fielders, Venkat and Solkar, who stood their ground fearlessly, and leapt about with acrobatic ease.

Yet if England's batting collapse was the main cause of defeat, the winning total of 173 required courage and coolness in the making. Thus with an historic win staring them in the face, India's batsmen diligently pieced together their final innings with care and patience. Wadekar made 45, Sardesai 40, Viswanath 33 and Engineer 28 n.o. A memo of sympathy should be written to Ray Illingworth – full marks to him for his handling of bowlers who never had runs behind them. It was top-class professional captaincy in the field.

The John Player title is still open. Essex, with 40 points from 15 games, hung onto top position by beating Kent with a faster scoring rate. Lancashire had no game so lie second, with 40 points from 14 games. Worcestershire beat Somerset but Leicestershire lost to Northants. So that would seem to halt the prospects of Somerset and Leicestershire and put Worcestershire in touch with the top. No one has strongly fancied them as champions with such a young inexperienced side, but having taken 36 points from just 14 games they have a very real chance.

## WARWICKSHIRE STUMBLE
### AUGUST 28–SEPTEMBER 3

THE home season, in all three competitions, has simmered gaily and now reaches boiling point. Lancashire meet Kent tomorrow (Saturday) to decide the fate of the Gillette Cup.

In the John Player League a mathematical brain is required to sort out the chances – Essex, Lancashire and Worcestershire are all involved.

The County Championship pennant looks destined for The Oval for the first time since 1958. By the end of the week the leaders, Warwickshire, had faltered against Gloucestershire though they took 23 points off Yorkshire. Surrey, however, beat Yorkshire and Derbyshire and lie only 14 points behind Warwickshire whose season is completed. Surrey have two games in hand.

## LITTLE MAN, LARGE LEAP
### SEPTEMBER 4–10

A little man leapt a long way off the ground to intercept a searing extra-cover drive and dismiss

**County Championship**
(as at August 27)

| | | P | Pts |
|---|---|---|---|
| 1 | Warwickshire | 22 | 230 |
| 2 | Lancashire | 23 | 220 |
| 3 | Kent | 22 | 208 |
| 4 | Surrey | 20 | 207 |

**ENGLAND**

| First Innings | | | Second Innings | | |
|---|---|---|---|---|---|
| J. A. Jameson run out | | 82 | run out | | 16 |
| B. W. Luckhurst c Gavaskar b Solkar | | 1 | c Venkat b Chandra | | 33 |
| J. H. Edrich c Engineer b Bedi | | 41 | b Chandra | | 0 |
| K. W. R. Fletcher c Gavaskar b Bedi | | 1 | c Solkar b Chandra | | 0 |
| B. L. D'Oliveira c Mankad b Chandra | | 2 | c sub b Venkat | | 17 |
| *R. Illingworth b Chandra | | 11 | c & b Chandra | | 4 |
| †A. P. E. Knott c & b Solkar | | 90 | c Solkar b Venkat | | 1 |
| R. A. Hutton b Venkat | | 81 | not out | | 13 |
| J. A. Snow c Engineer b Solkar | | 3 | b Chandra | | 0 |
| D. L. Underwood c Wadekar b Venkat | | 22 | c Mankad b Bedi | | 11 |
| J. S. E. Price not out | | 1 | lbw b Chandra | | 3 |
| Extras (b 4, lb 15, w 1) | | 20 | Extras (lb 3) | | 3 |
| **Total** | | **355** | **Total** | | **101** |

**Fall of wickets:** 1-5, 2-111, 3-135, 4-139, 5-143, 6-175, 7-278, 8-284, 9-352.
**Second Innings:** 1-23, 2-24, 3-24, 4-49, 5-54, 6-65, 7-72, 8-72, 9-96.
**Bowling:** Abid 12-2-47-0; Solkar 15-4-28-3; Gavaskar 1-0-1-0; Bedi 36-5-120-2; Chandra 24-6-76-2; Venkat 20-4-3-63-2.
**Second Innings:** Abid 3-1-5-0; Solkar 3-1-10-0; Venkat 20-4-44-2; Chandra 18-1-3-38-6; Bedi 1-0-1-1.

**INDIA**

| First Innings | | | Second Innings | | |
|---|---|---|---|---|---|
| S. Gavaskar b Snow | | 6 | lbw b Snow | | 0 |
| A. V. Mankad b Price | | 10 | c Hutton b Underwood | | 11 |
| *A. L. Wadekar c Hutton b Illingworth | | 48 | run out | | 45 |
| D. N. Sardesai b Illingworth | | 54 | c Knott, b Underwood | | 40 |
| G. R. Vishwanath b Illingworth | | 0 | c Knott b Luckhurst | | 33 |
| E. D. Solkar c Fletcher b D'Oliveira | | 44 | c & b Underwood | | 1 |
| †F. M. Engineer c Illingworth b Snow | | 59 | not out | | 28 |
| S. Abid Ali b Illingworth | | 26 | not out | | 4 |
| S. Venkat lbw b Underwood | | 24 | | | |
| B. S. Bedi c D'Oliveira b Illingworth | | 2 | | | |
| B. S. Chandra not out | | 0 | | | |
| Extras (b 6, lb 4, nb 1) | | 11 | Extras (b 6, lb 5, nb 1) | | 12 |
| **Total** | | **284** | **Total (6 wkts.)** | | **174** |

**Fall of wickets:** 1-17, 2-21, 3-114, 4-118, 5-125, 6-222, 7-230, 8-278, 9-284.
**Second Innings:** 1-2, 2-37, 3-76, 4-124, 5-134, 6-170.
**Bowling:** Snow 24-5-68-2; Price 15-2-51-1; Hutton 12-2-30-0; D'Oliveira 7-5-5-1; Illingworth 34-3-12-70-5; Underwood 25-6-49-1.
**Second Innings:** Snow 11-7-14-1; Price 5-0-10-0; Underwood 38-14-72-3; Illingworth 36-15-40-0; D'Oliveira 9-3-17-0; Luckhurst 2-0-9-1.

the batsman who, with unforgettable strokeplay, was winning the Gillette Cup for Kent . . . and the score-card read: Asif Iqbal c Bond b Simmons 89.

Of the nine Cup Finals, this North v. South confrontation was voted the best. Lancashire, the holders, retained the Cup after a day-long see-saw of agonising advantages. Kent's tactical approach in the field was full of good sense. To those most dangerous of stroke-makers, Engineer and Clive Lloyd, Derek Underwood bowled superbly, wide outside the Indian's off stump to restrict his onside appetite, and straight at the West Indian's legs around the wicket, offering no room for Lloyd's full, slashing swing to the off-side. Twelve overs, one for 26. Yet Clive Lloyd scored 66, Lancashire scored 224, and with Luckhurst out for nought the toss advantage seemed certain to put too many pressures on Kent.

But Asif shrugged them off and played a brilliant innings which won him the Man of the Match award. Lever with 11·2 overs, three for 24, and Shuttleworth with 10 overs, two for 25, bowled tightly and only Asif, who sloped sadly from the middle, with 25,000 people applauding a fine innings, rattled one of the steadiest attacks in the country.

In the County Championship the thrills were less instant and violent, but Glamorgan, after three days of palpitating cricket at the Oval, put Surrey to the misery of having to wait for their last game to take a further six points for the title.

The Oval wicket had no grass – we started the match "on the floorboards." Mickey Stewart played the captain's part by gleaning an important century (108). Pocock (five for 73) and Intikhab (three for 70) won five bowling points as Glamorgan went for 222. A Surrey declaration left Glamorgan 287 to win, but more importantly left themselves five hours to bowl us out on a worn wicket. A superb 78 by Majid Khan and some all-round support put a win for Glamorgan in prospect, but at the fall of the seventh wicket for 232 the game was set for a Surrey win or a long defiance for a draw. For 80 minutes Roger Davis (almost miraculously back in the side after that early season disaster) battled out the game, 17 not out, with Surrey fielders crouched in amazingly close positions.

This week one of Yorkshire's finest cricketers, Percy Holmes, died in Huddersfield aged 84. He was famous for his opening partnerships with Herbert Sutcliffe, especially the memorable record – 555 for the first wicket, after Essex had invited Yorkshire to take first knock. In the week's press there were many pleasant tributes from many of his contemporaries.

## BOYCOTT'S HISTORY-MAKING SEASON
### *SEPTEMBER 11–FINALE*

"THE strife is o'er . . ." Worcestershire sat back in their armchairs and watched Lancashire fall to Glamorgan in Sunday's televised game. Warwickshire suffered a worse fate. On the edge of their seats listening to radio bulletins, they heard that Mickey Stewart's wife Sheila had dashed onto the field at Southampton with champagne and kisses for the captain of the new champions. Harder still on Warwickshire, Surrey lost that match to Hampshire and ended with 255 points – the same number as Warwickshire. But Surrey won 11 matches to Warwickshire's 9 and that's how the issue is settled these days.

To the young Worcestershire side goes the accolade – the consistent batting of Ron Headley, Jim Yardley and Basil D'Oliveira. Last year Basil loudly proclaimed that Sunday cricket is a young man's game! The truth is that professional cricketers are bound to try always for their own self-respect, however much they dislike the Sunday game. Norman Gifford and his men have certainly done that, and with a side that is largely in transition.

Surrey are worthy champions – all good cricketers,

The Surrey squad in their Championship year. Back, left to right: L. Skinner, G. Howarth, R. Jackman, R. Lewis, G. Arnold, R. Willis, M. Hooper, G. Roope, C. Waller, Younis Ahmed. Front: P. Pocock, S. Storey, J. Edrich, M. Stewart (captain), A. Long (wicket-keeper), M. Edwards.

who have run close to the top so often. Mickey Stewart, who announced his retirement from the captaincy, is to rethink and possibly may continue in office. Perhaps his critics will retreat now the prize is won.

Can I, in conclusion, toast Geoffrey Boycott's history-making season? He ended with an unbeaten 124 against Northants and became the first Englishman to record a batting average of more than 100 in an English season. His full list of first-class scores is: 61, 110, 30, 75, 88, 112 n.o., 9, 169, 24, 121 n.o., 233, 58, 182 n.o., 6, 112, 13, 133, 34, 0, 3, 169, 151, 40, 111, 14, 66, 138 n.o., 84, and 124 n.o. Four times only he failed to reach double figures. He hit 13 centuries. In all, this brilliant season amounted to 2,503 runs at an average of 100·12.

## Final Table 1971

| | P | W | L | D | No dec | Bonus Pts Bt | Bw | Pts |
|---|---|---|---|---|---|---|---|---|
| Surrey (5) | 24 | 11 | 3 | 10 | 0 | 63 | 82 | 255 |
| Warwickshire (8) | 24 | 9 | 9 | 6 | 0 | 73 | 92 | 255 |
| Lancashire (3) | 24 | 7 | 4 | 11 | 0 | 76 | 75 | 241 |
| Kent (1) | 24 | 7 | 6 | 11 | 0 | 82 | 82 | 234 |
| Leicestershire (15) | 24 | 6 | 2 | 16 | 0 | 76 | 74 | 215 |
| Middlesex (16) | 24 | 7 | 6 | 11 | 0 | 61 | 81 | 212 |
| Somerset (13) | 24 | 7 | 4 | 13 | 0 | 50 | 89 | 209 |
| Gloucestershire (17) | 24 | 7 | 3 | 13 | 1 | 50 | 81 | 201 |
| Hampshire (10) | 24 | 4 | 6 | 14 | 0 | 70 | 82 | 192 |
| Essex (12) | 24 | 6 | 5 | 13 | 0 | 43 | 84 | 187 |
| Sussex (9) | 24 | 5 | 9 | 10 | 0 | 55 | 77 | 182 |
| Notts (11) | 24 | 3 | 7 | 14 | 0 | 58 | 83 | 171 |
| Yorkshire (4) | 24 | 4 | 8 | 12 | 0 | 47 | 75 | 162 |
| Northants (14) | 24 | 4 | 8 | 12 | 0 | 36 | 83 | 159 |
| Worcestershire (6) | 24 | 3 | 7 | 14 | 0 | 46 | 76 | 152 |
| Glamorgan (2) | 24 | 3 | 5 | 15 | 1 | 55 | 63 | 148 |
| Derbyshire (7) | 24 | 1 | 4 | 19 | 0 | 51 | 81 | 142 |

Leicestershire's record includes 5 points in drawn match when scores finished level and they were batting. Figures in brackets 1970 positions.

## 1971 FIRST-CLASS AVERAGES

### BATTING

| | I | NO | R | H'est | AV |
|---|---|---|---|---|---|
| G. Boycott | 30 | 5 | 2,503 | 233 | 100·12 |
| K. W. Fletcher | 41 | 12 | 1,490 | 164* | 51·37 |
| M. J. Harris | 45 | 1 | 2,238 | 177 | 50·86 |
| M. J. K. Smith | 48 | 9 | 1,951 | 127 | 50·02 |
| B. W. Luckhurst | 41 | 3 | 1,861 | 155* | 48·97 |
| R. B. Kanhai | 41 | 9 | 1,529 | 135* | 47·78 |
| B. A. Richards | 45 | 4 | 1,938 | 141* | 47·26 |
| J. H. Edrich | 44 | 1 | 2,031 | 195* | 47·23 |
| G. S. Sobers | 38 | 6 | 1,485 | 151* | 46·40 |
| Asif Iqbal | 34 | 6 | 1,294 | 120 | 46·21 |

### BOWLING

| | O | M | R | W | AV |
|---|---|---|---|---|---|
| G. G. Arnold | 632 | 171 | 1,421 | 83 | 17·12 |
| P. J. Sainsbury | 845·5 | 332 | 1,874 | 107 | 17·51 |
| T. Cartwright | 976·4 | 407 | 1,852 | 104 | 17·80 |
| D. Wilson | 527·2 | 210 | 1,095 | 60 | 18·25 |
| N. Featherstone | 131·3 | 34 | 336 | 18 | 18·66 |
| L. R. Gibbs | 1,024·1 | 296 | 2,475 | 131 | 18·89 |
| M. J. Procter | 535 | 149 | 1,232 | 65 | 18·95 |
| D. Underwood | 945·5 | 368 | 1,986 | 102 | 19·47 |
| J. Balderstone | 162·5 | 59 | 354 | 18 | 19·66 |
| R. Illingworth | 633 | 230 | 1,269 | 64 | 19·82 |

*Politics, yet again.* The scheduled MCC tour of India, Pakistan and Ceylon did not take place because of Government advice that domestic conditions in India might make the tour unsafe. Following the dangerous and riotous end to the 1968–69 tour of Pakistan, there seem to have been few qualms at the United Kingdom end about the decision to postpone the tour for twelve months, although India cabled the Cricket Council after the first of two statements, protesting that conditions were normal in the wake of the Indo-Pakistan war.

This time only a few of the leading English players had the consolation of tasting alternative international cricket during the winter. Richard Hutton, Norman Gifford, Tony Greig and Bob Taylor all played for a Rest of the World team which toured Australia instead of the South Africans, whose side had been officially selected only for the Australian Board to decide, for much the same reason as England in 1970, that to go ahead with the tour would invite trouble. During the summer of 1971, in fact, the full members of ICC had disagreed about whether to make an official end to cricketing relationships with South Africa and had left the decision to each nation to make for itself. England's administrators made it clear that they would not again play against South Africa until cricket was played and organised on a multi-racial basis. The Rest of the World tour of Australia did not arouse the same interest as the one to England in 1970 but it was nevertheless notable for one of the great innings, the 254 by Gary Sobers at Melbourne, an innings hallowed, like Stan McCabe's great one at Trent Bridge, by special comment from Sir Donald Bradman. At Trent Bridge he had instructed his team to come and watch every ball because "they would not see its like again". This time Bradman, not a man to offer gratuitous praise in public, said; "I believe Gary Sobers's innings was probably the best ever seen in Australia. The people who saw Sobers have enjoyed one of the historic events of cricket."

The Rest of the World won the series by two games to one, with two drawn, after a nasty shock at Perth when a young tearaway fast bowler of rare speed and hostility and with a lovely action, Dennis Lillee, took eight wickets in the first innings on the hard and bouncy Perth pitch. He ended the series with 24 wickets and, apart from Peter Pollock, the World side had nothing with which to counter him, although Tony Greig, like Lillee about to emerge as one of the great names of the 1970s, was the most successful bowler of anything above medium pace. The World side, led by Sobers, were saved by the skill of their two spinners, Bishen Bedi and Intikhab Alam, and by the immense power of a batting order which also included Kanhai, Ackerman, Graeme Pollock, Clive Lloyd and Zaheer Abbas.

# ✦ 1972 ✦

A diary is a personal record and I must tell you, if this journal is to make any sense, that I find myself injured at the beginning of the season, unable to practise or play with Glamorgan. Yet I have been summoned to Arundel, and Arundel in April means, of course, the grand entry of the tourists. My role there is as correspondent for the *Daily Telegraph*. Jim Swanton must attend a wedding so I find that my first-ever commission as a cricket reporter is not at a Haig preliminary between Nantymoel and Kimbolton, but at the season's first savouring of Australian spices.

## APPETITE FOR BATTLE
### APRIL 21–28

IT is difficult to say whether Ian Chappell's Australians are quite as aggressive as their captain has suggested, but on this occasion they certainly adopted all the abrasive qualities of their predecessors. Well, we expect it of them. The Aussie accent rang out loud and clear in this most perfect of English gardens, and the appetite for battle was pleasantly sharpened.

A final thought for this first week of 1972. Well known, established players always seem unreal to me when they turn out for new counties, though I suppose I am getting used to it. But who can reconcile himself to the sight of Ken Higgs of Lancashire and England bowling day in day out at Grace Road in a Leicestershire sweater? I suppose there is no room for romanticism in sport at the professional level.

Ken Higgs providing additional experience for Leicestershire.

## PRESIDENT-ELECT AN OPENING BAT
### APRIL 29–MAY 5

THE nomination of a new President for MCC always ends a few weeks of speculation in the corridors of power even though the change of office passes unnoticed by many cricketers in the street. However the choice of Mr Aidan Crawley as President designate will send ripples of recognition throughout a wide circle of cricketing people.

Mr Crawley is chairman of the National Cricket Association which tends to the well-being of all British cricket outside the first-class game. Yet in the professional world too he can claim understanding, because in his day he was an opening batsman of style who played for Oxford University and Kent.

Much of this week's cricket was ruined by rain and the Benson and Hedges Competition had a sticky debut. In some cases three days were required to complete the 55 overs apiece.

Of course the week's great expectations were of the Australians and their progress against Worcestershire and Lancashire. Rain disrupted both matches but there were definite points of interest. They beat Worcestershire after two quick first-innings declarations, but then the home county were legitimately bowled out by Massie (six for 31). Massie is medium-paced, with a high, straight arm action. It appears that swing is his major art and one supposes that conditions in this extremely wet, overcast weather are going to suit him.

The Old Trafford game was drawn. Ken Shuttleworth's four for 38 was a performance which may impress England's selectors. However, one of the best cricketing performances of the week was by Clive Radley, who rescued a Middlesex innings against the formidable Leicestershire attack at Lord's. He scored 112.

## FRED'S BACK
### MAY 6–12

YOU have to get used to change and innovation by the day in modern cricket. Players joke and claim that they often forget in the middle what competition they are playing . . . 40-over John Player, 55-over Benson and Hedges, 60-over Gillette, or that positive marathon of a contest, the three-day first-class match. Certainly captains reach into their cases each morning for the relevant documents. "What happens if it rains, skip?" "Do we cover the whole pitch or just the ends?" "Who wins if we tie?"

I see pressures building up on captains and this week Gary Sobers announced his resignation from the leadership of Notts. He has been troubled by an injured knee for some time. Another resignation came from Essex secretary, Major "Topper" Brown. He was not seeing eye to eye with the Essex Committee.

However, one must note too that there is a spectacular comeback as well, that of Fred Trueman. He bowled the statutory eight overs on Sunday for his new county, Derbyshire, for 35 runs and one wicket, but found John Edrich in brutal form. Fred's comeback at the age of 41 has more than a tinge of optimism about it.

Some sort of history was made at the close of the week by Surrey CCC. Their manager, Arthur McIntyre, refused to release Edrich or Roope for the MCC side which meets the Australians at Lord's in a week's time. The reason – Surrey have a vital Benson and Hedges match with Middlesex which clashes. The tail of sponsorship wags the dog.

*But, in truth, it has, in England at least, very rarely done so. This preference for county over MCC was something not heard of since the early days of Test cricket.*

## OPENERS' RECORD
### MAY 13–19

IT is always pleasant to bring the record-keepers out of hibernation and so many cricket-lovers are devoted to statistics. At Southampton Australia's opening batsmen Keith Stackpole and Graeme Watson broke the record for Australian openers in this country. Their 301 beat 239 made by Ponsford and McCabe at The Oval against Surrey in 1934. The victims this time were Hampshire, who can consider themselves a trifle unfortunate because they had dominated the game for two days only to lose it on the last. Richard Gilliat set 305 to win. It was accomplished for the loss of only one wicket.

In this game Hampshire's diminutive David Turner (131) played an innings of immense promise. He is a batsman without flourish – a short backlift, power from the wrists and skilled timing. More significant, if he is going to make the Test scene, he is left-handed, and this could help his claim. The point of this observation is that Turner's hundred was no flash in the pan. He is a player of quality and obvious potential.

*Sadly it was potential which the likeable Wiltshire man never fully developed, although he still bats for Hampshire with success and fields brilliantly.*

Australia's cause advanced steadily in better weather. Ian Chappell took an aggressive century off Surrey at the Oval, his last 71 runs coming in an hour. Then Dennis Lillee, who had undergone a manipulative operation on his back, bowled with genuine pace in Hampshire's second innings on Thursday. A healthy sign for England too – Edrich scored 110 against the Australians, and D'Oliveira 107 against Surrey later in the week.

Sussex followed Surrey's controversial example when they withdrew Tony Greig from MCC's side to play the Australians. Billy Griffith, Secretary of MCC, was prompt to make a public criticism. "Not many years ago the counties said they supported this match 100 per cent," he said. "I feel very strongly on this point because I believe the match is good for the future of cricket, and not just cricket in the short term."

Yet whatever is said on this subject, no criticism has been intended of the new Benson and Hedges competition. Indeed the outstanding individual and team performances of the week came from it. Leicestershire raced to an amazing 327 for four in the 55 overs and then routed Warwickshire for 143, Ken Higgs taking four for 31. Brian Davison was the hero. He hit an astounding 158 in 29 overs. Inevitably his century, struck in 68 minutes and including 10 sixes and 11 fours, was the fastest of the season so far. It was also the highest score ever made in top-class limited-over cricket in this country.

*Had the Rhodesian Davison, like Greig, set out early enough to play cricket for England, he would probably have done so.*

## LILLEE WINS FIRST ROUND WITH BOYCOTT
### MAY 20–26

LILLEE is fast, I have that on the authority of those who faced him at Lord's for MCC this week. Journalists have chosen to emphasise the Lillee v. Boycott confrontation for obvious reasons. Lillee won this first round comfortably. He trapped Boycott lbw in a half-forward position. Boycott retired from the game with a stomach upset before the second innings. The battle will be a long and fiery one, no doubt.

Also retiring hurt in this first day of big cricket was Bob Massie. He left the field troubled by a muscular injury to his side. Luckhurst (50) and Denness (68) were the only MCC batsmen to make first innings runs, though neither struck form. Alan Ward bowled with hostility and spirit. He took the wickets of Stackpole, Francis and Ian Chappell in the first innings – 15 overs, three for 40. Barry Wood and Ray Illingworth had a profitable partnership in the second innings, both passing fifty. Australia eventually won this declaration match, a carefree affair, by four wickets. Ray Illingworth set the target of 192 in two hours and five minutes, and two sparkling fifties, a dashing affair by Ian Chappell and a more paced effort by Francis, took the tourists easily to a win.

Money apart, there is an exciting incentive for success on Sundays this year. John Player have announced that the winning team will be financed on a short cricketing tour of West Indies early in the new year. Middlesex have also announced that they are to field ball-boys at Lord's in 40-over matches to save time. That is really taking it seriously.

## HELPFUL LEGISLATION
### MAY 27–JUNE 2

TO the relief of many, new legislation has arrived to rule that players not already capped by England must either have (1) been born in the UK, (2) resided in the UK for the past eight consecutive years and not represented another country in that period, (3) begun to reside permanently in the UK before the age of 14. These provisions are designed to restrict the honour of playing for England to those who, if they have not been born here, at least have played their cricket in this country. Players have felt the narrowing of chances since the large influx of overseas cricketers four years ago. It should greatly assist the development of young potential Test cricketers in Britain as well as ensuring that other countries are not denuded of their native talent.

## FIRST TEST A TIGHT STRUGGLE
### JUNE 3–9

THERE can hardly have been a more rainy first month of a season, and just when the worst seemed

over, and a splendid week's cricket lay in prospect, the heavens opened once more.

Then to England's team for the First Test, and few would have chosen otherwise – Boycott, Edrich, Luckhurst, M. J. K. Smith, D'Oliveira, Greig, Knott, Illingworth (captain), Snow, Gifford, Arnold. The twelfth man is Barry Wood of Lancashire, quite an elevation for him, though one never truly knows if it is just convenient for the selectors to pick a twelfth man on his home ground; or have they a serious eye on him?

By Friday night the Test is evenly balanced and it has been fascinating viewing, albeit on television. First there was the Boycott v. Lillee business, and bang on the elbow, Boycott was struck. He retired only to fall to Gleeson for eight. Lillee is forging ahead on points. It was Ray Illingworth's toss, and he batted on a wicket which bounced surprisingly and seamed. It tested all the skills and the courage too. Catches flew through the slips for two days. How John Snow got to first slip in a Test match I would not know. Sounds like he drew the "short straw" to me.

249 was England's muster, Edrich 49 and Greig 57, Lillee two for 40, Colley three for 83. Australia in their turn have reached 103 for four; Stackpole is out for 53 and much depends on the not-out pair, Greg Chappell and Walters. The seam bowlers continue to find help and a certain finish approaches if the weather remains fine.

No response from umpire Charlie Elliott to this confident shout from Geoff Arnold and the ring of slip fielders (left to right) Edrich, Boycott, Snow, Illingworth, Greig, Luckhurst and Knott. Doug Walters is the batsman in Australia's first innings at Old Trafford.

## ENGLAND WIN
### JUNE 10–16

THE weather held – just – and the modest crowd which had braved all sorts of grey, gusty, squally

| County Championship (as at June 6) | | |
|---|---|---|
| | P | Pts |
| **1** Yorkshire | 4 | 51 |
| **2** Leicestershire | 5 | 48 |
| **3** Warwickshire | 5 | 42 |
| **4** Northamptonshire | 5 | 40 |

conditions at Old Trafford saw England go one up in the Test series. It was a result which swung on high-quality fast bowling and brave, sometimes dogged, innings by the batsmen.

On the final day, if Australia had a chance of holding out – they needed 342 for a win – it was given them by rain which lost time for England on the fourth day. It was Greig who finally polished off the resistance, Marsh 91, Gleeson 30, and the main bowling figures were Greig four for 53, Snow four for 87. A fine win by England, the first win in a First Test match against Australia in this country for 40 years, and no team changes were anticipated. However today, Friday, it was announced that John Price is added to the successful eleven.

## MASSIE HAS ENGLAND GROPING
### JUNE 17–23

A new Test name, Bob Massie, and a little-practised art – that of bowling away- and in-swing at medium pace from around the wicket – have already made this Lord's Test match rather special. Australia's Massie took eight wickets for 84 in England's first innings of 272. English batsmen of pedigree and experience groped like novices. They had obvious difficulty in "reading" Massie's action and they must certainly concentrate on doing just that in the hard, businesslike

Dennis Lillee claims the first England wicket at Lord's but it was to be Massie's match. Edrich is the batsman to go.

way of English county cricket "professors".

When I call it a little-practised art I am not forgetting Mike Procter, or before him Len Coldwell, but they were primarily in-swing bowlers. Richie Benaud presented similar problems off the wicket from that angle.

England's middle-order rescued the show after Boycott, Edrich and Luckhurst had mustered just 22 between them. Australia began no better, Stackpole falling to Price who was included instead of the unfit Arnold, Francis and Walters failing too. Another Test result looks imminent.

This card does not necessarily include the fall of the last wicket

(5p)  **LORD'S**  **GROUND**  (5p)

# ENGLAND  v.  AUSTRALIA

THURS., FRI., SAT., MON. & TUES., JUNE 22, 23, 24, 26 & 27, 1972    (5-day Match)

| ENGLAND | | First Innings | | Second Innings |
|---|---|---|---|---|
| 1 G. Boycott | Yorkshire | b Massie | 11 | |
| 2 J. H. Edrich | Surrey | l b w b Lillee | 10 | |
| 3 B. W. Luckhurst | Kent | b Lillee | 1 | |
| 4 M. J. K. Smith | Warwickshire | | | |
| 5 B. L. D'Oliveira | Worcestershire | | | |
| 6 A. W. Greig | Sussex | | | |
| *7 A. P. E. Knott | Kent | | | |
| †8 R. Illingworth | Leicestershire | | | |
| 9 J. A. Snow | Sussex | | | |
| 10 N. Gifford | Worcestershire | | | |
| 11 J. S. E. Price | Middx | | | |

Geoff Boycott is Massie's first victim.

## MASSIE DOES IT AGAIN
### JUNE 24–30

THE 211th match between England and Australia will forever be known as "Massie's Match". In my diary last week I wrote about the threat of Massie, but I also suggested that England would "work him out". That never happened, and Massie's match figures of 16 for 137 tell of the highest personal success as well as of a splendid victory for his team.

*Massie never again found the magic formula which had enabled him to swing the ball so prodigiously at Lord's in this match.*

Ray Illingworth and Geoff Boycott on Wednesday saw their county sides through to the final of the Benson and Hedges competition. Leicestershire's spin was too much for Warwickshire, who were bowled out for 96. Grace Road has been the centre of the most dedicated effort over the last ten years or so, with secretary Michael Turner right at the heart of the action. Leicestershire have never won a major competition, but under Ray this year they must have a chance of one title or other.

Ray Illingworth is caught by Stackpole to become Massie's thirteenth victim.

## GLENN TURNER STRIKES A RICH VEIN
### JULY 1–7

I must be excused for finding Cambridge University's first win in fourteen years in the University Match at Lord's top of my notes this week. As one who played in three drawn matches in the early Sixties, I felt strongly for Majid Khan and his team. The margin of success was wide. Declaring on the first day at 280 for six – Owen-Thomas collecting a fine century – Cambridge then bowled out Oxford twice for 121 and 134. In the first innings John Spencer took five for 21, Robert Hadley four for 30, and in the second, M. P. Kendall took six for 43.

A man who enjoyed his weekend at Edgbaston was Worcestershire's opening batsman, Glenn Turner. On Saturday he took 122 off Warwickshire, on Sunday in the John Player game he took them apart again for 108 (including a record partnership of 182 with Headley), then on Tuesday continued where he left off by thrashing 128. Warwickshire's main response was from Dennis Amiss, 156 not out, and the three-day game drifted into stalemate. This was Willis's first county match for Warwickshire and Turner gave him a warm welcome.

Geoff Cope has been banned from bowling for a suspect action. Yorkshire had been warned in 1968 that his basic action showed a slight straightening of the arm immediately before delivery and the warning was repeated in July 1970. Remedial coaching will again try to make Geoff's action conform to the "fair delivery" required by rule 26.

Another disrupted season for Geoff Cope.

## SELECTORS LOOK TO PARFITT
### JULY 8–14

ENGLAND'S Test selectors announced their team for the Third Test at Trent Bridge. There were thirteen names . . . Price was left out, Boycott and Arnold are unfit and the newcomers are Hampshire, Lever, Hutton and, would you believe it, Peter Parfitt! Parfitt has not been on the Test scene for three years, though he is in good form with the bat and clearly with the series balanced so finely, Alec Bedser and Co. considered it best to seek experience. There are other considerations,

not the least Parfitt's excellence as a slip fielder. England have been grassing the catches in this department. For Australia, Mallett is added to the winning combination.

Well, by Friday night Parfitt had picked up four catches at slip in Australia's first innings and a duck. Australia 315 all out, Snow yet again got five, a superbly consistent performance, and England in return are 117 for four. Keith Stackpole characteristically fought and flashed his way to a fine century, 114. Lillee, Massie and Colley have shared the wickets.

Mushtaq is first to the 1,000 runs, passing the total in the grand manner with a century against Leicestershire. David Steele partnered him in a stand of 234 and Mushtaq then aired his all-round talents by taking six for 58. But the younger Steele still scored 91, giving his brother no chance to crow.

## EDWARDS IMPRESSES
### JULY 15–21

ENGLAND saved the Test at Nottingham and Ray Illingworth can rightly claim that his decision to put Australia in that first morning was justified. The wicket was absolutely docile and Luckhurst (96), Parfitt (45), D'Oliveira (50 n.o.) and Greig (36 n.o.) provided much of the resistance which held off Australia from twenty-to-three on Monday afternoon.

Before that Ross Edwards had written his name clearly in the annals with a magnificent innings of 170 not out in only his second Test. He opened the innings because of Francis's indisposition and was helped along by the Chappells, Greg getting 72. Edwards's own handiwork was a stream of high-quality strokes, especially on the off-side off the back foot. Like Greg Chappell he positively leapt down the wicket to meet the spinners and followed through with a clean swing of the shoulders.

It was bowlers' day again at the first Benson and Hedges final. Without Boycott, Yorkshire could never seize the initiative from Ray Illingworth's experienced attack. Graham McKenzie as always responded to an occasion making the batsmen struggle from the start. Even against the spin of Illingworth, Yorkshire could never raise the scoring rate much above two an over. At least they were the first side to avoid being bowled out

County Championship
(as at July 12)

| | | P | Pts |
|---|---|---|---|
| **1** | Gloucestershire | 11 | 109 |
| **2** | Warwickshire | 11 | 104 |
| **3** | Leicestershire | 11 | 96 |
| **4** | Northamptonshire | 11 | 91 |
| **5** | Essex | 11 | 89 |

by Leicestershire in the 55 overs – but 136 for nine left little hope.

Leicester were 50 for two overnight and another Yorkshire exile, Chris Balderstone, battled well enough to see them home by five wickets and win the "Man of the Match" award.

## AUSSIES CAUGHT ON A LEEDS TURNER
### JULY 22–28

IT is so refreshing to feel the cricket world rivetted by nerve and sinew to this Australian Test series. Already Association Football is under way, but for a change is confined to some of the smaller spaces in the press. There is a big build-up towards the Olympic Games in Munich, but this week all eyes and ears are turned to Headingley for the Fourth Test.

The details so far read: Australia 146 all out, Underwood four for 37; England 252 for nine, Mallett five for 111. Already the difference is plain. Mallett got good wickets, but a top-class English spinner would not have expected to concede over a hundred runs in taking five wickets on a turner. Oddly enough some of the most resolute batting on both sides came from down the order. Inverarity and Mallett put on 47, then for England Illingworth and Snow put on 104 for the eighth wicket. Team changes involved the dropping of Gifford, Mike Smith and Peter Lever. Their replacements are Underwood, Fletcher and Geoff Arnold.

Ray Illingworth has announced that he is not available to lead MCC to India, Ceylon and Pakistan this winter. He has had three rigorous years as England's captain, and very successful too. He is justified in missing this one "with the utmost reluctance for domestic and business reasons". To my mind he has shown marvellous durability under pressure. Whatever your cricket knowledge, and a captain is only judged on success by the majority, Ray Illingworth has personal qualities which breed loyalty in his side. The selectors must have received his decision with mixed feelings.

It should be mentioned that Sussex beat the Australians, before this Test, for the first time since 1888, thanks to a sporting declaration by Ian Chappell and a fine century by Geoff Greenidge.

## TOUR MATCHES

**v SUSSEX**
at Hove, July 22, 24, 25
Sussex won by five wickets

**AUSTRALIANS**

| First Innings | | Second Innings | |
|---|---|---|---|
| R. Edwards c Parks b Spencer | 41 | lbw b Greig | 14 |
| K. Stackpole b Greig | 0 | not out | 154 |
| I. Chappell lbw b Buss | 58 | | |
| G. Chappell c Parks b Phillipson | 20 | | |
| P. Sheahan not out | 34 | (3) c and b Joshi | 50 |
| D. Walters c Griffith b Buss | 24 | (4) not out | 42 |
| R. Marsh c Greenidge b Buss | 54 | | |
| J. Inverarity b Buss | 9 | | |
| G. Watson c Snow b Buss | 1 | | |
| A. Mallett c Parks b Greig | 29 | | |
| J. Hammond not out | 18 | | |
| Extras | 6 | Extras | 2 |
| Total | 294 | Total (for 2 wickets dec) | 262 |

Bowling: Snow 14-2-43-0, Greig 16·1-4-64-2, Spencer 12-1-40-1, Buss 29-9-69-5, Phillipson 11-1-32-1, Joshi 8-3-40-0.
Second Innings: Snow 7-0-35-0, Greig 9-4-12-1, Phillipson 14-0-50-0, Spencer 8-4-9-0, Buss 8-2-33-0, Joshi 24-4-89-1, Graves 4-0-32-0.

**SUSSEX**

| First Innings | | Second Innings | |
|---|---|---|---|
| G. Greenidge c Marsh b I. Chappell | 99 | not out | 125 |
| P. Graves lbw b Mallett | 48 | c Hammond b Mallett | 45 |
| R. Prideaux c I. Chappell b Watson | 55 | st Marsh b Inverarity | 47 |
| M. Buss b Watson | 22 | c Edwards b Inverarity | 10 |
| A. W. Greig c Mallett b Watson | 35 | lbw b Inverarity | 4 |
| J. Parks not out | 13 | b Inverarity | 5 |
| M. G. Griffith not out | 10 | not out | 14 |
| Extras | 13 | Extras | 11 |
| Total (for five wickets dec) | 296 | Total (for five wickets) | 261 |

Did not bat: J. Snow, J. Spencer, C. Phillipson, U. Joshi.

Bowling: Hammond 23-3-89-0, Watson 24-4-85-3, Mallett 30-12-68-1, Inverarity 10-3-24-0, Stackpole 4-1-5-0, I Chappell 7-1-12-1.
Second Innings: Hammond 7-0-41-0, Watson 10-0-47-0, Mallett 15-0-63-1, Inverarity 13-0-60-4, Walters 7-1-34-0, Edwards 0·2-0-5-0.

**v NORTHANTS**
at Northampton, August 5, 7 8.
Northants won by seven wickets.
Australians 191 (B. S. Bedi 5 for 57) and 143 (G. D. Watson 52, Bedi 4 for 53).
Northants 210 (Mushtaq Mohammad 88°, G. Cook 62, Watson 5 for 36) and 125 for 3 (D. S. Steele 60°).

## UNDERWOOD CLEANS UP
### JULY 29–AUGUST 4

OH dear! I was right – and I did not want to be quite so right. England (Underwood six for 48) won this Test match in three days and therefore retained the Ashes.

*Lewis did not, at this stage, mention the "fuserium" disease which affected the pitch at Headingley. It suited Underwood nicely and, to this day, some Australians believe it was all a deliberate plot.*

If ever a man has earned the respect of the watching public here it is Keith Stackpole. He fought it out, tooth and nail, for 28 runs in Australia's second innings of 136. Paul Sheahan, too, applied himself academically for 41 not out. But in these conditions of slow but sharp spin Englishmen, Welshmen too, cannot be bettered by touring teams. Remorselessly England ground down their opponents' confidence until they reached the point of no return, and no threat.

I write on this Friday night, August 4, 1972, about that Test match, the wicket, the comments and all sorts as if nothing has happened to me at all. I must try and be cool and dispassionate, but I see in my notes that A. R. Lewis of Glamorgan has been invited to lead MCC to India, Ceylon and Pakistan this coming winter. He has never played a Test match, by the way, and that in the eyes of many would seem to be taking a chance. We shall see. All I know, as I sit in my hotel room at Canterbury, is that the most marvellous challenge presents itself. Only the Muhammad Alis of the world dare say, six months before, that they will be standing when the opposition falls. I can but hope.

## FINAL TEST – KNOTT'S GEM
### AUGUST 5–11

The end of Barry Wood's first Test innings – caught Marsh bowled Watson.

THE Fifth and final Test against Australia began on Thursday and six days have been laid aside for it, so a definite result should be forthcoming if the weather holds. Barry Wood opened with Edrich in Boycott's continued absence, the first new cap of the season. The theory of selecting in a four-year cycle for the Australian challenge hardly stands up these days when other countries are so formidable as well. Wood has taken his chance. Although only scoring 26, he looked the part, and one wonders how many others would do just that.

England were bowled out for 284, Parfitt 51, Hampshire 42, aggressive and stylish runs, and Alan Knott in an absolute gem of attacking extemporisation, 92.

Australia have batted and amassed 274 for three and look set for a considerable first innings lead. Their captain, Ian Chappell, is not out 107 and his brother, Greg, departed this evening with 113.

The John Player League progresses at its usual furious rate. Middlesex close on the leaders. Mike Brearley, with an innings of 66, led them to a victory over Worcestershire; Leicestershire remain top with 36 points from 13 games. Middlesex have 34 from 13.

Alan Ward is a tragically disappointed young man

this year. He bowled with much fire for MCC against the Australians at Lord's early in the season, but has since nursed along various injuries. At the moment he has a thigh strain and is not in Derbyshire's side. It must be a depressing existence for a man with so much potential, to be confined to the fringes of the first-class game.

While the Test enters its crucial phase so does the County Championship. Warwickshire nose in front with a record 24 points from a win over Nottinghamshire, Kallicharran (165), Amiss (120) piled on the batting points, Rouse and McVicker took the vital wickets. But Gloucestershire kept up the chase with 18 points against Derbyshire, aided by five for 63 from David Graveney, nephew of Tom.

## AUSTRALIA WIN – CRICKET WINS
### AUGUST 12–18

THE weather is now continually fine. Grounds are hard, fielders moan and groan and call for drinks; batsmen drop their anchor and hope to see the day out; bowlers are scheming hard.

Stackpole is already walking and certainly there is no doubt in the minds of Tony Greig, Peter Parfitt and Alan Knott. But this was not to be the breakthrough England had hoped for. Sheahan was joined by Marsh and together they scored the 70 runs needed to win the final Test and square the series.

Geoff Boycott scores 204 for Yorkshire against Leicestershire, and Brian Bolus, having a difficult time in his first year as captain of Nottinghamshire, opens and gets 140 not out against Lancashire. It is good to see Zaheer Abbas in full flow for Gloucestershire (75 against Middlesex) and a double century by Roy Marshall against Derbyshire.

Yet, I suppose, the interest is at The Oval and I do concede a regret that the county game is so eclipsed by the Test game. Australia forged ahead to make 399 in their first innings following the centuries from both Chappells. England went in again 115 behind and Barry Wood treated us all (again I was loving every ball on television and I have become a fan of Benaud, Laker and Dexter) to a splendid innings of 90. Australia had 241 to win on a good wicket which lacked pace, and they made it for the loss of five wickets, led to their much desired conclusion by Keith Stackpole who scored 79. What a consistent fighter he has been.

The end of a fascinating series. If I could pay tribute to Ian Chappell it would be for the truly competitive way in which he has played his cricket, yet he has not chosen to be boorish or disinterested when it came to the games around the counties. Indeed Australia have tossed open many games, they have given great pleasure and have tried to gain results.

The Australian team celebrate their victory. Left to right: Edwards, Mallett, Colley, Sheahan, Marsh, Francis and Lillee.

*Chappell, for all his rough edges, was an outstanding captain and his 1972 side was an exceptional one, lacking only experience.*

## CLOSE PICKED AS PRUDENTIAL CAPTAIN
### AUGUST 19–25

AFTER the Fifth Test, MCC announced their team to tour India and Pakistan this coming winter. With A. R. Lewis go Amiss, Wood, Denness (vice-captain), Fletcher, Roope, Greig, Knott, Taylor, Underwood, Gifford, Arnold, Cottam, Birkenshaw, Pocock, Old.

*If Lewis had had his way, this side would have included Boycott and Snow, the twin pillars of Illingworth's side in Australia two winters before.*

Warwickshire head strongly for the County Championship and with three matches to go are 21 points ahead. Gloucestershire have tailed off rather with 176 points from 18 matches. Essex are way behind with 165 off 18 games.

At the County Pitches Committee it was discovered that the Headingley Test wicket was diseased. Fuserium disease had killed off much of the grass and this is one of the reasons why the pitch was sub-standard. The light colour of the wicket was nothing to do with a low-cut by the groundsman. Indeed the groundsman was exonerated on all points.

Brian Close has been invited to captain England in the Prudential series of one-day matches. Boycott is now available, so his competition with Lillee can be renewed. He has some leeway to make up.

It is announced that Mike Griffith no longer wishes to captain Sussex next year. Tony Greig will take over.

Mickey Stewart is resigning after ten years of captaincy with Surrey. Brian Bolus departs Nottinghamshire after one year of captaincy and may agree terms with Derbyshire. All eyes now on the final stages of the Championship and, of course, the Gillette Cup.

## ENGLAND TAKE ONE-DAY SERIES
### AUGUST 26–SEPTEMBER 1

THE one-day internationals are something of an anti-climax for the players after the sustained excitements and tensions of this wonderful Test series. But they have proved enjoyable contests and the close finish maintained interest even if support was not as great as the sponsors might have hoped.

*These games began to have more significance once they were placed ahead of the Test matches in the annual itinerary of an English season. The Australian Board was slow to see the worth of one-day internationals. Having done so, with great assistance from Mr Packer, they indulged in the biggest overkill in cricket history.*

England had won the first international easily enough at Old Trafford thanks to a fine century by Dennis Amiss. How odd that we should score none in the five- and six-day Tests then start the one-day internationals with one.

Bob Woolmer has been helping Kent make a late run in the Championship reminiscent of their win in 1970. In two games at Canterbury he had 19 wickets and he had a promising start in the international at Old Trafford, his 11-1-37-3 containing the Australians to 222 for eight, despite useful contributions from Stackpole (37), Ian Chappell (53), Greg Chappell (40) and Ross Edwards (57). Boycott gave England the fast start they needed and when he was out Amiss (103) and Fletcher (60) made sure of a win with nearly six overs to spare by their stand of 125.

So to Lord's. And now it was Australia's turn, despite a 50 from Alan Knott and a good score of 236 for nine. Stackpole at his most belligerent saw Australia maintain a rate of six an over for the first fourteen overs – aided by 12 wides. That set them up for an easy five-wicket win.

The deciding match at Edgbaston was again won by the side batting second though England made heavy weather of it at the finish. The consistent Stackpole (61) and some brave hitting by the tail helped Australia to 179. Geoff Arnold's bowling (11-3-27-4) seemed to have won the match particularly when Boycott and Amiss cruised to 76. But some careless batting left Greig to see us home by two wickets. Man of the Match was Barry Wood for his all-round performance.

Brian Close, back to captain England to success in the Prudential Trophy series.

## GILLETTE FINAL

THE Gillette Cup Final last season was a breathtaking contest. This year Clive Lloyd and Lancashire contrived to heighten the excitement in an occasion that is now as much a showpiece of cricket as the Cup Final is for soccer.

The press have exhausted every superlative in describing Clive Lloyd's 126, so one only needs to say that the great man had saved a great innings for a great occasion. There is no more thrilling sight than Clive Lloyd in full flow hitting sixes with effortless ease and the capacity crowd at Lord's had its fill of enjoyment. Even Warwickshire could not forbear to cheer though it cost them the match.

Their 234 looked a good score, its backbone some sound batting by Whitehouse (68), M. J. K. Smith (48) and Kallicharran (54). The odds are heavily against a side chasing a total of over 200 and batting second. But

then came Lloyd – with support from Pilling and Hayes. A wonderful match was won by four wickets with 3·2 overs left. What a climax to Bond's career.

All this overshadowed the Championship but Warwickshire are pushing closer to victory, with Gloucestershire defeated at Bristol by Nottinghamshire. The Player League may turn on the tightest of finishes between Leicestershire and Yorkshire. Lumb (55) and Leadbeater (40) saw Yorkshire to 176 for nine. Despite Dudleston's 61 that was three runs too many and Leicestershire could only reach 173 for eight. With Kent easily defeating Derbyshire – the whipping boys of the season – those three runs could be the difference between taking the title or being runners-up. The season is full of close finishes.

## WARWICKSHIRE CHAMPIONS
### SEPTEMBER 2

WARWICKSHIRE have won the Championship and well deserved to do so for their attractive batting which has brought them 68 bonus points. They won in style at Edgbaston beating bottom-of-the-table Derbyshire by 10 wickets. Kanhai has been in brilliant form this season and had a sparkling 124 in their 351 total. But it was Bob Willis (eight for 44) who made sure of the bowling bonus points with Derbyshire out for 188 – an impressive performance with his new county which included a hat-trick.

Warwickshire chairman Cyril Goodway pours the champagne for skipper Alan Smith, Steve Rouse, John Jameson and John Whitehouse.

## CONCLUSIONS

IT was a fine year for Leicestershire, winning their first major tournament. For months they careered along with bounce and confidence, almost arrogance. They expected to win before they took the field. They attacked their cricket, and special recognition should be made of Roger Tolchard's leadership in Ray Illingworth's absence. Mick Norman and Barry Dudleston have achieved a true understanding as openers. Their running between the wickets makes up for any lack of stroke power. Brian Davison was always likely to electrify, a powerful athlete. However, the various run-gatherers will not mind my giving laurels to Graham McKenzie, Ken Higgs, Terry Spencer, Jack Birkenshaw and Ray Illingworth. Add to those Steele

Don Shepherd –
retirement after 23 seasons
with Glamorgan.

and Balderstone and you have enough variety in attack to take on anyone.

Finally there will be players retiring and the cricket fraternity is a generous one. To me, you will understand, the retirement of Don Shepherd brings a large tear to the eye. "Shep" is universally respected and a career which brought over two thousand two hundred wickets is ample evidence of the heart he put into his daily endeavours. In the mid-Fifties he took 177 wickets in a season. Years later, in 1970 he was top of the national bowling averages and a *Wisden* Cricketer of the Year. Someone in Glamorgan has to bowl an awful lot of overs, straight, on a length, and take an awful lot of wickets if his retirement is to pass unnoticed – and that adds up to a lifetime's art and craft.

## Final Championship Table

| | P | W | L | D | Bonus Bt | Bw | Pts |
|---|---|---|---|---|---|---|---|
| Warwickshire (2) | 20 | 9 | 0 | 11 | 68 | 69 | 227 |
| Kent (4) | 20 | 7 | 4 | 9 | 69 | 52 | 191 |
| Gloucestershire (8) | 20 | 7 | 4 | 9 | 38 | 77 | 185 |
| Northamptonshire (14) | 20 | 7 | 3 | 10 | 34 | 77 | 181 |
| Essex (10) | 20 | 6 | 4 | 10 | 50 | 63 | 173 |
| Leicestershire (5) | 20 | 6 | 2 | 12 | 43 | 68 | 171 |
| Worcestershire (15) | 20 | 4 | 4 | 12 | 59 | 68 | 167 |
| Middlesex (6) | 20 | 5 | 5 | 10 | 48 | 61 | 159 |
| Hampshire (9) | 20 | 4 | 6 | 10 | 50 | 64 | 154 |
| Yorkshire (13) | 20 | 4 | 5 | 11 | 39 | 73 | 152 |
| Somerset (7) | 20 | 4 | 2 | 14 | 34 | 71 | 145 |
| Surrey (1) | 20 | 3 | 5 | 12 | 49 | 61 | 140 |
| Glamorgan (16) | 20 | 1 | 7 | 12 | 55 | 61 | 126 |
| Nottinghamshire (12) | 20 | 1 | 6 | 13 | 38 | 73 | 121 |
| Lancashire (3) | 20* | 2 | 3 | 14 | 42 | 56 | 118 |
| Sussex (11) | 20 | 2 | 8 | 10 | 46 | 49 | 115 |
| Derbyshire (17) | 20* | 1 | 5 | 13 | 27 | 60 | 97 |

Figures in brackets indicate 1971 positions.
*No. times declared.

*Flushed, no doubt, by the prospect of his forthcoming tour, Tony Lewis, whose vivid and informed writing in these Journals helped to pave the way for his subsequent career in journalism, omitted to mention in his 1972 Diary that Kent had won the John Player League. They did so under the captaincy of Mike Denness, who was about to embark as the author's deputy on the tour of the Sub-Continent.*

*By any yardstick the tour must be judged a success, thanks in no small way to the positive way in which Lewis himself tackled the tremendous challenge of leading England onto the field without having previously played in a Test. He not only conducted proceedings on and off the field with an effective mixture of charm, humour and determination, but also proved himself at once with a fine innings of 70 not out to win the First Test against the odds at Delhi. What followed was unfortunately anti-climax. India's spinners, aided by vociferous crowds and fine close fielding, enabled the home country to win the series two-one, although Lewis himself showed that they could be successfully attacked when compiling a commanding and enterprising hundred at Kanpur, as it turned out his only Test century.*

*In Pakistan neither side could achieve mastery on pitches of deadly slowness. There were, too, the inevitable threats of political disturbances. Donald Carr, who was an imperturbable and popular manager, took home to Lord's a recommendation that in future the tours to India and Pakistan, where the cricket is played in surprisingly different conditions, should be separated. No-one appreciated the slow wickets in Pakistan more than Dennis Amiss, who scored two hundreds and a 99 in the three Tests after failing in India. A prolific batsman was embarking on a most profitable 12 months.*

*Pakistan had prepared for the MCC visit by making a hectic visit to Australia, during the course of which they lost three Tests in as many weeks, and a more successful trip to New Zealand, where, with Intikhab Alam and Mushtaq Mohammad (a double century and five wickets in an innings in the same Test) to the fore, Pakistan won the only match in three to be decided.*

*Australia, much more of a team now than when they had arrived in England the previous summer, went to West Indies where the meteor that was Bob Massie faded into almost nothing in the hot sun and Dennis Lillee broke down with a serious back injury. Into the breach stepped yet another devastating bowler, the cheerful, six-foot four-inch Max Walker. "Tanglefoot" took 41 wickets on the tour and 26 at 20 each in the five Tests against a team which included Clive Lloyd, Rohan Kanhai, Roy Fredericks, Alvin Kallicharran and Lawrence Rowe. It was a singular triumph for Ian Chappell's side to win the series two-nil against a powerful team, but it was significant that Lance Gibbs was far and away the most successful West Indian bowler. The era of the fast bowling juggernaut, however, was soon to begin.*

# ╋ 1973 ╋

## *WATERLOGGED BEGINNINGS*
### *WEEK ENDED MAY 8*

Agreen journalist views a new project with a little apprehension. Jim Swanton, wishing to reassure me about the *Cricketer* Journal, wrote this encouragement: "I don't think that a mind as facile as yours will find this job a burden." I leave the reader to interpret this genial ambiguity as he thinks fit.

It must always have been difficult to offer a wide geographical spread of first-hand stories in a personal Journal of this kind, but the present fixture structure makes insularity even more likely. Each county plays every other once in the Championship and once in the John Player League. Each also plays four other sides in their part of the country in the Benson and Hedges Cup, and four traditional rivals in the extra Championship games. For Middlesex, this means that we will play most sides twice in the season, Yorkshire and Essex three times, Kent, Sussex and Surrey four times each. We even play Sussex three times in two weeks.

So the reader is asked to forgive me if he finds eye-witness accounts of the goings-on in, say, Lancashire and Glamorgan few and far between. He must also forgive me if he finds this opening instalment verging on the lugubrious. For since the season opened we have spent more time waiting for waterlogged grounds to dry than playing or practising. John Price reckoned that the most sensible net practice he could get would be with a bar of soap under a cold shower.

The rain has not, however, frustrated everyone all the time. Two week-ends of the Benson and Hedges competition have now been completed. The Southern group – by far the strongest – is again being closely contested. Last year Kent, perhaps the best one-day side in the country, failed to qualify for the quarter-finals. This year, against Middlesex, the depth of their batting enabled them to recover from 22 for three and 96 for five to 210 for seven; we never batted well enough to worry them. Last week we narrowly beat Surrey, who had beaten Sussex. Essex too won comfortably against Sussex. In the other zones, none of the non-Championship sides has looked likely to win. They have provided genial batting practice for Gordon Greenidge (173 not out) and Turner (123 not out) in the South, and for David Lloyd and Hayes in the North. Sadiq, who has matured quickly over the last couple of years, scored a century against Somerset.

## *NEW ZEALANDERS WARM UP*
### *WEEK ENDED MAY 15*

THE New Zealanders clearly have one of their best-ever sides. The batting, which hinges round Turner and Congdon, has depth to support their class. Parker must have improved since he played against us for Worcester last year; Redmond chances his arm, and Burgess, Hastings, and Pollard are experienced Test players. The seam bowling has menace and variety. Of the slow bowlers, only Howarth is known to be a top-class performer. I imagine that they will play the game tight, without too many flourishes. For panache we may have to wait for the West Indies, but New Zealand may prove the steadier side. Both teams will play three Test matches and two one-day internationals.

The touring teams play all their matches on covered pitches. The rest of us are not so well protected. I personally favour uncovered pitches, since they demand such a wide range of skills and courage in all departments of the game. They certainly lead to results, as this week's Championship matches showed. Close played as only he can on a wet pitch at Lord's to score a match-winning 153. This was his 10th century in the two years since his 40th birthday and his exile in the West Country. Mushtaq – you can't keep the Mohammads down – made 141 not out in a low-scoring match against Lancashire. And Keith Boyce with a superb all-round performance led Essex to a two-day victory over Surrey. Geoff Greenidge, on the other hand, found himself on the losing side against Hampshire, despite batting through the second innings for 100 not out.

Over the week-end, the outstanding performance was Oxford University's. They bowled Northants out for 172 on a docile pitch. After half their 55 overs, Oxford were only 60 for two; but Keith Jones, their captain, scored 82, and the University just made it in the last over. It is a remarkable fact that no Minor County side has either

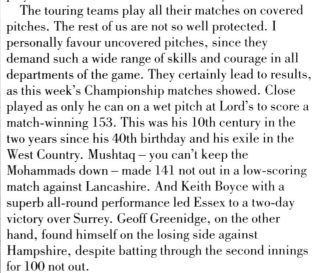

singly or blended yet beaten a first-class side in the Gillette Cup or in the Benson and Hedges Cup. Why have there been no giant-killers in all these matches? I suppose that the main reason is the scarcity of professionals in all areas of cricket except first-class (contrast the soccer scene beyond the First Division). And even limited-overs matches are less capable of being decided on the day by enthusiasm, dash, and instinct than football matches which last only 90 minutes.

## RUNS BEGIN TO FLOW
### WEEK ENDED MAY 22

FOR the second time this season Essex have won in two days. This week, they scored 337 for seven declared on a placid pitch at Chelmsford. The pitch was still easy on Thursday, but Derbyshire capitulated twice, for 119 and 190. East took 12 wickets for 130.

The other performance of the week was Hampshire's, and in particular Greenidge's. On a pitch which helped the seam bowlers, he scored 196 not out of his side's total of 341. Hampshire won by seven wickets.

Plenty of runs were scored at The Oval, where Intikhab, showing his winter form with the bat, hit a whirlwind – or was it a hurricane? – 139. Roope made 90 twice in the match, but even this batting was eclipsed by Gloucester's, for whom that well-known West Country trio of Sadiq, Zaheer and Procter scored fluently in their eight-wicket win.

We are now beginning to take seriously the possibility of Glenn Turner's scoring 1000 runs in May. He needs 201 with three matches to go.

On Friday, an important decision was reached by a special meeting of the TCCB. It was agreed that the Cricketers' Association should receive a lump sum of £3500 p.a. for four years, with a review after two years, which sum will represent their share of the income coming into the game. In addition, the TCCB will finance a non-contributory pension scheme which will cover all players. The 75 per cent of county cricketers who never receive a benefit or testimonial will now not leave the game without any retirement money.

*The Cricketers' Association deserved such an income, and the players – is it really as high as 75% who don't get a benefit? – deserved such a "pension". The Association has been excellently led throughout its existence, notably by its secretary, J.D. Bannister, and the TCCB, guided equally sensibly by D.B. Carr, have kept in close contact, to the benefit of all.*

## TEAMS FOR ENGLAND TEST TRIAL
### WEEK ENDED MAY 29

THE England selectors have chosen the following sides for the Test trial at Hove, which begins on May 30.

*Touring Team to India and Pakistan:* Lewis (captain), Denness, Amiss, Fletcher, Roope, Greig, Knott, Arnold, Gifford, Pocock, Cottam.

*The Rest:* Illingworth (captain), Boycott, Lloyd, Smith (M. J.), Radley, Hayes, Woolmer, Taylor (R. W.), Snow, East, Lever (J. K.).

The match is, of course, being billed as Lewis v. Illingworth. There are several places wide open, apart from the captaincy. Snow will have to show that he has fully recovered from his injured back. He bowled fast and accurately against Middlesex in the Bank Holiday match. He and Arnold should make a fine combination. One or two batting places will probably have question-marks against them at the moment. This match may produce a decisive innings from Smith, Lloyd, Roope, Radley or Hayes.

In the Sunday League, Leicester created an unenviable and unexpected record by being bowled out for 36 by Sussex. The crowd at Grace Road had been gloating – Sunday crowds are not, on the whole, too kind – as Sussex declined to 89 all out. But their glee turned to glumness as Denman (four for 5) and the other Sussex seamers removed one batsman after another. All this happened, apparently, on a slow but even pitch.

Two days remain in May. New Zealand play Northampton. Turner needs 93 for his 1000.

## ONE THOUSAND CHEERS
### WEEK ENDED JUNE 5

HE got them! Jim Watts put the tourists in at Northampton, where the start was delayed until 3.30. Turner was 70 not out overnight, and reached the target (93) on the morning of the last day of May. He is

Glenn Turner cuts Bedi for four to reach his target.

# Nerveless Turner joins 1,000 club

**By BRIAN SCOVELL**

GLENN TURNER, the record-br... New Zea...

INTO HISTORY, RUN BY RUN

'I was a bit irritable. I always am when I've had to struggle on a wicket which is favourable to bowlers. But I had a few snorters—gin and tonics—as...'

the seventh person to have scored 1000 runs by the end of May. The others were W. G. Grace (1895), T. W. Hayward (1900), W. R. Hammond (1927), C. Hallows (1928), D. G. Bradman (1930, 1938), W. J. Edrich (1938). It is today a feat only possible for a tourist, now that the counties play so little first-class cricket in May.

*No-one has done it since, although Graham Gooch had a brief sniff of the record a season or two back.*

The Test trial produced a few fine innings on a pitch favouring seam bowling. Roope scored 117 for the Tour XI, Hayes 88 and 51 for The Rest. Some artificiality crept in later, when slow bowlers bowled more than they would have done if the prime aim had been to win; and Boycott retired at tea on the last day with an alleged strain, to catch a train for Hull.

The captaincy problem was resolved by a compromise. Illingworth is to lead the side against New Zealand, with Lewis as his number two. Some fairly bland remarks were made by the chairman of selectors about Lewis learning tricks of the captaincy trade by this apprenticeship. Gifford was preferred to Underwood – a surprise to me – and Roope to Denness.

Elsewhere, Notts won their first victory at Trent Bridge for two years by beating Lancashire with two balls to spare. Randall, chosen as 12th man for the Test, scored an exciting 93. He is a young English player with flair, who catches the eye at once; he strikes me as a bright prospect. Sussex crushed Gloucester, thanks largely to a stand of 217 between Prideaux (170) and Greig (139), and to Snow's nine wickets in the match. New Zealand go into the first Test with the encouragement of a win over Lancashire. Collinge and the Hadlees did the damage on, I imagine, a pitch not unlike that on which the Test match against Australia was played last year.

Derek Randall – Nottinghamshire's promising new talent.

## MEMORABLE NOTTINGHAM TEST
### WEEK ENDED JUNE 12

THE First Test match at Trent Bridge turned out to be one of the most memorable Tests ever. New Zealand scored the highest fourth innings total in any Test in England – and yet lost by 38 runs. The bones of the match were as follows: England were bowled out for 250. On the second day New Zealand collapsed utterly, and were 97 all out. They fought back, and had England 24 for four when Greig joined Amiss. These two added 210 to enable England to set a target of 479 in two days and two hours. After two hours the score was 56 for two. After eight, 317 for five. New Zealand finally submerged, heroic, for 440.

Tony Greig returns to the pavilion after his valuable innings of 139.

Geoff Boycott is lbw to Bruce Taylor for 51 in the First Test at Trent Bridge.

On this occasion the mere scores cannot fail to indicate the pattern and excitement of the match. The pitch was sub-standard, with brown and green patches, and uneven bounce and pace. The ball swung and moved off the seam for most of the match. Boycott and

Amiss played well on the first day, but only Knott and Gifford showed much fight after they left. England's bowlers, especially Arnold, were a class above their opponents'. They were just too good on the day. Extras (20) were the highest score in the total of 97.

But when England collapsed to 24 for four in the second innings, it could have been anyone's game by close of play on Saturday. The rot started with a run out. Boycott and Amiss found themselves at the same end. In such circumstances Boycott usually shames his partner into self-sacrifice, but on this occasion Amiss outglared him. Muttering imprecations, the mighty Achilles retired to his tent. Greig joined Amiss when three more wickets had fallen quickly. He transformed the game. He drove "on the up", on either side of the wicket. The audience forgot about the vagaries of the pitch. Suddenly batting was once again a pleasure and an art. He scored 139 in little over three hours. Amiss made a fine 138 not out.

It was after tea on Saturday that the improbable marathon began. Congdon was hit in the face, but batted on. He carried on, never spectacular but always sound, playing mainly off the back foot with bat very straight, until 6.15 on Monday when, for no clear reason, Arnold bowled him. Pollard, of limited

Bev Congdon is eventually bowled by Geoff Arnold in the New Zealand second innings.

technique and unlimited courage, stayed until he was seventh out at 414. He had scored 116, his first Test century. The third new ball finished off the tail.

Only cricket, of all games, and only long two-innings matches at that, can produce such absorbing,

sustained, and varying possibilities.

The domestic cricket for the week has to take a back seat. Yorkshire had a champagne week. They beat Northamptonshire in two days at Middlesbrough. Chris Old took nine for 53 in the match. In India he improved all the time, returning, wondrous to relate, two stone heavier than when he went out. Yorkshire then crushed Somerset by nine wickets despite a colossal block-out by Brian Close, who succeeded in scoring 38 runs in four and a half hours. I should have enjoyed being a fly on one of his stumps while all this went on.

## DIFFICULTIES FOR LLOYD AND WARD
### WEEK ENDED JUNE 19

DAVID Lloyd, who is a brilliant short-leg, had an eventful week. Against Oxford he had his nose broken. In the next match, Majid struck him firmly on the head. It was a fateful ball, for as Lloyd bit the dust Pilling darted in from mid-wicket to catch the rebound.

Lloyd's injuries led him to say that he would not post a short square-leg again. The problem is that on many wickets, and against modern batting techniques, more catches go to short square-leg (often via bat and pad, or from the glove) than to the more traditional backward short-leg. But the modern position is far more dangerous. Not only can the bad ball be hit harder in that direction than in any other, but quite good balls can be clipped or slogged there at fearful velocity. The fielder, however brilliant, has literally no chance to see the ball. One accepts the dangers of batting against fast bowlers on lively pitches because one has a chance to use one's skill to avoid the danger.

The only answer, and I hope it is reached before we have a death on our hands, is proper protection. Batsmen and wicketkeepers have it, while the man who is in greater need of it might just as well be stark naked. A face mask and padded cap would help for a start.

*As usual, Brearley's thinking was ahead of its time.*

Yorkshire, fifth in the table, had one of their regular tedious draws with Derbyshire, the fault lying with the latter. This match will, however, be remembered little for its scores, much for its drama in being the stage for

Alan Ward's being sent off by the captain, Brian Bolus, for refusing to bowl. It was, I believe, the sad culmination of a situation in which Ward had become increasingly doubtful about his ability and almost pathologically afraid to bowl. One irony, of course, is that many a batsman was equally petrified.

## NEW ZEALAND AGAIN NEARLY SUCCEED

### WEEK ENDED JUNE 26

NEW Zealand have still never beaten England. With two hours of the Second Test to go, England in their second innings were only 70 runs ahead with two wickets left. Wadsworth twice dropped Arnold off Pollard, Fletcher took command, and England were safe. Scores: England 253 and 463 for nine, New Zealand 551 for nine declared.

The Lord's pitch was excellent. For most of the match it was a fine batting pitch, but it had pace and gave the spinners a chance later on. The weather on the first day was cloudy, and the ball moved enough to justify Congdon's decision to put England in. Boycott again looked in a class of his own; he scored 61 and 90, and got himself out each time. The New Zealand innings started badly, but Congdon and Hastings batted through from 10 for two to 200 for three. Congdon eventually made 175, Burgess and Pollard both scored centuries, and New Zealand declared with 10½ hours to go. England's middle order collapsed from 335 for four to 368 for eight, when Arnold came in, and the last act – so frustrating for New Zealand – began. Fletcher's 178 was a superb innings, crucial for the side and for his career. I was delighted, for he has always been a class player in county cricket, he always plays for the team, and he is a shrewd tactician.

*Successive Test centuries for both Bev Congdon (top) and Vic Pollard.*

🏃 *Until recent years, and certainly outside Essex, Fletcher was more a player's player than a spectator's.*

Northants had another convincing win, by an innings, against Notts at Newark. P. J. Watts, a man who shows the same calm good-humour in success as in disaster, scored 126. At Hove Frank Hayes scored his first first-class century. What I have seen of his batting (not much) makes me reserve judgment about his

# 5p LORD'S MCC GROUND 5p

## ENGLAND v. NEW ZEALAND

THURS., FRI., SAT., MON. & TUES., JUNE 21, 22, 23, 25 & 26, 1973  (5-day Match)

### ENGLAND

| | | First Innings | | Second Innings | |
|---|---|---|---|---|---|
| 1 G. Boycott | Yorkshire | c Parker b Collinge | 61 | c and b Howarth | 92 |
| 2 D. L. Amiss | Warwickshire | c Howarth b Hadlee | 9 | c and b Howarth | 53 |
| 3 G. R. J. Roope | Surrey | l b w b Howarth | 56 | | |
| 4 K. W. R. Fletcher | Essex | c Hastings b Howarth | 25 | | |
| 5 A. W. Greig | Sussex | c Howarth b Collinge | 63 | | |
| †6 R. Illingworth | Leicestershire | c Collinge b Hadlee | 3 | | |
| *7 A. P. E. Knott | Kent | b Hadlee | 0 | | |
| 8 C. M. Old | Yorkshire | b Howarth | 7 | | |
| 9 J. A. Snow | Sussex | b Taylor | 2 | | |
| 10 G. G. Arnold | Surrey | not out | 8 | | |
| 11 N. Gifford | Worcestershire | c Wadsworth b Collinge | 8 | | |
| | | B , l-b 1, w 1, n-b 9, | 11 | B , l-b , w , n-b , | |
| | | Total | 253 | Total | |

### FALL OF THE WICKETS

1—24  2—116  3—148  4—165  5—171  6—175  7—195  8—217  9—237  10—253
1—112  2—185  3—  4—  5—  6—  7—  8—  9—  10—

ANALYSIS OF BOWLING  1st Innings

| Name | O. | M. | R. | W. | Wd. | N-b | O. | M. | R. | W. | Wd. | N-b |
|---|---|---|---|---|---|---|---|---|---|---|---|---|
| Collinge | 31 | 8 | 69 | 3 | ... | 8 | ... | ... | ... | ... | ... | ... |
| Taylor | 19 | 1 | 54 | 1 | 1 | ... | ... | ... | ... | ... | ... | ... |
| Hadlee | 26 | 4 | 70 | 3 | ... | 1 | ... | ... | ... | ... | ... | ... |
| Congdon | 5 | 2 | 7 | 0 | ... | ... | ... | ... | ... | ... | ... | ... |
| Howarth | 25 | 6 | 42 | 3 | ... | ... | ... | ... | ... | ... | ... | ... |

### NEW ZEALAND

| | | First Innings | | Second Innings | |
|---|---|---|---|---|---|
| 1 G. M. Turner | Otago | c Greig b Arnold | 4 | | |
| 2 J. M. Parker | N. Districts | c Knott b Snow | 3 | | |
| †3 B. E. Congdon | Otago | c Knott b Old | 175 | | |
| 4 B. F. Hastings | Canterbury | l b w b Snow | 86 | | |
| 11 H. J. Howarth | Auckland | hit wicket b Old | 17 | | |
| 5 M. G. Burgess | Auckland | b Snow | 105 | | |
| 6 V. Pollard | Canterbury | not out | 105 | | |
| *7 K. J. Wadsworth | Canterbury | c Knott b Old | 27 | | |
| 8 B. R. Taylor | Wellington | b Old | 11 | | |
| 9 D. R. Hadlee | Canterbury | c Fletcher b Old | 6 | | |
| 10 R. O. Collinge | Wellington | Innings closed | | | |
| | | B , l-b 5, w , n-b 7, | 12 | B , l-b , w , n-b , | |
| | | Total | 551 | Total | |

### FALL OF THE WICKETS

1—5  2—10  3—200  4—249  5—330  6—447  7—523  8—535  9—551  10—
1—  2—  3—  4—  5—  6—  7—  8—  9—  10—

ANALYSIS OF BOWLING  1st Innings

| Name | O. | M. | R. | W. | Wd. | N-b | O. | M. | R. | W. | Wd. | N-b |
|---|---|---|---|---|---|---|---|---|---|---|---|---|
| Snow | 38 | 4 | 109 | 3 | ... | 3 | ... | ... | ... | ... | ... | ... |
| Arnold | 41 | 6 | 108 | 1 | ... | 3 | ... | ... | ... | ... | ... | ... |
| Old | 41.5 | 7 | 113 | 5 | ... | 1 | ... | ... | ... | ... | ... | ... |
| | | 15 | 0 | ... | ... | | | | | | | |

potential, for I should have thought that at present he could too easily be restricted on the leg stump. But others speak glowingly of him. Fred Titmus, never one to go out on a limb about someone who has yet to produce the goods, was even in favour of sending him to Australia on the last MCC tour.

Cricket at the end of the week was largely washed out. The West Indians, having almost beaten Essex in a rain-affected match at Chelmsford, beat Hampshire convincingly. Steve Camacho suffered a nasty injury when his glasses were smashed by a bouncer. Fortunately, no long-term damage is predicted. Perhaps batsmen as well as short-legs should wear face masks.

Alan Ward announced his retirement from the game.

Taunton
Somerset v. Australians,
May 1985.

**Leicester**
Leicestershire v.
Northamptonshire,
County Championship,
August 1980.

**Chelmsford**
Australia v. India,
World Cup, June 1983.

**Uxbridge**
Middlesex v.
Worcestershire,
County Championship,
July 1984.

**Basingstoke**
Hampshire v. Sussex,
John Player League,
May 1981.

Chesterfield
Derbyshire v.
Nottinghamshire,
County Championship,
June 1982.

He has been a bright comet, burned out early. I hope he may in time face up to his inner fears, and come back to county cricket.

 *He never did. It was a pity, perhaps, that he did not have Brearley as his captain and mentor.*

## KENT TO THE FORE
### WEEK ENDED JULY 3

IN the Benson and Hedges Cup Kent will meet Worcestershire in the final on July 21. One cannot avoid writing about Kent these days; their supporters cannot avoid watching: 15,000 crowded in to Canterbury to see them win a tense match against Essex by 46 runs, Ealham scored 48 and took another diving catch. Essex, chasing 169 for nine, looked well placed at 68 for one, but their batting is thin after the first three or four, and they collapsed against Shepherd and Woolmer. The other semi-final was a nightmarish cliff-hanger for Lancashire. Worcestershire won by scoring the same number of runs (159) but having lost nine wickets instead of being all out.

The achievement of the week, possibly of the season, occurred in the Gillette, where Durham beat Yorkshire (who better?) by five wickets. Their captain, Brian Lander, took five for 15. Sussex did well to win at Northampton, and Gloucestershire at Cardiff.

Rodney Marsh's brother won a golf tournament in Scotland to take his winnings for the season to "well over £30,000". I wonder if Rodney reckons he chose the right game?

*Shrewd again, Brearley. The imbalance in the incomes of the equally talented Marsh brothers is said to have been one of the catalysts of the "Packer Revolution".*

## COWDREY'S GREAT LANDMARK
### WEEK ENDED JULY 10

IN the Third Test New Zealand took what Robin Marlar described as "a gigantic step backwards into the bad old days". They failed to bowl anywhere near a good length on a pitch which should have helped their seamers, especially after Friday's rain. Boycott scored 115, Fletcher 81, and Illingworth 65. The fast-bowling trio of Snow, Arnold and Old kept up the pressure wonderfully, and England won by an innings and one run. Turner at last came good, with a precarious 81. He might willingly have traded, say, 400 of his May runs for 250 in the Tests.

Now for the West Indians. Middlesex played them this week. I had a good match, scoring 87 and 70 not out. I saw enough of them to realise how very, very good they can be . . . and how horrid. The fielding, for example, varies from the highest peaks of brilliance to pathetic and absurd panic. Boyce and Holder can be quick and hostile; they can move the ball; they can also be relatively gentle. Inshan Ali ought not to trouble our Test players too much. The batting is of course the strongest in the world.

A second great target has now been reached this year. Colin Cowdrey scored his 100th hundred. He is the 16th to achieve this record. He is now 40; didn't Jack Hobbs score 100 hundreds *after* his 40th birthday?

*Not quite. 98.*

Cambridge, underdogs in the University match, had the best of a draw. Hadley and Edmonds are good prospects; as, clearly, are Khan, Lee and Jones from Oxford.

*"Khan" was Imran. Like Edmonds, a good prospect indeed!*

## OVER RATES PUBLISHED
### WEEK ENDED JULY 17

THE TCCB have been trying for some years to think of ways of improving the over rate. In county cricket it has dropped from 20 per hour to 18 per hour in ten years, which represents a difference of 12 overs a day. In Test cricket the decline has been ever steeper. Exhortations via captains have been unsuccessful. As I know, it is hard for a captain to achieve very much in this respect.

There has been pressure from overseas to limit run-ups, which has been rightly resisted by the TCCB. They have decided that the only way to get our house in order is to threaten pockets, and that the only pockets to threaten belong to the players.

So this year each county which averages less than 18·5 must pay a fine of £500; the proceeds to be shared among counties which average 19·5 or more. The June figures have recently been published. To date, Middlesex are the only county to average over 19·5 (with 19·63); seven sides average under 18·5. It would be ironical if we were to end the season at the bottom of the table but £3500 richer. The champions will earn £3000.

 *Similar ironies have indeed occurred with this system.*

## BENSON & HEDGES CLIMAX
### WEEK ENDED JULY 24

I see no reason why one-day internationals should not become a routine feature of the calendar. Part of their interest will lie in seeing how overseas teams approach limited-overs cricket. So far, the practice in it has been to England's advantage.

Against New Zealand, England won comfortably at Swansea; the Manchester match was rained off after England had scored 167 for eight in their 55 overs. In the match that did finish, Arnold and Snow once again created havoc, and reduced New Zealand to 15 for four. One may see it either as a fascination or a drawback of this sort of cricket that there is a limitation on each bowler's allowance. This rule enabled the tourists to make a partial recovery, mainly through Pollard; but 159 was too small a score. Amiss played a wonderful innings, scoring 100 out of 135 in 39 overs. Strong forearms and good timing allow him to hit the ball

extremely hard for a player with so short a swing.

The other centre piece this week was the Benson & Hedges Final. This year it was played on an excellent pitch, and plenty of runs were scored. Kent, the favourites, won by 39 runs after scoring 225 for seven. They looked winners most of the time. Only when Gifford (33) and D'Oliveira (47) added 70 in 12 overs did their grip slacken. Asif, the quickest-footed batsman I've ever seen, scored 59 and took four for 43 to be Man of the Match. Luckhurst, who has emerged as one of the great and perhaps unexpected successes of one-day cricket, made a fine 79.

## WEST INDIES RENAISSANCE
### WEEK ENDED JULY 31

SINCE the decline of Hall and Griffith, West Indies had gone 20 Tests without a victory, until this week at The Oval they regained their pride with a convincing win by 158 runs. Sobers, the "four in one", was always a lesser captain than player, partly because of that generosity which makes him so charming a man. Now Kanhai, perhaps more ruthless a competitor, has had the satisfaction of leading a side in which Sobers played a vital role to this elusive win. They must now be the most talented and probably the best side in the world. They lack a second class spinner to support Gibbs, and an opening batsman to join Fredericks. They have impressive fast bowling and wonderful batting.

Lloyd and Kallicharran annihilated England on the first day in a stand of 208 which started when the score was 64 for three. Boyce followed his 72 at number nine

Mike Denness with the Cup and Asif Iqbal with the Gold Award are chaired by the victorious Kent team.

Alan Knott becomes one of Keith Boyce's eleven wickets at The Oval.

Frank Hayes – a century in his first Test.

with five for 70 and six for 77. For England, there was Frank Hayes. In the second innings of his first Test he scored 106 not out. He is the new hope of English batting. He is a fine off-side player off front and back foot. On the leg side, he is much more limited, but no doubt fluency here will come. He is a fine fielder. Hayes apart, only Boycott, who scored 97 despite being slightly below his best, and Illingworth had a reasonable game with the bat. Arnold once again bowled beautifully to take eight wickets in the match.

Hampshire had two splendid wins to take the lead in the Championship. They beat Lancashire by an innings and Worcester by 185 runs. Northants kept in touch by beating Sussex, but Essex lost ground with a two-day defeat at the hands of Leicester. Warwickshire took 13 points from their draw with Kent (4), but played it exceedingly cautiously on the last day, leaving Kent and themselves with no chance of a win.

The International Cricket Conference, impressed perhaps by the women, have agreed to hold a men's World Cup in England in 1975. The Conference also, more controversially, decided to restrict the number of fielders on the leg side to five. This new regulation will count unfairly against the off-spinner. One might as well restrict the slow left-armer or away-swing bowler to five on the off. The change, initiated, I gather, by Australia, argues an ignorance of the skills involved in bowling off-spin or in-swing, and of the varied resources available to the inventive batsman to deal with a leg-stump attack.

*This was, in fact, only a "strong recommendation" and the regulation was not applied in England, although only two men were permitted (and still are) behind the wicket on the leg side.*

The Conference were unable to offer anything but groans in respect of the over rate. They have however settled on a new umpire's sign, arms diagonally crossed above the head, to indicate "dead ball".

## LANCASHIRE TOPPLED
### WEEK ENDED AUGUST 7

LANCASHIRE'S record in the Gillette may never again be approached, let alone defeated. They came to Lord's to play Middlesex having won their last 14 matches in the competition, including three finals. When they had scored 224 for six (Pilling 90) the trainloads of vociferous supporters who turned parts of genteel St John's Wood into Stretford Road outposts were confident that the march would go on. But Smith (90) and Featherstone (46) added 135 for the first wicket; still the Lancastrians (at least those in the crowd) expected to win. We lost three wickets and in appalling light almost ceased to score. A thunderstorm stopped everything until the next day, when we just managed to score the 62 needed in 13 overs, with one over and four wickets to spare.

Their astonishing run owes a lot to Jack Bond who brought in a young team all of whom have matured together, plus Lloyd and Engineer. Lloyd was of course crucially missed this time.

The other favourites, Kent, also fell, by a large margin at Hove. Sussex amassed 263 for six, Snow struck with two quick wickets and the game was over bar the shouting. We will now play Sussex at home in the semi-final.

The other semi-final will be between Worcester and Gloucester. Both batted first and won fairly comfortably (I maintain that in good conditions it is worth perhaps 30 runs to bat first).

## PRESSURES OF TEST CRICKET
### WEEK ENDED AUGUST 14

THE Second Test was a disappointment, marred by negative attitudes, controversy, slow over rates, and a good deal of undistinguished batting. West Indies won the toss again and subsided to 39 for three and 128 for five. Fredericks (150) and Murray saved them with an extended stand of 114. They eventually reached 327. England started confidently; but once Boycott had retired hurt the batting looked fragile especially against the ubiquitous bouncer. England were at last out for 305. West Indies bowled 62 overs in the first 4½ hours of the innings. They batted more entertainingly in the second innings; but Kanhai did not declare and the match ended tamely with England on 182 for two (Amiss 86 not out).

The controversy arose in response to a decision by Arthur Fagg, when he gave Boycott not out; Kanhai and

County Championship
(as at August 7)

| | | P | Pts |
|---|---|---|---|
| **1** | Hampshire | 15 | 169 |
| **2** | Northamptonshire | 14 | 150 |
| **3** | Kent | 14 | 138 |
| **4** | Essex | 14 | 132 |

others made it clear that they disagreed. Next morning Fagg did not take the field for the first over. He was quoted in the press as having disparaged the standards of behaviour and the pressures put on umpires in modern cricket.

Certainly players should avoid showing disagreement with umpires; if they do err, they should apologise. But I have two further points to make. One is that if cricket has gained a worse name, then the source of it lies in Test cricket and in the television and Press coverage. County cricket has kept a remarkably fine standard of behaviour. Most umpires would not, I think, share Arthur Fagg's generalised distaste. Secondly, I think the umpires are themselves slightly responsible for such failings as exist. They have many actions open to them through official channels; and they could be firmer and more positive about some issues (e.g. timewasting) on the field.

Kent have now definitely won the John Player League for the second consecutive year. They are unquestionably the best one-day side in the country (at least while Lancashire lack Clive Lloyd); which is a consolation to those of us who have harboured hopes in this direction.

## GILLETTE SEMI-FINAL THRILLERS
### WEEK ENDED AUGUST 21

IT was a quirkish freak (or a freakish quirk) that in both Gillette semi-finals the margin of victory should be five runs. Five little runs! That's how you feel if you're on the wrong side of the gap, as we were against Sussex and Worcester against Gloucester. Our match was played on a poor pitch, worn and loose. The groundsman at Lord's has prepared fine pitches for the big games this year, but pressure of space has led to rather ropey ones for some of the other matches.

The selectors have chosen Willis for the last Test next week. Hendrick is omitted: so is Snow.

## DEBACLE AT LORD'S
### WEEK ENDED AUGUST 28

NOT even football, encroaching on the sports pages since July, could push West Indies into second place this week. Their supporters danced over Lord's

Rohan Kanhai clears the air with a handshake for Arthur Fagg.

for hours after the game in which England suffered their heaviest home defeat ever, by an innings and 226 runs.

The match, fantastic enough in purely cricketing terms, also took its place in that list of sporting events used and disrupted for political ends – unless the hoaxer who phoned on Saturday afternoon had nothing to do with the bombs that have been exploding in London and Birmingham.

Play was held up for almost two hours. By then the cricketing issue was scarcely in doubt. West Indies had scored 652 for eight declared with superb centuries from Kanhai, Sobers, and Julien. England, with eight wickets down, were more than 400 runs behind. The day's crude drama ended with England 42 for three in their second innings; off the last ball Boycott was caught from a hook off Boyce in a well-publicised ploy by Kanhai, and as he ran from the field he was mobbed and manhandled by jubilant supporters.

Only Fletcher really did credit to himself with the bat, scoring 68 and 86 not out. Only Willis can have helped himself with the ball. Illingworth's career as captain of England looks precarious to say the least. But what a side the West Indies are on fast true pitches such as this! At last they have recognised the potential of Boyce, who took 19 wickets in three Tests at 15 runs apiece; he and Holder made a formidable pair, though most bowlers will look better when they have 650 runs to play with.

*This puts later West Indian sides into perspective. Boyce and Holder were certainly fine bowlers, but much less mean than some of those who followed.*

The hot dry summer continues. As bowlers flag, some batsmen cashed in. Harris scored 201 not out, but was on the losing side against Glamorgan. Francis made 188 not out against Yorkshire. At The Oval, the Bobby Riggs of English cricket, Reg Simpson, steered the Old England XI to victory over the women with 71 not out.

## WEST COUNTRY TRIUMPHS
### WEEK ENDED SEPTEMBER 4

IT has often been claimed in recent years that one major drawback of the old amateur/professional set-up was that the amateur captain was often not worth his place on ability alone. It is odd that England's last three – professional – captains would also have been uncertain of a place had they not been captains. Denness has now the strongest claim of the three – the others are Illingworth and Lewis – for selection as a player alone. He is a handsome batsman with a great ability. He is a good fielder and a conscientious captain, though anyone could do an adequate job with the Kent side. I suspect that he does not appreciate or know how to use slow bowlers; but then he has not had much genuinely slow bowling in his side. He is a friendly and likeable person, who will probably be a good diplomat in West Indies.

Illingworth has done a good deal for English cricket, and deserves better than this epitaph-like memorial: "He will be remembered for his single-minded pursuit of the attritional style." (*The Times*). His virtues are wider than this. He is very open, a lover of argument; he will have a dispute out with anyone, face to face. He supports his players, but expects 100% at all times. He is a devoted captain, never losing concentration, confident in his own ways; he has done marvellously at critical moments. The severest criticism that can be levelled at him is that he did not sufficiently discourage that element of selfishness which is a part of the make-up of most successful cricketers.

Gloucester have won the Gillette Cup for the first time. They are an attractive side, which plays cricket properly. Tony Brown has done very well, not least insofar as he was responsible for the acquisition and retention of Procter, Sadiq, and Zaheer. Procter (94) and Brown (77 not out) won the match against Sussex. They came together at 106 for five and added 74. The total – 248 for eight – was the second-highest in a Gillette final. Sussex started well, though always a shade behind the rate they would have liked. Greenidge scored 76. But wickets fell: with Greig's run-out 121 for one had become 156 for four, and in the gloom Sussex had no chance. They were all out for 208.

The West Country takes all the honours not already won by Kent. Hampshire are now certain of the Championship. This achievement rivals Glamorgan's in 1969, for who could have given either side a chance before the event? It is especially remarkable that they have scored more bowling points than anyone else. Six of their bowlers average 26 or less, which speaks for

Hampshire enjoy their success. Left to right: David Turner, Bob Herman, Bob Stephenson, Trevor Jesty, Tom Mottram, Richard Gilliat and Peter Sainsbury.

itself. They too have found the right players from elsewhere. Apart from Richards, Greenidge, and O'Sullivan, they have made successes of other's discards. All credit to Herman and Taylor, and to Gilliat for his part in it.

## THE SPREAD OF HONOURS
### THE FINAL DAYS

DONALD Carr will manage the side to West Indies this winter; the 16 players do not include Snow. I think they will miss him. The last batting places went to Jameson by a whisker, I imagine, from Smith. If he scores runs, which he may well do, he will get them quickly. The spinners are Pocock, Underwood, and Birkenshaw. They all have something to prove. There are no real surprises; only Hendrick is from outside the Test scene, and he had come into the picture recently. He is a very good bowler already; but his method is similar to that of Arnold, and it is possible that neither will find much to help him in the Caribbean except the Caribbean itself for tired feet. I hope that in a year Randall and Edmonds will have done enough to go to Australia as young hopefuls.

In the Prudential Trophy series the West Indies again showed their superiority, though England regained some face by winning by one wicket in the last over at Leeds. Scores: West Indies 181, England 182 for nine. Denness scored 66. In the second, we struggled even more with the bat, on a better wicket, to finish 189 for nine. West Indies made no mistake, winning by eight wickets in only 42 overs. Fredericks scored 105. Lance Gibbs, lithe and quick as ever, with only those small traces of white in his hair to disclose his age, bowled beautifully in each match, as he did also in the Tests.

Last winter Doug Insole said that if any side averaged less than 18½ overs per hour this summer he was a Dutchman. Ergo, he is a Dutchman. Lancashire with 17·83 and Somerset with 17·79 were below the rate. Middlesex (19·68). Essex (19·58), Glamorgan (19·55), and Derby (19·51) were above the 19·5 mark, and so qualify for shares in the Lancashire and Somerset players' money (£1000 in all). One has to admit that the overall rate – 18·91 – is ·91 higher than last year and the highest since 1966.

Finally, a short roll of honour, for those elsewhere unsung. Cartwright, Lee and Jackman, all skilled and hard-working performers, take pride of place. Cartwright's wickets cost him two runs less each than anyone else's. Lee joined Bedi with 100 wickets, and Jackman not only took 92 wickets at the remarkable striking rate of a wicket every seven overs, bowling much of the time on the placid Oval wicket, he also made such use of his batting talents as to score 620 runs at 36. Intikhab too had an agreeably successful season with 86 wickets and 644 runs. Shepherd was nearest the double with 92 wickets and 802 runs. Of the batsmen no-one hitherto unremarked stands out; and ten of the first 13 in the averages are from overseas; which gives us something to ponder this winter!

### FINAL
### COUNTY CHAMPIONSHIP TABLE

| | | P | W | L | D | Bonus Bt | Bw | Pts |
|---|---|---|---|---|---|---|---|---|
| 1 | Hampshire (9) | 20 | 10 | – | 10 | 84 | 81 | 265 |
| 2 | Surrey (12) | 20 | 9 | 3 | 8 | 71 | 73 | 234 |
| 3 | Northamptonshire (4) | 20 | 8 | 4 | 8 | 53 | 75 | 208 |
| 4 | Kent (2) | 20 | 4 | 3 | 13 | 98 | 59 | 197 |
| 5 | Gloucestershire (3) | 20 | 6 | 4 | 9* | 63 | 70 | 193 |
| 6 | Worcestershire (7) | 20 | 6 | 4 | 10 | 56 | 75 | 191 |
| 7 | Warwickshire (1) | 20 | 5 | 5 | 10 | 74 | 62 | 186 |
| 8 | Essex (5) | 20 | 6 | 5 | 9 | 46 | 72 | 178 |
| 9 | Leicestershire (6) | 20 | 4 | 3 | 12* | 66 | 60 | 166 |
| 10 | Somerset (11) | 20 | 7 | 2 | 11 | 29 | 60 | 159 |
| 11 | Glamorgan (13) | 20 | 4 | 8 | 8 | 44 | 68 | 152 |
| 12 | Lancashire (15) | 20 | 4 | 6 | 10 | 44 | 67 | 151 |
| 13 | Middlesex (8) | 20 | 4 | 5 | 10† | 49 | 54 | 148 |
| 14 | Yorkshire (10) | 20 | 3 | 5 | 11† | 28 | 69 | 132 |
| 15 | Sussex (16) | 20 | 2 | 10 | 8 | 42 | 67 | 129 |
| 16 | Derbyshire (17) | 20 | 2 | 10 | 8 | 15 | 67 | 102 |
| 17 | Nottinghamshire (14) | 20 | 1 | 8 | 11 | 28 | 63 | 101 |

Figures in brackets 1972 positions.
*Including Gloucestershire v Leicestershire abandoned without a ball bowled. †Including Yorkshire v Middlesex tie, 5 points each.

*Mike Brearley's Journal showed all the shrewd judgment and firm opinions of his captaincy. Most of what he said proved right. He had doubts, for example, about aspects of Frank Hayes's batting; he immediately spotted the special talent of Derek Randall; he staunchly defends standards of behaviour in county cricket but accepts the need to hasten over-rates; he is astute, balanced and fair in his assessments of Ray Illingworth and Mike Denness.*

*Denness it was who took the MCC team to the West Indies, without John Snow, whose bowling he needed although whose temperament he may have felt unable to control. As Brearley had predicted, neither Arnold nor Hendrick got much help from Caribbean pitches. Hendrick took 12 first class wickets at 26, the most economical of the faster bowlers although he was not selected for a Test. Arnold's 12 first-class wickets cost him 50 apiece; Old took nine at 51 each!*

*For most of the tour Denness personally, and his team, straggling behind, were trudging up a very steep hill in great heat. But at Denness's left and right hand were two men of oak, Dennis Amiss, who made 1,120 runs in nine first-class games and who at Sabina Park led one of the most heroic of all Test rearguards – 262 not out – and Tony Greig whose 430 runs, 24 wickets and seven catches represented the finest all-round performance by any man in a series in the West Indies. Not far behind, as crucial supporters of Moses in the flight out of Egypt, were Alan Knott, whose 365 Test runs were mainly contributed at important moments, and Geoff Boycott, whose 112 and 99 in the last Test at Sabina Park, where England had been thrashed in the opening match of the rubber, helped to make possible an unlikely victory and a drawn series. The hero, however, was Greig who, bowling off-spin to everyone's surprise, became the first English cricketer since Jim Laker to take more than 12 wickets in a Test match.*

*The down side of Greig's tour was his sneaky running out of Alvin Kallicharran during the First Test. Diplomacy saved the tour from imminent disaster at this stage and Greig won respect from the West Indian supporters by dint of natural charm and brave and brilliant cricket. But his moment of instinctive opportunism, bordering on sharp practice, was not forgotten.*

*The English achievement in drawing the series had been instrinsically worthy but it had not deceived anyone into thinking that a powerful or cohesive Test team had yet been formed; and an Australian challenge was only a few months away.*

# — 1974 —

## MENUHIN WITH HIS COAT ON
### WEEK ENDED APRIL 27

**B**ARRY Richards sounded-off the most brilliant fanfare to greet the new season at Lord's on Wednesday. An innings of pure gold for Hampshire the champion county. Swathed in many layers of Hampshire sweaters he defied the biting cold and swung his bat freely through a myriad arcs to score one hundred and eighty-nine unforgettable runs. A most reputable MCC attack of Hendrick, Jackman, Knight, Acfield and Edmonds appeared to be sending down half-volleys and long hops all day. It was not so, of course. They bowled as well as they were allowed, but were treated to graceful drives through every possible chink in the covers; sadistic slashes which almost put the square third man in physical danger; as well as gentle persuasions to fine leg and lofted golf shots for six wide of long-on. The MCC captain, and author of this Journal, tinkered with his field placings all day long but eventually concluded that he had taken the field four or five short!

The month of April has been rainless. Thirty-four days of drought at Lord's made a perfect batting wicket and a lightning outfield. The ball fairly flew around, as indeed it did at Eastbourne a few days before. There, Dennis Amiss, 152, John Jameson, 110 and 111, as well as India's newcomer, Patel, scored centuries in the tourists' match with Derrick Robins' XI.

## RETURN OF THE PRINCE
### WEEK ENDED MAY 4

**T**HE past week's sport calls for a royal salute, certainly from the cricket world, for it brought the good tidings that Prince Philip had accepted the presidency of MCC by Lord Caccia's nomination, the office to change hands on October 1.

It will not be his first term as president, though it was smartly pointed out that, war years excepted, only two others had held the post more than once. Prince Philip's return to Lord's twenty-five years after his last tenure has much significance for the game, as well as endowing the whole cricketing fraternity with pride in the royal connection. Next summer the plans are laid to stage a knockout cup competition in England in which all the major cricket countries will take part. Prince Philip's close affiliation to the game in this year will raise the enterprise way above the level of "just another one-day contest". His will be an absolutely essential contribution.

The Indian tourists endured what is by now our traditional freezing reception at Worcester. Conditions underfoot were firm enough, but they were trapped in a bitter east wind with gusts of rain. Basil D'Oliveira produced his best timing and concentration with 108 and 44 not out, while Holder, Brain and Inchmore made batting an uncomfortable test for the tourists. Eventually, after looking a beaten side, the Indians rallied to Norman Gifford's declaration of 221 in 3½ hours.

Sunil Gavaskar, who always looks so dangerous when he is playing his shots, scored 88 and led the way in a spirited run-chase. India ended up 18 runs short with six wickets down, but their greatest encouragement from this match was the performance of the new young seam bowler Madan Lal, taking seven for 95 in Worcestershire's first innings, and it is clearly his presence on this tour which has prompted Ajit Wadekar, the captain, to describe his team as the best-balanced for many years.

Finally the name of Jim Edmonds meant nothing to anyone in first-class cricket until he walked onto the practice ground at Old Trafford and asked for a trial. Well you cannot get more direct than that! Left-arm fast, he bowled well enough to be offered a contract. He has played only club cricket before in the Birmingham area and is studying for a chemistry degree at Salford University. Pleasing to hear of young cricketers getting their chance. Too often, these days, the bleat is that overseas players are keeping them out.

## DON BRADMAN IN LONDON
### WEEK ENDED MAY 11

**S**IR Donald Bradman, England's most famed adversary, came to London this week after a long absence. He is here primarily at the invitation of the Anglo-American Sporting Club which, in conjunction with the Lord's Taverners, will put on a glossy evening of fund-raising next Monday. "The Don" is guest of honour. What a draw! It is sold-out, of course.

As to the current tourists, my good friends the Indians. They comfortably extricate themselves game by game from awkward corners, and this week slipped out of the noose at Southampton and Leicester. Ashok Mankad hit some form with a 60 and Madan Lal is emerging as a considerable player. He is getting good runs and bowls lively stuff with a fairly good line.

Ajit Wadekar scored 138 to hold off Leicester and there was more high scoring around the country: Dennis Amiss 195, Kallicharran 127, both versus Middlesex, and at Taunton, Barry Wood, 101, and David Lloyd put on 265 for the first wicket. David Lloyd is my choice for England. A left-hander must be included against Indian spin.

## ENTER ANDERSON ROBERTS
### WEEK ENDED MAY 18

THERE is much talk around the counties about Hampshire's new fast bowler Andy Roberts from Antigua. I faced him in the first match of the season, MCC v. Hampshire at Lord's, and one could see his potential. He does not appear physically large, like say Wes Hall. He is spare, lithe and flexible. His run-up is inconsistent at present, but that should work itself out during the year.

Andy Roberts – Antigua's first Test cricketer and Hampshire's gain.

*Andy Roberts had made his Test debut against England in the Third Test in Barbados in March as a replacement for Keith Boyce. Boyce returned to displace Roberts for the final two Tests.*

I also note in the Press this week mention of a coloured South-African all-rounder, Kaya Majola, who has signed to play cricket for Derrick Robins' XI next month.

The two ominous performances of the week in my book are Chris Old's century against India. He then turned round and took five for 30. He must feel good about that. Also David Lloyd's 103 against the tourists at Manchester. We shall see.

## IMPORTANT CENTURY BY DENNESS
### WEEK ENDED MAY 25

SATURDAY, the first day of my week, was a glorious day. May Day in fact, and one hundred years after the birth of the immortal Gloucestershire all-rounder Gilbert Jessop. Yet more than that, it was a day away from cricket for Glamorgan and I found myself with my team-mate Roger Davis ambling round from the Tavern at Lord's to our lofty observation point on the higher deck at the nursery end, pint of beer in hand, to watch MCC take on the Indian tourists.

How that sun shone! It was marvellous. The cricket was at first tentative, as Test players of both countries felt the first tang of international competition on their lips. Boycott and Amiss fell cheaply to Solkar. I rubbed my eyes. Only a winter ago I saw Solkar take the new ball in India against England in nine Test innings without taking a single wicket.

I am not one of those who revel in the occasional failures of Geoff Boycott. His personal motivation is so intense that he has built himself a high, scorching funeral pyre which sizzles him each time he hits poor form. The biggest favour you can do for him in lean times is to offer yourself as a net bowler, because he *will* be back. No, my delight was to see Mike Denness score a splendid century; Fletcher too, but then he is a better player and more established in popular favour.

Mike Denness has just returned from West Indies, unpopular with many of his side and with many of the Press, who in their blindness take their cues from those in the side who criticise most. Cheap journalism from cheap players. Some of the writing sent back from the MCC tour was simply character assassination.

## TROUBLE UP NORTH
### WEEK ENDED JUNE 1

MUCH talk of captaincy this week. Mike Denness is firmly established as England's leader after the Test Trial at Worcester. He is appointed for three Tests against India – and the very best of luck to him. (Happily A. R. Lewis batted well enough in the trial game to jog a few memories!) Next I learn that Clive Lloyd will be the new captain for the West Indies. I am not at all sure what experience Clive has had as a leader, except as vice-captain of Lancashire, but good fortune to him too in India next winter.

Sadder moments came the way of two county captains, Jack Bond and Geoff Boycott. Since he joined Notts this season as captain, Jack Bond has been in dismal form with the bat himself, and the whole side was rather ignominiously scuttled by Hampshire early this week. The Trent Bridge members have requested a meeting with the committee to discuss results and playing standards. At the age of 42 I believe Jack Bond was a wrong choice. However the choice was the Nottinghamshire committee's and they must be loyal to their captain. If his brief was to reshape the Notts side over the next few seasons then he must be allowed to work without the harassment of the members. In turn the members should be put in the picture. The captain's lot is . . . ah well . . . you will only understand if you have done it.

What will Geoff Boycott tell the Yorkshire committee, who have summoned him to appear before them? His crime? Failing to pursue a Lancashire declaration, asking Yorkshire to score at a rate of 70 an hour; 244 in 3½ hours. The pitch was not quite perfect, so reports say, and the occasional ball squatted or lifted. Geoff himself used the time up with an innings of 79 not out. Just the preparation he required to milk the bowling of The Rest in the Test Trial.

The Test side is Denness (captain), Boycott, Amiss, Edrich, Fletcher, Greig, Knott, Old, Birkenshaw, Underwood, Arnold, Willis. That is twelve and I should think it is odds on Jack Birkenshaw not making his home début.

## HOW HOME CONDITIONS CAN HELP
### WEEK ENDED JUNE 8

INDIA and England are once more in the Test arena, the one side bristling with famous spinners, the other baring the teeth of youthful speed and aggression. Two days have gone: England 328 for nine declared; India 25 for two, which includes the wicket of Venkat, the nightwatchman.

Manchester offered a bleak welcome, not only with icy winds and squalls, but also by the absence of

spectators. India froze, but they had their bright moments. Only Keith Fletcher dominated them for a long period. Amiss (56) and Greig, with a flamboyant 53, added support, but Fletcher scored his fourth hundred for England, 123 not out.

At the same time Pakistan are grouping to prepare their assault in the second half of the season. Majid Khan, Glamorgan's captain, announced publicly (and he is not a man to communicate with the Press on many matters) that he would not accept the Pakistan Board's offer of £350 for the tour. He felt that his Board were asking the county clubs indirectly to subsidise the English-based players. Clearly the counties were not going to withhold the season's wages from these players but Majid feels that Pakistan should pay the right rate for the job. £350 is "on the cheap". The Pakistan Board then announced from Lahore that no further offer would be made to Majid.

Majid is certainly a man who does not aim to be controversial at all. Yet he holds his principles high. If the Pakistan Board are acting true to form, and I know them well, they have failed to communicate properly with the player – yet again!

## GRAND GAVASKAR AND LLOYD FOR BOYCOTT
### WEEK ENDED JUNE 15

WELL, it is Geoffrey Boycott out of the England side, David Lloyd in. The reason, I suppose, is that Geoff has made just 58 runs in six innings against the Indians this summer. There is talk of exclusion rather than dropping; that he asked to be dropped. Maybe, but that is eyewash. Having fielded for his two centuries in the recent Test Trial I can assure him that he is in decent enough form. However, where a tougher personality than Boycott would ride the storm and play if required, he has descended again into his trough of despair and has no wish to see Solkar and Abid Ali after his scalp again. That is weakness not strength.

His poor relationship with England's captain Mike Denness cannot help matters. This is one sad aspect of England's team over the past year. Talk of internal strife comes with every Test match. There is only one remedy – success; and that is the best news of the week. England defeated India by 113 runs at Old Trafford,

Keith Fletcher enjoying the Indian bowlers.

County Championship (as at June 7)

| | P | Pts |
|---|---|---|
| **1** Hampshire | 5 | 74 |
| **2** Surrey | 5 | 63 |
| **3** Worcestershire | 4 | 58 |
| **4** Warwickshire | 5 | 46 |

putting them one-up in this three-match series.

Yet for me the performance of the match came not from an Englishman, but from Sunil Gavaskar. With calm and faultless judgment he took on the pace of Willis, Old and Hendrick and was eventually run out for 101 in the first innings. In the second innings too he looked authoritative and controlled. He was dismissed for 58. Staunch supporters were Viswanath, 40 and 50, as well as Abid Ali, 71 in the first innings.

Almost predictably John Edrich scored a century. He is back in his very best form and the Indian spinners are not half as menacing when bowling to a left-handed batsman.

## ADDING MACHINE NEEDED AT LORD'S
### *WEEK ENDED JUNE 22*

T HE sun has been a constant spectator this week. Cricketers look their suntanned best, outwardly glowing with good health even if their feet are beginning to feel the spikes beneath them rejected by the bone-hard ground.

England have put up the mightiest performance with the bat in the Second Test! In fact they "slumped" towards the end from 591 for six to 629 all out. The Indian sign has been erased. No longer do the names of Bedi, Prasanna and Chandra bring an uneasy look to the countenance of my friends of the 1972-73 tour to India – Dennis Amiss lbw b Prasanna 188; Mike Denness c sub b Bedi 118; or to Tony Greig c and b Abid Ali 106. Add to those the names of David Lloyd,

who overcame his first Test nerves to get 46, and John Edrich, who fell lbw to Bedi for 96. On a perfect batting strip this was cricket of attack and style, not of graft and endurance.

We await India's reply with the bat. Incidentally, Willis withdrew from England's side. Arnold replaces him.

Pakistan have made their presence felt. They beat Leicestershire in the opening game of their tour. Yet Barry Dudleston is the pride of that particular county at present. Against Notts this week he scored his third hundred in successive County Championship matches and this was his fourth against Notts in successive games against them. Then just for good measure he nipped in with 109 not out v. Gloucestershire on Sunday.

## ARNOLD AND OLD WREAK HAVOC
### *WEEK ENDED JUNE 29*

O N a heavy morning, cool and cloudy, the new ball did enough in the experts hands of Geoff Arnold and Chris Old to scourge the Indians into abject submission in the Second Test at Lord's. The lowest Test match total at the game's headquarters was recorded, 42. Added to their first innings effort of 302 this still amounted to defeat by an innings and 285 runs, and with it went the series to England.

Outside the Test, most attention was focused on the Benson and Hedges semi-finals. Leicestershire cracked off to a fine start at home to Somerset. Dudleston, 54, and Steele, 91, laid strong foundations for Davison to strike 73 in 65 minutes. A sad sight for the many coachloads from the West Country. Worse still, rain interceded with the situation overnight Leicestershire 270 in 55 overs; Somerset 20 for two in six overs. With the minimum of bother Leicestershire polished them off the next day, so qualifying for their second Benson and Hedges final in three years. Ray Illingworth took five for 20 in 11 overs.

At Old Trafford the other semi-final went to Surrey, even in the "lions' den". Limited-overs cricket brings 'em in up there. Lancashire were all out for 130 in the 48th over in reply to Surrey's 193 for eight. John Edrich, 62, Jackman, 32, were the chief batting contributors, but the bowling honours went to left-arm

seamer Butcher. He took three for 11 in 11 overs, the wickets of David Lloyd and Clive, as well as Pilling. You cannot ask more than that.

In the final, Leicestershire would be my choice. I can only be wrong.

## PAKISTAN OPEN IN STYLE
### WEEK ENDED JULY 6

PAKISTAN have made an immediate impact on the first-class scene. This time they beat Middlesex at Lord's in great style. Majid having somehow resolved his differences with the Pakistan Board, opened the batting in Sadiq's absence and scored 105 not out. Asif got 64, and that was pretty attractive stuff. Asif Masood played the next vital part, helping Mike Brearley's side back in to the pavilion for 77 only with a performance of five for 33.

Hereafter Middlesex applied themselves to the task of recovery. Mike Smith, on the day he was called to stand by for John Edrich in the Third Test in case of illness, scored his first century of the year, 101. Even so they were winkled out by Mushtaq (seven for 59) and Intikhab (two for 54) – the value of top-class leg-spinning never more plain. Now the Pakistanis faced the formidable task with time almost expired of scoring 112 in 16 overs. Majid and Aftab Gul went after two overs but Intikhab promoted himself from number eight to four in the order and with precision and force struck 61, Mushtaq 31 not out. It was a wild and wonderful piece of hitting – a challenge which most touring teams would have coldly ignored.

## WHITEWASH OF INDIA; NOW PAKISTAN
### WEEK ENDED JULY 13

THE Indians were, for the third time, crushed by England. Not at any single moment during these Tests have they looked dangerous opposition. Gone is the biting spin and acrobatic close catching which is their great art. None of the wickets turned, and they lurched around blindly, almost without hope.

Anyway, for the record, England beat India in the Third and final Test by an innings and 78 runs. So let us toast Mike Denness, who has been appointed captain

against Pakistan, and also David Lloyd, who put together a marvellous innings of 214 not out.

### ENGLAND v INDIA
### Averages for the series

**ENGLAND**

| Batting | M | I | NO | HS | R | Av | Cght |
|---|---|---|---|---|---|---|---|
| D. Lloyd | 2 | 2 | 1 | 214* | 260 | 260.00 | 1 |
| K. W. R. Fletcher | 3 | 3 | 2 | 123* | 189 | 189.00 | 1 |
| J. H. Edrich | 3 | 3 | 1 | 100* | 203 | 101.50 | 1 |
| M. H. Denness | 3 | 4 | 1 | 118 | 289 | 96.33 | 2 |
| D. L. Amiss | 3 | 4 | 0 | 188 | 370 | 92.50 | 0 |
| A. W. Greig | 3 | 2 | 0 | 106 | 159 | 79.50 | 2 |
| R. G. D. Willis | 1 | 1 | 0 | 24 | 24 | 24.00 | 1 |
| A. P. E. Knott | 3 | 2 | 0 | 26 | 26 | 13.00 | 15/1st |
| D. L. Underwood | 3 | 3 | 0 | 9 | 25 | 8.33 | 2 |
| G. Boycott | 1 | 2 | 0 | 10 | 16 | 8.00 | 1 |
| C. M. Old | 3 | 2 | 0 | 12 | 15 | 7.50 | 1 |
| G. G. Arnold | 2 | 1 | 0 | 5 | 5 | 5.00 | 1 |
| M. Hendrick | 3 | 1 | 1 | 1* | 1 | — | 4 |

| Bowling | O | M | R | W | Av |
|---|---|---|---|---|---|
| C. M. Old | 89 | 19 | 249 | 18 | 13.83 |
| M. Hendrick | 85 | 14 | 215 | 14 | 15.36 |
| R. G. D. Willis | 36 | 8 | 97 | 5 | 19.40 |
| G. G. Arnold | 65.5 | 13 | 204 | 10 | 20.40 |
| A. W. Greig | 70.1 | 16 | 176 | 6 | 29.33 |
| D. L. Underwood | 67 | 25 | 146 | 4 | 36.50 |
| D. Lloyd | 2 | 0 | 4 | 0 | — |

**INDIA**

| Batting | M | I | NO | HS | R | Av | Cght |
|---|---|---|---|---|---|---|---|
| S. S. Naik | 1 | 2 | 0 | 77 | 81 | 40.50 | 0 |
| F. M. Engineer | 3 | 6 | 1 | 86 | 195 | 39.00 | 4 |
| S. M. Gavaskar | 3 | 6 | 0 | 101 | 217 | 36.16 | 1 |
| G. R. Viswanath | 3 | 6 | 0 | 52 | 200 | 33.33 | 0 |
| A. V. Mankad | 1 | 2 | 0 | 43 | 57 | 28.50 | 1 |
| E. D. Solkar | 3 | 6 | 1 | 43 | 98 | 19.60 | 4 |
| S. Abid Ali | 3 | 6 | 0 | 71 | 101 | 16.83 | 1 |
| A. L. Wadekar | 3 | 6 | 0 | 36 | 82 | 13.67 | 0 |
| S. Venkataraghavan | 2 | 4 | 1 | 5* | 13 | 4.33 | 0 |
| B. S. Bedi | 3 | 6 | 1 | 14 | 15 | 3.00 | 2 |
| S. Madan Lal | 2 | 4 | 0 | 7 | 11 | 2.75 | 1 |
| B. P. Patel | 2 | 4 | 0 | 5 | 10 | 2.50 | 0 |
| E. A. S. Prasanna | 2 | 4 | 0 | 5 | 9 | 2.25 | 0 |
| B. S. Chandrasekhar | 2 | 3 | 2 | 2* | 2 | 2.00 | 0 |

| Bowling | O | M | R | W | Av |
|---|---|---|---|---|---|
| S. Abid Ali | 81.3 | 12 | 252 | 6 | 42.00 |
| B. S. Bedi | 172.2 | 28 | 523 | 10 | 52.30 |
| B. S. Chandrasekhar | 42 | 7 | 126 | 2 | 63.00 |
| E. A. S. Prasanna | 86 | 10 | 267 | 3 | 89.00 |
| S. Madan Lal | 73 | 19 | 188 | 2 | 94.00 |
| E. D. Solkar | 44 | 11 | 125 | 1 | 125.00 |
| S. M. Gavaskar | 1 | 0 | 5 | 0 | — |
| S. Venkataraghavan | 37 | 3 | 96 | 0 | — |

County Championship
(as at July 12)

| | | P | Pts |
|---|---|---|---|
| 1 | Hampshire | 10 | 136 |
| 2 | Worcestershire | 9 | 120 |
| 3 | Surrey | 11 | 119 |
| 4 | Leicestershire | 10 | 98 |

The result must be viewed with caution as Pakistan continue to beat all comers on the county circuit. It was Kent's turn this week, despite a century by Colin

Cowdrey. Sadiq got a hundred and Sarfraz five for 44. Of course Kent are suffering greatly from Test calls on Denness, Underwood, Knott and Asif Iqbal, as well as from injury to Bernard Julien. Even so there are two Test players of the calibre of Cowdrey and Luckhurst to hold the fort.

I find it sad to write that I believe that University cricket should cease to be first-class, but truly Oxford and Cambridge no longer play their important role in the game. The University match was a second-rate charade at Lord's last weekend. The only player of class, Imran Khan, was run out without facing a ball in Oxford's first innings. He did capture five for 44 in 20 overs, and three wickets in the second innings, and indeed as long as he was batting, for 46, Oxford looked likely to get the 187 required to win in five hours. They managed a dull unadventurous 184 for seven. "A sad end to a poor match," commented Rex Alston in the *Daily Telegraph*.

The answer probably lies with the tutors for admission at Oxford and Cambridge. If they refuse to accept the pupil who has outstanding cricket talent, who also will obtain a degree, even though not a spectacular one, then the opportunity to play first-class cricket should go to somewhere like Loughborough or St. Luke's, where sport is important.

## *SARFRAZ MAY SURPRISE*
### *WEEK ENDED JULY 20*

INDIA depart sadly as the Pakistan menace grows. Wadekar's men went through the motions of two one-day Prudential Trophy internationals without knowing quite what they were up to. Until they find players who can take on true pace bowling I fear they will be the poor relations in the World Cup competition next summer.

Not so Pakistan. They rolled over Notts by an innings and 49 runs. This was their ninth win of the tour. Truly impressive. Sarfraz Nawaz earns special mention here. Against Notts he took eight for 27 to dismiss them for 51 in the first innings. Sarfraz left Northants a few seasons ago with a reputation for being injury-prone. He was certain he was injured, and that to my mind is proof enough. When I encountered him in the Test series in Pakistan in 1972-73 his reputation had soared amongst

his colleagues. He had filled out physically, and although not lightning fast, he proved to be on the hasty side of fast-medium. He bowls a useful bouncer, but more important, he has a great liking for the ball when the shine has gone. He runs it away to slip in the middle of a hot afternoon when others have settled for the short-of-a-length restrictive style.

Perhaps I could stick my neck out this early and nominate the sixteen selections for the winter. Dangerous, but fun, and, in spite of the Pakistan series to come: Denness (capt), Amiss, Lloyd D., Fletcher, Boycott, Graves, Greig, Knott, Bairstow, Pocock, Birkenshaw, Underwood, Jackman, Arnold, Hendrick and Old.

Peter Graves – consistent performances for Sussex.

🏏 *Of those who did not, in fact, go on that ill-fated tour, Pocock and Jackman had other tours to come and Boycott returned from his self-imposed exile in 1977. Birkenshaw, however, was not to play for England again. Peter Graves continued to give fine service to Sussex but was never to play in Test cricket.*

## *CAPTAINS IN A TIGHT CORNER*
### *WEEK ENDED JULY 27*

IN the 1974 Benson and Hedges Cup Final, the day was won by Edrich's men of Surrey, and Illy will have a million reasons why it all went wrong for Leicestershire.

It was certainly no fault of Ken Higgs, who helped confine Surrey to 170 with a bowling stint of 7 overs 4 for 10. John Edrich anchored – a patient 40 – and Younis offered a characteristic 43, made with a bustle. Possibly Geoff Arnold struck the crucial blow for Surrey by trapping Dudleston lbw for nought on the first ball of Leicestershire's innings. Such a miserable reward for the courage of Dudleston, who had volunteered to play with an eye half closed and badly bruised by a ball from Bob Cottam during the week. Arnold proceeded to get three for 20 in his 10 overs, and Pocock three for 26 in 11. There was much talk afterward about Freddie Brown's award of Man of the Match to John Edrich. His innings of 40 had been painstakingly put together over 35 overs. It was Younis rather who got things going. Talk also of a bad lbw given against Roger Tolchard.

Indeed the chat was about giving umpire Bill Alley

Pat Pocock and the prized pennant.

the Gold Award for his four lbw decisions on the front foot. Ken Higgs was strongly considered too for a hat-trick when Surrey were throwing the bat. Yet captaincy in these tight fiery corners is crucial. The winning captain cannot have done badly.

On Thursday morning, the England team huddled in the centre of the playing area at Headingley while a grandstand was vacated and searched by police during a bomb scare. As at Lord's last summer these threats to innocent lives make the most incongruous scenes on playing fields. Thankfully the delay was brief and play continued. Pakistan won the toss and struggled fitfully on a wicket which seamed continually, at least for these first two days. The thought occurs that it could be a more benign strip in the fourth innings, which would suit England very much indeed because after one innings each they are 102 runs behind, and Pakistan are now 20 without loss in their second innings.

*Sarfraz Nawaz has David Lloyd caught behind by Wasim Bari in England's second innings.*

This is a personal diary, so I must be allowed the indulgence of recording that this week the author retired from first-class cricket. Struggles with painful knees are ended. Relief therefore, but mostly sadness to leave behind the good times. I just do not know whether to laugh or cry. I think I shall just have a drink and chat to a wife who has been very patient for the past 350 Glamorgan matches.

## WORLD RECORDS DON'T COME OFTEN
### WEEK ENDED AUGUST 3

I suppose if county cricketers had been asked what was the best-ever second-wicket stand, they would stare blankly and shake their heads. However we were sent rushing to the record books this week by John

Jameson and Rohan Kanhai. Warwickshire's opening bat Neal Abberley departed for nought in the first over of the day, and by the time the allotted 100 overs were through Jameson and Kanhai had sent Gloucestershire's young fielders scurrying after 465 runs without sacrificing a wicket. There must have been one or two thanksgivings offered to the TCCB by those fielders for limiting the first innings in this way. Just think: the world record second-wicket partnership which they broke was part of an innings of 826 for four. The batsmen were B. B. Nimbalkar (443 not out) and K. V. Bhandarkar (205) and their team was the state of Maharashtra, who bludgeoned Kathiawar to humiliation at Poona in 1948. In Warwickshire's case 800 would not have been necessary. Gloucestershire were sent on their way with an innings defeat.

I was personally pleased to see my old friend Mike Brearley in the big runs. He has clear credentials to lead an England side, but the absence of Championship hundreds has, I believe, halted his progress to the top. This week he scored a superb 163 against Yorkshire and with Mike Smith (105) put on 192 for the second wicket.

*Mike Brearley had scored only two centuries for Middlesex in more than 200 innings before 1974. He went on to score another 27 for Middlesex but never one for England.*

Perhaps this would be a proper moment to catch up with the John Player League. Leicestershire still lead: p 12, w 11, pts 44. Kent have games in hand. They have 36 points from 10 games and Somerset have 36 from 11. This is anyone's title, but when the luck goes with you it helps. For example, on Sunday Leicestershire actually won their match against Yorkshire with a six hit by Chris Balderstone off the last ball.

So to the First Test match. To me it was more than a game of cricket, it was a real battle. Rain ended it as a draw when it hung in the balance. On the last day, England chasing 282 to win required 44 for victory with Keith Fletcher at the crease, 67 not out, and Chris Old 10 not out. Only the tail was left. Anyone's game.

E. F. "Bunty" Longrigg has just died. Much loved as Somerset's captain before the war. After, he served the game quietly but lucidly as chairman and president, as well as contributing to many a sub-committee at Lord's. He was without question one of Somerset's most faithful servants for almost fifty years.

England Schools Cricket Association play host to the West Indies Youth squad which included future Test cricketers Richard Austin and Jeffrey Dujon. The ESCA XI also included many familiar names, left to right: Ray Dexter, Ashok Patel, Stephen Mitchell, Paul Wakefield, Mike Gatting, Chris Cowdrey, Mark Precious, Paul Allott, Stephen Lee, Donald Kayum, Neil Hartley and Paul Parker.

## KNOTT COMES GOOD AND ARNOLD CENSURED
### WEEK ENDED AUGUST 10

I was at Lord's for the first two days of the Second Test to see Pakistan badly treated by the weather. Majid and Sadiq, the former with a great deal of fortune outside the off stump, sailed along merrily and took the opening partnership to 71. Some time later, after a prolonged deluge of rain, Pakistan were declaring at 130 for nine, and Derek Underwood looked a happier young man than he has been of late. After the openers had gone only Wasim Raja got to double figures. Underwood claimed five for 20, Tony Greig three for 23.

Of course only the ends of the wicket are covered when it rains. The ball lifted and turned at such speed that no side in the world could have lasted out that first day. Yet when Intikhab made a positive gesture by declaring with nine wickets down so as to torment England before the turf dried out, he found Lloyd and Edrich unshakeable. Amiss went to Asif Masood for two but Pakistan lacked a finger spinner. The wrist spin was too slow. They must have longed for Pervez who, although not all that successful in Pakistan, would have been an essential item in England. No team should tour England without a finger spinner.

*Maybe we shall see a return to this practice before long. Certainly a real "sticky wicket" would be a novel and challenging test for many of today's leading batsmen.*

Even so, the next day England contrived to place themselves in a frail position, until Knott came good with the bat. He scored 83 and Old 41, the total 270. Everything now depends on whether Pakistan bat on a true surface. There is rain about so one sees this as England's major chance to go ahead in the series.

The controversy of the week involved Geoff Arnold. Umpire Peter Wight reported Arnold to the TCCB Disciplinary Committee for directing bad language at him. Wight had ruled in Surrey's John Player League match against Warwickshire that Arnold had bowled a wide down the leg side. Arnold disagreed with the judgment and was roused to use insulting language. The outcome was that Arnold has been suspended from two County Championship matches, but not from playing in the current Test.

Geoff is one of the game's greatest tryers, loyal to Surrey and to England. He is openly hostile to opponents, umpires, spectators, icecream sellers or even unsuspecting nannies who stroll across the sight-screen as he prepares to bowl. It is an attitude that spills over into unnecessary words and acts of bad temper. I believe he needs to be kept in line, but I deplore the public chastisement.

## SOBERS TO RETIRE
### WEEK ENDED AUGUST 17

HUGO Yarnold died this week; killed in a car crash, returning home after umpiring the Northants v. Essex match at Wellingborough. It happened at Leamington. What a generous contribution he gave the game. "The little General", we called him in his umpiring days. His voice resounded with kind authority "in the middle". When I was a county captain I recall Hugo sitting in the dark umpire's room in Swansea, peering earnestly at the law book; not even delicate spectacles could render that lined, weatherbeaten face studious. I went on to the Glamorgan dressing room where minutes later the "General" appeared, chin in, chest out, shoulders back and in his best parade-ground voice addressed me. "You may be unaware of the law pertaining to the tea interval, skipper. I have to inform you that tea will now be taken at 16.37." "Thank you, Hugo." "Thank *you*, Skipper."

Gary Sobers, on Friday, announced his retirement

County Championship
(as at August 6)

| | P | Pts |
|---|---|---|
| **1** Hampshire | 14 | 181 |
| **2** Worcestershire | 14 | 162 |
| **3** Surrey | 16 | 153 |
| **4** Leicestershire | 15 | 149 |

from the game but I do not think we have seen the last of him. Rather, I believe, that physically and mentally the professional circuit had become to much for him. He never enjoyed playing six days a week and travelling on the seventh. He was a less brilliant player for it.

Now, I am sure that Gary will play the cricket he wants, and as soon as he rediscovers his enthusiasm he will thrill us again. I say "thrill" because there are few opponents in one's professional life who actually excite while they are plundering one's bowling.

*Gary Sobers did not return to first-class cricket after 1974, although he was to appear at The Oval for an Old World XI v. the Courage Old England XI in 1982.*

The Test match took some unexpected twists before rain brought about a draw, which curiously enough almost everyone wanted. No-one minded seeing Pakistan struggle against Underwood in the first innings because the wicket had become legitimately wet after midday rain. However, it was quite a different matter when Pakistan were successfully managing their second-innings fight back, 173 for three, and were again caught on a rain-affected strip to slump to 226 all out leaving England just 87 to win. Lloyd and Amiss put on 27 without loss on the fourth evening. Thankfully there was no fifth day. The rain which affected the wicket the second time fell overnight and when the wicket was fully covered. Many precautions were taken to keep rain off, but the truth is that Pakistan were entitled by the rulings to resume their interrupted second innings on a wicket at least resembling the one that had been "wrapped up" on the Saturday night.

## PAKISTAN LAY IT ON
### WEEK ENDED AUGUST 24

**P**AKISTAN gave the country a batting treat at The Oval. Again they took the calculated chance of opening with Majid. It worked, and the bravery of the decision deserves success. He fell for 98, brilliantly stroked and hammered at rapid pace.

I know him well, of course, as a Glamorgan colleague, and he personifies the extreme attacking instinct which whispers inside a batsman and says "These cocks can't bowl". He has little respect for Old.

He takes a hundred off Willis and Warwickshire whenever he wants. He is annoyed by the petulance of Geoff Arnold and he believes Tony Greig to be the most over-rated player in the world. Well, I am not saying that those are my sentiments too; they are not, but this is the sort of mental spring-board which sends this fine player into the Test match arena to dominate. He is not interested in anything but showing up the opposition.

Not only did Majid do just that, but Zaheer (240) chose the occasion to score his second Test double-century. He is another who does not score slowly. On the huge baked surface of the Oval they ran fours, fives, hit sixes and ran short singles. An exemplary batting performance with Mushtaq, as ever, relishing the final turn of the screw with a solid 76.

The wicket is slow. England will settle for a draw. Well, who can blame them. Pakistan declared at 600 for seven, using up almost two days, and who can get 600 quickly? Yet David Lloyd has gone and Derek Underwood props it up at the moment with Dennis Amiss.

Bob Willis is in this match in place of Mike Hendrick. It will be a chance to play himself onto the boat for Australia. However, the truth is that it is "onto the plane" these days, and replacements can be flown out pretty quickly, as indeed Bob Willis was last time. How many fast bowlers will go? A key question.

*As it turned out it was Colin Cowdrey who got the call to leave his fireside that winter.*

The County Championship race has resolved itself into a final sprint between Worcestershire and Hampshire. Oddly enough Glamorgan, my own county, have a definite role to play because they face both. What an impact they made at Cardiff this week. They scored 284 for five to beat Hampshire and that after being bowled out for 90 in the first innings. Hampshire relaxed. They scored 234 and a curiously inept 139. Andy Roberts had routed the Welsh side with eight for 47 in the first innings but found Len Hill (90) and Eifion Jones (67) impossible to shift the second time around.

The Sunday League competition is also near the end. Leicestershire are still out there in front, 50 points from 14 matches. Somerset are second, 46 points from 14, and these two have to meet yet at Grace Road.

## WILL BEDSER'S PRESENCE HINDER TEAM SPIRIT?
### WEEK ENDED AUGUST 31

ENGLAND survived the Oval Test. They battled through, and thanks to a Fletcher century, the longest on record in England, the draw was achieved. England's batting was not half as attractive as the Pakistanis' but then how do you tell a side to go out and get 600 quickly! So Mike Denness survived to be elected captain of MCC in Australia this winter. His manager will be Alec Bedser.

I do not agree with the decision which makes a selector the manager. For example, there is much scope for accusations of favouritism on tour. Who eats most often at the manager's table? Who drinks with him most? Who has most in common with him? And so on. I am sure Alec Bedser would never dream of wavering from his duties as he saw them. But I believe the presence of one who after all just about controls the cricketing future of everyone in the party, will be a hindrance to team spirit, not a help.

In the cricket fraternity (and I emphasise these are not my views) there was comparative quiet when the team for Australia was announced mid-week. Titmus at 42? Not many complained at that. Certainly many thought that Birkenshaw had been flattered by his selection as twelfth man for home Tests. Most think Pocock the better bowler, though at The Oval it was recognised that he had not produced the goods this season. Titmus's selection surprised most, but not as much as the decision of pace – Old, Arnold, Hendrick, Willis and Lever – could make this the dullest Test series of all time to watch. Yet some say it is realistic. Test match wickets are so good, spinners only rarely win matches. Personally I favour a more balanced attack and would have taken Edmonds of Middlesex. Also, how will those fast bowlers be exercised? One of Mike Denness's first problems.

## A SPLASHING FINISH
### WEEK ENDED SEPTEMBER 7

THE battles are over; the prizes won and lost. During these last days of the 1974 cricket season, rainswept and completely lacking the romance of a grand finale, the Prudential Trophy went to Pakistan, the Gillette Cup to Kent, the Sunday League title to Leicestershire and the most cherished prize of all, the County Championship, to Worcestershire.

Mike Denness on his way to Australia.

A champagne soaking for Norman Gifford to celebrate Worcestershire's County Championship success. Joining in the festivities are (left to right) Glenn Turner, John Inchmore, Ron Headley, Jim Yardley, Brian Brain, Vanburn Holder and Alan Ormrod.

A week ago there was nothing but poor weather to stop Hampshire retaining their Championship title. The weather turned out worse than poor – absolutely diabolical! Day after day Hampshire watched the playing surfaces gather water, and loyal groundstaffs attempt to mop it up. They had a two-point lead on Worcestershire going into the last game. Then at Dean Park, Bournemouth not a single ball was bowled against Yorkshire. Their rivals did play, though not for long; yet long enough for Norman Gifford to put Essex in to bat at Chelmsford and take four bowling points before that game too was washed out for two whole days. So the final table read: Worcestershire p 20, w 11, l 3, d 6, pts 227; Hampshire p 20, w 10, l 3, d 6, pts 225.

The Gillette Cup Final was rained off on Saturday and was played on the Monday. Kent won a low-scoring game. Lancashire, 118 all out, fell to the seamers, who all got enough movement to prevent the bat from getting on top. Clive Lloyd was run out (that's a change!) the victim of a model throw by Alan Ealham from the fence. Kent found run-getting hard too. They got 122 for six. Shepherd top-scored with 19.

Let us leave the season, so dissatisfying to some and ripe with achievement for others, with a note of the finest innings played for many seasons. Majid Khan opened the innings for Pakistan against England in the Prudential Trophy match at Trent Bridge (Pakistan won two-nil by the way). 110 minutes later he had scored a brilliant hundred. Majid, when he has his "working boots" on, is a delight to the eyes. When he dons slippers for a royal performance, and many times I have been the lucky witness from the other end of the pitch, he sends old men to tears and the young to their dreams. "He's a proper player," said Don Kenyon to me. "Drop the ball short to 'im and he whacks it. They won't do it twice then will they?"

*Majid was largely responsible for the increased confidence and aggression in Pakistan's batting which made them one of the most formidable international sides in the late Seventies.*

True, but apart from whacking it, Majid played all the beautiful touches and turns of a virtuoso, and one short-arm pick-up off Derek Underwood's bowling over wide mid-on should be writ forever in the folklore of Sherwood Forest.

On that note I am happy to close my diary – with the sight of a "proper player", and the hopes of more like him to come.

## FINAL COUNTY CHAMPIONSHIP TABLE

| | P | W | L | D | Tie | NR | Bt | Bw | Pts |
|---|---|---|---|---|---|---|---|---|---|
| 1 Worcestershire (6) | 20 | 11 | 3 | 6 | 0 | 0 | 45 | 72 | 227 |
| 2 Hampshire (1) | 20 | 10 | 3 | 6 | 0 | 1 | 55 | 70 | 225 |
| 3 Northamptonshire (3) | 20 | 9 | 2 | 9 | 0 | 0 | 46 | 67 | 203 |
| 4 Leicestershire (9) | 20 | 7 | 7 | 6 | 0 | 0 | 47 | 69 | 186 |
| 5 Somerset (10) | 20 | 6 | 4 | 10 | 0 | 0 | 49 | 72 | 181 |
| 6 Middlesex (13) | 20 | 7 | 5 | 8 | 0 | 0 | 45 | 56 | 171 |
| 7 Surrey (2) | 20 | 6 | 4 | 10 | 0 | 0 | 42 | 69 | 171 |
| 8 Lancashire (9) | 20 | 5 | 0 | 15 | 0 | 0 | 47 | 66 | 163 |
| 9 Warwickshire (7) | 20 | 5 | 5 | 10 | 0 | 0 | 44 | 65 | 159 |
| 10 Kent (4) | 20 | 5 | 8 | 7 | 0 | 0 | 33 | 63 | 146 |
| 11 Yorkshire (14) | 20 | 4 | 7 | 8 | 0 | 1 | 37 | 69 | 146 |
| 12 Essex (8) | 20 | 4 | 3 | 12 | 1 | 0 | 45 | 51 | 141 |
| 13 Sussex (15) | 20 | 4 | 9 | 6 | 1 | 0 | 29 | 63 | 137 |
| 14 Gloucestershire (5) | 20 | 4 | 9 | 6 | 0 | 1 | 29 | 55 | 124 |
| 15 Nottinghamshire (17) | 20 | 1 | 9 | 10 | 0 | 0 | 42 | 66 | 118 |
| 16 Glamorgan (11) | 20 | 2 | 7 | 10 | 0 | 1 | 28 | 56 | 104 |
| 17 Derbyshire (16) | 20 | 1 | 6 | 13 | 0 | 0 | 23 | 62 | 95 |

1973 positions in brackets.

## First-class averages 1974

**Batting**
(Qualification: 8 innings: average 10.00)

| | I | NO | Runs | HS | Av |
|---|---|---|---|---|---|
| C. H. Lloyd | 31 | 8 | 1458 | 178* | 63.39 |
| B. A. Richards | 27 | 4 | 1406 | 225* | 61.13 |
| G. M. Turner | 31 | 9 | 1332 | 202* | 60.55 |
| G. Boycott | 36 | 6 | 1783 | 160* | 59.43 |
| R. T. Virgin | 39 | 5 | 1936 | 144* | 56.94 |
| D. L. Amiss | 31 | 3 | 1510 | 195 | 53.93 |
| J. H. Edrich | 23 | 2 | 1126 | 152* | 53.62 |
| J. H. Hampshire | 23 | 6 | 901 | 158 | 53.00 |
| R. B. Kanhai | 22 | 4 | 936 | 213* | 52.00 |
| J. A. Jameson | 42 | 2 | 1932 | 240* | 48.30 |
| G. S. Sobers | 27 | 4 | 1110 | 132* | 48.26 |
| D. Lloyd | 22 | 2 | 958 | 214* | 47.90 |
| B. F. Davison | 39 | 3 | 1670 | 142 | 46.38 |
| Zahir Abbas | 29 | 4 | 1159 | 240 | 46.36 |

**Bowling**
(Qualification: 10 wickets in 10 innings)

| | O | M | Runs | W | Av |
|---|---|---|---|---|---|
| A. M. E. Roberts | 727.4 | 198 | 1621 | 119 | 13.62 |
| G. G. Arnold | 487 | 139 | 1069 | 75 | 14.25 |
| V. A. Holder | 659 | 146 | 1493 | 94 | 15.88 |
| M. J. Procter | 311.3 | 80 | 776 | 47 | 16.51 |
| B. L. D'Oliveira | 345.3 | 105 | 697 | 40 | 17.42 |
| M. N. S. Taylor | 541 | 147 | 1259 | 72 | 17.48 |
| H. R. Moseley | 661.5 | 198 | 1420 | 81 | 17.53 |
| R. Illingworth | 535.1 | 204 | 1014 | 57 | 17.78 |
| P. Carrick | 405.4 | 167 | 840 | 47 | 17.87 |
| S. J. Rouse | 164.5 | 34 | 489 | 27 | 18.11 |
| D. L. Underwood | 563 | 228 | 1181 | 65 | 18.16 |
| R. P. Baker | 207.1 | 48 | 494 | 27 | 18.30 |
| S. Turner | 594.5 | 160 | 1265 | 69 | 18.33 |

*Tony Lewis is a humane and also a wise observer: "Mike Denness . . . unpopular with many of his side and with many of the press, who in their blindness take their cues from those in the side who criticise most. Cheap journalism from cheap players."*

Well, Denness made them feel cheap with his batting against India, showing both his ability and his character. Now he set off on what turned out to be "Mission Impossible". The association of Dennis Lillee and Jeff Thomson, for two seasons amongst the most destructive partnerships the cricket world has known, was blithely unforeseen when England flew out. Thommo had played one Test unsuccessfully, as it turned out with a broken bone in his foot. Lillee's recovery from a serious back injury was uncertain. But from the moment they got together at the Gabba, England's fate was clear.

Nor did England have any luck until it was too late. Denness was ill at the start of the tour and could find no form. Amiss was injured. Edrich, taking over as captain at Sydney, batted in forlorn defiance with broken ribs. Boycott, absent by his own will, was gravely missed. And there was no fierce return fire from England, for all the heroic efforts of Willis, bowling with a bad knee.

It ended better, with Denness and Fletcher hitting match-winning centuries in the last Test at Melbourne when Max Walker was left to carry the Australian attack by himself because of injury to the she-devil, "Lillian Thomson". Peter Lever belatedly bowled with the inspiration he had displayed under Illingworth four years before. But Australia's winning margin of four-one was no more than a tough, confident team deserved: apart from the fast bowling, Mallett bowled his off-spinners well, the close catching was sensational and with the Chappell brothers, Walters and Redpath reinforced by the formidable Rodney Marsh, they were seldom short of runs.

Meanwhile West Indies were starting to form the most powerful side in the world, though, as the following year was to prove, they were not yet quite ready for Australia. In India they won a memorable series three-two. The Antiguan, Andy Roberts, was the outstanding fast bowler and a young man from the same island, Vivian Richards, made his first Test appearances. At Bangalore he began with four and three, out in both innings to Chandrasekhar. In the Second Test at Delhi he made 192 not out. The star was born.

# ⊹ 1975 ⊹

## WINDING A FAVOURITE CLOCK
### WEEK ENDED APRIL 25

IT is an odd feeling. This is the first time since 1955 that I have not been involved in English first-class cricket as a player. I had no idea how little fuss is made by everyone outside the game when the opening overs of a new season are being sent down.

The player imagines fanfares greeting his fresh endeavours, his hopes and fears churning around in the overall relief to get on with it – get the first ball up there, on a length outside the off stump, or feel the new ball leap off the middle of the bat. For the followers it is different. It is just the rewinding of a favourite clock, the ticking strong and steady day after day after day right through to September – a familiar, comforting presence.

First the MCC v. Worcestershire match, which is the first chance for aspiring Test players to air their talents. This time, in front of the new selectors, Alec Bedser (chairman), Sir Len Hutton, Ken Barrington and Charles Elliott, Roger Knight of Gloucestershire stroked a splendid hundred.

He was exactly 100 not out when the MCC captain Richard Gilliat declared, leaving Worcestershire 281 to make at 65 an hour on a decent pitch. It was a stirring finish, a truly aggressive way to start the season, which left the champions 11 runs short with 11 balls to go: a win for MCC, who owed much to Mike Hendrick's demonstrating the value of bowling a full length, taking six for 40 – all six in succession by the way.

On Thursday Jack Bailey, secretary of MCC and the ICC, announced the calling of a special ICC meeting before the Prudential Cup series to discuss fast, short-pitched bowling. The suggestion originated with the Pakistan Board of Control.

So, the 1975 season is in motion, and it is well to remember that although it may seem like the same old clock ticking away, it has been fitted with some very special chimes this year. Who can face the first one-day World Cup series and four English Tests against Australia with anything but excitement? Certainly not me.

Roger Knight – the first century of the season.

## LEE'S SEVEN WICKETS FOR EIGHT
### WEEK ENDED MAY 2

THERE was a flurry of Benson & Hedges activity on Saturday for instant prizes which attracted our instant attention. Ted Dexter is the resident adjudicator of the "Team of the Week" and decided that the one really outstanding performance was by Somerset, who bowled out my former team-mates Glamorgan in 25 overs for a modest 81. This they achieved after Brian Close had won the toss and invited Glamorgan to bat first. It was at a very early stage in the day that the scourge of Welshmen over the years, Tom Cartwright, was let loose.

Cartwright once had a match analysis of 15 for 89 against Glamorgan in 1967 at Swansea and since then Welsh batsmen have tended to stand transfixed by the smooth, rhythmic approach of their tormentor. This time he took four for 13, Graham Burgess three for 12, and by 3.30 p.m. the contest was over.

Minor Counties North put up the strongest challenge against Derbyshire. Derbyshire were given a formidable advantage by their newly recruited openers Ron Headley and Phil Sharpe, 127 for the first wicket. Then a former Derbyshire player, John Harvey, demonstrated just how familiar he was with the bowling of Hendrick, Rhodes, Russell, Swarbrook and company. He opened the innings and got 56. Maslin managed 35 and the amateurs, with 179 for seven, fell just seven runs short of a surprise victory.

The captaincy of England will be hotly disputed over the next few weeks. The England selectors have much to decide. Is the Prudential Cup the place for experiment? To my mind the answer is yes. Change must come though I would expect Denness to keep his place.

Let me just list some of the form horses, ones I would not mind seeing in England Prudential colours this season: 1. Barry Wood, 2. Dennis Amiss, 3. Mike Denness, 4. Roger Knight, 5. Tony Greig, 6. Frank Hayes, 7. Alan Knott, 8. Derek Underwood, 9. Mike Hendrick, 10. Jack Simmons, and 11. Peter Lee. Lee's seven wickets for eight runs against Warwickshire, 12 for 62 in the match, was the bowling feat of the week.

 *Interesting to consider how effective Jack Simmons might have been in one-day internationals given his*

*consistent successes in more than a decade of limited-overs cricket for Lancashire.*

## A HURRICANE NAMED BOYCE
### WEEK ENDED MAY 9

KEITH Boyce, one of my favourite cricketers, scored a century in 58 minutes in a County Championship game against Leicestershire at Chelmsford this week – the fastest Championship hundred since 1937. He then turned around and returned match bowling figures of 12 for 73 – six for 25 in the first innings, and six for 48 in the second. Surprisingly this did not bring victory to Essex because Chris Balderstone battled away to score 101 after his side had followed on.

The Benson & Hedges competition produced three remarkable games on Saturday. First, trying my hardest to restrain an Oxbridge loyalty, the Combined forces of Oxford and Cambridge defeated last year's County Championship winners Worcestershire. The wicket at Fenner's was reported to be playing unpredictably and getting worse, so Worcestershire, chasing a total of 158, probably knew that they would have to play well to win. Basil D'Oliveira began to pull the effort together after Turner, Wilkinson, Ormrod and Parker had departed for 18 runs, but at that important stage the Gold Award performance was produced by the Cambridge seam bowler Peter Hayes. No wickets fell to him but he held the Universities' advantage with 11 overs, eight maidens for six runs.

Then at Bristol, Hampshire mustered only 129, but then dismissed Gloucestershire for 62. I can think of some stalwart seam bowlers who have toiled season after season on the unresponsive turf at Nevil Road, but it was a bonanza day for them this time. Bob Herman won the Gold Award by his seven overs for 24 runs and five wickets.

Finally at The Oval that king of aggressive cricket Brian Close got Surrey into the almost impossible situation. When the ninth wicket fell Surrey needed 28 runs with five overs left. Butcher and Baker swung happily away and increased their chances to ten runs off ten balls, then six off six. Then off the last ball (and I can just imagine how many pep talks "Closey" was firing around by then) with an almost hopeless three to win the Surrey pair set off on a leg bye. Incredibly, short third man misfielded. It was "Closey". They ran one, scampered two, and hared home for three and a shock win. Whose fault? Surely it wasn't Close's. No, there must have been some rough ground in front of him. But someone has got to get a dressing down. I'll bet that groundsman's ears are burning!

## DENNESS AND THE CAPTAINCY WRANGLE
### WEEK ENDED MAY 16

THE Boyce man does it again. Only two days after his amazing 58-minute hundred he smashed Minor Counties South for a century in 70 minutes. "It's too much smoking," said Robin Hobbs. "He just can't give it up."

The subject of the English captaincy too continues to stir some journalists to pure hatred of Mike Denness, some to equally partisan support of his cause, and some to a trouser-splitting state of compromise, calling for Denness as captain of the Prudential Cup competition, and Greig as the new Test captain when the Australians come. Oddly enough, cricketers themselves do not feel particularly heated about it all. Most feel that there is no captain ready for the job; no-one matured by long and testing seasons at the job; no-one with the seniority and flair.

I would ask first whether the England team play devotedly for Mike Denness? The answer is that you never know at that level. Certainly they all play for their *country* and with such an obvious motivation, the question of whether they are supporting their captain is obscured. New selectors may bring new deals. The time fast approaches when change will have to be made. The perpetual sniping at Denness is eroding his credibility. Skeletons are building up in the cupboard even though he has batted with reasonable consistency in recent Tests.

## HAROLD RHODES AT THIRTY-EIGHT
### WEEK ENDED MAY 23

IT is interesting to see Harold Rhodes back in action this season. He got two Lancashire wickets for 40 in his 11 overs. Coming back into the game as a fast bowler at the age of 38 would appear a rather optimistic move from a distance, and of course Rhodes brings with him the perpetual query about the legality of his action. I viewed the latest photographs taken of him bowling last week. They were taken for a feature which the *Daily Telegraph* Colour Magazine are publishing shortly.

The hyperextension of the bowling arm, which whips the forearm through as he delivers the ball, is very much in evidence. This was the medical justification which eventually cleared his action in his earlier career. Harold Rhodes certainly turned it to his advantage. Often it was said that he was able to bowl faster than others even at the end of the day when he was physically tired. Whipping the ball down when you should be too tired is one thing; whipping it down when you should be too old to bowl fast is another, equally interesting experiment.

## THE SADDEST BUGLE-CALL
### WEEK ENDED MAY 30

"FOR the first time in 18 months I have found peace and contentment in cricket. I am now enjoying the game and do not want anything to upset the present trend. I regard my main task as that of leading Yorkshire back to supremacy and the next two summers are going to be important ones. There is more to cricket than batting all day and getting plenty of runs. Now I want to concentrate on developing the future of the game in Yorkshire where, I believe, I am best appreciated." signed Geoffrey Boycott (May 24, 1975).

*Daily Mail, Monday, May 26, 1975*      PAGE 25

# This is the end, Boycott
A HALF-EXPECTED phone call to the Woking home of Test chief Alec Bedser has surely ended the ...tt (right)      REFUSAL TO      he says he is 'better appre-' answer was : 'No, I have made stated.' up my mind.' Yet he almost ...'    ...Middx contact ...

Retreat – the saddest bugle-call of all. England's best batsman no longer wishes to fight for his country. Hinting only now and then about the nature of the malaise which has consumed him, he has left us all guessing, inviting half-truths and home psychology.

Disaster always overshadows success but I just want to tell you about my first week's work as a full-time cricket correspondent. Last Tuesday I saw that admirable Worcestershire fast-medium bowler Brian

Brain produce the season's best bowling figures, eight for 55 against Essex. Five slips were on hand at one stage – a heartwarming sight. Then I watched two young Etonians, Mark Faber and John Barclay, restore much hope in the appetites of Englishmen to play fast bowling. At Hove they took all that Andy Roberts could send down, testing courage and the horse-hair in the batting gloves. What else? A perfect century before lunch in that same game, Hampshire v. Sussex at Hove, by Barry Richards. Incomparable. I do wish he would move his feet sometimes!

The Aussies are here. Mike Denness is captain in the Prudential series. Snow fell across the Cairngorms and there was an earth tremor in Lancashire. Otherwise it was a quiet week in the world of cricket!

Mark Faber (top) and John Barclay taming the West Indian attack.

## MURRAY REACHES THE SUMMIT
### WEEK ENDED JUNE 6

I shall take a glass before penning this week's diary. H'm, that's good . . . and a toast to old JT. You see, at Lord's last Saturday, John Thomas Murray, the man with the golden gloves, held onto a rising ball from Tim Lamb which Dudley Owen-Thomas had edged. It was an historic dismissal because no other wicketkeeper in the game's history has amassed 1494 victims. 1493 was the record which stood for so long as the proud possession of Herbert Strudwick. Just another incident of Surrey-Middlesex rivalry.

The elegance of John Murray's wicketkeeping is one of cricket's clichés. Behind the stumps you perceive graceful movement imposed on one of the most bruising jobs in the game. He is a man for the important occasion too. His current captain Mike Brearley declared, "He often saves his best performances for Yorkshire or Surrey, and is less likely to sparkle on a damp Thursday at Ashby-de-la-Zouch."

John Murray, the new record-holder.

JT retires at the end of the season after 23 years with Middlesex.

We are a day away from the Prudential Cup competition. I have just left the Duke of Edinburgh's reception to the eight teams, a unique gathering in the game's history. The MCC Committee and others enjoyed drinks in the Long Room and a speech of welcome from the Duke himself. The players admitted that there was a strange disbelief about every handshake. What on earth is Ross Edwards doing in the same room as Viswanath, as Roy Fredericks, as Javed Miandad, as Hedley Howarth, as Zulfiqar Ali, as Michael Tissera, as Tony Greig? There never can have been such a medley of Test cricketers in one room at the same time.

I lunched with the Sri Lankans. They were apprehensive and urgently discussed techniques for limited-overs cricket. I believe they acknowledge that it is rather too late to learn, but they will relish the experience.

 *How quickly they have come of age in international cricket with some impressive Test match performances and a convincing series of one-day wins over the visiting England "B" team.*

## INDIA GIVE PRUDENTIAL CUP A STUTTERING START
### WEEK ENDED JUNE 13

IF the Prudential Cup stopped now, rained off for a week if you like, it will be remembered as a wonderful venture which prospered under blue sunny skies. The players have taken to it; that eradicates my doubts, held rather shamefully I confess, that first-class cricketers do not consider the one-day game a valid test of talents and so accept defeat too readily.

Yet my week started with a performance of Indian mysticism which defied explanation. In front of a full house at Lord's, including many of their supporters, India in the person of Sunil Gavaskar *refused* to chase England's total. Dennis Amiss stroked a brilliant century, 137, leading England to the highest score ever achieved in one-day cricket, 334 for four. India replied with 132 for three. Sunil Gavaskar blocked out the 60 overs for 36 not out. G. S. Ramchand, the manager, made a Press statement afterwards that Gavaskar had considered the England score unobtainable and had taken practice. Crazy! Did he not read the rules of the competition which state that teams tied with the same number of wins at the end of the Group stage will be judged on overall run-rate.

However, up at Headingley, the competition was given wings. In a hard fluctuating match Australia beat Pakistan by 73 runs. Australia batting first stumbled from 63 for one to 124 for four when Ross Edwards, as

he has done so often, re-upholstered the innings.

278 for seven was too much for Pakistan, though Majid was at his brilliant best. Majid will always respond to a challenge, the tougher the better. The pressure of Thomson and Lillee, the twin scourges of England's past winter, would be enough to persuade him to take them on. He scored 65. Asif, 53, joined him and as long as these two were together, Pakistan hopes were alive.

On the Wednesday I saw one of the finest cricket matches in my life. At Edgbaston, West Indies chasing Pakistan's 266 for seven were first 166 for eight, then 203 for nine, yet still won the match with a miraculous last-wicket stand of 64 between Andy Roberts and Deryck Murray.

England comfortably overcame New Zealand – Keith Fletcher 131. India swamped East Africa and Australia beat Sri Lanka. Just a word for the Sri Lankans. They scored 276 for four in pursuit of 328 – admirable form. I was not surprised, but it is nonetheless a happy event for them to prove their talents at a moment when their application for membership of the International Cricket Conference comes up for consideration.

Colin Cowdrey announced on Monday that he will retire at the close of the season. On Wednesday there were rumours of his joining Sussex. We had best wait and see!

## CLASHES OF THE MIGHTY
### WEEK ENDED JUNE 20

THIS was the week when it was resolved that the semi-finalists in the Prudential Cup competition would be West Indies, England, New Zealand and Australia. After those matches mid-week, tomorrow's final is between West Indies and Australia. So England fail to make it. Who beat them? Why, Australia of course. Old ghosts walked at Headingley to haunt Denness's side. A new one too; Gary Gilmour has assigned his name to a match in the way that Bob Massie did in the Lord's Test in 1972.

On Wednesday at about four o'clock Australia were 39 for six in reply to England's 93 all out. It was incredible. I was at The Oval watching West Indies make easy progress to the final at the expense of New Zealand. In the box at The Oval run by that generous host Frank Russell of the Cricketers' Club was a television, and there a few of us stayed for a while until depression set in. "Lillee or Thomson?" we asked at first. "Gilmour," came the reply. That was when he had dismissed the first six batsmen for 10 runs in nine overs. That is where *I* was. Where were you when England fell? It is like asking where you were when war broke out, or St Paul's was bombed. The ultimate humiliation, to be mopped up by the same bunch of Aussies, but this time in our own country in swinging conditions on a pitch of uneven bounce, which should have favoured us.

Gary Gilmour begins his demolition act. Dennis Amiss is the first English batsman to go.

The gods were with Gilmour, because as England fought back miraculously and squeezed Australia into that prickly corner in mid-afternoon, he lunged into drive after drive off Old, tucked Snow down to third man a couple of times, and that was that.

England's only consolation was the bowling of Snow, which got better and better and may find him in the Test side in three weeks' time.

## JUNE 21 — CRICKET'S DAY OF GLORY
### WEEK ENDED JUNE 27

WEST Indies are the Prudential Cup champions. At Lord's, on the most perfect summer's day, they never once allowed Australia to lead the struggle, not even by a short head. Yet, after a marathon day's cricket which lasted from 11 a.m. until 8.42 p.m., the margin of victory was only 17 runs.

Ian Chappell put in the West Indies when he won the toss, probably because in previous rounds Clive Lloyd's side had preferred to field first. Gilmour no-balled three times in the first over. The flags waved, the bells rang and the rhythms beat out from the West Indian encampment near the Tavern. Beside Clive Lloyd's innings, all other batting was commonplace; a performance of surpassing skill and power; 102 runs scored with panache. He met Lillee's bouncers with a swishing hook of the bat, just as if he was scything the head off a cobra with a samurai sword. The sun beat down on a rock-hard surface, the ball sizzled over the light brown outfield. It is not often you will see the herringbones of the Lord's drainage system turn the field into a grid. Lloyd struck Walker for four through the covers off the back foot in his first over, and thereafter put together all manner of destructive strokes. The one which kept me shaking my head from the Press box was the "pick-up" shot off the front foot, sending the ball which approached down the line of middle-and-leg whistling for four through square leg. 291 for eight meant that Australia would have to bat with exceptional distinction.

Just think how close they came, and this in spite of an unbelievable five run-outs. Ian Chappell's was the best innings, typically ebullient and threatening; 130 wanted off the last 22 overs; 76 off 10 with four wickets standing; but at 233 in the 53rd over the last pair, Lillee and Thomson, were at the crease. No hope . . . or so it seemed.

Yet they set about the job as if they meant to win it. After a few firm thumps over the ring of fielders they had the West Indians set back in the field, and they took a load of singles. They won Australia a lot of friends by their bravado and obvious enjoyment, 21 wanted off two overs, but then, true to luck and the form of the side, they were sunk by a fifth and final run-out.

The Duke of Edinburgh made the presentation in front of thousands, testifying in front of the pavilion that "the Pru" had achieved something memorable for cricket.

Colin Cowdrey, whose retirement has taken up far too little space in this diary, sent memories racing back to his prime with a brilliant century, 151 not out, for Kent, to win the game against the Australians. Grace, power from timing, scarcely a jerky or uncomfortable movement – things that have been written and said of him so many times before. The perfect reminder of his talent.

Clive Lloyd hooks Dennis Lillee for six.

## A B & H SURPRISE
### WEEK ENDED JULY 4

SUNNY days persist with scarcely a breeze, and the batsman is "king". Hundreds click off wide bats and footsore bowlers spit their impatience into dusty footholes.

The Benson & Hedges semi-finals threw up one surprise – Middlesex beat Warwickshire at Edgbaston, a noble effort by Mike Brearley's side, who are scarcely equipped for the one-day game. Leicestershire beat Hampshire. The comment I enjoyed most was by Alan Gibson writing in *The Times* from Edgbaston. He summed up a splendid innings by Clive Radley which had been crammed with energy, high-class strokes, as well as pushes and prods, dabs and deflections, and scampering singles, as a mixture of "the classical, the baroque and the Old Kent Road." One look at Radley's scuffed pads, straw hair and red face at the end bore out the marvellous description.

Mike Denness was nominated England's captain for the First Test against Australia at Edgbaston. His own position was hardly in dispute as a batsman because he has continued the run of form which began with the Sixth Test in Australia and took him through New Zealand. That 188 against Australia was the highest by an England captain in a Test in Australia, exceeding A. E. Stoddart's 173, also in Melbourne in 1894-95. Criticism of his captaincy often masks his ability as a batsman pure and simple.

## MIKE DENNESS LOSES MORE FRIENDS
### WEEK ENDED JULY 11

I suppose the Test match claims most of our attentions, but there were many fine achievements and several hard, fluctuating matches in the County Championship. Graham Gooch and Bob Woolmer won places in the England thirteen. Gooch made his début; Woolmer and Hendrick did not play.

In fact, I have a shattering tale to recall. Mike Denness won the toss at Edgbaston, and presumably after seeking opinion from senior players, put Australia in to bat. The weather was chill, cloudy and rather unsettled, and Australia's attack was bulging with the sort of bowlers who can take advantage of those conditions. Perhaps the disaster which followed emphasised more than anything else the professional's unwritten law "Never put in the opposition if there is rain about."

England's bowlers bowled short, McCosker and Turner put on 80 easy runs, but fine bowling by Snow, Arnold and Old managed to winkle out five on the first day for 243. This was extended to 359 all out on the second. Amiss and Edrich went in for one over, the heavens opened, a thunderstorm descended, and the square was flooded. They came out again at 4.45 and by the close England are now 83 for seven. The first Test is virtually lost.

John Edrich hung on better than most, with some luck going his way. He got 34, Knott 14; no-one else had double figures. Dennis Lillee needed no coaxing; three wickets for 13 in 12 overs; Max Walker four for 35 in 15. It was sickening to see the opposition so arrogant, to see old skeletons leap out of the cupboards. I know it is a sticky rain-affected wicket, but there looked to be no hope from the time the batsmen left the pavilion. Before the Test I felt, and wrote, that new men with fresh approaches were needed. I think I am right, though poor Graham Gooch, the newcomer, tickled one down the leg side to Marsh and left for a duck off his third ball.

John Snow – often at his best against the Australians.

Max Walker enjoys his fourth success of the innings as Rod Marsh catches Tony Greig and England are 54 for five.

The University match was drawn, the batsmen dominating in the end in spite of a breakthrough by Cambridge on the first morning which should have been enough to win the match. Their left-arm opening bowler Jackson found swing in the air and took seven for 98. Oxford's sensible fight-back was led by Fursdon, 112 not out. Pathmanathan for Oxford played neatly in both innings, 50 and 72, while Peter Roebuck, one of many promising players to come out of Millfield School recently, held Cambridge's second innings together with 158.

Lancashire went to the top of the County Championship with 132 points from 11 matches. Hampshire, Essex, Kent and Yorkshire pursue them keenly.

## CARNAGE BY RICHARDS AND GREENIDGE
### WEEK ENDED JULY 18

FOLLOWING on 258 runs behind Australia, England made 93 for five on the Saturday and by 3 p.m. on Monday, with time lost for rain as well, England had lost the First Test by an innings and 85 runs.

Australia thumped the ball in on a pitch that was never dry. They collected like eight green vultures behind the bat, willing every false shot. Whatever England had in mind by way of retaliation it was going to need extraordinary luck. It was all rather like a poorly-written mystery thriller. Every horror was totally predictable; no sleight of hand, no trickery, just plain murder by the Australians, and English corpses heaped up in their wake. It was Keith Fletcher this time who

Dennis Lillee runs to congratulate his partner Jeff Thomson as Graham Gooch departs for a "pair" in his first Test.

battled most successfully. He made 51. Gooch received a ball from Thomson which pitched just short of a length, lifted and left him. He touched it to Marsh – a tough debut indeed.

It was while England limped to defeat that Mike Denness himself suggested to the selectors that a

change of leadership may benefit the side. That again was a brave and honest thing to do. We need new soldiers and someone as flamboyant as Tony Greig to follow. Indeed just hours after the game ended, Greig was announced captain for the next three matches.

The Gillette Cup was the other main attraction of the week. A few days ago I was lauding Glamorgan (with some bias perhaps) and enjoying the annoyance they have given Hampshire over the past two seasons. I have heard of turning the tables, but this Gillette result is ridiculous. Barry Richards and Gordon Greenidge put on 210 for the first wicket. Greenidge was first to his fifty, out of 91. Richards surged from behind and seven minutes before lunch he reached 100 out of 177 in the 34th over! The shots exploded all round Southampton, Greenidge looking as if he had stored up two seasons of vengeance. After the 60 overs, 371 runs were scored, a world record in one-day cricket. Gordon Greenidge thundered on and on to an individual English record of 177. Glamorgan did not win.

*News had obviously not reached England of Graeme Pollock's 222 not out in the Eastern Province innings of 373-5 against Border in October 1974 – two one-day records which still stand today. It is possible that at the time these scores were not considered eligible as this was the first limited-overs match to experiment with the "fielding circle".*

## LEICESTERSHIRE TAKE SEASON'S FIRST CUP
### WEEK ENDED JULY 25

THE Benson & Hedges Cup final comfortably went to the favourites, Leicestershire. Middlesex, Mike Smith (83) apart, failed with the bat. Norman McVicker – "Nice wun Norman, let's have anuther wun" – took the wickets of opener Phil Edmonds, Clive Radley, Mike Brearley and Norman Featherstone for 20 runs in 11 overs. I believe Brian Davison's catch at cover to dismiss Brearley to be the finest catch I have seen for many seasons. He dived low to his left and held the ball, which was driven not more than a foot above the ground at any stage, inches above the turf in his left hand. John Steele (49) and Roger Tolchard (47 not out) carried Leicester through, though at 121 for five they were not without the need for caution. They won by five wickets in the end.

Ray Illingworth with another trophy for Leicestershire.

🏏 *Phil Edmonds was back in his more traditional role of No 9 when Middlesex appeared in the Gillette Cup Final in September.*

It was Lancashire who got to the top of the table this week: 132 points in 11 games, with six wins. Kent and Essex have 131, Leicester 130 and Yorkshire 129.

## RENOVATIONS OF STEELE AND WOOD
### WEEK ENDED AUGUST 1

THERE were five new names announced in the England party for the Lord's Test which began yesterday. David Steele is possibly the most surprising because he is winning a Test cap at the ripe age of 33 and this is his benefit year. Barry Wood came in to open the innings. Peter Lever to open the attack, and Bob Woolmer and Phil Edmonds completed the selectors' remedies. Out of the side go Denness, Fletcher, and Arnold. Hendrick is unfit, Edmonds and Old were omitted.

David Steele quickly proved why he was chosen. England were again heading for disaster, 49 for four, Dennis Lillee taking the wickets of Amiss, Edrich, Wood and Gooch. Amiss batted at number four. I feel that he should have begun the series in that position as England's most fluent run-getter. There is no way you can be fluent against Australia's attack within the first hour and a half. However, by moving him down now, Amiss is landed with heavy personal pressures, the feeling of having his last chance. The Lillee threat was soon pointed at him and he succumbed to a ball fairly well up which came back off the seam and trapped him lbw. Graham Gooch at least got off the mark this time. He looked composed, without signs of panic, but he went to a catch by Marsh off a ball from Lillee which looked a little wide. Steele, however, marched in to lunch to a hero's reception, 36 not out. The one difference in his play from others is that he plunges forward on the front foot. Lillee, Thomson and Walker in Australia may sort him out, but on this wicket at Lord's which had no special bounce, he had the confidence to recognise that he could play forward to balls well up to him. Amiss, Edrich and Wood rather lingered on the back foot. Yet the balls dug in short Steele hooked downwards and in fact was as quick as anyone to move onto the back foot. Why has he been in the background so long without being chosen for England? Is this one innings, which he extended after lunch to 50 exactly, a chance affair? I suppose he has never *looked* an outstanding player. His runs have often been grafted cheerlessly. Most seasons he averages just over 30. This one he is up to 45-plus. More than anything he is recognised by professional players as a man of heart and determination, the qualities which appeared to have gone from the England side at Edgbaston. For the moment all one can say is that he did every bit as well as everyone hoped for him.

Let us not take credit from two other fine

County Championship
(as at August 1)

| | | P | Pts |
|---|---|---|---|
| **1** | Hampshire | 13 | 148 |
| **2** | Yorkshire | 14 | 147 |
| **3** | Kent<br>Lancashire } | 13 | 144 |

performances. Tony Greig greeted the potential disaster of the early collapse with his very best batting. His height is a clear advantage in the playing of this sort of bowling, but again it was a triumph for nerve, temperament and personality. Runs came at a good rate too. Alan Knott joined in as well, a marvellous competitor. Both appreciated that the wicket was slow and both had the good sense to recognise a situation in which they were taking on the dreaded enemies on equal terms. 315 was England's total – not exceptional, but at least we are in the game.

Ross Edwards – unlucky not to reach his century.

It was almost better than that after John Snow and Peter Lever got to work. Snow four for 66 and Lever two for 83 did most to remove the front-line Australian batting. Only Ross Edwards (99) stayed and he was aided from the most unexpected and annoying quarter, Dennis Lillee (73 not out).

Australia 268. Two exciting days' cricket and a joy to see English players huddling in the middle of the wicket to celebrate the falling of yet another Australian wicket. Greig's revival is far from complete but there will be a new spirit born if success like this can be sustained.

Lancashire, like Essex last week, lost their position at the top of the County Championship table. They were beaten by Glamorgan in spite of Ken Shuttleworth's five for 42. John Hopkins, 87, Majid Khan 79 and 62, did much for Glamorgan but perhaps Roger Davis did most, 61 and five for 86. Yorkshire beat Surrey to send them to the top. Cope, five for 123, and Carrick, four for 63, were the decisive wicket-takers.

When Yorkshire are strong, England are strong, the old saying used to be. It is many seasons since Yorkshire's succession of Championship wins through the Sixties, but it is probably good for the country at large that the county which has excluded overseas players and built up their own youngsters is at the top. Great credit to Geoff Boycott too that the harsh policy of ending the careers of old and trusted players like Phil Sharpe, Don Wilson, and more recently Tony Nicholson has come off. No-one minds Yorkshire being at the top if they are as good as the adage, and take the rest of us with them.

*Sadly this was not to be the beginning of a golden period for Yorkshire. They eventually went on to lose*

*the Championship to Ray Illingworth's Leicestershire and little has gone right for them since.*

## EDRICH OVERCOMES WORST MEMORIES
### WEEK ENDED AUGUST 8

I felt this week as if I would be recording a great English victory over Australia in the Second Test, but such matters are not resolved without a desperate fight by those under pressure. Maybe the victory was for the Lord's pitch, placid throughout. Australia were left 484 to win, and Tony Greig left himself 500 minutes in which to bowl them to defeat. England trouped off the pitch an exhausted, frustrated but inwardly satisfied team with the tourists 329 for three at the close.

Still, it is a joy to tell a tale of English ascendancy after the previous winter of humiliation and the Edgbaston debacle. Greig made the most of it. He interrupted batsmen at the crease to adjust fielders, so upsetting their concentration. He took up his position at silly point and gave them as much verbal pressure as they are renowned for handing out.

David Steele scored 45 in the second innings, but the honours go to John Edrich, who got 175. His runs came slowly on the Saturday. His timing was not right. I felt he was not getting his front foot out far enough to the pitch of the ball to lean into the drives with any strength. On Monday, however, he had clearly worked out many things for himself and runs came at a steady pace. For one who suffered the physical terrors of the winter in Australia, it was a performance of character born of long experience.

Whereas others looked shattered by the old traumas down-under, Edrich, Greig and Knott have emerged as the men of special aptitude for the game at the top.

The John Player League is bustling along, and this year has attracted a larger following at grounds than ever before. Worcestershire this week achieved something else never done before in the competition – they scored a record 307 for four against Derbyshire. Then up at Old Trafford Barry Dudleston hammered 152 in an amazing 28 overs against the Sunday specialists, Lancashire. He was three runs short of Barry Richards' Sunday League record, though Richards used up all 40 overs.

## EDMONDS THE MAN OF THE MOMENT
### WEEK ENDED AUGUST 15

CHANGES were made for Headingley, one of them surprising. Keith Fletcher was recalled to the ground he probably hates most of all and against the bowling which has reduced him to a nervy player well below his true class. He and "Greigy" are good mates and it might just work out that Keith responds. He will if he can, but so far it has not gone too well for him. The devil in the shape of Dennis Lillee is rarely to be denied his victim once he scents uncertainty at the other end. Mallett held on to a catch which I suppose was typical of those offered in Australia, from a fencing shot outside the off stump. Keith Fletcher scored eight in the first innings and now needs the luck to get in, next time around.

John Hampshire was brought in too. Obviously it is felt that staying at the wicket is not enough in itself. To win this series from a position of one-down, someone has to put bat to ball and John Hampshire is as likely to manage that as anyone. He never settled in his innings of 14, but it may come to him next time in familiar Headingley surroundings.

The miracle of the match, however, involves Phillippe Henri Edmonds of Middlesex. Another attacking move rightly brought him into the side with the positive intent of bowling out Australia. Derek Underwood is still in, but he is faster and flatter through the air. They can possibly complement each other. Yet Edmonds is the man of the moment because in this, his first Test, he has taken five for 17 in 12 overs. Australia are in trouble, 107 for eight in response to England's 288.

Edmonds will bowl better than this and take no wickets at all, but no-one can begrudge him his luck. Ian Chappell and Doug Walters both mis-pulled shortish balls; Edwards padded up to a straight one first ball; Greg Chappell swept and was beautifully held by Underwood at square leg; and Greig held a catch hit by Gilmour to mid-wicket. Heady days for England and surely this is the basis of a win.

David Steele, bless his Staffordshire heart, did it again: 73 valuable runs. He scored a century against the tourists for Northants in the game before the Test.

David Steele shows the full face of the bat.

They certainly know he is around!

In an exciting match, Yorkshire beat Middlesex by five runs with eight balls left at Lord's. Clive Radley got yet another hundred, and he must be close to the Test side if Fletcher or Hampshire cannot put together an innings next time. Geoff Cope took five for 63. Yorkshire also beat Derbyshire by eight wickets with those two young bowlers Cooper and Carrick to the fore again, Cooper six for 44 in the first innings, Carrick eight for 72 in the second as well as an innings of 87.

 *Clive Radley has been such an effective and reliable batsman over the years that it is perhaps surprising that he was not given more opportunity in Test cricket. In only eight Test match appearances, all in 1978, he made two centuries and two fifties and averaged 48.10.*

Fred Swarbrook, Derbyshire's Pickwickian-looking left-arm spinner, rose from the luncheon table at Hove today, Sussex 64 for one, to see the sun out, blazing down on a wicket which had been saturated in an over-night thunderstorm. He turned his arm over after the interval and in less than half an hour had turned in the best bowling performance of his career, by a long way, and the best figures of the season. From the sea end he turned the ball and it lifted too. In six overs he took nine wickets for 20 runs. Sussex lost by 179 runs. I can just see the water in that communal bath at Hove swell as young Swarbrook, ample size that he is, plunged in jubilation – a couple of pints of beer inside him no doubt, and can you blame him!

## OUTRAGE AT HEADINGLEY
### WEEK ENDED AUGUST 22

GEORGE Cawthray, the groundsman at Headingley, pushed back the covers from the Test wicket on Tuesday morning to find that lumps of soil had been gouged out from the creases and oil poured onto the part of the pitch where the ball would bounce just short of a half-volley. He talked to the nightwatchman, who had not heard a whisper all through his vigil, then sent for the police. On the walls outside the ground were painted slogans which announced "George Davis is innocent." The name of George Davis does not appear in *Wisden*, though he is certain of a place next year.

Wicket inspection at Headingley – Tony Greig, Joe Lister, David Constant and Ian Chappell examine the damage.

He is, in fact, a man convicted of armed robbery and serving a 20-year jail sentence. Cricket has again been used for political purposes. The Test was abandoned; Australia retain the Ashes.

It was quickly ascertained by the captains and umpires that no other pitch could be produced which was similar in wear to the existing one, on which the ball had turned slowly over the four days. The game was poised for a victory either way. England left Australia 445 to win and they were in the middle of a noble effort to make it. The highest score ever made to win a Test in England is 404 at Headingley by Australia in 1948. Ian Chappell's side had reached 220 for three overnight. Just 225 to get, but they could not afford a mistake. McCosker looked solid, 95 not out; Doug Walters, 27 not out and untroubled. Much depended on the initial assault by John Snow, who had bowled superbly throughout the match without getting his rewards into the scorebook. As it turned out, George Davis ended the excitement, but in truth, if he had not, the weather would have. Just after noon rain fell and a draw was inevitable, barring miracles.

There was hope among the general public for an extra Test but within an hour or two Lord's came out with this statement on behalf of the TCCB: "Following the incident at Headingley this morning, the senior representatives of the Test and County Cricket Board and of the Australian cricket team have, in conjunction with the manager, considered the possibility of playing a further Test match. Both parties agree that an incident of this nature, in the circumstances prevailing, does not justify the playing of an additional match. In any event there would have been considerable practical difficulties in staging a five- or six-day match at the only possible time, the 11th to the 16th/17th Sept.

Further, a number of the Australian players are committed to return to their employment at home immediately after the Oval Test."

On Wednesday in the Gillette Cup semi-finals, Gloucestershire went the same way as they had in the twilight in 1971. This time with no less hope of winning up to the very last moments. Lancashire were in pursuit of a total of 236, composed mainly of Sadiq's brilliant strokeplay (122). With three wickets standing Lancashire made it, but there were only three balls to spare. Hughes was the man who mauled John Mortimore last time, and this time he stepped down the wicket, when 37 were needed from five overs, to hit Knight for a tremendous six over long-off. He and Simmons took 12 off that over, six off the next, and the pressures subsided.

Opposing them at Lord's will be Middlesex, who beat Derbyshire at Chesterfield by 24 runs. Middlesex scored 207, Featherstone responsible for an aggressive 70, but Derbyshire's start, given them by Headley and Sharpe, of 81 looked decisive. Yet one-day cricket goes all wrong sometimes. It turns hitters into blockers, blockers into sloggers; throw in a couple of run-outs and there you have it – Derbyshire's tumble to defeat, leaving Middlesex sharpening their claws for a second major cup final in one season.

## FIREWORKS AT CHELMSFORD
### WEEK ENDED AUGUST 29

R. N. S. Hobbs c Laird b Higgs 100; that is the scorecard line of the week to me. Even more, this was the fifth-fastest hundred in the history of the game. Percy Fender's 35 minutes looked a bit shaky at one stage, but eventually "Hobbsy" had to settle for 44 minutes. It was certainly the fastest against an Australian side. Who did he hit, you ask? Well, four sixes were struck off Mallett, all of them well clear of the fence at the end of the Chelmsford ground, a good 80 yards away. His longest hit landed on the river bank about 90 yards away. Higgs was twirling his legspinners from the other end and ended up with figures of 13 overs, two for 91; Mallett 7.4 overs, one for 76.

Yet story-book endings are few and far between in first-class cricket. Essex lost the match by 98 runs and

Robin Hobbs – the batsman.

**County Championship**
(as at August 29)

| | P | Pts |
|---|---|---|
| **1** Yorkshire | 18 | 192 |
| **2** Hampshire | 17 | 190 |
| **3** Leicestershire | 17 | 189 |

Hobbs was left out of the side for the next match at Northampton.

*Percy Fender's record still stands – but only just. Steve O'Shaughnessy of Lancashire equalled the 35 minutes in his innings against Leicestershire in 1983.*

Peter Johnson, who was a Blue at Cambridge in 1970-72, and who left first-class cricket to qualify as a solicitor, has given steadiness to the Notts middle-order in his first season back. His century against Leicestershire this week was his first, but it was achieved in the teeth of men chasing the Championship title hard. In fact Leicestershire raced home to a win by eight wickets, Barry Dudleston making a magnificent hundred in 111 minutes.

Finally from the county scene I should mention the record fourth-wicket partnership for Northants between Mushtaq, the new acting captain, and Wayne Larkins. Mushtaq (138) and Larkins (127) put on 273 against Essex.

I write about the counties before the Test because a marvellous conclusion is stirring up in the Championship. Also the Australians won the toss and put any hope of an English win out of the question in two days of sound, stylish batting. Alan Turner went early, but then Ian Chappell and Rick McCosker stayed together all day to make the score 280 for one at the close of the first day. Not a good feeling in the home dressing room! The massacre continued, although McCosker went early next day for 127. It was pleasant justice to see him reach his first Test century when the vandals at Headingley had dug up the pitch just as he was about to make it there. Ian Chappell played superbly, 192. He left in a huff, failing to acknowledge the standing ovation offered to him by a huge crowd. Australian journalists in the Press box could not excuse him. To me it was a classic case of a cricketer getting too close to his pursuit. Certainly the last thing Ian Chappell would want to be associated with would be anything that smacks of accepted courtesies. Not that he is ungracious, but I think formalities freeze him. It was a set-piece ovation for the touring captain and he shunned it.

Someone who did not behave in similar fashion was Ross Edwards, who announced today that he is retiring

Ian Chappell – unhappy not to reach 200.

from Test cricket. Ian Chappell gave him the honour of leading out Australia. Both then and when he walked alone to bat he was warmly received because he is known as a warm person as well as an inflexible competitor. His is the reputation I would think all schoolboys should pursue. He has been a perfect ambassador for Australia, and Perth in particular.

Australia 532 for nine declared, England 19 for no wicket on Friday night. Need I say more?

## MARATHON AT THE OVAL
### WEEK ENDED SEPTEMBER 5

ENGLAND staged a massive rearguard action at The Oval and the Fourth Test was drawn. Of course, once Australia had batted so well in the first innings there was never a way we could square the series. England got 191 and there was only defeat to contemplate in a six-day Test. Max Walker bowled superbly, four for 63. He has a deceptive action. First of all he is tall and extracts sharp movement off the seam. Secondly he appears to be angling the ball into the bat from outside off stump because he drops his left shoulder and arm at the moment of delivery, but in fact he can run the ball away to slip as well as anyone. Jeff Thomson sent the ball down quicker than at any time on tour, as far as one could judge from the ring. It looks as if he has lengthened his run. He gathers momentum on the way to the stumps now, rather than jogging and straining for pace just out of his action. Accuracy has come with it. Here is a bowler who has learned much in this country and has certainly gone back to Australia a better performer for the trip. I do not know how much he has learned from Dennis Lillee, but Lillee is a man who would be in any side in the world. Apart from the enormous courage involved in his fight-back to fitness after those stress fractures of the spine, he has other qualities. He is aggressive, physically and verbally, which is absolutely essential in the fast-bowling game; he can take "stick," as he did in the Prudential competition against the West Indians, and come back snorting fire. Yet he has learned the true art of bowling which lifts him far above the ordinary. Variation of pace, length and line are all under his control. His presence has made the Australian side of 1975 a memorable one. I also believe that the wicketkeeping of

Rod Marsh has enhanced it too. Apart from the acrobatics which he was required to go through to take Jeff Thomson, especially with the new ball, he moved and took the ball with great certainty; simple, straightforward 'keeping with no frills.

So England went in 347 behind and grafted to safety. Edrich 96, Steele (yes, once again) 66, Roope 77, Woolmer a maiden century, 149, and Knott 64. Only in one respect could Tony Greig be criticised and this is for his rejection of the prospect of winning. That sounds a harsh statement, but in fact if he had batted with Roope instead of sending another nervous newcomer, Woolmer, to the crease, and had runs come at 20 more to the hour, Australia would have been left an awkward 200 or so to get on a wicket which had seen six days' cricket. Still it must have done the team in the dressing room the power of good to watch the tourists footslog around The Oval for 13 hours. Ian Chappell has announced that he is to give up the captaincy. Greg Chappell might succeed him, though the Australian Board may yet find Ian Redpath the better candidate.

## LANCASHIRE TAKE GILLETTE WITH IMPUNITY
### WEEK ENDED SEPTEMBER 12

IT was impossible to build up the fervour for yet another sunny day, another shirtsleeved crowd, another glossy day of one-day cricket at Lord's. Perhaps it was because the Gillette final was won by Lancashire so early in the day. They were never extended by Middlesex once they had bowled out three important players for 33 – Mike Smith, Mike Brearley and Clive Radley. There were efforts of determination and even style by Gomes, Barlow and Edmonds, but 180 in the 60 overs was never going to be enough. Unfortunately too for Middlesex John Price had been forced out of the game by injury. Lancashire scored 182 and there was no way the runs could be checked off Clive Lloyd's bat.

John Murray walked to the middle for the last time in a fine career. It is the way so many would love to end their careers: Lord's, a packed house, and a standing ovation.

John Murray has been a model of style behind the wickets – familiar mannerisms, the touch of the cap, fingertips to fingertips with the gloves, and the poise of

a true MCC coaching manual. Rhythm, "giving" with the ball, neatness of dress, tidiness of mind – all these attributes will leave a lasting impression on all who saw him play.

However, Clive Lloyd was the Man of this particular Match and one can only pay tribute to Lancashire, who have made this one-day game into an exciting spectacle as well as being expert at the negative bowling arts which success requires.

At Darley Dale in Derbyshire, Hampshire won the John Player League. Their 222 was much too good for Derbyshire's 152. In the Championship, however, Hampshire were baulked by John Ward, not the best known of cricketers, an Oxford Blue who has just retired from Derbyshire. He scored 104 to stand between Hampshire and victory. That innings pushed his career average up to 11! His previous highest score was 83 for Oxford University.

Lancashire beat Gloucestershire by 10 wickets, Peter Lee five for 66, so it now becomes a straight fight between Lancashire, who play Sussex at Hove tomorrow, and Leicestershire, who meet Derbyshire at Chesterfield. If Leicestershire take seven bonus points they will win. Lancashire will have to get something close to the maximum 18.

## LEICESTERSHIRE MAKE THE LAST HEADLINE
### WEEK ENDED SEPTEMBER 19

LEICESTERSHIRE for the first time in their history end on the top. They struggled at first against Derbyshire on Saturday, but so did Lancashire against Sussex.

A tribute is due to the county champions. Anyone who wins the title deserves it and their number of wins emphasises that. Ray Illingworth is obviously a first-class captain and the team has a host of varying talents which dovetail to bring success. However, one thinks back to the years before Tony Lock took over, when Mike Turner, the secretary, was feeling his way. Leicestershire were a side of memories but of no strong reputation. In the club's president, Bill Bentley, Mike Turner found an ally who believed in success not just participation. Turner recognised the players his county wanted because he himself had been a leg-spinner on

Colin Cowdrey leaves the field at the end of his final innings in first-class cricket.

the staff. Bentley backed his judgment. There are others, of course. Charles Palmer, the club's former captain, is never far from the action. The ground has been bought and renovated, the pavilion improved and the cricket along with it. They meant to succeed.

### FINAL COUNTY CHAMPIONSHIP TABLE

| | P | W | L | D | Bt | Bw | Pts |
|---|---|---|---|---|---|---|---|
| 1 Leicestershire (4) | 20 | 12 | 1 | 7 | 61 | 59 | 240 |
| 2 Yorkshire (11) | 20 | 10 | 1 | 9 | 56 | 68 | 224 |
| 3 Hampshire (2) | 20 | 10 | 6 | 4 | 51 | 72 | 223 |
| 4 Lancashire (8) | 20 | 9 | 3 | 8 | 57 | 72 | 219 |
| 5 Kent (10) | 20 | 8 | 4 | 8 | 59 | 70 | 209 |
| 6 Surrey (7) | 20 | 8 | 3 | 9 | 55 | 67 | 202 |
| 7 Essex (12) | 20 | 7 | 6 | 7 | 61 | 67 | 198 |
| 8 Northamptonshire (3) | 20 | 7 | 9 | 4 | 40 | 72 | 182 |
| 9 Glamorgan (16) | 20 | 7 | 8 | 5 | 45 | 66 | 181 |
| 10 Worcestershire (1) | 20 | 5 | 6 | 9 | 55 | 63 | 168 |
| 11 Middlesex (6) | 20 | 6 | 7 | 7 | 45 | 59 | 164 |
| 12 Somerset (5) | 20 | 4 | 8 | 8 | 51 | 65 | 156 |
| 13 Nottinghamshire (15) | 20 | 3 | 9 | 8 | 59 | 67 | 156 |
| 14 Warwickshire (9) | 20 | 4 | 10 | 6 | 48 | 65 | 153 |
| 15 Derbyshire (17) | 20 | 5 | 7 | 8 | 33 | 69 | 152 |
| 16 Gloucestershire (14) | 20 | 4 | 10 | 6 | 43 | 62 | 145 |
| 17 Sussex (13) | 20 | 2 | 13 | 5 | 37 | 62 | 119 |

1974 positions in brackets.

*"Temperamentally, the West Indies have always been suspect . . ."*

*"Man for man, the West Indies side was at least as talented as Australia's. The difference lay in their response to pressure . . ."*

*"The first match . . . revealed Lloyd's weakness as a captain . . ."*

*"Lloyd was all the time trying to block the gaps rather than trying to take the initiative."*

Few, at the time, would have disagreed with Henry Blofeld's Wisden summary of the 1975-76 tour when Australia, led for the first time by Greg Chappell, with his brother Ian lending valued support, produced one of their greatest sustained performances in beating the West Indies by five matches to one. No-one could confidently have predicted that Lloyd's West Indies team was about to embark upon almost a decade of consistent success in both Test and limited-overs cricket. Time and again during that period Lloyd himself was to rescue his side with cool, determined batting, and the old theory that West Indians buckled under pressure was finally to be laid to rest.

Apart from the gradual evolution towards an attack based on four fast bowlers, the biggest reason for this was the increased professionalism of the players, due partly to rapidly increasing rewards, especially in Australia. At this stage Lloyd was still a novice as a tactician and his side altogether too happy-go-lucky in their approach, and these were costly failings. Roberts and the emerging Jamaican fast bowler Michael Holding did not once share the new ball throughout the series, for instance, while on the opening day of the First Test West Indies managed to lose six wickets for 125 runs in 18 overs! Even in a limited-overs match this would have seemed bizarre tactics; in a Test it was unbelievable.

Four men scored over 400 Test runs: Lloyd himself, Kallicharran, Fredericks (who set up the one victory with an amazing hundred off 71 balls on the fast pitch at Perth) and Richards, who found his form belatedly, but finished the tour in a blaze of brilliant batting. All these men, however, were outdone by Greg Chappell who averaged 117 in compiling an aggregate of 702 in 11 innings, whilst his brother made 449, Alan Turner 439 and Ian Redpath, with three separate hundreds, 575.

Of the bowlers Gary Gilmour, with 20 wickets, displaced Max Walker as the main supporting act to Thomson (29 wickets) and Lillee (27), while for the West Indies Roberts was much the most dangerous bowler, though this was the series in which Lance Gibbs finally overtook Fred Trueman's Test record of 307 wickets.

In the other Test series of the winter, India drew one-all in New Zealand, for whom young Richard Hadlee took seven for 23 at Wellington; and, back home again, West Indies defeated India two-one in a four-Test series, although the rubber ended in unpleasant circumstances when India, suffering a spate of injuries on a spiteful pitch, could find only six batsmen fit enough to take guard in the second innings.

# ᐩ 1976 ᐩ

## THE SPICES AWAITING
### WEEK ENDED APRIL 24

HARD as I have tried to digest the early-season action which in this first week has involved only MCC, the Universities and their opponents Leicestershire, Somerset and Gloucestershire, I have the feeling that the significant happenings are in Port of Spain.

It is the week of the deciding Test between India and West Indies – one-all so far. It is reported that the West Indian fast men Michael Holding and Wayne Daniel virtually assaulted the Indian batsmen (at least that has been claimed by Polly Umrigar, the Indian manager, and Bishan Bedi, the captain). Bouncers have struck Gaekwad on the temple; Patel was hit in the mouth; Viswanath has broken a finger and India were forced to declare their first innings at 306 for six.

Lillee and Thomson have gone back to Australia for the moment, but there looks likely to be no release for the England players. Soon they will be face to face with fast, dangerous bowling again, five Tests against West Indies.

Around the counties, Eddie Barlow is sure to help Derbyshire to make progress. Bob Willis is fit again and so is Alan Ward. How quickly will Dennis Amiss and Keith Fletcher repair their wounded spirits?

The West Indies touring side has been announced and there is no-one, not even the player himself, who is not surprised to see the name of Larry Gomes on the list. Larry did score a fighting century for Trinidad against the Indians recently, but his form in the Middlesex middle order has been nothing to raise interest. If he was English he would not even be considered for a Test trial.

Larry Gomes playing for Middlesex during 1975.

🏏 *How well Larry Gomes has repaid the selectors for what certainly seemed a surprising choice at the time.*

The MCC v. Leicestershire game was notable not for the centuries by Dennis Amiss (164), Mike Brearley (137 not out), Barry Dudleston (103 not out) and Brian Davison (103), but for the one bowler who made an impact on the game, which was played in conditions favourable to the batsmen, Paddy Clift. This 23-year-old Rhodesian took eight for 17 in the MCC first innings in only 16.5 overs.

That old favourite Robin Hobbs this week accepted a trophy which he could never ever have expected to possess – the Walter Lawrence Trophy for the fastest century of 1975. It was against the Australians at Chelmsford as many will remember. A century in 44 minutes, the fastest for 55 years. He was right . . . when that happens it really is time to retire!

## CENTURIES ALREADY – EVEN A DOUBLE
### WEEK ENDED MAY 1

SO the County Championship got under way on Wednesday, the weather fine, wickets firm, and the bowlers got stick rather than easy prey. Everyone watches the form of Dennis Amiss. After his century for MCC last week he piled up 167 against Warwickshire. Zaheer got 188 against Yorkshire, and you might say that the Leeds wicket favoured the bat – Johnny Hampshire 155 not out, Colin Johnson 102. Ray Illingworth scored 135 to rescue Leicestershire, the county champions, from collapse against Notts; Mike Brearley, on his 34th birthday, presented himself with 135 against Kent. Then just to remind us how much he believes in serving his country and the game of cricket until the "ole legs can run no more," Basil D'Oliveira stroked his first century for two seasons, against Warwickshire at Worcestershire. At the younger end of the scale, Tony Borrington announced good form with 102 not out against Sussex at Ilkeston, and Paul Parker of Cambridge University scored 215, his maiden first-class century, against Essex at Fenner's. This was the highest innings for Cambridge since David Sheppard's 239 not out against Worcestershire in 1952.

Paul Parker – a promising start to the season.

## INJURY TO ARNOLD A BLOW TO SURREY'S HOPES
### WEEK ENDED MAY 8

ONE of the most worrying features of Surrey cricket so far is the injury of Geoff Arnold. He has worked so very hard over many seasons to fight off a recurring hamstring condition; he has run up to the wicket with great spirit for England all over the world, winter after winter, and now, after the well-merited rest has come, he has developed Achilles tendon trouble.

Cecil Paris, president of MCC, this week announced his successor, who will take up that office in October next. It is W. H. "Tadge" Webster, a sportsman who has a colourful record both in cricket and soccer. He is now retired, but was formerly a stockbroker, who played for Middlesex from time to time during the summer after he went down from Cambridge in 1932. In cricket administration he has been chairman of MCC's Grounds and Fixtures Committee and also a past treasurer of Middlesex.

## THE WEST INDIANS ARE HERE
### WEEK ENDED MAY 15

IT was a hot, sunny day at Arundel Castle, the most perfect setting for cricket. The West Indians took their first bow of the 1976 season, and it appeared proper that they should do so in a friendly encounter at a location which, with all its ancient trees and glades, expresses the traditions of the game outside the Test and county grounds.

It is to perpetuate her late husband's memory that Lavinia, Duchess of Norfolk, has sought help to

Lavinia, Duchess of Norfolk with rival captains Colin Cowdrey and Clive Lloyd.

maintain cricket at the castle. Under the guidance of former MCC secretary Billy Griffith, the Friends of Arundel Castle Cricket Club was formed. There are already 1,000 members, and 2,000 more are required to establish the renaissance of an institution which had

lapsed since the Duke's passing.

West Indies won the match by seven wickets, but, more important, their presence has set the tongues wagging about the fast-bowling skills of Roberts, Daniel and Holding. Who can play them? Can Dennis Amiss come back? What about Keith Fletcher? The hunt is on again for brave men.

*Although Dennis Amiss returned to score 203 in the final Test and took 179 off India in the First Test of the winter tour, he was to play no more Test cricket after 1977. Keith Fletcher never reestablished his previous form in Test matches and despite his undoubted skills as a tactician his one series as England captain in India in 1981 – 82 was a disappointment.*

On Monday there was an even more succulent aperitif to the Tests. Clyde Walcott and Clive Lloyd, at a lunch given by the British Sportsman's Club at the Savoy Hotel, claimed that the Indians had "surrendered" that controversial Test at Port of Spain which, by the way, West Indies won because Bedi refused to allow his injured men to bat a second time.

## GREIG IS CAPTAIN: LET THERE BE STYLE
### WEEK ENDED MAY 22

IT was a week which ended with the certain information that Tony Greig has been chosen to captain England in all five Tests against West Indies.

Let me start with the simple story. Greig was obviously going to be invested with the charge of our international affairs after his three-match reign against Australia last summer. He is a junior county captain, but he has instincts of aggression which can earn England respect in world competition. I feel certain that he will not see the job simply as a mission to draw matches against the major powers. I hope he is mindful of West Indies' poor showing in Australia and assesses England's chances of winning a few Tests as a real possibility.

After decades of bashing on the door at Lord's the England Women's cricket team have been tentatively allowed to set foot on the Mecca. This is their Golden Jubilee Year and the Australian Women's side is over here to help them celebrate. There are three Tests and a one-day international. It is this last fixture which MCC have said can be moved from Sunbury to Lord's if Middlesex are not using the ground that day for a home draw in the quarter-final of the Gillette Cup. So they are not quite home and dry yet.

The biggest boost for the ladies is the arrival of a sponsor, Unigate, who are putting something in the region of £9000 in the kitty.

## *IN A SPIN AT BRISTOL*
### *WEEK ENDED MAY 29*

THE Test matches came into focus with a week of trial cricket – MCC v. West Indies at Lord's and the official Trial at Bristol. It is a time of scrutiny for the selectors and of agony for many players. Although Alec Bedser has the understanding to assure candidates that they will not be condemned to failure if they miss out this week, there is always the fear that the wrong evidence will be offered.

*There has always been much debate on the value of Test trials as too much can often be read into one outstanding or disappointing performance. The MCC game against the tourists remains the traditional "trial" and it is perhaps no bad thing that the official trial match has now been dropped from the calendar.*

For example, it was essential for Dennis Amiss to succeed against the West Indian fast men. He did not. Here was a batsman who had scored massively in 1973 and 1974, even in West Indies, but who had been reduced to a shellshocked veteran by Dennis Lillee and Jeff Thomson. England wanted him to do well this week. Yet at 6.26 p.m. on Saturday evening, in the sunshine making Lord's a glorious place to be, Dennis ducked away from a short ball sent down by Michael Holding and as soon as I saw the blood spatter his shirtsleeve and gloves I knew that it was the end for him. He was not dazed, and walked steadily from the field to have his head stitched. There could surely be no comeback now. Graham Roope padded up and was bowled by a straight one. He shaped hesitantly against the fast bowling. Randall jumped about without any obvious technique. Only the former University men

Mike Brearley and Richard Gilliat stood their ground, watched the ball instead of ducking willy-nilly.

The sight of Holding is something special. His run-up is long but every pace looks natural and necessary. He does not look built for power but his thin body whips down the ball at frightening speed.

Christopher Cowdrey, son of Colin, is chosen to lead the England Young Cricketers to West Indies in July, August and early September. The idea was to visit at this unusual time because school holidays were on. Yet most of the players, like Gatting, Williams, Athey, Jones and others, are on the staffs of first-class counties. They would have found West Indies a better place to tour earlier in the year.

Mike Gatting in action for Middlesex against Northants before his departure for the West Indies.

## *FIRST TASTE OF RICHARDS*
### *WEEK ENDED JUNE 5*

GLORY be! Old Closey is back. I have just checked, and it is nine years since he last played Test

14 *The Daily Telegraph, Monday, May 31, 1976*

# CLOSE (45) RECALLED TO ENGLAND TEAM AFTER 9-YEAR BREAK

### By MICHAEL MELFORD

BRIAN CLOSE, 45 and Mike Brearley, 34,
~~ England side

cricket. He is 45 and England want him for the First Test against West Indies at Nottingham, which starts on Thursday. I am staggered.

I respect his talent, his guts and the romance of selecting a player at this advanced age, but normally the great comebacks are made by Test heroes. Brian Close has hardly been a success in Test cricket, save for his captaincy against West Indies in the Final Test of 1966.

He has played 19 Tests, 31 innings. His highest score is 70 and his average is 24.03. He has taken 18 wickets for just under 30 apiece and 20 catches. I am no believer in averages and can quite understand what has made Close such an attraction to Tony Greig. Greig wants fighters. The sheer pace of the West Indian fast bowlers scattered some of the younger talent last week and left Dennis Amiss, our best player, cut and bruised. Amiss is not chosen. He has wisely been taken out of the firing line.

One of our "younger selections" is Mike Brearley, 34, again chosen for solid courage against fast bowling, which he demonstrated in the MCC match against the tourists last week. If we are simply going to be satisfied with parrying the blows, are we ever going to get to a position of winning the match?

If all this smacks of defensive selecting then the tactics employed by Greig in the first two days of the Test confirmed that England fear the West Indians rushing away with an early win. Greig set incredibly defensive fields. Close, whose menace in the field is the sight of his bald pate shining out of the corner of your eye when you are batting, his chewing, scuffling presence, was placed at square leg! The bowling was not accurate. Vivian Richards hammered a brilliant 232, Kallicharran 97 and Fredericks 42. England never put pressure on them close to the bat.

Mike Brearley – a late-comer to Test cricket.

## A CENTURY FOR STEELE AT LAST
### WEEK ENDED JUNE 12

THE Nottingham Test by Saturday had cast England in the usual defensive role. Yet our team was selected for such contingencies and the grafters grafted out of trouble into the inevitable draw. It was slow pleasure. The only spin bowling on the West Indian side was by Fredericks, 17 overs, Richards six, and

Kallicharran 10 – not exactly a threatening array of spin, and this in two England innings. Otherwise the occasion was likely to be only a slow funeral for England, yet in the persons of David Steele, Bob Woolmer, Brian Close and John Edrich, the British corpse refused to lie down. Steele got the century which eluded him last summer and how can one fail to admire the scores if not, truthfully, the style of a man who, against the fastest bowling in the world over two years, has collected Test scores of 50, 45, 73, 92, 39, 66, and now 106. Magnificent.

Bob Woolmer looked comfortable and stylish, playing some shots in the style of Colin Cowdrey. He got 82, and in the second innings the old warhorses gave the defiant performance for which they were billed. Edrich never looked like getting out, and Close, brought in to fight off the fast men, found himself playing out time to safety against third-rate spinners.

On Wednesday the quarter-final of the Benson & Hedges competition was completed, sending Warwickshire to play Worcestershire and Surrey to take on Kent in the semi-finals. The Gold Awards of the week went to Bob Willis, five for 27 against Lancs; Jarvis four for 54 against Notts; Edrich, 57 not out against Essex; and Imran Khan, one for 29 and 56 not out against Leics.

Fighting broke out among the fans at Worcestershire. Ray Illingworth was quoted at the end of the match as saying, "It was a great game played in competitive spirit, but the fighting was a disgrace. If you can't behave better then don't come to the game."

## RULE BRITANNIA (FOR A WHILE)
### WEEK ENDED JUNE 19

AFTER the moan about slow over rates, and the disappointment of going to the Lord's Test to find that Viv Richards was forced out of the game by a virus, there came a most marvellous day; a Friday. Lord's turned into a feverish theatre as the stumbling, bumbling, blocking England leapt to her feet and put the Carib dragon to the sword.

England were 197 for eight at the close of the first day. Brearley (40) and Close (60) had done their stuff. They were chosen to wear down the pace attack and this they did with a partnership of 84 in 140 minutes. Yet do not quarrel with the run rate. England received only 13 overs to the hour.

So now to this incredible Friday. Derek Underwood led the home charge with the bat. His 31 helped the last two wickets to put on an amazing 53 runs.

Old bowled a short one to Fredericks and the little Guyanese was betrayed by his love of the hook. Snow held onto a catch down at long leg which would have turned many hands to jelly.

Maybe there was a look about John Snow which should have hinted at the excitement to come. He enjoys bowling at Lord's and was given the proper encouragement by his captain, who encircled the West Indian batsmen with close fielders. Old Closey's armourplated pate dazzled in the sunshine as he thrust his chin out into the batsman's domain around the crease. Greenidge cut and hooked superbly, but Underwood was brought on first change. Greenidge reeled off superb strokes but then, aiming to pull a ball from Underwood which was not as short as the stroke required, skied it to deep mid-on, where Snow judged an awkward catch well.

That started the final collapse. Two balls later Snow bowled Murray, and two overs later he trapped Julien lbw. Snow had previously had Gomes caught by Woolmer and Kallicharran by Old for a duck. Clive Lloyd fell to the other executioner, Underwood, for 50. Snow took four for 68, Underwood five for 39. England's best bowlers had produced the goods so badly needed and Greig had excelled as a captain·in the field. He hustled the batsmen, probed their nervous systems, crowded them and cajoled them. West Indies were bowled out for 182, so from the first defiance of the morning it had been a day of English domination. Can they now set up the win?

The crowds are willing them to do so. I was sitting with friends in one of the boxes when the swell began. It took a few rehearsals but soon *Rule Britannia* drowned the calypsos for the first time this summer. The promenaders in front of the Tavern roared "Britons never, never, never shall be slaves" as Mike Brearley put his broad bat to Andy Roberts and Barry Wood hooked a bouncer into the Tavern. At the close John Snow was cheered to the balcony; the dark mysterious man of moods had a curtain call after only the second act. It was deliriously England's proudest cricket

moment for many seasons.

## CAPTAINS "COURAGEOUS"
### WEEK ENDED JUNE 26

AGONY of agonies. It rained all day on Saturday, and on Tuesday the Second Test match was drawn. England plodded in their second innings, leaving the tourists 323 to win in 295 minutes. In reply, Roy Fredericks compiled a responsible, skilful, defensive century to ensure that England would not win, but then suddenly out marched Clive Lloyd to make a gesture of attack which bore no relationship to the situation of the moment. Kallicharran, presumably batting to order, had taken two hours 25 minutes to make 35, yet with 12 overs left West Indies were surging with the full range of strokeplay to get the 120 required to win. One minute blocking, the next slogging. It was a crazy sequence. When Lloyd was out, he waved off Julien, the batsman at the other end. Greig called back his fielders from the outfield, uncoiled from his own distant corner and started spitting back. No, he would not go off. There were four West Indian wickets down; he claimed his chance to bowl them out while they were defending. Two more wickets did fall, but quite honestly, there was never a moment when either captain attempted to "make" his luck by taking the slightest chance.

On Wednesday the semi-finals of the Benson & Hedges Cup were resolved, Worcestershire beating Warwickshire by 12 runs at Edgbaston and Kent accounting for Surrey by 16 runs at The Oval. In both cases the home captain won the toss and chose to bat second.

## COMRADE JACKMAN
### WEEK ENDED JULY 3

IT has been possible to have many sorts of weeks in cricket this week, and I do not believe anyone has shared mine.

First of all can I tell you that it was hot enough to melt the paint off the seat wherever you spectated. At least I was honoured to be sweltering on the new blue accommodation at Old Trafford which Crown Decorators have just finished. I saw one of my favourite bowlers too, Robin Jackman, sensing a pitch of uneven

Robin Jackman – a fine bowler but also no mean performer with the bat.

bounce, and firing the ball tantalisingly just outside off stump, begging the suicidal square cut. I have written before, though no more times than the Bristol bard, Alan Gibson, has about Jack Davey, that Jackman personifies all I enjoy in cricket. He shouts, swears, puffs and pants, whacks in the bouncer and hopes to crack you on the knuckles, but he is gentleman enough to ask you if you are still alive, and sport enough to buy you the first pint; in short, the cricketer who does not get so close to his task that he loses sight of the daily comradeship. Jackman took six Lancashire wickets for 51 on Saturday. Hayes played well, as he usually does when he gets runs, Charlie Elliott watched intently. I think he may conclude, having seen the irregularities of the wicket, that Hayes might be an asset in the next Test, which, of course, is at Old Trafford.

To avoid crowds I attended the University match on Wednesday and Thursday. It was white hot, with just the gentlest breeze waltzing around the huge ground under the top tier of the stands at the Nursery end. Tavaré, from a distance, looked every bit as promising a player as he had looked at Fenner's. He has the style. Does he have the heart?

Parker is much hailed but I do not see the rhythms so strong in him. Judges I respect assure me I have it wrong, and that is good. Gurr, the big Oxford quickie, looks hostile enough. He will play for Somerset.

*Perhaps Tony Lewis was right after all – certainly Tavaré was to be much more successful in Test cricket.*

Almost no-one watched the University match, yet there was more talent involved than there has been for many years. I wish they would wear their colours. Alastair Hignell and others wore dark blue caps. Lack of identity is the last thing the teams want in an era when they are trying to re-establish themselves.

## IGNOMINY AT MANCHESTER
### WEEK ENDED JULY 10

THERE has been a surge to the top of the County Championship table this week by Essex. They defeated Surrey and Northants, the latter being potential leaders themselves.

Essex beat Surrey mostly with spin bowling, but first placed their opponents in a difficult situation by brilliant batting. Graham Gooch, 99, Keith Fletcher, 78, and Ken McEwan, 53 and 117, created time for the winkling-out process. McEwan has played superbly this summer, but this contribution on a wicket that turned more and more was one of adventure and class against Intikhab and Pocock.

David Acfield took four for 96 in the first innings and seven for 57 in the second. He has made the most of his opportunities since the retirement of Robin Hobbs, and certainly life as a county cricketer is much more enjoyable for him with a regular place in the side. He came down from Cambridge in 1968, and his patience has paid off. His selection for MCC against the West Indians was significant. His 11 for 153 in this match will not have done harm to his claims for higher recognition.

David Acfield bowling against Surrey.

A lot of professional players have told me that a young Yorkshire man called C. W. J. Athey is going to be a very good player. Against Sussex at Leeds on Tuesday he scored his maiden century, 131 not out. Yorkshiremen are always slightly begrudging about outstanding young talent, insisting that youth has to be fired by long and testing experience among the professionals before easy praise is offered. Still, Athey is "on the map."

*How sad for Yorkshire that the "long and testing experience" is now producing so many runs for Gloucestershire.*

England. Ah! What has happened to England? Depressing stuff from Old Trafford. First of all, the selectors were put in an unenviable position when the fitness count was taken. They first made voluntary changes – Edrich for Brearley, Hayes for Wood, who is unfit, and Hendrick for Ward. By Wednesday we were reading how Selvey, Willey and Balderstone, three players who have no Test experience, had been called up in case Edrich's thigh was still troublesome, Snow's hamstring was unfit and Woolmer's shoulder injury was likely to impair his batting. Willis, Ward, Jackman and Arnold, other fast-bowling candidates, are also unfit.

It turned out that only Mike Selvey was required and he made a huge impact on his first Test. West Indies made only 211 and of those Gordon Greenidge made a

Derek Underwood and Gordon Greenidge – both tired men.

most pugnacious 134. Selvey, pitching the ball well up to the bat, and getting some movement late in the air, took the wickets of Fredericks, Richards, Kallicharran and Holding for 41 in 17 overs. Very promising bowling.

England were ignominiously extracted for 71 – Roberts three for 22, Holding five for 17, Daniel two for

No allowances for the England tail – Underwood just manages to avoid a Holding bouncer.

13. Only against Australia had England ever failed to reach 100 in an innings. Yet not even against Lillee, Thomson and Walker in the winter of 1974-75 were England so humbled. Relentless fast bowling on a wicket of uneven bounce gave the West Indians a riotous time.

It was no good blaming the pitch entirely. Fredericks got a half-century in the second innings and Gordon Greenidge is once again sailing towards a century with 71 not out.

## WEST INDIES ONE-UP: TWO TO PLAY
### WEEK ENDED JULY 17

WE are passing through the most unusual spell of dry weather but the fields are no more arid than our reservoir of British cricket talent. Everyone shouts "rebuild" to the selectors. Yet where is the straw to rebuild the shambling edifice? England reached the final day of the Manchester Test requiring rain, or the little matter of 427 by the last two batsmen, Selvey and Hendrick. They put on one run, and after 12 minutes, 20 balls, England were one-down in the series. West Indies had won by 425 runs.

In the Gillette Cup second-round tie, Essex, top of the table, were beaten by Hertfordshire at Hitchin. Keith Fletcher, honourably, did not complain about the pitch, though one witness, to whom I talked on the telephone, believed that Essex had much the worst of the conditions. Be that as it may, congratulations are due to Herts. R. L. Johns, an Oxford Blue of 1970 and an off-spinner, took four for 31. Doshi, the promising Indian left-arm spinner, won the Man of the Match award with four for 23.

*To Robin Johns this may well have been a personal highspot in his career in Minor County cricket. But Doshi was to move on to a Test debut in 1979 and in his first season for Warwickshire, the following summer, he was one of only two bowlers to take more than 100 wickets (Robin Jackman was the other).*

The man of the week, however, must be Gordon Greenidge, who on Saturday became only the second man in the England-West Indies Test series to score two centuries in one match. George Headley did it twice. No England player has done it.

## KENT'S BENSON & HEDGES CUP
### WEEK ENDED JULY 24

A strange week. I do not have to write any longer that the sun shone; or that not a drop of rain fell. Basil D'Oliveira limped out to bat in the Benson & Hedges Cup final with a Falstaffian optimism about his ample frame. He had decided, as he could hardly walk because of a leg injury, to swing rapid blows with the bat and let his runner, Glenn Turner, sort out the rest. Worcestershire were well adrift of Kent's 236 for seven, but he gave them spirit and helped them go down with belligerence, as he clobbered a half-century. The crowd loved his brilliant improvisations.

It was Kent's cup and Graham Johnson was awarded the Gold Award for his 78 runs and three catches down at long leg.

The England selectors chose new caps, and new opening bats. I can't see the sense in that. Woolmer and Steele will now open and Balderstone and Willey are in the side, which has Ward, Snow and Willis to bowl fast. Hendrick and Selvey are dropped, Old is injured,

Edrich and Close are left out too, probably for ever.

The ICC, meeting at Lord's for two days, decreed that the next World Cup will be in England in 1979, and that bouncers must not be bowled against non-recognised batsmen. I suppose once a tailender has scored 30 the umpire holds up a white card which gives the bowler the right to let him have one!

Geoff Boycott is back in the Yorkshire side after a long recuperation from a broken hand. His back has been extremely painful too.

The Headingley Test is a sanctuary from the never-ending television reports from the Olympics, the most sizable bore as far as I am concerned. West Indies stroked a superb 450, Fredericks 109 and that man Greenidge again, 115. Tony Greig (fingers crossed) is 89 not out. I am glad for the captain, sad for David Steele, who failed as an opener. The wicket is perfect; surely we can hold out in this one, but win it? . . . And whose army?

## GREIG AND KNOTT — AND WILLEY AND WILLIS
### WEEK ENDED JULY 31

A dejected but undefeated Tony Greig leaves the field as Deryck Murray celebrates the West Indian win.

WEST Indies have won the rubber. They went two-up with a decisive victory at Headingley by 55 runs. Tony Greig got his hundred, but so did Alan Knott, who one thought would never get double-figures again! They played really well, nothing attributed to luck. Greig stood up high and handsome and played his full range of belligerent shots.

In the second innings he was left alone, 76 not out. No-one could stay long enough to help him win the match. Bob Willis gave rise to hope with five for 42 in the second innings, Snow four for 77 in the first. Also, Peter Willey's 45 gave him a confident start in Tests.

England scrambled out of another kind of Test at The Oval. The Australian Women were just about to have the audacity to beat us in our own country and take away the St Ivel Trophy when Rachael Flint dropped anchor and scored 179 to save the game. Next week the women play their first-ever match at Lord's.

The batsman of the moment is Zaheer Abbas. "Z", as he is known to all Gloucestershire, scored his seventh century of the season, and on his 29th birthday too.

I watched him this week at Cheltenham. The game

before, at The Oval, he had scored 177. His cover-driving is dazzling. Glamorgan bowled tidily but they could not contain him in the first innings. He got 78. Then when Glamorgan bowled poorly in the second he took 50 off them. His great art is to hit the fairly straight ball which is well up through cover. I suppose he plays slightly inside the line. Whatever the method, he is almost impossible to restrain in this form.

Another international player who has been comfortably restrained so far is Eddie Barlow. The South African was hired at a reputedly high cost to rescue Derbyshire. Bob Taylor gave up the captaincy in favour of Barlow mid-season. Eddie has found form elusive but this week hit a career-best 217 against Surrey. It seems to have been that sort of a week for the lads from The Oval.

Majid Khan has resigned the Glamorgan captaincy. There is clearly trouble in the camp there. Alan Jones has taken over for the remainder of the season.

The England Young Cricketers tour is under way in the West Indies. The boys are managed by former Sussex and England player Hubert Doggart, and coached by Les Lenham, a former Sussex player and NCA regional coach.

## GILLETTE TIME AGAIN
### WEEK ENDED AUGUST 7

THE West Indians lost their first match on tour, though they were judged by the critics to have collapsed rather spiritlessly to Middlesex. More important for Middlesex they are top of the Championship table. It reads: Middlesex 156 points; Hampshire 137; Essex 136; Northants 133; Leicester, the holders making a late run, 132; Warwicks 131; Gloucester 131. There is obviously a spectacular finish in prospect.

A sadness. Chris Aworth, a batsman of much promise, is to leave cricket and pursue a business career. At Cambridge he was one of the outstanding players and his promise has been confirmed in Surrey colours. He is 23 years old and his predicament highlights the decisions young men have to make. Is the presence of overseas players, and their accessibility for the right money, stifling the enthusiasm of our young hopefuls? Surrey do not have a good record for holding

August 4th – Ladies' day at Lord's.

on to their Oxbridge men if the example of Aworth, Roger Knight, Dudley Owen-Thomas and Mike Selvey is a proper guide. I always thought that Michael Hooper, a Carthusian, was far too good a player to leave the game. He was on Surrey's staff for a while. He is now working in the City.

## LLOYD'S TWO-HOUR MURDER
### *WEEK ENDED AUGUST 14*

WE are now in drought conditions, reservoirs are dried up and water is rationed in many parts of the country. Watering of gardens is forbidden. Cricket pitches have just about retained their green, but the outfields are light brown, fast and uneven. Some wickets pour out runs; others break up and spin.

You simply cannot keep the West Indians quiet in these circumstances, which are very like their own at home. On Monday I witnessed the mutilation of the Glamorgan attack by Clive Lloyd. He scored 201 not out, which, by coincidence, was his score against my old county on the tour of 1966. This time however he nudged an existing world record for fast scoring. His double-century came up in 120 minutes, which equalled the time set by Gilbert Jessop for Gloucestershire v Sussex at Hove in 1903.

There was poor news also at Swansea. Majid Khan, my friend and former team-mate, informed Glamorgan that he will never play again for them. A short while ago he resigned the captaincy because of "administrative interference". My immediate reaction is that Glamorgan will be best served by a revolution! There should be no way that a man as talented, as honest and as loyal to the "daffodil" as Majid should be forced out of the game.

Test match time. West Indies win the toss and by Friday night they have scored no less than 687 for eight declared. Bob Woolmer and the recalled Dennis Amiss have survived the initial attack. Amiss is on 22, Woolmer 6.

The innings to remember was by that man again, Viv Richards. He scored 291, taking his aggregate for the series to 829, with an average of 118. I was amazed by the machine-like quality of his batting. He just never looked likely to get out. Yet he played all the extravagant and flamboyant shots for which West Indies have won their fame. Anything this ordinary England attack pitched on the stumps he smashed through mid-wicket; anything outside he sent skimming through the covers. He hit Willis, the fast man, over extra-cover for four, and went down the wicket to Underwood with a total commitment to the most savage drive. An unforgettable concoction of method and magic.

Middlesex continue their charge for the top of the County Championship table. They beat Derbyshire at Lord's, Fred Titmus taking six for 72. Then to end the week they beat Essex, one of their pursuers, by 36 runs at Chelmsford. Barlow and Radley are scoring lots of runs.

## LAURELS FOR AMISS AND HOLDING
### *WEEK ENDED AUGUST 21*

THE selectors have taken a fair amount of criticism. Let us offer congratulations. They chose Dennis

Amiss for the Fifth Test, at The Oval, knowing that they were putting on him the pressure of a career ended or reborn. They knew too the fear that has sent his body rigid when fast bowlers have bounced the ball at him; how he has ducked away from the ball without looking at it; how Michael Holding hit his head and cut it open in the MCC match at Lord's.

Yet Dennis succeeded. Not only did he look more comfortable, albeit on a remarkably slow pitch, but he scored a double-century. His strokeplay was memorable, but more than that, his courage from the time he went to bed in the "condemned cell" in his London hotel room on the eve of the match was demonstrated to the whole cricketing world.

He has evolved a new technique, the result of begging advice from many former players. He almost leaps back and across to off stump. He is therefore in a ducking position, or alternatively he can stand up and play the ball from where he is deep in the crease. This was the most precious of all his Test innings. He should now have a safe passage to India.

Lest he be forgotten in the praise for the return of the wounded warrior, it should be said that Michael Holding achieved the most amazing bowling figures imaginable on such a peaceful wicket, eight for 92 and six for 57.

England were routed. West Indies won the series three-nil and quite frankly possessed too many good players for us. Even without spin, England were outplayed. There must now be a policy of team-building, young players mixed with the more experienced for the tour to India this winter.

*Two more summer series and the Caribbean tour of 1980–81 have passed but still no Test match victory against the West Indies. The last win was at Port of Spain at the end of Mike Denness's tour of 1974.*

## CHAMPIONSHIP HYSTERIA
### WEEK ENDED AUGUST 28

WOULD it surprise you to know that it still refuses to rain? No, I suppose it would not. It has become a national concern, however, even though cricket marches on uninterrupted. The wickets are dry and most are turning by the second day.

This does not perturb those at Lord's who are cheering Middlesex on to a likely Championship, nor those rooting for Northants, Gloucestershire, or Leicestershire. By Wednesday some matters were much clearer. Middlesex, Leicestershire and Northants all won, which rather left behind Gloucestershire, who had been playing against the West Indians.

Scarborough beat Dulwich in the clubs' final at Lord's. I am not sure whether or not it is an indictment against English cricket, but the Man of the Match was nominated as George Murray, an Australian who is into his fifties and who is over in this country studying our systems and philosophies of education. He must wonder where have all the players gone? Just to emphasise the point, the Dulwich side contained five Australians, two West Indians and a Pakistani! At least Scarborough, whose side we may guess was made up of Yorkshiremen, won the title.

## RAIN-PRAYERS ANSWERED
### WEEK ENDED SEPTEMBER 4

RUNS from Zaheer have become commonplace, though always bewitching; victories by West Indies, three in a row, in the Prudential one-day internationals, were expected; dazzling runs yet again from the bat of Viv Richards would have been a predictable conclusion, and one felt that eventually the violent instincts of Gordon Greenidge were bound to ignite the fastest hundred of the season. And so these things occurred to our great delight, but a popular, rare feat came to pass which few would have anticipated when the year began – Middlesex won their first outright County Championship since 1947.

It was in the home of the old enemy, Surrey, that the final five points came which made the title certain. A sparkling innings of 61 by Graham Barlow gave them the impetus in the last act. Middlesex had perfect balance, a credit to their cricket committee. Even so, many played above themselves.

Barlow rose in one season from a county hopeful to a possible Test player. Allan Jones, the fast bowler who left Somerset, found new heart at headquarters. Lamb produced figures that promised more in his courage than in his bowling action. Mike Selvey learned new tricks, developing a useful inswinger as well as the one

Three promising young cricketers, Chris Tavaré (top), David Gower (centre) and Ian Botham.

which runs away from the bat, all from a full length. Sheer volume of wickets and match-winning figures got him an England place. They say that Phil Edmonds did not improve this season, though I saw him bowl only once. So the support for Titmus forthcoming from "Smokey" Featherstone with his off-spinners was of maximum importance on dry wickets. The close fielding was excellent, the batting start solid, with Mike Brearley, Mike Smith and Clive Radley experienced enough to weather most storms.

The wicketkeeping was a problem in that young Gould went off to West Indies with the England Young Cricketers; so did Gatting. Gould's replacement behind the stumps kept on getting injured until Michael Sturt was extricated from his employment outside the game to take over. He was J. T. Murray's deputy for some time in the Sixties. He did superbly. Immaculately dressed, neat and stylish, he had the audacity to stump people out – almost unheard of in modern cricket!

Most important of all, Mike Brearley's captaincy was accepted by other counties as being fair and reasonable. Everyone was inclined to play cricket with Middlesex. There were no grudge, drawn games as there were against the club in the late Fifties and early Sixties. Indeed, Geoff Boycott, having explained very properly that Yorkshire were likely to be up there with a chance had not he, Chris Old and John Hampshire been struck down with injuries, confessed that Middlesex deserved to win because they made their own luck.

Talk about winning: England Young Cricketers beat West Indies in their Test at Port of Spain. Thanks were due to Agatha Christie Ltd for their sponsorship. Specks of hope appear at the end of the tunnel!

The England Young Cricketers to tour the West Indies. Back, left to right: I.M. Wilks (Surrey), A.L. Jones (Glamorgan), N.J. Kemp (Kent), M.K. Fosh (Essex), P.J.W. Allott (Cheshire), S.J. Still (Sussex), D.J. Munden (Leicestershire), I.J. Gould (Middlesex), A.S. Patel (Middlesex). Front: G.H.S. Doggart (Sussex, manager), D.I. Gower (Leicestershire), M.W. Gatting (Middlesex), C.S. Cowdrey (Kent, captain), P.R. Downton (Kent, vice-captain), R.G. Williams (Northamptonshire), C.W.J. Athey (Yorkshire), L.J. Lenham (Sussex, assistant manager and coach).

## NORTHANTS DO IT
### JOURNAL END

SO it all ends, 1976, leaving me with the impression that cricket is more popular a spectator sport now than it has been since the immediate post-war years. The Oval was sold out for the final Test even though West Indies had settled the series at Headingley. There are signs of young cricketers – Gatting, Gould, Tavaré, Parker, Gower, Athey, Botham, Randall, Barlow and more.

I was happy, like everyone else, bar Lancastrians, to see Northants win the Gillette Cup, the first touch of success for 98 years. Theirs is a tough assignment, to keep the game alive and well in a sparsely populated county. Much credit to Ken Turner, their secretary, to Mushtaq also, and to Roy Virgin, who settled down to playing hard for the captain who replaced him.

On the flimsy basis that underdogs deserve to win more than others, then it was a sadness to see the John Player title snatched from Somerset on the last ball of their season. At Cardiff, they required three to tie and four to win off the last ball. Dredge was run out on the third (a tie would have still won them the title) and the cup went to Maidstone, where Kent beat Gloucestershire, Asif scoring a brilliant 106. Sussex were in the hunt too at Edgbaston but they lost.

The MCC team for India is announced. Tony Greig is captain but goes very much on trial as a leader. Ken Barrington is manager, and Mike Brearley is the vice-captain. David Steele is left out and so, unluckily, is Peter Willey. The others included are – Amiss, Fletcher, Knott, Barlow, Randall, Cope, John Lever, Miller, Old, Selvey, Roger Tolchard, Underwood, Willis and Woolmer.

It looks to be a proper balance of youth and experience. I am glad that Keith Fletcher is going, and I concede little to the many opponents to his selection.

I think Geoff Cope, on an individual level, would agree that many fine things can come from mournful situations. He has suffered the private agaonies of an action going wrong. Eventually, with the aid of former Yorkshire bowlers like Johnny Wardle, he straightened the offending arm and still found enough skill in the fingers to get spin, and enough understanding of the game to blend in his flight. This summer he was at his

126

best. His action was filmed and found to be perfectly good. Now he has been chosen for his first national honour, a tour to India with MCC. That is the sort of success story that makes one long for next season.

## FINAL COUNTY CHAMPIONSHIP TABLE

1975 positions in brackets.

| | P | W | L | D | Bt | Bw | Pts |
|---|---|---|---|---|---|---|---|
| 1 Middlesex (11) | 20 | 11 | 5 | 4 | 57 | 67 | 234 |
| 2 Northamptonshire (8) | 20 | 9 | 3 | 8 | 54 | 74 | 218 |
| 3 Gloucestershire (16) | 20 | 9 | 5 | 6 | 54 | 66 | 210 |
| 4 Leicestershire (1) | 20 | 9 | 3 | 8 | 51 | 68 | 209 |
| 5 Warwickshire (14) | 20 | 6 | 7 | 7 | 65 | 70 | 195 |
| 6 Essex (7) | 20 | 7 | 4 | 9 | 57 | 62 | 189 |
| 7 Somerset (12) | 20 | 7 | 8 | 5 | 47 | 63 | 180 |
| 8 Yorkshire (2) | 20 | 6 | 6 | 8 | 49 | 67 | 176 |
| 9 Surrey (6) | 20 | 6 | 4 | 10 | 54 | 61 | 175 |
| 10 Sussex (17) | 20 | 5 | 8 | 7 | 49 | 71 | 170 |
| 11 Worcestershire (10) | 20 | 6 | 3 | 11 | 50 | 59 | 169 |
| 12 Hampshire (3) | 20 | 4 | 10 | 6 | 52 | 67 | 159 |
| 13 Nottinghamshire (13) | 20 | 4 | 7 | 9 | 58 | 60 | 158 |
| 14 Kent (5) | 20 | 5 | 7 | 8 | 48 | 57 | 155 |
| 15 Derbyshire (15) | 20 | 4 | 7 | 9 | 39 | 70 | 149 |
| 16 Lancashire (4) | 20 | 3 | 7 | 10 | 43 | 75 | 148 |
| 17 Glamorgan (9) | 20 | 3 | 10 | 7 | 37 | 60 | 127 |

*Thrashed at home by the West Indies, well beaten the season before by Australia and without a win in a series overseas for six years, England were not expected by many to come home with the bacon from India. They had not beaten India, indeed, on their own soil in any of the four previous rubbers played there since the inaugural tour under Douglas Jardine over 40 years before. But, under the prophet Tony, deliverance was at hand.*

*Tony Greig began the tour with a growing reputation, but with no great success as a captain. He finished it a hero in his adopted country. Yet during the last few days of the long journey across the world, he began sowing the seeds which brought him a personal fortune but which tarnished his shining image for ever.*

*In India, Greig was cunning, charming, inspirational and brave, the master of all situations from the moment that he beamed his first smile at the hordes waiting at the airport to meet the team before dawn on a warm and smelly Bombay morning. With him Greig had in Ken Barrington a manager whom everyone liked and respected and for whom nothing was too much trouble. He also had shrewd tactical advice from Keith Fletcher and, making his first overseas tour in a senior role, Mike Brearley. His team was well balanced, both in its range of abilities and in its mixture of canny experience and youthful zeal. Nor were India, who had no fast bowler of any worth and an uncertain batting side, the most*

*fearsome of opponents. With Viswanath badly out of form, the batting relied heavily on Sunil Gavaskar, who did not have one of his happier series (though he was, inevitably, the leading run-scorer) and the bowling was almost entirely in the hands of the three great spinners, Chandrasekhar, Bedi and Prasanna, who were by now very well known to most of the MCC team.*

*England put their faith in seam, swing and pace. Bob Willis had never bowled faster overseas; John Lever enjoyed a triumphant first tour, with ten wickets and a fifty in his first Test at Delhi; Chris Old was always contributing usefully and managed, unusually, to be fit for four of the five Tests, and Greig himself, usually bowling off-spin, took 10 wickets to add to his 336 runs in a low-scoring series. His trump-card, however, was Derek Underwood who never bowled better overseas than he did on this tour. Not only was he brilliantly accurate, but also more confident than sometimes in the past and therefore more prepared to vary his pace and trajectory. He took 29 Test wickets at 17 each.*

*Dennis Amiss had another admirably consistent series with the bat, and not the least heartening aspect of a very happy tour was the fielding. Greig, Brearley, Fletcher, Old and Willis were all brilliant at times close to the wicket, and in the covers the fullest use was made of the wonderful speed, agility and enthusiasm of Randall and Barlow, whenever they were on the field. With Alan Knott at his brilliant best behind the stumps, England were a hard combination from whom to take the initiative. It was hardly to be expected that, even after a convincing three-one win in the series (heavy wins too, by an innings, 10 wickets and 200 runs) Greig's side could adapt quickly enough to defeat Australia in the Centenary Test match at Melbourne at the end of the tour, but in fact they contributed fully to an unforgettable occasion, bowling Australia out cheaply on a damp pitch at the start of the match and then, when faced with ignominious defeat, being baled out by Derek Randall's famous innings of 174.*

*The senior members of the Australian Cricket Board, understandably preening themselves after the immense success of a superbly organised and staged cricket match, were blithely unaware of the mighty storm which was about to break about their heads, shattering, as completely as the 1914-18 war had changed the world, the established order of all cricketing things.*

# ✦ 1977 ✦

## DAMP AND CHILLY, SUNNY AND CHILLY
### WEEK ENDED APRIL 29

I HAVE a heavy cold. I always start the cricket season with a cold. Is it the weather, or is it all in the mind? I must remember the precept of P. J. K. Gibbs: "Ne'er chance a clout till June be out, and even then not before lunch." Not one of the first batch of Benson & Hedges Cup matches was finished on the Saturday. I have had two damp, chilly days in The Parks, the second almost a complete washout, and one sunny, chilly day at Arundel. The warmest place my duties have taken me so far has been to the Waldorf Hotel, where the Australians held their opening Press conference.

Arrival of the Australians. Jeff Thomson, David Hookes and Greg Chappell about to join Max Walker on the team coach.

The Australians won by 20 runs at Arundel, against Lavinia, Duchess of Norfolk's XI, with more than three overs to spare (it was a 45-overs match). Not a significant one, though it was a modest encouragement that England's younger batsmen did better than the veterans. Even so, I thought M. J. K. Smith was going to win the match, until he was out to a fine, diving catch by Malone at point.

## TWO NOTABLE INNINGS
### WEEK ENDED MAY 6

A NOTHER dismal week, sniffing and sneezing in the rain. I saw two notable innings at Taunton by Vivian Richards, one in the Sunday League, and one in the Championship match against Glamorgan. He was out in the second to a memorable catch by Llewellyn at backward square leg, one that Milton (Arthur, I mean, not the poet John) would have been proud to hold. There were those who felt that Richards had thrown his wicket away, at a time when Somerset still needed some runs, by taking an unnecessary risk, but catches like that are acts of God rather than man. Besides, it is the way he takes the occasional risk which makes Richards so compelling to watch. And additionally and alternatively, as the lawyers say, he does not take so many risks as a casual glance might suggest. His bat sometimes wanders from the classical line, but not his eyes. Maurice Tate thought that Bradman would never score many runs in England unless he kept his bat straighter. Hm.

## IN AFFECTIONATE REMEMBRANCE
### WEEK ENDED MAY 13

I AM not going to try to assess the consequences of the Greig/Packer affair, partly because I know no more than I read in the papers, and partly because by the time these words appears in print, long and learned and up-to-the-minute reports will be published on the adjoining pages. I would just like to risk a couple of points, sitting here at The Oval, waiting without much hope for Surrey and Essex to resume play, and with precious little else to write about. The first is that I expect the experiment will be a successful one, whatever attitude the cricketing authorities take. The second is that Greig's reputation, as a captain of England, has been destroyed. I deplore the whole thing, but I expect that the people (Australian journalists, I understand) who put an obituary notice in *The Times* "in affectionate remembrance of international cricket, which died at Hove" may have got it right. If you are laughing at these comments in the autumn I shall be only too pleased.

In the Benson & Hedges Cup, all the leaders won again, except Sussex, who were not playing. The weather mucked about with most of the matches. Gloucestershire, Glamorgan and Middlesex must be almost sure of a place in the knockout stages.

## SOMERSET TOPPLE AUSTRALIANS
### WEEK ENDED MAY 20

THIS has been the first proper week of the season, the weather positively warm towards the end. Yesterday I watched without my overcoat, though still keeping it handy. Everyone has been looking much more cheerful, except possibly the Australians. Their first day at Swansea was washed out, but Glamorgan still came near to beating them in the next two. There was some disappointment among Welshmen that the Australians held on in the last hour, but not very much, because Glamorgan have beaten them twice since the war. There was a good deal more excitement at Bath, where the Australians lost, the first time they have ever been beaten by Somerset. Chappell scored a century (99 of them before lunch) against his old colleagues, and Hookes scored a century in the second innings, but they were outplayed. Somerset might have missed their chance (they did not have all that much time to spare at the end) by failing to press sufficiently hard on the second evening. The third-day gate, and the arc of sponsors' tents, may have had something to do with that.

It would be a mistake, though, to infer from the evidence so far that the Australians are a weak side. Some of their strongest sides – for example those of 1902 and 1909 – have made disastrous starts to the season in damp Mays.

Somerset have a lot of young talent, much of it home-grown, or at least home-nursed: Rose, Denning, Botham, Slocombe, with Marks, Roebuck and Gurr in the background. Botham is already near the England side, still rather an erratic player, but a true all-rounder. Marks, now in his second year as Oxford captain, will surely be a Somerset captain one day if he decides to devote his time to the game. They have all come to the front under the captaincy of Close, who has been criticised in the past for showing insufficient sympathy towards youth. Has anyone, even Kent, got a potentially stronger hand of young men?

## A LOST OVERCOAT
### WEEK ENDED MAY 27

I WRITE just returned from Ilford, a ground I knew as a boy. You could walk round it in those days. Now it is impossible, unless you are prepared to clamber over awkward fences and slink through sponsors' enclosures. But I still like the Ilford ground. I met several members of the Poet's and Peasants' CC, an organisation of which I have the honour to be Poet, though I have not quite managed to write the Annual Poem yet. I did make a start today:

> Hail, cricket! glorious, manly, British game!
> Thou art no better; thou art much the same

– a touch plagiaristic, I fear. However, I lost my overcoat, temporarily, which shows that the weather is improving. Essex won in two days, against Nottinghamshire. I thought East bowled very well. If Underwood is going to debar himself from England sides, I think East has as strong a claim to replace him as Edmonds.

The Australians were in trouble again on the first day against Gloucestershire, but bucked up and won the match in two, with handsome assistance from the Gloucestershire batsmen, who threw their wickets away on the second evening. However, it was a win for the Australians and now they have beaten MCC at Lord's,

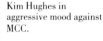
Kim Hughes in aggressive mood against MCC.

Geoff Miller – all-round potential.

without suggesting that their new batsmen have come quite to terms with current English pitches. Of the English prospects (assuming that Randall has passed from the prospective to the assured stage, at least for the time being) Botham, Barlow and Miller did themselves a bit of good. Miller is the one about whom I have most doubts, almost certainly because I have not had much luck with him. This matter of being "lucky" with a batsman is bound to affect one's judgment. I remember I was always shocked when Willie Watson was not chosen for England, because every time I saw him he seemed to make a pile of runs. I probably underestimate Brearley as a batsman because there have been few times when his best innings have coincided with my presence. All the same he is the obvious, almost the only, choice to captain England in the first Test, as his selection as captain of MCC implies.

# ENGLAND'S PRUDENTIAL VICTORY
### WEEK ENDED JUNE 3

THE Prudential trophy matches have begun, and England have won the first. The name of Packer still reverberates around the grounds, but not until the emergency meeting of the ICC in the middle of the month will we learn much more, and probably not then. In the meantime Greig is playing for England under Brearley's captaincy. This was only to be expected. He clearly had disqualified himself from continuing as captain, but unless and until his arrangements with Packer cause him actually to decline an invitation to play for England there is no reason not to consider him on his merits as a player. Some people have suggested that he is not really good enough as a player, pointing to his poor first-class figures last season, but his Test record confutes them. There is much talk of the possible return of Boycott to Test cricket, and a clear statement, that he was willing to be considered irrespective of who is captain, would make this possible. Not that his return would be universally welcomed. Noboby doubts his genuine dedication to Yorkshire, but unfortunately he *was* out of the way when the fast bowling was at its fiercest, and some of those who took the blows instead do not forget it.

Warwickshire beat Northants, their first win of the season. They looked a strong side, even without some of their famous West Indians. Northamptonshire did not have a happy match, and probably regretted winning the toss. Brown, the Warwickshire captain, is still a more than useful cricketer. Then to Worcester, where Lancashire were beaten early on the third day. The Lancashire captain complained about the pitch, and

Mike Brearley and Tony Greig at Old Trafford.

Bernard Flack was summoned to have a look at it. Certainly it was not a good one, especially for Worcester. Bradman would have been taxed to make one of his customary double-hundreds on it.

The early finish enabled me to pick up the last day's play at Taunton, though there too it was over by four o'clock. Warwickshire had to make 229 and never looked like it once Kanhai and Humpage were out. This was one of the matches played with Kookaburra balls (each county has to play two) a subject on which Brian Close expressed himself briefly and forcefully.

# WHOLEHEARTED PROCTER
### WEEK ENDED JUNE 10

THE Benson & Hedges semi-finalists are Gloucestershire, Hampshire, Kent and Northants. I saw Gloucestershire beat Middlesex by 18 runs, after they had seemed to be on the wrong end of it for most of the day. The final tilt was given by Procter, who seemed to be bowling nearly as fast as he did in his prime. I only hope his knee, and sundry other parts of his anatomy, stand up to the strain. Procter differs from many overseas players in English cricket, in the wholeheartedness with which he identifies himself with his adopted county; an unflagging trier. If, in the old anology, I had to choose a side to play for my life, I would ask him to captain it, and if he declined I would count myself a dead man.

The hero of the quarter-finals, however, was Christopher Cowdrey, who in the presence of his father scored a century against Sussex at Canterbury. The Sage of Longparish records that Colin said to him in the morning, "Let us go and have a strong drink; they've got Christopher going in first. He wanted to do it, mind you, but it's asking quite a lot." Christopher is 19 years old, and it was his sixth innings for Kent. Against a Sussex score of 264, nearly always enough to win a 55-overs match, Kent lost three for 111, but Cowdrey and Ealham put on 146 in 20 overs. Cowdrey was out only when the match was almost won.

Earlier in the week I watched Middlesex beat Sussex, their chief danger the weather rather than the opposition. Middlesex looked a good side, even without Brearley and Barlow, and their 20 points took them to the top of the Schweppes Championship table, just

| County Championship (as at June 3) | | |
|---|---|---|
| | P | Pts |
| **1** Yorkshire | 6 | 66 |
| **2** Kent | 4 | 56 |
| **3** Middlesex | 5 | 48 |
| **4** Gloucestershire | 4 | 45 |

Dennis Amiss – a century in England's one-day win.

above Yorkshire, who had the worst of what play was possible in the Roses match. Brearley played a useful innings in the third of the Prudential internationals, which was apparently played in pouring rain, and has been confirmed in his captaincy of England, at least for the first two Tests.

## NEARLY A "STICKY" AT GLOUCESTER
### WEEK ENDED JUNE 17

I SAW the latter part of the Australian match at Chelmsford. The prospects seemed so grim that I rang up from London, expecting to turn round and go home again, and I was a little sceptical when told that they were hoping to make a start at two o'clock: but when I got there, the sun was shining really warmly. The match was a destined draw, but the Australians played some attractive strokes, and it was pleasant to see bare backs and summer frocks instead of overcoats and umbrellas.

Then to drenched Gloucester: no play on Wednesday, but a start on Thursday, and a win over Leicestershire in two days, by eight wickets, after Leicestershire had won the toss. The pitch on the first afternoon was for a while as near a "sticky" as we often see nowadays. *Autres temps, autres moeurs,* but I do really think Goddard and Parker would have had almost any side out, in the conditions, in a couple of hours. As it was, Leicestershire struggled to 225 for eight and declared; but in their second innings, when the fast bowlers did the damage, they were all out for 49. Zaheer and Brain made important contributions, but it was a captain's match if ever there was one, destructive bowling allied to a masterful innings by Procter. I was pleased to see Shuttleworth taking wickets again. It is through ill-luck, not lack of talent, that he has never lived up to his worthy tour of Australia under Illingworth. And of course it was good to see Illingworth himself again, worth all the other spinners in the match put together.

Ken Shuttleworth in his first season for Leicestershire.

## PACKER VIS-A-VIS ICC
### WEEK ENDED JUNE 24

THE First Test was a good game on the whole, a draw always likely after the weather weighed in. Brearley

made a competent start. John Woodcock summed it up by saying that Australia had the better of the match, yet it was England who were closer to victory at the end. Boycott has informed Bedser that he is willing to play for England, irrespective of who is captain. A loud snort of "Big of him!" echoes round at least the southern counties. All the same, it would be tactless, to say the least, to make him captain, even if Brearley does not establish himself. He ought to work his passage – which does not just mean scoring runs – before any such idea is considered.

Packer and the ICC have not reached agreement, to put it mildly. There was no joint communiqué, which even the Commonwealth Prime Ministers managed. ICC have, however, succeeded in demonstrating that this is really a row about television rights.

There were two very close Benson & Hedges semi-finals, won by Gloucestershire and Kent. Gloucestershire got through because of Procter's bowling – six for 13, including the hat-trick. Especially remembering that knee, I would call it staggering, though in another sense that was precisely what it was not. He was everybody's Player of the Week (and practically everybody now seems to select one). The Gibson award for Umpire of the Week (prize only a pint, and the honour and glory) went to Jack Fingleton, who took over in that capacity in an emergency. I suggested to him that he has a secret contract as umpire for Packer, and was getting in a little practice.

The Universities held the Australians to a draw in a two-day match, and Marks's declaration (six an over), while you could not call it an inviting one, was, given all the circumstances, understandable. They have plenty of good players at present, who could do well in county cricket if so inclined. Wingfield Digby, moving in a mysterious way as usual, took some wickets.

## JOLLY OVAL CROWD
### WEEK ENDED JULY 1

THE University match has been drawn, but seems to have been played with spirit on both sides. Oxford made a good chase in the last innings, but as soon as I read in the stop-press that Wingfield Digby was run out, I knew that the higher powers had deserted us. I had to spend the early part of the week at home, with some

John Edrich – looking for runs.

tiresome infection of the eyes, but saw a good match between Surrey and Warwickshire at The Oval, won by Surrey with just seven balls to spare. In the first innings it looked as though Edrich might get his 100th hundred, but he will have to wait a little longer. Surrey's supporters were as boisterous in their praise of their side, on the last day, as they had been severe in their condemnation on the first. Only Lancashire supporters, in my experience, share this trait to the same extent.

But I like the Oval crowd: a jolly, mixed lot they are. For one thing, it seems to be only around the Elephant & Castle that you can still hear the fine Old Cockney affirmative, "Ho, yus." In the rest of London, and for that matter in most of the country, from the Conservative Ladies' coffee morning to the public bar, it has become "Uh yuh."

It is time I said a word about the John Player League, now halfway through its course, approximately. Leicestershire, seven wins out of eight, are the leaders. Their bowlers grow older but accuracy and experience can compensate for age over eight overs. Essex and Sussex have won six matches. Yorkshire have won one (this pleases me, as I like to see Yorkshire concentrating on better things), Worcestershire one, and Northamptonshire, which is odd even in this odd sort of cricket, none at all.

## TOURISTS AT LORD'S
### WEEK ENDED JULY 8

I WATCHED cricket during the week at Taunton, Lord's, and Maidstone. I say "watched", but there were times when I saw precious little of it, because of this eye trouble. The high pollen count? New glasses needed? Or something nasty in the woodshed? The medical men do not seem quite sure. The prospects for a blind cricket-writer must be limited. One old friend kindly said that it could hardly make much difference, since I never wrote about the cricket anyway. Another, a player, suggested I took up umpiring. Anyway, it quite spoilt my visit to the pretty Mote ground, my first for many years.

Lord's on Sunday was full of tourists, taking a look at this curious English pastime. Some of their couriers seemed to have been inadequately briefed. I heard, for instance, a good deal about "the referees" (though when you come to think of it there is nothing sacrosanct about the term "umpire"). Leicestershire were beaten by Middlesex, but stay narrowly at the top of the Sunday League. Middlesex stayed at the top of the Schweppes Championship after their win over Notts. They had to overcome stubborn resistance from White, playing against his former colleagues. Kent were close behind them, but took only three points at Maidstone against Surrey. Now Gloucestershire, for whom Procter continues to be in marvellous bowling form, have climbed into second place. I was impressed by the play of Downton, who looks as if he will become another in the line of distinguished Kent wicketkeeper-batsmen.

*It was only after his move to Middlesex that Downton really established himself as a useful contributor with the bat and although he toured the West Indies in 1980–81 it was not until 1984 that he took over from Bob Taylor as England's first-choice wicket-keeper.*

England chose an unchanged side for the Second Test, and seem to have made a useful start. Boycott, against the Australians at Scarborough, made nought in the first innings, and a century in the second. There is a general feeling that he will have to come back soon. After all, if you continue to play men who have thrown in their hopes with Mr Packer, what case is there for excluding someone who, whatever his reasons, has not?

## EDRICH DOES IT
### WEEK ENDED JULY 15

JOHN Edrich has reached his 100th hundred, after missing it narrowly several times earlier in the season. He is the 17th cricketer to do so. The next will no doubt be Boycott, who has just reached his 97th.

*Interesting to note that John Edrich's 100th century was accumulated in much the same way as so many of his runs – in businesslike style with very little beating of the drum. How different from Geoff Boycott's Headingley performance in front of a television audience of millions.*

Edrich has never been such an eye-catching batsman as cousin Bill (who scored 86, despite losing six years to the war), but more consistent, especially at the highest

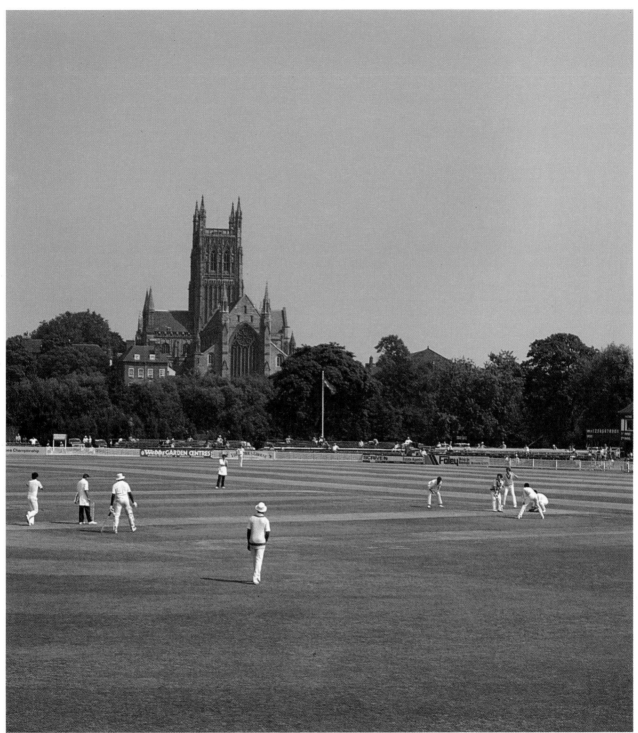

**Worcester**
Worcestershire v.
Lancashire,
County Championship,
August 1983.

Hastings
Sussex v. Lancashire,
County Championship,
June 1985.

**Milton Keynes**
Northamptonshire v.
West Indies, June 1984.

**Swansea**
Glamorgan v.
Nottinghamshire,
May 1980.

Tunbridge Wells
India v. Zimbabwe,
World Cup, June 1983.

level. His record against Australia bears study.

England had a very satisfactory win in the Test. The Packer arguments rumble on. In the Schweppes Championship, Middlesex lead Somerset and Gloucestershire. I wonder when last Somerset and Gloucester simultaneously occupied such exalted positions. Theoretically, Gloucester are the best-placed, but games in hand are often illusory benefits, especially in so uncertain a summer.

England lose their fourth wicket at 325. Bob Woolmer is caught by Ian Davis off Kerry O'Keefe for 137, his second successive century in the series.

I saw Middlesex at Southend, where they failed to beat Essex, despite a long lead on the first innings. A century by Fletcher thwarted them. They chose to bat on for as long as they could, in the hope of bowling Essex out a second time; which was not unreasonable, since Championship leaders cannot expect anything very generous in the way of last-day declarations. The Southend pitch did not co-operate. Often Southend pitches look as if they are going to be dreadful by the end, but they have a disconcerting habit of survival.

## PROCTER'S MEN TAKE B&H CUP
### WEEK ENDED JULY 22

SO Gloucestershire won the Benson & Hedges Cup, to their delight, without too much difficulty – and without the necessity of any miracles from Procter, though he has stamped his character on the side, and the victory in the competition is his so far as these things can ever belong to one man.

Scotland beat Denmark by 158 runs, at Broughty Ferry. This is about all I can tell you of the three-day contest between the old Scandinavian rivals, because newspapers consider that Scottish cricket is of no interest to English readers, and possibly not even to

Scottish ones. But you could pick a strong all-time Scotland XI: reasonable qualifications have been held by Jardine, Peebles, Greig, Denness, P. A. Gibb, Robertson-Glasgow, to name a few.

## THE STATISTICAL FRONTRUNNERS
### WEEK ENDED JULY 29

EVERY week I intend to have a good look at the averages. This week I remembered. According to *The Times*, which is no more likely to be accurate than the rest, but I have to keep in with them, you understand; according to the sacred papyrus, the leading batsmen are: Richards (the Somerset and West Indian one), Boycott, Woolmer, Hayes (who is out of cricket at present with a broken cheek-bone, the result of a ball from Roberts in that unfortunate match at Old Trafford), McEwan, and Greenidge. Richards has scored nearly 300 more runs than anybody else.

The leading bowlers are Hendrick, Procter, Emburey, Daniel, Underwood, and Miller. The only name in either of these lists which is a bit of a surprise is that of Emburey, whose four wickets for Middlesex last year cost 90 runs each. Here, it seems, is the successor to Titmus – not "ready-made", as I have heard it said by the Tavern, but carefully prepared. He has spent some years on the staff learning, and awaiting his opportunity.

Of the top six bowlers, Procter has most wickets, 73 (Brain, who is seventh, has 62, which tells you a good deal about Gloucestershire's successes). The man with more wickets than anybody, though well down the list, is young Botham, of Somerset, with 75 (and five more in Australia's first innings in the current Test, in which England appear to be doing rather well). Several people and places claim a share in Botham. There is Cheshire, where he was born in 1955. There is Bill Andrews ("one of my boys"). There is Lord's where he spent two years on the staff. There is Bill Andrews ("spotted him at once, natural genius"). There is Yeovil, where he lives and where his interest in the game developed. Down in Somerset they have been saying for some time that he is the best all-rounder they have had (not counting importations) since Arthur Wellard. Some reservations on the last point from Bill Andrews ("course Arthur did

John Emburey – working for success.

play for England, but I wasn't very fit at the time").

*It was, of course, Arthur Wellard's six-hitting record that Ian Botham was to pass in 1985 – the Somerset supporters were not to be disappointed.*

Boycott is in the England side again, to universal interest, though not universal approval. After making some favourable reference to him recently, I received a stern letter from a lady in Isle of Wight, accusing me of succumbing to "boycottitis". (She has already stopped reading the Sage of Longparish, "because he always brings Boycott in", and I fear that between us we have lost a reader.)

The Packer ramifications mount, and are getting very boring, quite spoiling the season. He is reported to be having trouble with one or two of his signatories, notably Thomson, whom I heard described as "the nigger in the woodpile", not the most felicitous of analogies. The Test and County Cricket Board have threatened a ban, on county cricket as well as Test cricket, for those who join the enemy. I do not propose to write about this again, until something amusing happens, like Mr Packer entering a round-the-word yacht race with Rachael Heyhoe Flint as crew. I record my expectation that the outcome will be determined by two things: the courts, and money.

## BOYCOTT'S WEEK
### WEEK ENDED AUGUST 5

IT HAS been Boycott's week, no doubt about it: perhaps less for the runs he scored in the Trent Bridge Test than the way he hid his eyes when he had Randall run out. He has always been a bad runner between the wickets, and is not likely to get much better at it. Still, Boycott has learnt a touch of shame, which used not to be noticeable in these situations, and the consequence of shame is atonement, which he certainly made.

The Australians, two-down with three played in the rubber, are not doing as well as they could. Many observers attribute this to divided counsels in the party, and a general anxiety about the future. But you could say much the same of the England side.

I saw most of the Cheltenham Festival. Despite

almost two days lost, it made record profits, and if in the Old Patesians' tent you dared to suggest that Gloucestershire might not win the Championship, you went thirsty. They had two good wins. Procter scored a hundred before lunch and keeps on taking wickets. Zaheer scored a double-hundred and a hundred in the same match, the third time he has achieved this improbable feat.

Thence to Cardiff, where before a crammed crowd (I can't imagine why they didn't play it at Swansea, or perhaps I can) Glamorgan entered the semi-finals of the Gillette Cup for the first time. The others are Middlesex, Somerset, and Leicestershire.

## A BAN IS PROPOSED
### WEEK ENDED AUGUST 12

BOYCOTT has scored his 100th hundred, and done it at Headingley, before his own people, in a Test match against Australia. How very like him! England have made an excellent start to the match. Already it is hard to see how anything can save Australia except the weather, and that has been behaving itself rather better lately.

The TCCB proposes a two-year ban, applying to all English cricket, for the Packer players. Its validity will have to be decided by the courts. There are some who would like to have seen the ban limited to Test cricket, and some who would like to have seen a life ban. Certainly there is no particular logic in the arbitrary period of two years. But on the whole I think they have taken the sensible course.

Middlesex began the week with a remarkable win over Surrey in little more than a day. They bowled Surrey out for 49, declared their first innings at 0 for 0, bowled them out for 89, and won by nine wickets. That he bowled throughout an innings without conceding a run was not much consolation to the Shoreditch Sparrow, who was captaining Surrey.

I have been sorry to miss the Weston Festival this year. There were high jinks on Wednesday, when Somerset scored 492 in their first innings against Surrey, further diminishing the chirp of the unfortunate Jackman. Vivian Richards scored a double-century, which took him past 2,000 for the season, and put on, with Roebuck, 251 for the fifth wicket, a Somerset

County Championship
(as at August 2)

|   |   | P | Pts |
|---|---|---|---|
| **1** | Kent | 15 | 175 |
| **2** | Middlesex | 16 | 173 |
| **3** | Gloucestershire | 15 | 163 |
| **4** | Derbyshire | 16 | 135 |

record. The previous record-holders were J. C. White and C. C. C. Case: so any of you young men who think that Case was a figment of Robertson-Glasgow's imagination are wrong.

## ASHES TO ENGLAND
### WEEK ENDED AUGUST 19

ENGLAND beat Australia by an innings and 85 runs in little more than three days, winning the rubber and regaining the Ashes: as conclusive a win as was Australia's in the last full series. The last time England won three consecutive Tests against Australia, indeed the only time in this country, was in 1886, when A. G. Steel was captain. Why have the Australians,

Ian Botham bowls Jeff Thomson to take five wickets in an innings for the second time in only his second Test match.

who seemed to have plenty of talented young men early in the season, and looked as good a side as England in the first Test, gone to pieces? A common opinion is that they have been worried about their futures, and thinking about the problems of life as superstars when they should have been concentrating, especially on their catches. But most of the English side must have had similar uncertainties on their minds, and better concentraiton has had as much to do with the victory as anything. I am more inclined to think it was lack of experience of English pitches in a wet summer which caused Australia's bright hopes to fade.

*In the incredible see-saw tradition of England-Australian competition over the years, Australia were to take three in a row against England in 1979 – 80 while*

*England did the same to them in the historic summer of 1981.*

The Gillette Cup semi-finals were an anticlimax to the Test. There was no play at either Swansea or Lord's on Wednesday, but Glamorgan and Leicestershire managed a start on Thursday afternoon, and Glamorgan have won today, by five wickets, with 15 balls to spare, not too uncomfortable a margin as these occasions go, though they had some anxious moments. Poor Middlesex and Somerset, like Goebbels in the song, had noebbels at all. They will try again next Wednesday.

## A SAD, SODDEN WEEK
### WEEK ENDED AUGUST 26

THE delayed Gillette Cup semi-final between Middlesex and Somerset was a sad farce. After two blank days it had been decided, if necessary, to settle it by spinning a coin, but in fact a 15-overs game was possible on the last (sixth) day. Close said wryly afterwards that they should have made Smith man of the match for winning the toss, and there is no doubt that to bat second is a heavy advantage in so brief a match. All the same, Somerset seem to have given Middlesex an easier task than they should have done.

## PIED PIPER OF CORNHILL
### WEEK ENDED SEPTEMBER 2

ANOTHER week for ombrologists. The Australians had the better of the last Test, substantially so on the figures, but as the weather increasingly made a draw certain, there was little excitement or satisfaction for anybody. The news of the sponsorship of cricket in England by the Cornhill Insurance Company, on a large scale, is no doubt good; though I am less exuberant about it than some. Few benefits in life are free, and he who pays the piper calls the tune, as they learnt in Hamelin, and come to that in Hambledon. I do not much care for the thought of England matches being called "Cornhill Tests", though to be sure it is a dignified name. I wonder if in a quarter-of-a-century's time there will be two sets of records in *Wisden*, for Tests (Cornhill) and Tests (Packer).

With three days set apart for the Gillette Cup final, we have a long weekend to contemplate the Championship possibilities. Gloucestershire have scored 216 points, Kent and Middlesex 211 each. They all have one match to play, starting next Wednesday: Gloucestershire at Bristol against Hampshire, Kent at Edgbaston, Middlesex at Blackpool. Gloucestershire have won a match more, so that five points will secure the Championship unless one of the others wins its last. There is no sign of a spell of settled weather.

Earlier in the week I saw Gloucestershire lose at Taunton. The disappointment was that Close was out for 87 after looking as if he was bound to get a hundred in his last innings there. He let the thought bother him too much. There was no special need to hurry, but he was swinging the bat wildly towards the end, as if he were back at Old Trafford in 1961. We all stood up and cheered him in.

## WEEPING OVER CRICKET
### WEEK ENDED SEPTEMBER 9

K ENT and Middlesex have tied for the Schweppes County Championship. It is no use pretending I am pleased about it. I wanted Gloucestershire to win, less

Bob Woolmer catches Steve Perryman and Kent beat Warwickshire to share the County Championship with Middlesex.

Brian Close at the end of his 29th season in first-class cricket.

for any reasons of local patriotism than because such a pleasing historical symmetry (1877 and all that) would have been worthy of Procter's farewell to Gloucestershire – if such it should prove to be. I wept for Gloucestershire's failure, as I had wept when Close was out at Taunton last week. I was, on reflection, puzzled that I should start crying over cricket matches

at my time of life. Then I remembered that the drops they have given me for my eyes, among their other qualities, are supposed to stimulate the tear-ducts, so I have an excuse (not counting the whisky).

Gloucestershire must be wondering whether they will ever win a Championship again. So often, during the last 100 years, they have been so close. Looking back through the records, I was particularly struck by their misfortunes in 1930. That year they lost the Championship by three points, after winning three more matches than any other county, and five more matches than Lancashire, the champions. Under almost any other points system than the one which obtained, they would have won at a walk.

Sharp disappointment, also, in Essex. They remain one of only two counties – Somerset is the other – who have never won anything. A few weeks ago it seemed that they were on their way to victory in the John Player League, but Leicestershire crept up, winning comfortably over Glamorgan last Sunday. Essex duly beat Worcestershire, but knowing that their labour would be in vain, so long as Leicestershire won. The John Player people had already sent the trophy to Leicester, and only a replica to Chelmsford.

*Essex and Somerset were both to put matters right in 1979 when they shared all the honours – Somerset winning the Gillette Cup and John Player League while Essex took the Benson and Hedges Cup and the Championship.*

Glamorgan had lost the Gillette Cup final the previous day, putting up a fight acceptable to their numerous (and well-behaved) supporters, after a poor start.

So Middlesex have had the best of the season, with a share in the Championship, and a win in the senior limited-overs competition. Kent have the other half of the Championship, Gloucestershire the Benson & Hedges, Leicestershire the John Player. England have beaten Australia. This summary makes it clear that, for all the triumphs of Procter, and Boycott, and Vivian Richards, it has been Brearley's year. Let us hope, as he sets off for the winter's tour with his diminished England side, that the wind will be tempered to the shorn lamb.

## SCHWEPPES COUNTY CHAMPIONSHIP FINAL TABLE

| | P | W | L | D | Bonus Bt | Bonus Bw | Pts |
|---|---|---|---|---|---|---|---|
| 1 Kent (14) | 22 | 9 | 2 | 11 | 54 | 65 | 227 |
| Middlesex (1) | 22 | 9 | 5 | 8 | 43 | 76 | 227 |
| 3 Gloucestershire (3) | 22 | 9 | 5 | 8 | 44 | 70 | 222 |
| 4 Somerset (7) | 22 | 6 | 4 | 12 | 58 | 64 | 194 |
| 5 Leicestershire (4) | 22 | 6 | 4 | 12 | 44 | 73 | 189 |
| 6 Essex (6) | 22 | 7 | 5 | 10 | 38 | 65 | 187 |
| 7 Derbyshire (15) | 22 | 7 | 3 | 12 | 38 | 64 | 186 |
| 8 Sussex (10) | 22 | 6 | 5 | 11 | 52 | 60 | 184 |
| 9 Northants (2) | 22 | 6 | 6 | 10 | 43 | 68 | 183 |
| 10 Warwickshire (5) | 22 | 4 | 8 | 10 | 61 | 72 | 181 |
| 11 Hampshire (12) | 22 | 6 | 5 | 11 | 53 | 54 | 179 |
| 12 Yorkshire (8) | 22 | 6 | 5 | 11 | 36 | 63 | 171 |
| 13 Worcestershire (11) | 22 | 5 | 10 | 7 | 29 | 55 | 144 |
| 14 Glamorgan (17) | 22 | 3 | 7 | 12 | 36 | 60 | 132 |
| Surrey (9) | 22 | 3 | 6 | 13 | 42 | 54 | 132 |
| 16 Lancashire (16) | 22 | 2 | 4 | 16 | 36 | 57 | 117 |
| 17 Nottinghamshire (13) | 22 | 1 | 11 | 10 | 34 | 52 | 98 |

1976 positions in brackets

It is interesting to read Alan Gibson's account of the 1977 season again, if only because he viewed with detachment the bitter dispute which followed the news that a large proportion of the best cricketers in the world had signed to play for Kerry Packer's World Series Cricket organisation in rivalry to established Test cricket. Unlike many cricket writers, myself I fear included, Alan can see the wood for the trees; the game is never too solemn for him and the more solemn it becomes, the more he enjoys poking gentle fun at it.

This said, 1977 will always be remembered as the Year of the Cricket Revolution. *The passions it aroused were profound, wherever cricket was played at first-class level, and they spilled over into the case in the High Court in London in the winter, wherein Mr Packer routed his opponents. The attempt by the established Cricket Boards to ban from Tests and from domestic cricket in their own countries those players who had signed, clandestinely, for what then seemed relatively huge sums of money, to play the "privately" promoted matches in Australia, was declared illegal. It was a long and painful case, with much dirty linen washed in public.*

*The course of World Series Cricket has been well enough documented elsewhere. Suffice to say here that it made a slow start in its first season, despite the determination of those involved to gain acceptance from a largely sceptical Australian public and press. But the innovation of floodlit cricket was a success, and the turning point was to follow a season later when, after another legal battle, Mr Packer won the right to take his matches to the scene of so many great sporting occasions, the Sydney Cricket Ground. Not only this, but the right also to erect huge floodlights.*

*The battle went on in different ways in different countries. In Pakistan where England were touring under Mike Brearley and, after he had broken his arm, under Geoff Boycott, there was an attempt by Packer to persuade the Pakistan selectors to play some of "his" men – Mushtaq, Zaheer and Imran – in the Third Test in Karachi. The England team threatened not to play the match if the Packer players were actually selected, having been flown in from Australia in dramatic circumstances in an attempt to show that Packer did not wish to debar his players from taking part in Tests when they were available to do so. In the event the Pakistan Board stuck to the ICC's hastily formed policy of not selecting the Packer players.*

*Later, at the end of March, 1978, the bitterness spread to the West Indies. The Board here had gone against ICC policy in selecting their Packer players for the first two Tests against Australia. The latter had just won an enthralling home series against Bishen Bedi's Indians. Australia were captained by the old favourite Bobby Simpson, who had emerged from retirement to lead a largely untried team into battle for the official "Fair Dinkum" Aussies. For the Third Test the West Indies selectors, aware that the Packer men would not be available for a forthcoming tour of India and Sri Lanka, dropped three of the Packer men. Clive Lloyd promptly resigned as captain and the remaining Packer players withdrew leaving the West Indies to take the field with six new caps. Two of the original selections, Alvin Greenidge and Larry Gomes, made centuries, but Australia scored over 300 in the fourth innings to win a splendid game by three wickets. The series, incidentally, ended on a bizarre note when a riot ended play early on the fifth day just when Australia appeared likely to win. The West Indies Board offered to extend the match into a sixth day, but one of the umpires, Ralph Gosein, refused to stand, as there had been no provision in the laws or the playing conditions for an extension. One way and another, cricket seemed in a vulnerable, confused and embattled state when the 1978 season began.*

# — 1978 —

## THE PARKS NEVER LOOKED BLEAKER
### *WEEK ENDED APRIL 28*

YOU may remember that, when I left you at the end of last season, I was bothered about my eyesight, and I was deploring the weather. I am relieved to say that the eyesight, thanks to some new pills and new glasses, is greatly improved. The weather seems to be carrying on just where it left off. I began my season at Fenner's. The first morning had a touch of the sun. But it soon grew cold and grey. On the second day it rained, and there was no play until five o'clock. The match petered out when Essex did not enforce the follow-on. They were not to be blamed. The players who took the eye were those you would have expected to – McEwan, Gooch and Lever for Essex, Parker and Hignell for Cambridge.

It had rained at Cardiff on the Saturday, so I was off there on Monday for the Somerset match. It was a tolerably fine day. Somerset scored 196. From the last possible ball of the match, Glamorgan could score only one run, which made the scores level, but meant that Somerset had won, since they had lost fewer wickets. The last few overs were very exciting, but there had been some mediocre cricket earlier on. Both sides threw away positions from which they should have made the game safe.

Then three days at Oxford. I have never seen the Parks look bleaker. This was not just because of the weather. The trees are late to foliate, and many of them are dying. Nobody was there, except those on duty, or walking their dogs. Spring and youth seemed far away. The University and Warwickshire had two empty days, and nothing of significance happened on the third.

## ONE VAST PUDDLE
### *WEEK ENDED MAY 5*

ON Saturday, in the Parks, Kent batted for two and a half hours, but that was all for the whole match. I then travelled nearer home, to Bristol (not quite home any longer, since during the winter we have moved out to the Somerset countryside, and damned lucky we are, I think, as I look out of my study window and see on the horizon Glastonbury Tor and Downside Abbey). There was no play on any day of the intended match between Gloucestershire and Northamptonshire. That was, for me, two and a half hours of play in a week. Not that I have been the only one to suffer. In the round of championship matches just ended, all eight were drawn, and all eight lost at least one full day's play. The whole of England and Wales is one vast puddle.

## PARTRIDGE OF BIRDLIP
### *WEEK ENDED MAY 12*

A little better, thank you. In the Benson and Hedges, there was, again, no play on Saturday at Bristol, but they managed to finish the match by Tuesday afternoon. On Monday, Gloucestershire had to bat in a light as bad as I can recall in a county match. This spell of batting in a gloom, not exactly inspissate, indeed at times markedly spissate, put Gloucestershire so far behind the clock that they lost the match, when they had bowled Derbyshire out for 148. Nevertheless, Derbyshire had deserved their win. If they had the best of the weather, they also had Barlow, who takes his task of leading them seriously, keeps them fit, and contributed at tender moments with both bat and ball. In this match seven Derbyshire men were home-born, thus fulfilling the Longparish Standard. The Sage of that place, Johnny Woodcock, has declared that five men in every county side should be born in the county. I do not quite agree with him about this – what about the counties in England, Wales, Scotland, who, in acreage and (I should think) population, far surpass the 17 "first-class" counties? Are these men to be handicapped in their first class careers because they were born at, say, Chippenham? All the same, the Sage is trying to assert an admirable principle: it is natural and becoming for a cricketer to wish to play for the village, the town, the county, the country in which he was born.

Gloucestershire had only four home-born men, but think Partridge should be counted as two. He is known among fellow-cricketers as "Pheasant", and by a pleasing chance was born at Birdlip, a village up in the north of Gloucestershire, near Stroud. Still, a couple from Devon and one from Worcestershire are not unneighbourly. I think Derbyshire must have a chance of winning something this season, and I know Barlow's heart is into his work, just as Procter's is for Gloucestershire.

I have not left myself much space to tell you about the cricket at Taunton, where Glamorgan were beaten, with plenty to spare at the end, by Somerset. I wonder if Somerset will make a mark on this season? I am suspicious of them, because they have begun so well. If Somerset are ever to win a championship they will do it by moving up from the bottom with six consecutive wins against the strongest sides in the last month of the season. Nash hit Breakwell for four consecutive sixes, from the first four balls of an over, and there was a fine hint of odd history in the making, but that was where it ended.

*Somerset's leadership was not, unfortunately, maintained and in 1986, after all the intervening years of success, they were still without a Championship title.*

## WHO WILL LEAD IN AUSTRALIA?
### WEEK ENDED MAY 19

WHERE cricketers gather, the question most frequently discussed is: Who will lead England against Australia this winter? Brearley, or Boycott, or Some Other Basket as I heard it delicately put at Lord's lately. I cannot see there will be any problem, so long as

Pakistan fielders celebrate the departure of Boycott for only three in the Prudential match at Old Trafford. Iqbal Qasim, Sarfraz Nawaz (the bowler), Sadiq Mohammad and Haroon Rashid rush to congratulate the wicket-keeper Wasim Bari.

Brearley is fit, gets a tolerable number of runs, and makes no flagrant mistakes in the Tests this summer, when the opposition is unlikely to be taxing (the weather has given the Pakistanis hardly a chance of getting their talented side together).

## A DEMON WHO CAN BAT
### WEEK ENDED MAY 26

ALTHOUGH I have dated this, as is customary, on Friday, I am in fact writing on a Saturday afternoon at Taunton, where Somerset and Gloucestershire are playing the Spring Bank Holiday match, and after the memorial service to Harold Gimblett. The noble church of St James, by the ground, was nearly full. As one of the participants it may not become me to say so, but I felt that the entire proceedings struck the right note, something like triumphant consolation, for a thanksgiving service for a Christian man. In the pause after the Bishop of Taunton had given his blessing, a gentle ripple of clapping drifted over from the ground.

I have been nowhere all week but Taunton, off and on. Last Saturday was a disappointment, chiefly because on such a rarely lovely day the match should have been over by a quarter to three. The Combined Universities were bowled out, before lunch, in 32 overs. They were below strength, because of the inexorable examiners, but even so, they can play much better, as they had shown against Glamorgan, a match lost by lack of experience rather than talent. The win put Somerset into the Benson & Hedges quarter-finals. The others are Nottinghamshire, Kent, Derbyshire, Middlesex, Sussex, Warwickshire and Glamorgan.

The championship match at Taunton, against Kent, may have been an important one, for Kent and Somerset, with Essex, are making the early spurts in the Schweppes, if I may be permitted the phrase. Kent won with runs to spare, though not much time. Kent had the better of the luck, I think it fair to say, and still were not secure from defeat until Richards was bowled, first ball, on the last morning. Dredge, the Demon of Frome, had a successful match with both ball and bat. Oh yes, he can bat a bit, our Demon. It is not the first time I have seen him take part in a stand of 50. The last was at Northampton, when he vigorously supported Moseley in a last-wicket partnership. Moseley made the first 49

Colin Dredge – the Demon of Frome.

runs, and Dredge the 50th. You don't open the innings for Frome all those years, against giants such as Midsomer Norton and Shepton Mallet, for nothing.

Kent do look a formidable side, I suppose the best in the country. Ealham has installed, or it might be better said distilled, a fine spirit from a rich, though mixed, field of grain.

I will long remember an incident one morning on the train to Taunton. As we were passing through Backwell (to be distinguished from Breakwell) a lady came marching through the buffet car, where we were genteelly sipping our coffee, crying in bell-like tones, "A Gentleman has Dropped his Trousers in the Corridor!" She had her evidence, too, a neat pair of dark-blue pin-stripe. Waving them above her head like Boadicea flourishing a captured Roman Eagle, she swept on. Her mission must have been in some way achieved, because she returned at Creech St Michael, without them.

## LEATHER-JACKETS AND OTHER BUGS
### WEEK ENDED JUNE 2

Willis bowls Mohsin Khan in the First Test at Edgbaston.

A rather dismal week, for me, though I should be comforted by England's good start to the Test match. I should have been at Swansea earlier in the week, but was abruptly copped by one of those internal bugs which make it necessary to have plumbing facilities within easy reach. I did manage Lord's, for Middlesex and Northamptonshire.

Middlesex scored 280 in their 100 overs, which was a good score, since the pitch did not behave itself very well. It was not that it was slow – that was only to be expected after all the rain – but that the bounce and turn were variable. It is 1935 that is still remembered as the year of the leather-jackets at Lord's (where South Africa won the Test and their first rubber in England) and I dare say something of the same kind has happened again.

Northamptonshire lost three wickets overnight, effectively four on Thursday morning, since Lamb's damaged finger caused him to withdraw from the match. The innings never looked like re-establishing itself. When eight were down, for 100, the follow-on seemed a formality, but in fact a vigorous last-wicket stand brought them within a run of saving it. This caused some tension between me and my old friend Rex Alston. His paper do not pay him for a lost day (very mingily, I think, since after all they have booked his time). Mine does, and besides I was not averse from a quiet day at home with my bugs – not the leather-jackets. So Northamptonshire followed on after lunch, and when they lost two wickets for three, and the third at 13, there was a rustling of railway timetables, a sparkle in the eyes of the caterers, poised as ever at the shutters, and a crease in the distinguished brow of Rex Agonistes. I do not know to what strange gods these Cambridge men pray, but they were unexpectedly efficacious during the afternoon, and in the end Middlesex had to take the extra half-hour for their two-day win.

Not that the week was totally in vain. I became a grandfather. They have called the child Joanna, against my advice. Her destiny will obviously be to marry Henry Blofeld, who falls in love with every woman he meets, as long as she is called Joanna.

## THE CURSED BOUNCERS
### WEEK ENDED JUNE 9

BY the time you read these words it will be old history. The song and dance will have ended, though the smell will linger on, as of a bad drain. England won the Edgbaston Test by an innings, which was satisfactory enough, the performances of Gower and Botham more pleasing still. But all was marred by the bouncers bowled by Willis at Qasim, and the serious consequent injury not only to Qasim, but to the good

County Championship
(as at June 2)

|  | P | Pts |
|---|---|---|
| **1** Nottinghamshire | 4 | 54 |
| **2** Somerset | 5 | 52 |
| **3** Middlesex | 5 | 49 |
| **4** Kent | 4 | 44 |

name, or what is left of it, of cricket. You will find it all in the records, and there is no point in my rehearsing it now. No doubt the first bouncer against Qasim in the morning was intended as a warning – "Get out, night-watchman, or else . . ." No doubt Brearley, his position as captain for Australia still in some doubt, was anxious to avoid any action which might have been construed as a weak one (though, for many of us, he produced the opposite effect. He miscasts himself as an Iron Chancellor.)

Though I should be sorry. Far from the sound and fury, I had an enjoyable week. Three more days at Lord's, in good weather: Kent beat Middlesex with plenty of time and wickets left. Kent's young and local men did well. I hope they will be faithful to them in giving them full opportunities. I was impressed by Dilley, a tall, young, quick bowler. It was, to be sure, another tricky pitch, and the man who did most for Kent was probably their acting captain, Shepherd. His first innings, which swung the match, had some whacking strokes – a six, which hit the pavilion balcony, was one of the best – but he had some luck with dropped catches. One of them went so high that anybody on the field might have caught it. While Middlesex were still drawing lots for the honour, or waiting for Brearley to catch a train from Birmingham, the ball fell to earth about 15 yards from the place where it had departed.

## SOMERSET'S DOUBLE TRIUMPH
### WEEK ENDED JUNE 16

IT ought to have been a lovely week, because it was the Bath Festival, which I always enjoy. Because of my wife's illness (she is in hospital in Bath, but the operation is over, and she seems to be well) I was allowed to do it all. My special thanks to the Sage, who I know also likes coming to Bath. Somerset won both matches: against Lancashire by four wickets, after a Lancashire recovery in the third innings which gave Somerset quite enough to do in the fourth (Richards, Roebuck and Denning did it, in that order of skill); and then against Sussex, easily, by an innings.

Two championship wins for Somerset in a week, and they up at the top already! "'Tes unbloodyblevable," I heard it said, countless husky voices clamouring for their close-of-play cider. I met lots of old friends, and

received warm hospitality, as you always do at Bath, whether the game be cricket or rugby. But I was fretting all the time, not so much about Rosemary, whom I knew was in good hands, but about the children's supper. The worst day was Thursday, when Adam said that he thought he was going off chips, and Felicity said that she thought she was going off baked beans. Fortunately I produced a bag of peaches, bought from that splendid fruiterer's on the Bath Bus Station (heartily commended to you all), so they did not quite starve.

There were good moments in the cricket, apart from the aura of Somerset success. Lancashire set Somerset to score 231 in 163 minutes, which I considered generous, considering they had dug themselves out of a deep hole. They were enabled to do this by a last-wicket stand between Croft and Hogg. I was glad to see Roebuck batting so well; and Burgess, another Millfield boy, hit the six which won the match.

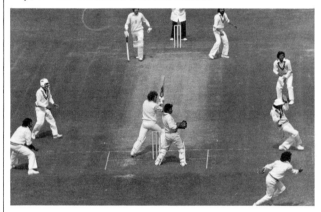

Geoff Miller watches Graham Roope take four runs off Wasim Raja in the Second Test at Lord's.

## BOTHAM PRODIGIOUS
### WEEK ENDED JUNE 23

ROSEMARY was restored to me, on Father's Day, and not before time. Felicity was just about to go off peaches. I had the week-end free and saw some of the Second Test on television. There was no play on the first day, and less than 13 hours on the next three, which was still sufficient for England to win by an innings and 120 runs. There was another prodigious performance by Botham, who scored a century and took eight for 34 in the second Pakistan innings. Nobody has ever before taken eight wickets in an innings and scored a century in the same Test match. On Wednesday I was at Taunton for the Benson & Hedges semi-final. Kent won, and will meet Derbyshire in the final. Derbyshire, I suppose, have been the surprise of the competition. Barlow's stress on physical fitness has had its critics, but it does make them a hard side to score runs against quickly in the one-day competitions.

## LORD'S DWARFS THE UNIVERSITIES
### WEEK ENDED JUNE 30

ONE of the interesting things about the averages used to be the proportion of amateurs to professionals. For many years most of the leading batsmen were amateurs, most of the leading bowlers professionals. Nowadays the comparison we make is between home and overseas players. I notice that in the current batting list the only Englishmen are Randall, Ormrod, Roope and J. F. Steele, of whom only Roope is in the Test side. The first three bowlers, however, are Hendrick, Underwood and Willis, with Lever at 6, Edmonds 7, Ratcliffe 9, Pocock 10 – and Old and Botham nearby. One of the reasons why the Pakistanis have looked a poor batting side is the strength of English bowling at present.

*This is an interesting observation in the light of recent lamentations about the poor state of England's native bowlers. After all, the effects of limited-overs cricket had by now had plenty of time to filter through. But of Alan Gibson's list here, only Willis was genuinely fast. In subsequent years it was the overseas fast bowlers who tended to dominate the county bowling averages.*

Randall was one of those who played well at Lord's, where I saw the first day of Middlesex and Nottinghamshire. Randall's innings was only marred because he was connected, or mis-connected, with three run-outs, for two of which at least he was to be blamed. His judgment, so unerring in the field, seems to desert him between wickets.

It was a long time since I had seen the University match. I knew it had gone down in the world, but it was still a shock, in the morning, to see only four people scattered around the top tier of the "free seats." I thought there were five, but the fifth turned out to be a

dustbin. I think it is time the University match left Lord's. The players are keen enough, and the standard of cricket is still high. The Combined Universities have done much better than the Minor Counties in the Benson & Hedges. There were a dozen players in this match, who would establish their places in county sides without difficulty, should they make the game their career. Why, then, has the match lost its support? Why do the undergraduates no longer come? Why do the country parsons no longer come? Partly just because it is at Lord's, and the ground dwarfs the occasion.

The crowd at Headingley for the Third Test – much in need of happiness.

The match was ruined by rain. Cambridge won the toss and were all out for 92, batting slowly. Marks batted very well for Oxford. He had some luck, but rightly took the attack to the bowlers after two wickets had fallen quickly. There was no play after the first day until half-past three on the third. Cambridge, 0 for 0, needed 100 runs to avoid an inning defeat. They could not win, but Oxford just might, especially if the sun came out and shone on the wet pitch. This it only briefly did. Parker, after a stodgy first innings, unworthy of his talents, played just the right game, going for his strokes and not letting the bowlers get on top. So the game was honourably saved.

## HISTORY MADE IN THE GILLETTE CUP
### WEEK ENDED JULY 7

TEN hours' cricket in the Third Test at Headingley, and of course a drawn match, and the series to England. I was glad to see that Sadiq, a likeable and loyal cricketer, scored 97. Brearley took two hard slip catches, scored 0, and has been named captain against New Zealand, which I think is what most of the team would wish.

I had a look at the New Zealanders at Taunton. Somerset fielded a weak side. It always strikes me as a little discourteous, and possibly unwise – from the financial point – for counties to use matches against touring teams so casually. But Somerset are under heavy pressure, the New Zealanders have injury problems, and, as one senior Somerset supporter said to me, "If you remember the way things were, and not so many years ago either, 'twould have seemed a bloody miracle that we had four players to leave out." The New Zealanders did not look a particularly strong side, but everything would be different if only the sun would shine.

### Gillette Cup

## Record Somerset win as Richards hits 139

**By A SPECIAL CORRESPONDENT at Taunton**

MAGNIFICENT Somerset batting, highlighted by an unbeaten 139 from Viv Richards, clearly the man of ·tch. ·e···e· · ··me· · ···· · ·ver Warwick-

In the first round of the Gillette Cup, I saw an astonishing match between Somerset and Warwickshire. Warwickshire scored 292 for five, which meant that Somerset had to make more than any side batting second had ever done in the competition. This they did, with two overs and five balls to spare, and also with five runs to spare, since Richards (139 not out) hit the last ball for six.

I thought that Whitehouse, whose sturdy (and in its later stages dashing) innings had done much for his side, made a mistake in taking off Willis after only five overs of his allotment. When he first faced Richards, Willis bowled him three very fast balls – not bouncers – any of which might have had him out. Two more overs of Willis, or even seven, would have been a good swap for Richards's wicket. But I do not suppose that Whitehouse, any more than I, really contemplated Somerset getting the runs.

## INTO THE SHREDDER
### WEEK ENDED JULY 14

AFTER a dead draw at Cardiff, I moved back to Bristol, for Lancashire against Gloucestershire. I had to broadcast a television commentary on this match, as well as report it. It is some time since I have done this, and I was surprised to find how difficult it was. There was a good moment at the beginning. The lady in the secretary's office, carrying the stencil from which the scorecards were to be printed had it blown from her tray by an unexpected draught, and it swept gracefully into the shredder. Only later did I realise where the responsibility for this disaster lay, when a once-familiar voice on the public address system reminded me that Puff the Magic Dragon was again amongst us.

Lancashire were behind on the first innings but won by lunch-time on the third day. As it turned out, they had the best of the pitch in the last innings. Fortunately there was no shortage of major sporting activities in the neighbourhood for the disappointed spectators. I repaired to the High Littleton School Sports. Adam came second in the 70 metres sprint, and second in the sack race, which he was expected to win. He maintains that the chap who beat him had a hole in his sack, and could slip out a crafty foot, but I am afraid Adam has learnt to think the worst of everybody after the World Cup. Felicity came third in the under-seven sprint, but failed to live up to training form in the blue bean race.

I see that the New Zealanders have beaten both Middlesex and Warwickshire, in a week, by an innings. Hadlee must be bowling well.

## BETTER AFTER THE TESTS
### WEEK ENDED JULY 21

KENT duly won the Benson & Hedges, by six wickets with more than 13 overs to spare. It is their third win in the seven years the competition has existed. Derbyshire, although they had four Test players, and Kirsten, who is good enough to be another, had not the reserve strength to compensate if the great men failed. Barlow scored one, and Hendrick did not take a wicket – though he had Woolmer, who made top score, dropped off consecutive balls. This just about

Alan Ealham displays the Benson and Hedges Cup.

extinguished Derbyshire's hopes, never more than flickering after they had scored only 147.

Somerset had a good week. I saw them beat Leicestershire in the championship. Richards scored 99 and 110. Breakwell made another half-century, and so did Roebuck. I shall keep a picture of Richards when he was out, leg-before, in the first innings, pausing at the wicket for a long time with bowed head, less from disagreement with Bill Alley's decision than simple disappointment.

Then at Cardiff, in the Gillette Cup, although Richards scored a mere 52, Denning made 145, and Somerset arrived at 330 for four. Glamorgan made a plucky answer, but there was never any chance that they would win. This match went into the second day, as did all the others except at Northampton, where Kent won easily.

England won both one-day Prudential matches against New Zealand, the first by a little, the second by a lot. It is strange how little these matches appeal to me. I liked them much more when they were played *after* the Tests, as at first they were: a kind of super-frolic to mark the end of the tour. Even the John Player League is more interesting. This reminds me it is time I wrote about the John Player League.

## *A HOUSE DIVIDED*
### *WEEK ENDED JULY 28*

WHICH I now do. The trouble with the John Player League is that it has reduced the extraordinary to the commonplace. A close finish has always been one of the delights of cricket (not least if it ended in a draw): but, when you get three or four every week, you become bored with them. At least, I do. Last Sunday, Worcestershire beat Essex by a run, and Glamorgan beat Sussex by two wickets. In the other six matches play was abandoned. The difficulty is that 40 overs is not enough for a match between first-class cricketers, nor indeed most adult cricketers of *any* class, and the supplementary rules – the 15-yard run-up for bowlers, the complications about reaching results when the weather interferes – make it artificial. In the longer one-day competitions, there is, with luck, just space for a good match. It would be best for Sunday cricket, I think, to abolish the over-limit altogether, and leave it

to the captains to get a result between two o'clock and seven. Two points for a win, one for a tie, nothing for anything else. Much good cricket, in clubs and leagues, has been played on this basis.

*A clever idea but, I fear, with professionals involved (if they will excuse me) the time element would be open to much abuse. With a set number of overs this cannot happen.*

I spent the week at Leeds and Leicester, and enjoyed a variation from the western scene. Yorkshire cricket, not for the first time, is a house divided – you only had to sit among the crowd at Headingley to realise it – and it is high time Raymond Illingworth arrived to cry "Order! Order!" The division concerns whether the county should be led by Hampshire or Boycott: or to be more precise, whether it should be led in the *style* of Hampshire or Boycott. The Kirkstall-Laners are mostly, at present, on Hampshire's side. The play on Monday illustrated the difference between the styles. New Zealand had declared at 263 for four, the overnight score, which was an indication that they would like a match. Yorkshire soon lost two wickets, which brought Boycott and Hampshire together. Hampshire scored a

Success for England in the First Test of the Under-19 series against the West Indies.

**SCARBOROUGH CRICKET GROUND**

| WEST INDIES | First Innings | | | Second Innings | |
|---|---|---|---|---|---|
| 1 T Etwaroo | c French b Thomas | 28 | | c Carter b Parsons | 4 |
| 2 L Lewis | b Thomas | 10 | | c French b Parsons | 13 |
| 3 C Best | c Sharp b Carter | 68 | | c French b Carter | 38 |
| 4 H Roach (wk) | c Taylor b Thomas | 8 | | lbw b Parsons | 0 |
| 5 L Reifer | not out | 24 | | c Sharp b Carter | 15 |
| 6 A M White (Capt) | c Carter b Parsons | 49 | | c Forster b Parsons | 29 |
| 7 S Haye | b Thomas | 2 | | st French b Carter | 8 |
| 8 S Jumadeen | c Sharp b Carter | 6 | | c & b Parsons | 24 |
| 9 K Persaud | c & b Mellor | 38 | | not out | 8 |
| 10 W Davis | lbw b Persons | 0 | | lbw b Parsons | 8 |
| 11 E Grant | run out | 0 | | c Forster b Carter | 8 |
| | b 1 lb 7 w ... nb 9 | 17 | | b 1 lb 1 w ... nb 3 | 5 |
| | Total ... | 249 | | Total ... | 160 |

Fall of the Wickets

1 2 3 4 5 6 7 8 9 10   1 2 3 4 5 6 7 8 9 10
23 96 129 135 148 157 237 241 246 249   7 55 65 59 72 109 136 136 147 160

| Analysis of Bowling | First Innings | | | | | | |
|---|---|---|---|---|---|---|---|
| | Overs | Mdns. | Runs | Wkts. | Overs | Mdns. | Runs | Wkts. |
| Thomas | 21 | 3 | 84 | 4 | 8 | 1 | 60 | 0 |
| Parsons | 18 | 7 | 51 | 2 | 20 | 8 | 46 | 6 |
| Carter | 18 | 2 | 63 | 2 | 13.5 | 1 | 49 | 4 |
| Forster | 4 | 0 | 18 | 0 | | | | |
| Mellor | 9.3 | 3 | 16 | 1 | | | | |

| ENGLAND | First Innings | | | Second Innings | |
|---|---|---|---|---|---|
| 1 K Sharp (Cpt) (Yorkshire) | c Grant b Davis | 7 | | b Grant | 96 |
| 2 M Brearley (Yorkshire) | c White b Davis | 70 | | hit wkt b Persaud | 30 |
| 3 R Carter (Northants) | not out | 63 | | | |
| 4 C Forster (Northants) | not out | 0 | | | |
| 5 B French (wk) (Notts) | lbw b Grant | 20 | | | |
| 6 A Mellor (Derbyshire) | | | | | |
| 7 G Parsons (Leics) | c Best b Davis | 13 | | | |
| 8 D Pauline (Surrey) | lbw b White | 0 | | | |
| 9 N Taylor (Kent) | c Best b Davis | 10 | | not out | 41 |
| 10 P Terry (Hants) | b White | 4 | | not out | 3 |
| 11 D Thomas (Surrey) | | | | | |
| | b 6 lb 6 w 6 nb11 | 29 | | b 7 lb10 w 4 nb 3 | 24 |
| | Total (7 wkts. dec.) | 216 | | Total | 194 |

Fall of the Wickets

1 2 3 4 5 6 7 8 9 10   1 2 3 4 5 6 7 8 9 10
17 48 48 72 178 195 214   81 180

| Analysis of Bowling | First Innings | | | | | | |
|---|---|---|---|---|---|---|---|
| | Overs | Mdns. | Runs | Wkts. | Overs | Mdns. | Runs | Wkts. |
| White | 14 | 2 | 46 | 3 | 8 | 1 | 22 | 0 |
| Davis | 19 | 6 | 51 | 3 | 10.2 | 1 | 39 | 0 |
| Grant | 7 | 1 | 25 | 1 | 8 | 0 | 37 | 1 |
| Best | 5 | 0 | 17 | 0 | | | | |
| Haye | 8 | 1 | 21 | 0 | | | | |
| Persaud | 7 | 2 | 21 | 0 | 1 | 0 | 33 | 1 |
| Jumadeen | 4 | 2 | 6 | 0 | 5 | 0 | 39 | 0 |

Umpires G. Mounfield, G. D. Newport    Scorers : L. Franklin, B. Pantin

Cricket Balls for all Matches Supplied by ALFRED READER & CO. LTD.

fast 90, batting as if he was interested in winning the match. Boycott scored a slow century, looking as if he was interested in scoring a slow century.

Technically, there is no English batsman today to compare with Boycott. Hampshire is more handsome to watch, when he is going well, but at the beginning of this season he had scored 29 centuries in 423 first-class innings, and you would expect better from an England No. 4 or 5. Yet he seems to have the knack of getting his team on his side, and this, given a tolerable efficiency in play, has marked many captains, both of Yorkshire and England.

## SOLACE OF PYJAMAS
### WEEK ENDED AUGUST 4

STILL on my travels, I saw Essex beat Lancashire by an innings, in two days, at Southport, and take themselves to the top of the championship. The second day was mostly played in darkness, which accounts to some extent for Lancashire's collapse.

On Wednesday, we had the Gillette Cup quarter-finals. I went to Old Trafford, where Lancashire won. Their hopes are centred now on this competition, in which they usually play well.

Lancashire scored 279 in their first innings, which should have been safe enough. Play was shortened on the first day, and there was very little on the second. What is more, it had been an unsettled night because my pyjamas had vanished from my hotel room. I suspect some mischief by the correspondent of the *Daily Telegraph*, a notorious oriental prankster, but no dusky gentleman had been seen loitering in the corridor. He was entirely innocent. The pyjamas turned up in the morning, lodged in a tangle of sheets in the laundry. I am sorry if I make too much of this trifling incident, but when a man gets to my age, and is away from home, he needs the solace of pyjamas.

## GOWER RIDES LUCK AND RESCUES ENGLAND WITH 111

By M̶ ̶ ̶ MELFORD

England won the First Test against New Zealand, comfortably in the end. Gower's century was reassuring – I say no more than that, because his quality always shone. Brearley scored two and 11, which is a little bothering. Surrey's committee, and ground staff, made a finish possible by thought and diligence, borrowing tarpaulins from Wimbledon and Lord's to keep off the worst of the rain.

## THUNDEROUS POWERS
### WEEK ENDED AUGUST 11

I had a week at the Weston-super-Mare Festival, which I always enjoy, though there are usually 11 journalists for one telephone. Somerset beat Warwickshire by nine wickets, and drew with Hampshire. We were, compared with most other places, lucky with the weather. The clouds kept missing us. It rained in High Littleton, it rained in Bristol. I wondered whether it was raining at Hinton Blewett, where the editor of *The Times* lives. Ever since *The Times* began the column "Today's Arrangements" with "11.50 a.m., Eclipse of the Sun," I have assumed that they control the elements. Whatever magical, not to say thunderous, powers, were set in motion, we managed some cricket at Weston.

Not much else seems to have been happening, though on the first day of the Second New Zealand Test Boycott, recalled to the side, made a century, batting for six hours, and dropped in the slips in the third over. Well, as my North Country aunts used to say, "Soom moothers do 'ave 'em."

## ONE OR TWO MEMORIES
### WEEK ENDED AUGUST 18

ENGLAND won the Second Test against New Zealand all right. Brearley, dropping down to No. 5 in the order, as was inevitable with Boycott's recall, scored 50: a great relief, I imagine, to the selectors. Botham took nine wickets in the match. New Zealand were unlucky when the umpires, on Saturday morning, allowed play to start in bad light, and called it off after two balls. This meant, as learned readers will know, that the pitch remained uncovered until play was resumed, four hours later – when it was quite a different

David Gower on the way to his first Test century.

animal. This has led to a clamour for light-meters, though you need only a minimal experience of filming to know how fallible these devices are.

Well, England won by an innings and 119, in four days. I do not know that their victories mean very much, though obviously the fast-medium bowling is good, and there are some promising young players. We shall know more about them after the Australian series. If we should win that, then we ought to have a strong side for several years.

And so to Taunton again, for the semi-final of the Gillette Cup – Essex the visitors: the only two sides who have never won anything. I have still hardly got my breath back, and I am not, not now, a man liable to be carried away by the result of a cricket match.

Somerset scored 287 for six, with a hundred by Richards. This meant that Essex would have to come near to Somerset's own second-innings Gillette record, set up on the same ground earlier this season, if they were to win. There were several times when it looked as if Essex would do it. In the end, with the scores level, and off the last possible ball, Essex lost their last wicket, run out, and therefore, according to the rules of the competition, the match.

One or two memories. The catch by Denness, at midwicket, falling as he held it when it seemed to be past him, which made a worthy end to Richards's innings. The way Richards stepped back outside his leg stump to clout the ball through the covers, choosing his gap, everyone knowing what was to come, everyone powerless to avert it. Gooch's innings, confident as a Metropolitan policeman directing the traffic (I have stolen the analogy from the Sage), unhurried in manner though in fact hurrying all the time. The last over, with 12 needed, the Demon of Frome to bowl it. In the middle of it he bowled – Oh! horror! – a no-ball – but he also bowled East. Essex needed three from the last ball, Lever and Smith ran furiously for them, but a calm return from the Somerset captain stopped them getting the third, by about a yard and a half.

*Of all the hectic one-day finishes I have witnessed, this was just about the most breathless. It is not often that two batsmen come so close to running three to win the match off the last ball. Poor Essex were shattered by the experience – but they were also hardened by it and it was*

*not long before they were bobbing up in most of the one-day finals – with Somerset, it seemed, often their main rivals!*

Sussex won the other semi-final with plenty to spare against Lancashire. But nobody in Somerset, except for a few crabbed and ageing critics, believes that Sussex can possibly win the final.

## EAST IS EAST
### *WEEK ENDED AUGUST 25*

OFF to Folkestone, in time to see Kent beat Gloucestershire by 10 wickets in two days, Gloucestershire did not, I am afraid, look much of a side, though they had the worst of a tricky pitch; however, I saw two innings by Jack Davey, and nearly an over by David Shepherd. These two Devonians are never happier than when doing one another's jobs.

There was hardly time to get back to High Littleton, so I had a pleasant day off before attending the Essex match in the last three days. Essex had to win this match if they were to have any real hopes of the championship. Without Gooch and Lever, who had both been chosen for England, they never looked like doing it.

Essex made a good fight of the match, but did not win it. Indeed, they were 7-5 down on first innings points. Kent now lead the championship by 43 points with two matches to play. Essex have three matches to play.

Tavaré batted very well, confirming, or so I trust, the England selectors in their intention to take him to Australia. Underwood bowled well, and it is sad that he has debarred himself from Test cricket. East also bowled well. He took some punishment, but kept his length and his sense of humour. The 100th over of the Kent first innings, which he bowled to Tavaré, ostentatiously offering a single so that he could get at Underwood, was full of comedy, not overdone. Before it began, Tavaré and Underwood held a consultation and East, hand cupped to ear, crept up behind them, crouching. The crowd's laughter gave him away. I wish I could make this report as funny as it was.

*Ray East was that rare phenomenon, a natural visual comic. He would have made a brilliant career in silent films.*

## ICICLES ON THE SIGHT-SCREEN
### WEEK ENDED SEPTEMBER 1

ENGLAND won the Third Test against New Zealand, on the fourth day, although for more than two days New Zealand seemed to be having the better of it. They were bowled out by Botham and Willis in their second innings, for 67. I am afraid it has been a disappointing tour for them; twice in the Tests they reached good positions, and faded away. You can attribute this to the English fast-medium bowling, or to inadequacies of

Early success for New Zealand in England's second innings. Left to right are John Wright, Richard Hadlee (bowler), Bev Congdon, Geoff Howarth, Mark Burgess, John Parker, Bruce Edgar (wicket-keeper) and Brendon Bracewell. Geoff Boycott is the batsman to go but Graham Gooch, at the other end, stayed to see England home.

batsmanship, or to the miserable summer, which gave the New Zealanders little more chance to find their best form than it did the Pakistanis. However you judge it, Brearley will have a useful side to take to Australia.

I went to Bournemouth, to see Hampshire play Kent, expected to be the match which would settle the championship. On Monday morning, I heard the caterers ringing for champagne. On Tuesday evening it remained bottled. Hampshire needed to score 312 in the last innings, and did it with no obvious difficulty, rather as if they were having a gentle pre-season practice. Greenidge scored two centuries, and I remembered how he had thwarted Gloucestershire on the last day of last season. The first was a particularly fierce innings: in 136, he hit three sixes, sixteen fours, a vulnerable greenhouse and a slightly less vulnerable police car. So Kent, as things stood, needed 10 points from their match against Sussex next week.

So on the next day I was off to Southend. Our marvellous highspeed train from the west was stopped outside Didcot because a herd of cows was on the line. When I did reach Southend, after a long and shivering wait in the taxi queue, I found a driver who had never heard of the cricket ground, and only vaguely of cricket. He made strenuous efforts to drive me to Shoeburyness, Chalkwell, and even Chelmsford, and it was about three o'clock when I arrived at Southchurch Park. I glanced at the board, which showed 141 for nine, and saw to my surprise that Derbyshire were in the field. The tenth wicket fell almost immediately. Fortunately I had a mine of information at my elbow in the person of T. E. Bailey, who not only told me what had happened, but what was going to. Derbyshire, he said, would make about 120. They were 102 for six at the close. Since Essex had taken no batting points, Kent could now win the championship on first innings points alone.

On the second day Derbyshire took a first innings lead of five, and Essex, with four bowling points, made sure of finishing at least second in the championship, the highest position in their history. It was very cold. My oriental colleague gravely pointed out to me the icicles on the sight-screen. Essex were five runs ahead at the end, with two second innings wickets down, after a day much interrupted by rain and bad light.

And then, on the Friday, the match ended in a draw, and Kent were the champions. It was not the most dramatic way to win a championship, but Kent will not be perturbed about that. Also, we had some bold and sporting play. Essex made a declaration which gave Derbyshire a chance, and Derbyshire responded by going for the runs. Perhaps they should have stopped whacking in the very last over, when they had nine wickets down and still needed 13. A Kent supporter near me emphatically thought so. But they did score 10 of them, and did not lose another wicket. East bowled the last ball to Mellor, who pulled it round the corner. They ran three, but reluctantly recognised that there was no chance of more.

## FAREWELL, FROM WORCESTER, WITH THANKS
### WEEK ENDED SEPTEMBER 8

NO, I am not being wise after the event. I told Sir John Elliot, whom I had the pleasure of meeting at Southend – he is one of the pillars of Essex cricket – I told him that Somerset were not going to win the Gillette Cup, and very likely not the John Player League either.

County Championship
(as at August 29)

| | | P | Pts |
|---|---|---|---|
| **1** | Kent | 21 | 285 |
| **2** | Essex | 20 | 254 |
| **3** | Middlesex | 21 | 236 |
| **4** | Somerset Yorkshire } | 21 | 221 |

This was not a judgment of form, or a case of betting against your wishes, but a respect for history, which I have often found to be a good guide to cricketing events. Somerset have always been a side who win the matches they are expected to lose, and lose those they are expected to win. This is a large part of their appeal.

You will have read reports of the match, and shall not suffer another from me. I must, however, say a word about Sussex. Who, at the beginning of the season, would have thought that a win for Sussex would be widely popular? Yet it was – more popular, much, than Kent's in the championship. Now that their Old Man of the Sea is off their backs, and with the sensible captaincy of Long, Sussex are rapidly regaining their old place in public affection. I was glad, too, that Parker was the man of the match. If he is encouraged to

play his natural game, which is full of strokes – and always assuming he likes the game sufficiently to take it up as a career – he might easily become another of Cambridge's long and distinguished list of England captains.

And so to Sunday, and the culminating disappointment for the Taunton crowd. It was known, before the end, that Hampshire had won, and that Somerset therefore *had* to win, or tie, to win the League – for Hampshire had the higher run-rate. For the third time this summer, the gates at Taunton were closed. The crowd was prospectively jubilant, and remained so, undauntedly, till the very last ball. From this Somerset needed four runs, with nine wickets down. They ran two, before the inevitable run out.

I feel I should apologise that in this journal I have written so much about Somerset. As I have explained, this was partly due to circumstances beyond my control, as Stuart Hibbert used to say with incomparable elegance. I am pleased, though, that I saw so much of their most successful season, particularly as it has meant I have seen a lot of Vivian Richards. Now that Barry Richards has decided to leave us – more mourned than Greig – there is no question who is the best batsman in the country to watch, greatly though I admire the assiduity of Boycott.

I spent the last few days, still with Somerset, at Worcester. Worcester makes as gracious a setting in autumn as in summer. I visited the cathedral. I did not have the nerve to reprove God for the weather, though I had framed a prayer ("Two shocking summers running, Lord, gets a bit much"). There, in the silence, and with more thanksgiving than sorrow in my heart, I said farewell to it.

Victory in the Gillette Cup final for Arnold Long and his Sussex team.

**Schweppes County Championship Final Table**

|  | P | W | D | L | NR | Bt | Bw | Pts |
|---|---|---|---|---|---|---|---|---|
| 1 Kent (1) | 22 | 13 | 6 | 3 | 0 | 56 | 80 | 292 |
| 2 Essex (6) | 22 | 12 | 9 | 1 | 0 | 55 | 74 | 273 |
| 3 Middlesex (1) | 22 | 11 | 5 | 5 | 1 | 48 | 75 | 255 |
| 4 Yorkshire (12) | 22 | 10 | 9 | 3 | 0 | 58 | 55 | 233 |
| 5 Somerset (4) | 22 | 9 | 9 | 4 | 0 | 44 | 76 | 228 |
| 6 Leicestershire (5) | 22 | 4 | 13 | 5 | 0 | 57 | 68 | 173 |
| 7 Nottinghamshire (17) | 22 | 3 | 12 | 7 | 0 | 63 | 67 | 166 |
| 8 Hampshire (11) | 22 | 4 | 11 | 6 | 1 | 53 | 60 | 161 |
| 9 Sussex* (8) | 22 | 4 | 11 | 7 | 0 | 39 | 64 | 151 |
| 10 Gloucestershire (3) | 22 | 4 | 9 | 8 | 1 | 42 | 55 | 145 |
| 11 Warwickshire (10) | 22 | 4 | 13 | 5 | 0 | 39 | 56 | 143 |
| 12 Lancashire* (16) | 22 | 4 | 9 | 8 | 1 | 28 | 59 | 135 |
| 13 Glamorgan (14) | 22 | 3 | 11 | 8 | 0 | 43 | 54 | 133 |
| 14 Derbyshire (7) | 22 | 3 | 12 | 7 | 0 | 33 | 63 | 132 |
| 15 Worcestershire (13) | 22 | 2 | 15 | 5 | 0 | 56 | 51 | 131 |
| 16 Surrey (14) | 22 | 3 | 12 | 7 | 0 | 36 | 58 | 130 |
| 17 Northamptonshire (9) | 22 | 2 | 12 | 6 | 2 | 41 | 56 | 121 |

**1977 positions in brackets.**
*Six points deducted for breach of regulations.

# FIRST CLASS AVERAGES

**Batting**

(Qualification: 8 innings average 10.00)

* Not out

| | I | NO | HS | Runs | Av |
|---|---|---|---|---|---|
| C. E. B. Rice | 37 | 9 | 213* | 1871 | 66.82 |
| G. M. Turner | 38 | 7 | 202* | 1711 | 55.19 |
| C. G. Greenidge | 34 | 1 | 211 | 1771 | 53.66 |
| D. L. Amiss | 41 | 3 | 162 | 2030 | 53.42 |
| J. H. Hampshire | 36 | 6 | 132 | 1596 | 53.20 |
| B. F. Davison | 35 | 3 | 180* | 1644 | 51.37 |
| G. Boycott | 25 | 1 | 131 | 1233 | 51.37 |
| M. J. Procter | 36 | 3 | 203 | 1655 | 50.15 |
| K. S. McEwan | 37 | 3 | 186 | 1682 | 49.47 |
| Asif Iqbal | 25 | 6 | 171 | 934 | 49.15 |
| A. J. Lamb | 27 | 8 | 106* | 883 | 46.47 |
| D. W. Randall | 40 | 7 | 157* | 1525 | 46.21 |
| I. V. A. Richards | 38 | 4 | 118 | 1558 | 45.82 |
| J. A. Ormrod | 41 | 7 | 173 | 1535 | 45.14 |
| Zaheer Abbas | 35 | 1 | 213 | 1535 | 45.14 |
| C. J. Tavaré | 39 | 5 | 105 | 1534 | 45.11 |
| R. W. Tolchard | 35 | 16 | 103* | 841 | 44.26 |
| A. I. Kallicharran | 29 | 5 | 129 | 1041 | 43.37 |
| B. L. D'Oliveira | 22 | 5 | 146* | 728 | 42.82 |
| Imran Khan | 37 | 5 | 167 | 1339 | 41.84 |
| G. A. Gooch | 33 | 3 | 129 | 1254 | 41.80 |
| K. W. R. Fletcher | 35 | 8 | 89 | 1127 | 41.74 |
| M. J. Harris | 36 | 4 | 148* | 1315 | 41.09 |
| G. P. Howarth | 37 | 3 | 179* | 1375 | 40.44 |
| G. R. J. Roope | 29 | 7 | 113* | 888 | 40.36 |
| R. A. Woolmer | 34 | 3 | 137 | 1245 | 40.16 |
| B. R. Hardie | 33 | 7 | 109 | 1044 | 40.15 |
| E. J. O. Hemsley | 37 | 7 | 141* | 1168 | 38.93 |
| R. D. V. Knight | 38 | 6 | 128 | 1233 | 38.53 |
| M. N. S. Taylor | 29 | 9 | 103* | 770 | 38.50 |
| P. A. Slocombe | 40 | 8 | 128* | 1225 | 38.28 |
| D. S. Steele | 36 | 5 | 130 | 1182 | 38.12 |
| J. F. Steele | 34 | 3 | 133 | 1182 | 38.12 |
| D. I. Gower | 31 | 2 | 111 | 1098 | 37.86 |
| Javed Miandad | 32 | 6 | 127 | 983 | 37.80 |
| P. W. G. Parker | 37 | 6 | 112 | 1192 | 37.25 |
| C. H. Lloyd | 36 | 6 | 120 | 1116 | 37.20 |
| Sadiq Mohammad | 42 | 3 | 176 | 1449 | 37.15 |
| W. Larkins | 44 | 5 | 170* | 1448 | 37.12 |
| C. T. Radley | 26 | 1 | 106 | 923 | 36.92 |
| P. N. Kirsten | 35 | 4 | 206* | 1133 | 36.54 |
| E. J. Barlow | 25 | 4 | 127 | 765 | 36.42 |
| J. N. Shepherd | 28 | 6 | 101 | 785 | 35.68 |
| C. J. C. Rowe | 35 | 5 | 85 | 1065 | 35.50 |
| P. Willey | 35 | 9 | 112 | 921 | 35.42 |
| F. C. Hayes | 35 | 5 | 136* | 1055 | 35.16 |
| B. C. Rose | 41 | 5 | 122 | 1263 | 35.08 |
| P. A. Neale | 40 | 6 | 103* | 1182 | 34.76 |
| M. J. Llewellyn | 31 | 6 | 82 | 849 | 33.96 |
| K. D. Smith | 39 | 4 | 132* | 1187 | 33.91 |
| G. Miller | 25 | 5 | 95 | 674 | 33.70 |
| J. A. Hopkins | 44 | 3 | 116 | 1371 | 33.43 |
| M. W. Gatting | 39 | 4 | 128 | 1166 | 33.31 |
| R. O. Butcher | 14 | 0 | 142 | 464 | 33.14 |
| P. M. Roebuck | 37 | 8 | 131* | 944 | 32.55 |
| P. Carrick | 32 | 11 | 105 | 679 | 32.33 |
| R. C. Ontong | 34 | 4 | 116* | 969 | 32.30 |
| G. Cook | 40 | 2 | 155 | 1226 | 32.26 |

**Bowling**

(Qualification: 10 wickets)

| | O | M | Runs | W | Av |
|---|---|---|---|---|---|
| D. L. Underwood | 815.1 | 359 | 1594 | 110 | 14.49 |
| R. A. Woolmer | 135.4 | 46 | 292 | 20 | 14.60 |
| W. W. Daniel | 453.3 | 113 | 1114 | 76 | 14.65 |
| M. Hendrick | 473.5 | 167 | 895 | 59 | 15.16 |
| J. K. Lever | 681.1 | 160 | 1610 | 106 | 15.18 |
| P. H. Edmonds | 503 | 174 | 912 | 60 | 15.20 |
| M. W. Gatting | 168.3 | 37 | 411 | 26 | 15.80 |
| R. J. Hadlee | 497.1 | 120 | 1269 | 78 | 16.26 |
| R. E. East | 700.2 | 226 | 1506 | 92 | 16.36 |
| I. T. Botham | 605.2 | 141 | 1640 | 100 | 16.40 |
| C. M. Old | 520.1 | 166 | 1108 | 64 | 17.31 |
| R. G. D. Willis | 473.2 | 116 | 1197 | 65 | 18.41 |
| G. G. Arnold | 401 | 102 | 910 | 49 | 18.57 |
| C. E. Waller | 371 | 125 | 861 | 46 | 18.71 |
| M. W. W. Selvey | 743.5 | 199 | 1929 | 101 | 19.09 |
| G. W. Johnson | 510.4 | 173 | 1084 | 56 | 19.35 |
| H. R. Moseley | 348.1 | 103 | 813 | 41 | 19.82 |
| P. E. Russell | 235.4 | 88 | 423 | 21 | 20.14 |
| C. E. B. Rice | 322.3 | 82 | 835 | 41 | 20.36 |
| W. Hogg | 256.4 | 58 | 775 | 38 | 20.39 |
| J. E. Emburey | 799.3 | 243 | 1641 | 79 | 20.77 |
| B. M. Brain | 573.2 | 138 | 1589 | 76 | 20.90 |
| J. P. Whiteley | 172.5 | 46 | 475 | 22 | 21.59 |
| R. M. Ratcliffe | 571.3 | 151 | 1532 | 70 | 21.88 |
| E. J. Barlow | 214.5 | 58 | 528 | 24 | 22.00 |
| N. Phillip | 583.1 | 113 | 1591 | 71 | 22.40 |
| K. Higgs | 381 | 112 | 923 | 41 | 22.51 |
| C. E. H. Croft | 431.3 | 101 | 1266 | 56 | 22.60 |
| A. M. E. Roberts | 254.1 | 74 | 617 | 27 | 22.85 |
| K. B. S. Jarvis | 598.5 | 139 | 1863 | 80 | 23.28 |
| D. P. Hughes | 191.1 | 54 | 517 | 22 | 23.50 |
| P. B. Clift | 519.4 | 156 | 1209 | 51 | 23.70 |
| M. J. Procter | 665.2 | 185 | 1649 | 69 | 23.89 |
| A. J. Harvey-Walker | 145 | 42 | 408 | 17 | 24.00 |
| J. C. Balderstone | 368.5 | 104 | 914 | 38 | 24.05 |
| P. I. Pocock | 662.4 | 201 | 1615 | 67 | 24.10 |
| J. W. Southern | 762.3 | 247 | 1833 | 76 | 24.11 |
| C. W. J. Athey | 93 | 26 | 268 | 11 | 24.36 |
| R. D. Jackman | 590.2 | 134 | 1707 | 70 | 24.38 |
| J. H. Childs | 521 | 155 | 1440 | 59 | 24.40 |
| J. M. Rice | 267.1 | 70 | 709 | 29 | 24.44 |
| G. A. Cope | 342.3 | 114 | 784 | 32 | 24.50 |
| D. Breakwell | 445.1 | 135 | 1007 | 41 | 24.56 |
| S. Turner | 531 | 149 | 1183 | 48 | 24.64 |
| Sarfraz Nawaz | 445 | 116 | 998 | 40 | 24.95 |
| S. Oldham | 485 | 115 | 1326 | 53 | 25.01 |
| J. Spencer | 496.5 | 143 | 1158 | 46 | 25.17 |
| R. Illingworth | 261.4 | 86 | 635 | 25 | 25.40 |
| J. F. Steele | 229.5 | 62 | 566 | 22 | 25.72 |
| P. D. Swart | 358 | 73 | 1112 | 43 | 25.86 |
| G. B. Stevenson | 375.3 | 79 | 1144 | 44 | 26.00 |
| L. B. Taylor | 300.2 | 50 | 1040 | 40 | 26.00 |
| K. F. Jennings | 442.3 | 148 | 1041 | 40 | 26.02 |
| M. A. Buss | 179.2 | 52 | 473 | 18 | 26.27 |
| C. H. Dredge | 573.1 | 135 | 1473 | 56 | 26.30 |
| D. S. Steele | 378.3 | 110 | 976 | 37 | 26.37 |
| Intikhab Alam | 623.2 | 197 | 1570 | 59 | 26.61 |
| V. J. Marks | 458.1 | 133 | 1217 | 45 | 27.04 |
| J. R. T. Barclay | 207 | 49 | 554 | 20 | 27.20 |

*Cricket's civil war continued furiously throughout the winter with Australia, inevitably, the major battleground. As in all wars, neither side claimed any victories without counting a large cost. The Australian Cricket Board announced at the end of the season that they had lost in excess of $A800,000 over the two years of WSC, and because of huge capital outlay on grounds, plus an enormous bill for salaries, the losses incurred by WSC themselves were considerably greater although contributions to advertising revenue from the cricket on Channel Nine reduced the losses as far as the wider Packer business interests were concerned.*

*The key to the improved fortunes of WSC in their second year lay in the inability of the reconstituted official Australian team to give England a serious challenge for the Ashes. The victory of Brearley's team by five matches to one exaggerrates the difference between*

*the sides but gates declined along with the fortunes of the national team and the night matches at Sydney proved an increasing counter-attraction for young spectators. Nevertheless, there was still a strong body of more conservative opinion in Australia, and a general feeling that attractive as the WSC night matches may have been, they did not have the same meaning as a traditional Test match against the old enemy.*

*To British eyes, England's retention of the Ashes was not in any way a hollow success. Brearley again led them shrewdly; the team were very fit and dedicated; and all the main bowlers, Willis, Botham, Hendrick, Old, Lever, Miller and Emburey had their moments. Australia did at least find one new hero, Rodney Hogg, a solidly muscled, curly-haired fast bowler who took 41 wickets in his first six Tests. In a series dominated by bowlers, in fact, only Gower averaged over 40 for either side, and only Randall, Yallop and Border over 30.*

*Later in the season, in an unhappy enterprise which led to the eventual compromise "peace" between Packer and the ACB, the "Circus" moved to the Caribbean, where there was little cricket to savour and an ugly riot developed at Georgetown. The "official" West Indies had earlier toured India under Alvin Kallicharran, and lost a rather colourless series by the only game in six to be finished.*

*India also toured Pakistan for their first encounters on the cricket field for 17 years. The rapprochement between neighbours was more significant than the cricket, but it was a more positively played series between these two than many before or since, Pakistan winning two-nil through the immense strength of a batting order which began: Majid Khan, Sadiq Mohammad, Zaheer Abbas, Mushtaq Mohammad, Javed Miandad and Imran Khan. Mudassar Nazar took over from Sadiq after one match.*

*When one recalls that there was also a tour of New Zealand by Pakistan, it was not surprising that the heads of cricket supporters were spinning from an attempt to keep up with it all. Nor, when the first ball was bowled in April, was there any real sign of the dramatic agreement which was to end the civil war at the end of May. By the terms of it, Channel Nine bought the right to televise official Test cricket in Australia, the cause for which General Packer had first led his troops into action. Several players were a good deal richer, and night cricket had come to stay.*

# ─ 1979 ─

## A RULE WHICH HANDICAPS
### WEEK ENDED MAY 4

IT looks like being a tricky season. The outlook is gloomy, not only here in High Littleton, where the south-westerly is pelting rain on the windows, but at New Printing House Square. *The Times* is looking after me generously, and I used to complain when they swished me around the country so much but, like the aged African Emperor, crowned triumphantly at the end of *Black Mischief*, after countless years in prison, I keep fumbling at my ankle, because I miss my chain.

The England Under-19 party which toured Australia in January 1979. Back, left to right: Freddie Brown (manager), Gordon Lord (Warwickshire), Norman Cowans (Middlesex), Russell Cobb (Leicestershire), Andrew Arundell (Yorkshire), Iain Anderson (Derbyshire), Colin Cook (Middlesex), Kevan James (Middlesex), Keith Andrew (assistant manager). Front: Grant Forster (Northamptonshire), Duncan Pauline (Surrey), Kim Barnett (Derbyshire), Nigel Felton (Kent, captain), Simon Dennis (Yorkshire), Mike Garnham (Gloucestershire).

So far, nothing much has happened, except the rain. I made a visit to the Parks, where there was no cricket, and the poor trees, smitten with the Dutch bug, gave the ground an even more gap-toothed look than last year. In the Benson & Hedges, two matches had to be continued on Monday, and at Trent Bridge Nottinghamshire and Middlesex could not finish on Tuesday. An odd thing, it seems to me that, while a drawn match is decided on run-rate (Middlesex thus winning this one), qualification for the quarter-finals, should points be level, depends on wicket-taking rate. This rule handicaps sides who have to play in truncated matches, because they do not get a chance to bowl at the tail-enders.

Even the Village Championship, where they take a pride in playing in the rain, did not do too well last Saturday. About a third of the matches was rained off. This competition is organised by *The Cricketer*, and sponsored by Samuel Whitbread. When it began, in 1972, it was sponsored by John Haig, but Haig have now transferred their support to the "club" championship, presumably on the grounds that the taste for whisky is urban rather than bucolic.

## SUPERFICIALLY INNOCUOUS
### WEEK ENDED MAY 11

I watched Somerset playing Northamptonshire at Taunton. It was very good meeting old friends again, though Bill Andrews was not among those present, at least so I judged because I could not hear him. It was also a very good win by Somerset, achieved in not much more than a day-and-a-half's play. The second day was washed out and, when I saw the rain at High Littleton this morning, I expected little from the third. But, though the clouds were never far away, Taunton stayed dry. I was doing some commentary for HTV, and the producer, sensibly, decided that we should record the entire morning's play, so that if it rained in the afternoon – when we were due to be on the air – we should not have an empty screen. Yet, in fact, we had an interesting afternoon's play, and a very satisfactory one for Somerset. Northamptonshire went in, second time, 122 runs behind, and scored exactly that number, which meant that tea was taken. It was a long 20 minutes for Somerset, because it might easily have rained again.

Marks had an admirable all-round match. His bowling does look, superficially, innocuous, but he takes some playing if the pitch gives him even a little help. It was disappointing not to see a longer innings from Larkins, a player of whom I constantly hear high praise, but with whom I have not so far had much luck.

*Like Frank Hayes, Wayne Larkins has been one of the "nearly" men of English cricket. Everyone in the game knows of his quite exceptional talent but, like Alan, Larkins himself has had little luck when the moment was right.*

## COCK-EYED CLOCK
### WEEK ENDED MAY 18

THE weather is still wayward. I went to Bristol on Saturday to watch Gloucestershire and Somerset in the Benson and Hedges, but there was no play. On

Monday, however, we had a full day in beautiful sunshine at least, rather less than a dull day, because Somerset had won easily by tea-time.

When Gloucestershire made the arrangement with an insurance company which guaranteed the continuance of county cricket at Bristol, not all their members were happy about it – some saw it as an erosion of their rights – but it is certainly making them more confortable. The newly panelled members' lounge and dining-room is handsome. The old Bristol pavilion used to be something of a joke. Now, though it looks much the same from the outside, with the cock-eyed clock two-thirds of the way along the roof, it is transformed within.

I saw my first Sunday League match, Hampshire and Essex, at Southampton. It was Hampshire's first win in the competition, and Essex's first defeat. I thought it quite a good match. I enjoy Sunday League better when we do not have one of those wild, scrambled finishes, when luck takes over from merit. Greenidge and Turner did most of the scoring for Hampshire. Turner is a good cricketer, and yet, to me, a slightly disappointing one. When he first came out of Wiltshire, all sorts of counties were said to be competing to sign him. I suppose it has been a lack of concentration that has held him back from the highest level. I have seen him get out to some silly strokes and, when he encounters a bad patch of form, he stays in it too long.

## CAPS OF ASSORTED COLOURS
### WEEK ENDED MAY 25

ON Tuesday the preliminary rounds of the World Cup began, and I went to Wolverhampton to watch Papua play East Africa. It struck me that this would have made a good theme for Beachcomber, whose

Action from the match at Wolverhampton.

recent death we mourn. Can life hold anything more when you have seen Papua play East Africa at cricket at Wolverhampton? The Papuans did not do very well; 101 for eight in the 39 overs that were possible. The cricket was, I thought, of a good club standard, especially considering how the conditions, miserable even by English standards, must have taxed both sides. The adjudicator for the Man of the Match award was Rachael Heyhoe Flint, which would have given Beachcomber another good line. The Papuans wore caps in the assorted colours of Bradford Northern. Most of the other matches were affected by the weather, but Singapore beat Argentina by one wicket, at a place called Pickwick, and the United States beat Israel at a place called Blossomfield. According to *The Guardian*, the high moment in the American innings came when

Concentration in the pavilion at Blossomfield.

Lashkari was caught by Zion Moses off Reuben. There's names again!

I went to Worcester on Wednesday for the Somerset match. No play. There was no play at Wolverhampton either, so Papua and East Africa had to split the points. On Thursday, though the weather was discouraging, I decided to try Worcester again. I reached the station a little late, and a kind porter, who knew what I had come for, immediately directed me on to the next train back to Bristol. He had heard the news from the county ground, and was angry, as a Worcester man had every right to be. But I will defer my thoughts about this until next week.

## TEMPERS RESTORED
### WEEK ENDED JUNE 1

CORRECTION: Somerset are out of the Benson and Hedges Cup, and Glamorgan take their place. The melancholy events at Worcester on May 24 will have been well chewed over in *The Cricketer* by the time you read this, so I will not recount them, just add a couple of points. I strongly disapprove of Somerset's action, and wrote to that effect in *The Spectator* before the TCCB decision was announced. I wrote that I hoped they would win nothing this season, and that they would immediately be knocked out of the Benson and Hedges. Since they have been knocked out even more immediately than immediately, and accepted the decision so gracefully, it is now happily possible to forgive them. All the same, I am not sure that exactly the right decision was reached. Whatever reserve powers the Test and County Cricket Board possesses, Somerset were essentially suspended by retrospective legislation. However unwise Rose may have been in his action, it was within the law. It would have been better if the Board had simply expressed censure, and invited Somerset to consider their position. They could then have withdrawn voluntarily.

The other good news of the week – or relatively good news – was the agreement between Mr Packer and the Australian Cricket Board. It is much too early to say how it will work out. The postponement of India's tour to Australia is a breach of faith, and an alarming indication of the extent of Mr Packer's victory.

## SRI LANKA AND CANADA GO THROUGH
### WEEK ENDED JUNE 8

THE Benson and Hedges semi-finalists are Yorkshire, Essex, Derbyshire and Surrey. Of these, only Surrey have won the cup before. Gooch made what must have been a noble hundred for Essex, and Younis what must have been, for him, a deeply satisfying one for Worcestershire against Surrey (who did not re-engage him this season), even though it did not suffice to win the match. Wright, a New Zealander, scored a hundred for Derbyshire. It was his second of the week – just the thing to set him up for the Prudential.

In the Schweppes championship, Essex have taken a useful lead. In the John Player there have so far, despite desperate efforts, been ten "no results", and it is still more or less a jumble. Yorkshire, with three wins out of five, are top, and Warwickshire, with none out of four, are bottom.

The ICC Trophy has managed to get itself completed, and the qualifiers for the World Cup are Sri Lanka and Canada. Sri Lanka's passage was predictable, after their previous achievements in one-day cricket – which include a win over England, apart from that remarkable performance against Australia at The Oval in 1975. But they have not endeared themselves to the public by their refusal to play Israel. Canada's success was unexpected and popular, though the cosmopolitan nature of their side does not quite suggest a revival of cricket in North America, where a hundred years ago it was so strong.

*This is a shrewd point. I suppose Canadian society is, anyway, cosmopolitan, but if any sport is really to take hold, it needs the interest and participation of the natives. This is why the explosion of interest in cricket in the Persian Gulf is spurious: the interest comes mainly from temporary immigrants.*

## BEST SEAT IN PLAYROOM
### WEEK ENDED JUNE 15

THE first day of the Prudential Cup proper was much as expected. Canada did not disgrace themselves, but duly lost; so did Sri Lanka; so did India, who have never come to terms with the limited-over game. England beat Australia without, in the end, much difficulty, after the Australian batting had failed on a Lord's green-top. The most remarkable aspect of the match was that Boycott took more wickets than he scored runs.

I doubted whether I should be able to get in at Lord's, since nobody has sent me a Lord's pass yet this season, so I decided to watch at home on television, something I have not in the past had much occasion to do. Watching cricket on television is not very satisfactory for, though you have an amplitude of information, there is a lack of atmosphere and contact. This is no criticism of the producers, commentators and engineers (though for myself I could do with fewer slow-motion replays): it is simply the nature of the medium. I did my best to create the right atmosphere. I took up my position in the best seat in the playroom, the children bravely accepting the decision that they would have nothing to watch all day unless they wanted cricket. I had, by my side, a bottle

of hock on ice, and at lunch Rosemary was to bring me salmon and cucumber sandwiches (I cannot stand cucumber, and would have to remove it, carefully, from the sandwich, as I have done countless times before on cricket grounds: what could be more evocative than that?) But it did not work. I was bored, without the wander round the ground, the old pals in the bar and press-box, the gossip. I left after lunch and took the dog for a walk.

## BOVINE-LOOKING
### WEEK ENDED JUNE 22

IT has been Bath Festival week, and the weather was not totally bad. Somerset needed to beat Essex, if they were to continue to think of the championship. They made a good try. The scores were: Somerset 277 for nine, and 284 for seven declared, Essex 302 for eight, and 87 for seven. Marks is still in extraordinarily good form. There was much discussion as to whether he or Roebuck will turn out to be the better. Myself, I think Roebuck's technique is superior, and that he will score more runs, but Marks has a gift of rising to the occasion, and he also has his bowling, which is not so milky as it is bovine-looking. They are both pleasant and personable young men. Marks, an Oxford Blue, was born in Somerset. Roebuck, a Cambridge Blue, was born in Oxford, but since he went to Millfield (like several more of the present side) and played his first match for Somerset seconds when he was 13, is reasonably regarded as a local. They will be pillars of Somerset for the next decade or more, provided they do not get bored with the game. When we mourn the days of the amateur we must remember that, without the abolition of his old status, players such as these might well have been lost to county cricket.

*It was Marks's bowling, not his batting, which won him some England caps. But Roebuck was preferred to him as captain of the county in 1986.*

## POCOCK'S LUCK
### WEEK ENDED JUNE 29

I WAS at Cardiff for part of the Surrey match. Surrey won easily, despite losing some quick wickets in the last innings. It was good to see Pocock still taking wickets: an unlucky cricketer in one respect, for he seemed destined for a long spell as an England player when Illingworth was recalled to the side as captain, thus sealing the off-spinner's place.

The atmosphere at Cardiff was not very happy. I am in no position to apportion blame, and did not seek to become better informed on the troubles. But I have noticed before that Welshmen, rather like Lancastrians, tend to be a little over-enthusiastic about their representatives when things are going well, and a little over-contemptuous when they go badly.

Pat Pocock – plenty of wickets for Surrey.

## ADMIRATION FOR PRINGLE
### WEEK ENDED JULY 6

REFLECTING on the second World Cup, I feel that though it could not be called a failure – it is reported that the attendances were higher than in 1975 – it was less gripping than the first. The novelty was wearing off. The weather did not help, though in such a summer as this it could have been much worse, and we could hardly expect a repetition of the 1975 heat wave. It was always fairly obvious that the West Indies would win. There was just a chance, some thought (indeed I was one of them) that, on an inspired day, the Pakistani batsmen might do enough to beat them: but this view did not sufficiently take into account the depth of the West Indies fast bowling. It is hard to score quickly when, having battled through the opening spells of Roberts and Holding, you are faced with Croft and Garner. The only real chance of the West Indies losing would have been in a series of drastic interventions from the rain. None of these things quite made for the drama of 1975, but the competition had to prove itself in less favourable conditions than it had then, and this it has done.

Collis King – a magnificent innings in the World Cup Final.

The Benson and Hedges finalists will be Essex and Surrey. I wonder if Essex can do it at last. They ought to be fairly sure of the championship, though it is early in the season to say it. I have an anxious feeling that, unaccustomed to winning as they are, they might falter on the brink, as Somerset did last year.

On the University match, which Cambridge won by an innings and plenty to spare, I would prefer not to dwell, though even an Oxonian must mention with admiration Pringle, a freshman who scored a century and took five wickets. In all the history of the match, not many freshmen can have done as much, though with telephone charges what they are, I am not going to ring up Bill Frindall or Irving Rosenwater about it. This performance, however, though it exacts tribute from an Oxonian, did not do so from the London public, who walked or drove blithely by, most of them unaware that the match was going on.

Derek Pringle – a significant contribution to the Cambridge success.

## EMERGING SHEEP
### WEEK ENDED JULY 20

THE Indians lost the Test at Edgbaston by an innings. They were unlucky: not in losing the toss, because somebody always has to do that, but because Bedi was unfit to play, and Chandrasekhar, brought in to replace him, clearly was not bounding with health. Even great spin bowlers grow older, and become more liable to injury (it is all very well saying that Rhodes, for instance, played Test cricket until he was 50, but he did not have to play in 10 or so five-day Tests a year). They must have regretted not bringing over Prasanna.

In the John Player League, the sheep are sorting themselves out from the goats, or perhaps one should say the tobacco from the ash. Kent and Somerset are joint leaders, 30 points from nine games, Worcestershire two points behind after playing the same number. Four points behind Worcestershire are Middlesex, who have played an additional game. For all the uncertainty of 40-over cricket, it will be surprising if the winner does not come from the present first three.

David Gower reaches his double century at Edgbaston.

## TOUCHES OF QUEEN VICTORIA
### WEEK ENDED JULY 27

ESSEX won the Benson and Hedges, without too much trouble, so the only county now which has never won anything is Somerset. They must fancy their chances both in the Gillette Cup and the John Player League, but they can hardly hope to catch Essex in the Championship, nor can anyone else. Essex now lead the Schweppes table by 69 points, with eight matches to go. It would take a series of disasters even more cataclysmic than those which overtook Hampshire in 1974 (so feelingly recalled to this day by John Arlott) to

Keith Fletcher and Graham Gooch enjoy the first Essex win in any major competition.

thwart them. I saw part of the Essex match at Bournemouth. They won by an innings, and I was impressed not only by their abilities, which were known, but by their confidence, which has not always been apparent at critical moments in the past. They played as though the thought of defeat did not enter their heads, so much so that I was occasionally reminded of Yorkshire in the Thirties and Surrey in the Fifties. (East, of course, has always had touches of Queen Victoria about him: "There is NO depression in this house, &c").

Nottinghamshire are second in the Schweppes. They beat Yorkshire quite easily, although Boycott carried his bat through Yorkshire's second innings for 175. Boycott's average now stands at 148, for 12 innings, five not out. It is a real disappointment to me that Yorkshire, after a promising start, have not done better. They had wretched luck with the early weather, but as the rain has hesitantly departed, they have not taken their opportunities. The championship table bears an odd look, with Kent no better than the middle bunch, and Yorkshire and Middlesex (who have also had shocking chances with the weather) near the bottom.

I must not forget to tell you about an excellent win by Gloucestershire against the Indians at Bristol (Procter in form again). This should be worth some extra money to them under the Holt sponsorship scheme for matches by the counties against touring teams. I am glad to see some attention being paid to such matches, which were once one of the most attractive fixtures of any county's season but, in recent years, have tended to become rather idle shams.

Mike Smith of Middlesex using protection at Scarborough against the widespread plague of greenfly.

Mike Brearley catches Sunil Gavaskar at Lord's to give Ian Botham the fastest 100 wickets in Test cricket.

## PROCTER STILL FORMIDABLE
### WEEK ENDED AUGUST 3

THE weather has been much better lately, but Lord's was flooded on the second day of the Test, and naturally I had chosen the occasion for a visit. It was a particular pity because the Indians, after some lamentable batting, had been showing much livelier form in the field. Yorkshire have had their second win in a week, after bowling Warwickshire out for 35 on a wet pitch. Whitehouse, the Warwickshire captain, had some sharp things to say about uncovered pitches. He was not taking the defeat unsportingly: he just takes the view that pitches should be covered at all times. There have, of course, been arguments about this for a long time, and various attempts at compromise. I am inclined to think it would be better to cover them completely, or not at all. My own preference would be for the latter, though I do not suppose I should have many county treasurers on my side. The majority of cricketers have to do without covers, and the fewer barriers there are between the first-class game and the rest of it the better. If you play a game like ours in a climate like ours, you must expect the weather will take a hand in it, as it has done since cricket began.

Before my abortive trip to London, I saw some fluctuating cricket at Bristol. Leicestershire made 314 for four, and took three Gloucestershire wickets for 38 on the first evening. Then Sadiq scored 137 and Procter 122. Procter reached his century in 90 minutes. Now I learn that, in Leicestershire's second innings, Procter took seven for 26 (five in 16 balls) and Gloucestershire won by eight wickets. Procter's form this season has not been, for him, especially impressive, but this was a reminder that he is still a formidable cricketer. I am astonished at the way he has kept up his fast bowling, after so much trouble with injury. This was Gloucestershire's first win at Bristol for three years.

We had another reminder of Procter's talents recently when he won a single-wicket match against Botham. These matches are becoming increasingly popular and, though they savour a little bit of stunts, traditionalists should not really complain. Single-wicket had a lot to do with the increasing popularity of cricket in the first half of the last century. There was as much interest when Marsden met Pilch and Mynn met Dearman as if the heavyweight championship was at stake. The trouble with these modern gladiatorial contests is that the rules are never quite the same twice running. The principals agree upon their own. It would be difficult to legislate for such private affairs, but might not MCC make some recommendations in the hope of securing a greater unanimity? It is not so long since the old single-wicket laws (which would not do in modern conditions) were printed with the rest in *Wisden*.

## SAGGING TAUNTON
### WEEK ENDED AUGUST 10

I WAS at Taunton on Wednesday for the Gillette Cup. Not that I saw much of it: the ground was so full that it was sagging. Somerset beat Kent comprehensively. Garner bowled them out, after Somerset had not batted particularly well. Sussex and Northamptonshire went through, and so did Middlesex, though the match against Yorkshire went into a second day. The matches of Middlesex and Yorkshire this season would make a saga in themselves. Several senior Somerset supporters (and I am not talking just of the committee room) expressed their anxiety to me about the behaviour of the one-day supporters. They were not too bad on Wednesday, but on Sundays, I gather, it can be a bit grim, when the lads charge in, attracted less by the cricket than the all-day licence.

| County Championship (as at August 1) | | |
|---|---|---|
| | P | Pts |
| **1** Essex | 17 | 215 |
| **2** Worcestershire | 18 | 154 |
| **3** Somerset | 18 | 131 |
| **4** Surrey | 19 | 130 |

## SLIP ONE IN, KAPIL
### WEEK ENDED AUGUST 17

THE latter part of the week produced just about the worst weather of the summer, as the poor Fastnet racers learned. Cricket suffered too, none more than the Indians. On an acceptable batting pitch at Headingley, they had taken four English wickets for 80, when it rained for the rest of the day – and all the next. They must, however, be pleased with the continuing development of Kapil Dev. I hear people saying "If only he was a couple of yards faster . . . " but if he was a fast bowler he would be a different one, and not necessarily a better. It would, no doubt, be a great advantage if he could learn to slip in, without advertising it beforehand, an occasional faster ball.

The county which had least reason to regret the weather was Essex. They had no match in the second part of the week, and neither Worcestershire nor Somerset, their nearest challengers – if the word is not too far-fetched – could get near a finish. Essex are still 61 points ahead, and need only 20 points from their last five matches to be certain of the championship.

## DELIGHT IN HIGH LITTLETON
### WEEK ENDED AUGUST 24

ESSEX duly won the championship at Northampton on Tuesday. They had been 14 behind on the first innings, but Hardie (with a century), Denness and, happily, Fletcher saw them through. They had to wait half an hour, for the Worcestershire result, before they knew they were champions, and it was a tense wait, because there were some extraordinary goings-on at Derby, where Worcestershire were playing. Worcestershire ended the Derbyshire second innings in the 19th over of the last hour, and went in with 10 minutes left and 25 to win. The umpires informed them that they had four overs to get them, but Derbyshire rang Lord's to confirm that play must stop on time (which seems an obvious enough point) and only two overs were bowled. Worcestershire scored 17 though, of course, they might have got the 25 in the two overs had they not been pacing themselves for four. A series of odd things has happened to Worcestershire this season. There was the declaration by Somerset in the Benson and Hedges, a groundsman's starting handle was rolled into the pitch, and they once had to follow on after Gifford had declared.

It has been a crowded week, so far as the weather has permitted. The Third Test, badly affected, drifted to a draw. The Gillette Cup semi-finals were won by Somerset and Northamptonshire. I was at Lord's for the Somerset–Middlesex match. Somerset won comfortably, by seven wickets, and no other result looked likely once Middlesex had lost their first five wickets for 74. A pleasing thing was the admirable innings of 90, not out, by Denning, one of the less publicised Somerset batsmen. He was made Man of the Match. This gave particular delight in High Littleton, where he is regarded as a local (born at Chewton Mendip down the road). His educational background is Millfield and St. Luke's, Exeter (alas! no more as a separate entity). He has never quite come into the England reckoning, perhaps partly through a lack of ambition, or "meanness" as they say in Yorkshire, but he has served his county very well. Northamptonshire won by 37 runs at Hove. It must have been a good match. A. J. Lamb and Willey made most of the runs for them, and T. M. Lamb took most wickets. Willey's repeated successes in limited-over cricket must be a strong recommendation for the Australian tour. Somerset are probably relieved not to have to meet Sussex, after uncomfortable recollections of last year: but Middlesex was the one they wanted out of the way. It is a measure of Brearley's skills as a captain that nobody ever feels quite safe against him.

Somerset are also on top of the John Player League. They have 42 points from 13 matches, two more than Kent. Worcestershire have 38 from 14. The resemblance to the climax of last season is becoming marked: let us hope the fates do not press it too far.

*They pushed the resemblance to the limit, but this time smiled finally on those whose hopes they had dashed the previous year.*

## OLD BALD BLIGHTER
### WEEK ENDED AUGUST 31

THE firm of Haig, to whose prosperity I have made a steady contribution, asked me to Lord's yesterday.

When I mentioned to my friends that I was going to "the final of the Haig", their reaction was to ask which villages were in it this year. In fact, the sponsorship of the village competition has now been undertaken by Whitbread, and Haig has given its generous patronage to the Club Cricket Championship, which is organised by the National Cricket Association. They clearly still derive some vicarious advantages from their former sponsorship!

The teams playing in the club championship were Reading and Scarborough. Scarborough were strong favourites, especially with Brian Close in their team. They did win, but only just, a stout effort by Reading, who did not score enough after a good opening partnership. It was grand to see the Old Bald Blighter again, looking the same age as he has for the last twenty years. I was surprised to see so large a crowd, getting on for two thousand, with a Test match on over the river. It was a delightful day, what I remember of it.

## PERSONAL PLEASURE IN SOMERSET'S DOUBLE
### WEEK ENDED SEPTEMBER 8–9

NO, it was not a replica of the end of last season: more a reversal. Somerset, you recall, then lost two titles in two days, and now they have won two in two. At the beginning of the season, Essex and Somerset were the only counties which had never won anything. Now they have each won twice. The final Test also had an exhilarating ending. Brearley made a declaration which required India to score 438 in the last innings. Nobody has ever made so many runs to win a match, in the fourth innings of a Test, but I was inclined at the time to think that the declaration was a little too generous, given that England needed only to draw to win the rubber; and the Indians again showed their capacity for second-innings recoveries. They were only nine runs short, with two wickets left, at the end and, if Gavaskar had managed to continue his marvellous innings a little longer (and Botham had not made a characteristic intervention, with two catches and three wickets) they must have won.

So the Indians ended their tour not, I imagine, dissatisfied. They won only one county match, and that was against Glamorgan (whose dismal season has

Sunil Gavaskar – so near to victory.

continued) but they did have poor luck with the weather. The famous spinners are not, on this evidence, the force that they were – though it would be unwise to write off a man of such classical method as Bedi. The batsmen took some time to run into form. Given their temperament, the Prudential Cup was not a happy preparation for them. They still look as if they will take some beating on their own pitches. It is sad that they will not be touring Australia, and that we are lumbered with this bastard tour instead, at the behest of Mr Packer. But I am glad that Brearley has accepted the captaincy, bravely when you consider that he has so much to lose and so little (barring the shekels) to gain.

Essex's championship win gave pleasure far beyond the boundaries of the county, not just because it was unprecedented. They are a popular side with a popular

The line-up for the International Batsman of the Year competition at the Oval. Left to right: Gordon Greenidge, Zaheer Abbas, Asif Iqbal, Barry Richards, Ian Chappell, David Gower, Graham Gooch, Clive Lloyd.

captain. Although Fletcher has scored more than 3,000 runs in Tests, at an average of over 40, he never quite became the dominant force in English cricket he once suggested. There was rarely anything violent about his methods. His off-drive would be made quietly, almost gently, and then you looked again, and the men in the covers were not bothering to chase it. Yet not many of his admirers thought that he had in him the makings of a captain. A shrewd adviser, yes, but hardly a captain. That is what we used to say of Fletcher. It is also what we used to say of Illingworth.

I also had a special personal pleasure in the success of Somerset. They beat Northamptonshire with only the occasional tremor. Richards played the innings he did not manage last year – not too restrained, not too aggressive. Garner took most of the Northamptonshire wickets. That the two West Indians were dominant on the day should not distract us from the thought that this has been a side constructed mainly from locally born-and/or-bred talent. Once the Gillette Cup was won, I thought it probable that the John Player League would be too, and sure enough a relaxed Somerset won at Trent Bridge, while Kent nervously lost at Canterbury.

It has been a frustrating season for me. It was the third wet summer running, and there has been no *Times*. But at the end of it we have some interesting and (again, for me) enjoyable results. I wish Yorkshire had done a little better. They did show their possibilities at times. The closing stages of the season were much cheered by a visit of the Poet's and Peasants' CC (please get the apostrophes right, editor). You will remember that I am the Poet of this excellent club. They were touring in the west, and their first match was washed out, and their second (at Newton Abbot, against South Devon), had to be abandoned because a water main had burst under the pitch. These disasters had the advantage that they were able to call on their Poet at High Littleton. It was a genial session at The Star, but they refuse to give me the statutory bottle of whisky until I write the statutory ode. It seemed an appropriate conclusion. Here were the Peasants, who mostly come from Essex, and they were visiting the Poet in Somerset. We were all happy.

## FINAL COUNTY TABLE

| | | P | W | L | D | Bt | Bl | Pts |
|---|---|---|---|---|---|---|---|---|
| | | | | | | **Bonus Points** | | |
| 1 | Essex (2) | 22 | 13 | 4 | 5 | 56 | 69 | 281 |
| 2 | Worcestershire (15) | 22 | 7 | 4 | 11 | 58 | 62 | 204 |
| 3 | Surrey (16) | 22 | 6 | 3 | 13 | 50 | 70 | 192 |
| 4 | Sussex (9) | 22 | 6 | 4 | 12 | 47 | 65 | 184 |
| 5 | Kent (1) | 22 | 6 | 3 | 13 | 49 | 60 | 181 |
| 6 | Leicestershire (6) | 22 | 4 | 5 | 13 | 60 | 68 | 176 |
| 7 | Yorkshire (4) | 22 | 5 | 3 | 14 | 52 | 63 | 175 |
| 8 | Somerset (5) | 22 | 5 | 1 | 16 | 56 | 55 | 171 |
| 9 | Nottinghamshire (7) | 22 | 6 | 4 | 12 | 43 | 54 | 169 |
| 10 | Gloucestershire (10) | 22 | 5 | 4 | 13 | 53 | 54 | 167 |
| 11 | Northamptonshire (17) | 22 | 3 | 6 | 13 | 59 | 58 | 153 |
| 12 | Hampshire (8) | 22 | 3 | 9 | 10 | 39 | 66 | 141 |
| 13 | Lancashire (12) | 22 | 4 | 4 | 14 | 37 | 55 | 140 |
| 14 | Middlesex (3) | 22 | 3 | 3 | 16 | 44 | 60 | 140 |
| 15 | Warwickshire (11) | 22 | 3 | 7 | 12 | 46 | 51 | 133 |
| 16 | Derbyshire (14) | 22 | 1 | 6 | 15 | 46 | 60 | 118 |
| 17 | Glamorgan (13) | 22 | 0 | 10 | 12 | 35 | 58 | 93 |

Draws column includes matches where no play was possible. 1978 positions in brackets.

**BATTING**
(Qualification: 8 innings, average 10.00)
* Not out

| | I | NO | HS | Runs | Av |
|---|---|---|---|---|---|
| G. Boycott | 20 | 5 | 175* | 1538 | 102.53 |
| Younis Ahmed | 30 | 8 | 221* | 1539 | 69.95 |
| A. J. Lamb | 34 | 8 | 178 | 1747 | 67.19 |
| G. M. Turner | 31 | 2 | 150* | 1669 | 57.55 |
| Sadiq Mohammad | 30 | 2 | 171 | 1595 | 56.96 |
| K. C. Wessels | 36 | 2 | 187 | 1800 | 52.94 |
| A. I. Kallicharran | 26 | 5 | 170* | 1098 | 52.28 |
| C. G. Greenidge | 30 | 2 | 145 | 1404 | 50.14 |
| D. L. Amiss | 37 | 3 | 232* | 1672 | 49.17 |

**BOWLING**
(Qualification: 10 wickets)

| | O | M | Runs | W | Av | BB |
|---|---|---|---|---|---|---|
| J. Garner | 393.1 | 137 | 761 | 55 | 13.83 | 6-80 |
| D. L. Underwood | 799.2 | 334 | 1575 | 106 | 14.85 | 8-28 |
| Imran Khan | 415.4 | 106 | 1091 | 73 | 14.94 | 6-37 |
| H. R. Moseley | 196.4 | 50 | 495 | 31 | 15.96 | 6-52 |
| R. J. Hadlee | 317 | 103 | 753 | 47 | 16.02 | 7-23 |
| R. D. Jackman | 628.1 | 173 | 1595 | 93 | 17.15 | 8-64 |
| J. K. Lever | 700 | 166 | 1834 | 106 | 17.30 | 8-49 |
| S. T. Clarke | 320.1 | 106 | 757 | 43 | 17.60 | 6-61 |
| G. G. Arnold | 435.5 | 147 | 950 | 52 | 18.26 | 6-41 |

Alan Gibson called England's visit to Australia in 1979–80 a "bastard tour". It is merely an excuse to say that England's heart was not in it, for they were roundly beaten by three matches to nil in the Test matches, Dennis Lillee taking 23 wickets. But the Ashes were not at stake and somehow there was not quite the traditional atmosphere. This was partly because England had been in Australia less than 12 months before and partly because their own games were mixed in with one-day internationals and Tests against the West Indies in a bewildering hot-potch. There was no pattern or rhythm to the season's cricket, the hybrid programme being the result of the agreement between Packer and the ACB at the end of May. This has bound the signatories to a long series of limited-overs matches between three nations, a format which has been a part of every Australian season since. It was overkill then and it remains so today.

The home team, born of a slightly uneasy marriage between the heavyweights of Australia's WSC team – the Chappells, Lillee, Marsh, etc. – and the best of the young hopefuls who had emerged unscathed from the defeats by England, notably Kim Hughes and Allan Border, may have been too good for Brearley's side this time, but they were no serious match for the West Indies.

WSC had completed the maturing process of Lloyd's team: they had emerged as a ruthlessly efficient combination of mean, accurate, fit and hostile fast bowlers and buccaneering batsmen. The West Indies won both the "World Series" Cup (beating England, not Australia, in the final) and also the Test series, two-nil. It was their first win in a series in Australia at the sixth attempt.

At the end of their messy and exhausting tour, England played a Test in Bombay to celebrate the Golden Jubilee of the Indian Board of Control. India had just had a six-Test series against Pakistan, winning it two-nil, and interestingly England's visit was, for once, muted. Those who went to the Wankhede stadium witnessed a virtuoso performance by Ian Botham. Swinging the ball prodigiously throughout, he took 13 wickets and also made a century in a low-scoring England first innings. Bob Taylor also broke a record, taking ten catches in the match. His opportunity to play regular Test cricket in the absence of Alan Knott had been one of the happier outcomes of the years of strife.

# — 1980 —

## THUNDEROUS INNINGS FROM GOOCH
### WEEK ENDED MAY 2

ONCE more on the bat's back I do fly, after summer merrily. Once more summer missed its cue, for it was grey and chilly in The Parks at Oxford where I began. But the match produced two notable innings. The first was by Broad, who scored a century for Gloucestershire before lunch, something that cannot often have been done on the first morning of the season. He is not a newcomer – he played for the second XI as

Chris Broad (far right) and David Graveney – early runs at the expense of the University bowlers.

long ago as 1976, and did well in his few championship matches towards the end of last season – but it was the first time I had seen him in the runs.

The other innings to remember was played by David Graveney. After the University had been bowled out cheaply, Brain (who was captaining Gloucestershire) decided not to enforce the follow-on, but to take some batting practice. He opened the second innings with Bainbridge and Graveney. These improbable successors to Hobbs and Sutcliffe put on 100 in 24 overs. Graveney went on to score his first century in first-class cricket. He had said to me, in that quizzical Graveney way, in reference to Broad's innings, that the Oxford bowlers were clearly working on the theory that Broad was vulnerable to half-volleys, and Broad might have said the same thing about Graveney.

From Oxford I travelled to Cambridge, where it was even greyer and chillier. East (Essex) at one time

attempted to field in an overcoat borrowed from a spectator, but the umpire, Bird, did not share his sense of humour. The University did not bat badly, though slowly, against the champions – who must have been pleased by the form of Pringle, since he is on their books. We had a thunderous innings from Gooch, his highest in first-class cricket. He had not a great deal to conquer, but 200 at nearly a run a minute takes some doing in any class of cricket.

## TOO MUCH ASKED OF BOTHAM?
### WEEK ENDED MAY 9

WE are on the captaincy arguments again. Brearley has said he will not tour again. The name most frequently mentioned as his successor is that of

Ian Botham listening to advice as captain of MCC and flanked by Chris Tavaré, David Bairstow and Peter Roebuck.

Botham. Botham, at 24, would be the youngest captain since Ivo Bligh (discounting M. P. Bowden, who was deputy for C. Aubrey Smith in one match – subsequently granted Test status – in South Africa in 1889). But Chapman and May were not much older than Botham when appointed. They were both, on balance, successful captains, and their principal successes came in the early part of their careers. So youth is not a barrier in itself. Another argument is that Botham has no experience of captaincy. This is not conclusive, either. Three Yorkshiremen, Jackson, Hutton and Illingworth, all of whom beat Australia, were never (except for the odd match) captains of Yorkshire. Chapman had been sacked from the English captaincy before he captained Kent. May had not reached the Surrey captaincy when he first led England.

There remains a further query: are we asking too much of Botham, with such heavy responsibilities as he already has? This was an argument used against Hutton, and it is true that, by his last season, Australia 1954-55, the strain had told upon his batting. There is a real risk that Botham might burn himself up too soon, especially because of an exceptionally demanding, and absurdly crowded Test programme in the next couple of years.

Botham has the physique for it. Has he the character? "A couple o' year, and he'll be a great captain. Pitch him in now and he could ruin. Still a touch too hot in the head." I will not give the source of this quotation, since I have not obtained permission, but it came in an authoritative, experienced and friendly Somerset voice.

Arriving at The Oval, I met my senior correspondent of *The Times*, John Woodcock, the Sage of Longparish, in the press box. We greeted each other warmly, and then a touch of perplexity crept into our well-chiselled faces. There was also some heartless laughter in the background, and what I suspect were coarse remarks in Hindi from the representative of *The Daily Telegraph*. But I was grateful for the clerical error which enabled me to meet Johnny, a rare event in the season. It was decided, after a couple of quick snorts, that it would be best if I returned to the west, and I arrived at the Bristol ground just in time to see the fall of the last Gloucestershire first innings wicket.

## GOWER UNWISE AFTER FIFTY
### WEEK ENDED MAY 16

I had another travel misadventure last Wednesday, but this was predictable, since it was the Day of Action, and as no trains were running from Bristol to the Midlands, I could not get to Leicester. I was there yesterday, when the West Indies polished them off in two days. Greenidge scored a rapid century. The most interesting thing, for English supporters, was Gower's innings. There is a feeling that he has to prove himself in county cricket after his Test uncertainties. Did he, or did he not? He took time to play himself in, and gradually began to make his strokes. He was caught in the slips soon after reaching his 50, just the time when, as has so often been said, he ought not to get out. It was a good ball from Holding, but an unwise and unnecessary stroke.

Other recollections: at Worcester, another useful innings by Broad of Gloucestershire and a handsome double-century by Turner, though the match was a dead draw. Turner hit nine 6s. He was particularly severe on Partridge. One pull to square leg soared to the highest branches of a horse-chestnut. It was a pity that it happened to be a horse-chestnut, because Worcestershire is perry country, and it would have been pleasing to say that we had had a partridge in a pear tree.

At Bristol, there was a noble hundred by Zaheer against Northamptonshire, followed by a collapse. On the same day, there was a gathering of the clan of Grace, though most of them were direct descendants, not of W. G., but of brother E. M., the Thornbury coroner. There were doleful Gloucestershire supporters saying that an inquest was needed on their batting. At Bristol, later, when Gloucestershire were beaten by Glamorgan, there was an innings by Miandad, which excelled Zaheer's. I wrote about it in glowing terms, but as my report ended halfway through ("subbing on the stone", it was mystically described to me) I am afraid I shall be confirmed as an anti-Glamorgan man: a totally false belief which has harassed me for years. It was encouraging to see Willis bowling fast and looking fit.

## PASSION IN THE AIR
### WEEK ENDED MAY 23

THIS has been a Benson and Hedges week, with matches, now restricted to an allocation of two days, beginning on Saturday, Tuesday and Thursday. I think, on the whole, this is a good idea, though it removes interest from the championship before it has properly begun. On Saturday I was at Taunton. It was a warm day for a change, with a large crowd, and Middlesex won by a run. Taunton, for so long one of the quieter, remoter county grounds, where you could enjoy the prospect of the Quantocks (and of empty seats in the foreground) now hums with enthusiasm. The skeleton of the new pavilion is built. I am afraid it is going to do nothing for the view, but it is needed.

I was there again on Sunday, and this time Somerset won, easily, against Yorkshire. There was passion in the air, but very little misbehaviour (it is a good idea closing the bars on Sunday afternoons). The only really nasty bunch of yobbos, at least in my proximity, were – and as one of the tribe I write it with regret – Yorkshiremen. Hampshire and Boycott opened Yorkshire's innings, and each was run out for 0. There ought to be a good tale here, but it was no more than a couple of exceptionally good throws by Slocombe.

*Phil Slocombe once played with distinction in an early season representative match, but his promise was not fulfilled. I wonder if he was not one of the victims of the "Overseas Stars" syndrome.*

## LOVELY UGLY TOWN
### WEEK ENDED MAY 30

ENGLAND, captained by Botham, lost the first Prudential Trophy match against the West Indies, but won the second. The West Indies won the Trophy

**WEST INDIES**

| | | |
|---|---|---|
| C. G. Greenidge | c Lever b Marks | 39 |
| D. L. Haynes | c Willis b Marks | 50 |
| S. F. A. Bacchus | run out | 40 |
| *I. V. A. Richards | c Lever b Botham | 26 |
| A. I. Kallicharran | c Willis b Old | 11 |
| C. L. King | run out | 33 |
| A. M. E. Roberts | not out | 25 |
| J. Garner | run out | 0 |
| M. D. Marshall | b Willis | 0 |
| M. A. Holding | b Willis | 0 |
| Extras (lb 9, nb 2) | | 11 |
| Total (55 overs) for 9 wkts | | 235 |

Did not bat: †D. A. Murray.
Fall: 86, 113, 147, 169, 186, 231, 233, 233, 235.
Bowling: Willis 10-1-25-2, Lever 7-1-23-0, Botham 11-2-71-1, Old 11-1-43-1, Marks 11-1-44-2, Willey 5-0-18-0.

**ENGLAND**

| | | |
|---|---|---|
| P. Willey | c & b Holding | 56 |
| G. Boycott | run out | 70 |
| C. J. Tavaré | c Murray b Holding | 5 |
| G. A. Gooch | c Bacchus b Marshall | 12 |
| D. I. Gower | c Bacchus b Roberts | 12 |
| *I. T. Botham | not out | 42 |
| V. J. Marks | b Holding | 9 |
| †D. L. Bairstow | run out | 2 |
| J. K. Lever | not out | 0 |
| Extras (lb 22, w 4, nb 2) | | 28 |
| Total (54.3 overs) for 7 wkts | | 236 |

Did not bat: C. M. Old, R. G. D. Willis
Fall: 135, 143, 156, 160, 178, 212, 231.
Bowling: Roberts 11-3-42-1, Holding 11-0-28-3, Garner 10.3-0-41-0, Marshall 11-1-45-1, Richards 5-0-28-0, Greenidge 6-0-24-0.
Umpires: D. J. Constant, D. G. L. Evans.
**England won by 3 wickets.**
Man of the Match: G. Boycott.

because of a higher overall run rate, an absurd way of deciding these things. Why cannot they be shared, as championships often have been? England's performance in the matches should do them good, and also their captain, whose appointment has been confirmed for the first two Tests. I was pleased to see that Marks was chosen for the second match, and played acceptably. I make very few correct prophecies about cricketers, but I did say, years ago, that Marks would play for England, and was mocked for saying it by a purple-sweatered *Guardian* man.

I spent half the week at Swansea, and half at Hove. Swansea is, as Dylan Thomas said, a lovely ugly town, and St. Helen's is a lovely ugly sports ground.

On the first day, Glamorgan let a good batting position crumble, though there was an admirable innings by Alan Jones, an underestimated cricketer. I see that *Wisden*, ridiculously, has just deprived him of his only Test cap, against the Rest of the World in 1970. Among the other week-end delights of Swansea were a barman who looks like Don Mosey, a senior member who looks like Jim Swanton, and a commentator who actually turned out to be Alun Williams. Nottinghamshire won comfortably in the end, and I was struck by an innings from a young man called Curzon, played primarily for his wicket-keeping. He showed a sound technique and a sound temperament, until he was caught at deep square leg, off Hobbs.

"There is about the game whenever Sussex play it the faint suggestion of sandshoes, of a breeze off the sea, and of people inordinately enjoying themselves." So wrote Dudley Carew many years ago but, though we had a breeze off the sea at Hove, there was no inordinate enjoyment. Sussex cricket, one way and another, has got itself into a proper muddle in recent years: more heavy clogs than sandshoes. Sussex held out on the third day when Kent looked to have the winning of the match. Booth Jones, from Hastings Priory, scored 0 in his first innings but 50 in his second, in his first first-class match. Head, the deputy wicket-keeper, from Lancing, had a good game. Woolmer played one of the best innings I have seen from him. Wells, from Newhaven, also had a happy match, both with bat and ball. He bears a cricketing name, and even initials (C. M.). Apart from the famous original C. M. Wells, there have been several others, including the father of H. G., who took four wickets in four balls for Kent against Sussex at Hove; and of course the "Bomber." I think the present C. M. will turn out to be a good one.

*So do I, but he must make his breakthrough into international cricket soon, if ever he is going to do so.*

## ELEGANT ROSE AND DENNING'S JOYFUL BANG
### WEEK ENDED JUNE 6

AT New Road, Worcestershire against Somerset, there was no rain. The weather was not so much hot as stuffy. The haze hid the Malvern hills. The match followed the familiar pattern imposed by the 100-over limit (a bane). Each side reached four batting points. There was another astonishing innings by Rose. Not only is he scoring more runs, but he is a much better-*looking* batsman than he used to be. Elegant, tall, upright and left-handed, he reminded me at times of the pictures, and faint boyhood memories, of Woolley (pause for laughter among purple-sweatered *Guardian* correspondents). Worcestershire set Somerset to score 291 in 215 minutes. It was a fair declaration, but for a long time I thought it would be beyond Somerset. With 20 overs to go, they needed 117, but Rose scored his second century of the match, and Denning had a joyful bang, and they got there by eight wickets with three overs spare. Denning does not consider himself a specially good batsman and, as a matter of fact, neither do I, but he is a cricketer who gives much pleasure, warm and cheerful, and as West Country as the bells of his home Chewton Mendip (which were used as an interval signal on the old West of England Home Service). Rose is in such form that I am sure it would be worth giving him another try for England. I cannot think of a precedent for a county captain playing in a Test under one of his own charges.

## JONES THE STEEPLE
### WEEK ENDED JUNE 13

THE First Test can be regarded as a lost opportunity for England, or a brave and encouraging effort. I prefer the second interpretation, but all the same I rather agree with those who say that we are unlikely to have a better chance of beating the West Indies this summer (or next winter), than when they were 129 for five in their second innings, 79 still needed on what was apparently a scary pitch.

I spent most of my week at Derby and Northampton. It must be about five years since I watched cricket at Derby, partly because first-class matches there were suspended for a time. When I heard of this, I was in one way not sorry, because the facilities at Derby had always made the Wagon Works at Gloucester look like the Yankee Stadium. But in another way I was, for it was at Derby, in 1966, that Sobers bowled out the county before lunch on the third day, thus giving me time to travel to the west via London, and take out a young lady, and (successfully) propose marriage to her. I am glad to see that, since county cricket has been restored to Derby, they have improved the ground, though I do not count among the improvements the cinema organ in the clubhouse.

There might have been a good moment on the last day, when Kirsten was batting. He mishit a steepler, and every Jones in the Glamorgan side circled underneath it. Nash, the captain, kept his head, and called "Eifion!", and Eifion duly caught it. Supposing, I thought, he had called "Jones", or even "Alan" (for there are two Alans among the Joneses, and a third in reserve). That's captaincy.

## HEREDITARY HOICK
### WEEK ENDED JUNE 20

IT has been Bath Festival week, and confoundedly wet. Still, the rain did give me opportunities to consider the wider scene. Middlesex are at the top of the championship, and are playing so well at the moment that they look as if they might win that and everything else as well. Their temporary acquisition of Van der Bijl, and the unexpected bonus that the West Indies did not choose Daniel, has made a big difference.

In the Test match, Gooch has scored 123 for England in 162 balls. When Gooch was beginning, the Sage of Longparish aptly likened him to a policeman, and he has much the appearance of your traditional bobby on the beat. This season he seems to have joined the Flying Squad.

Chris Smith – quick to make his mark with Hampshire.

And now to Bath. Tremlett and C. L. Smith had a long partnership. Smith is a South African on a one-year contract, who was with Glamorgan last year. It was the second time this season I have seen him look as if he might become a formidable batsman.

*He has done so, and is no longer called a South African!*

It seems odd to see a Tremlett playing *against* Somerset. Timothy is the son of Maurice, a much-loved Somerset captain. Timothy was born in Somerset, which his father, though a Somerset man in all other essentials, was not. He made his highest score in first-class cricket. He does not have the majesty of his father's drive but, for his age, a sounder defence. He fell to a hereditary hoick to long-leg, and was warmly applauded by the Bath crowd, who would actually have liked to see him get his hundred. The match was drawn, as had always seemed probable. Jesty scored a good century, and Hampshire made a reasonable declaration but Gavaskar, the likeliest man to give the lead, was caught at deep mid-off in the first over.

## THREAT OF MIANDAD LIFTS GLAMORGAN
### WEEK ENDED JUNE 27

MIDDLESEX received a check to their triumphant progress at Lord's in a semi-final of the Benson and Hedges. They were beaten by Northamptonshire, by 11 runs. It was their first defeat, of any kind, in the season. The match went into the second day, and the other semi-final, in which Essex beat Worcestershire, went well into the third. That is what the weather has been like.

Worcestershire made enough runs to win a Benson and Hedges semi-final more often than not – three out of four, I would guess, though I have not counted – but were thwarted by another formidable innings from Gooch. In this week's Test match, he made the rest of the England batting look puny – and even, for a time, the West Indies fast bowlers, which was much more difficult. England would probably have lost, but for the rain.

Earlier in the week, I was at Cardiff. There is a lifting

of spirit in Glamorgan's cricket season. They had just won their second Championship match, a happy change from the calamitous 1979, when they won none. Miandad has made a big difference to the batting, as much for the threat he poses as the runs he scores. Nash, an intelligent, pleasant man, has settled in well as a captain. Glamorgan scored 300 on the Saturday against Somerset, but rain allowed only a couple of hours' play on Monday, and none at all on Tuesday.

## GARNER'S MAIDEN CENTURY
### WEEK ENDED JULY 4

TO Bristol for the West Indies match, where everyone was still talking about Garner's maiden century the previous day. He could not have made it at a better time, because the West Indies were 100 for eight when he went in. The West Indies duly won, despite good efforts by Sadiq, Graveney and Procter, but this must have been about the best performance against them by a county so far, putting Gloucestershire in the running for the Holt Products Trophy (which they already hold).

Earlier in the week I had been at a damp Southampton. There was no play on the Saturday. We were not the only sufferers. There was none in five other matches, including the University match. (There was at Swansea, where Richards made 100 in 66 minutes, the fastest of the season.) Rain stopped play again at Southampton at tea-time on Monday, and the match ended in a draw, as was always probable. Cope and Carrick bowled well, and among those who helped to thwart them was Tremlett. There was a real touch of father when Tremlett was out. As he walked in, clearly finding the whole thing inexplicable, he removed his cap in response to the applause, and rubbed the nape of his neck with the back of his hand. I have seen Maurice do this hundreds of times. Whether it is an argument for heredity or environment I am not sure.

Tim Tremlett – like father like son.

## HAPPY BIRTHDAY!
### WEEK ENDED JULY 11

ON Saturday at Taunton the West Indies scored 400 for seven, with centuries by Richards and Lloyd, but I was not there (I was at Bristol, where Nottinghamshire were playing: nothing much exciting happened). On Sunday I was at Taunton, when the weather allowed Somerset to score 77 for no wicket. There were loud cheers for Rose, upon his selection for England, but it was one of those hopeless hanging-about days. On Monday there was no play. On Wednesday I went to Lord's, and, again there was no play.

It has been pointed out in the correspondence columns of *The Times* that this is not the first time a captain of England will have his own county captain under his charge in a Test. R. W. V. Robins, when captain of Middlesex, played under G. O. Allen. But I wonder when was the last time Somerset have had two men in an England side (apart from Rose and Botham, who played together once in a Test in New Zealand). Braund and Palairet?

The batting averages are headed by A. J. Lamb, and there are five other overseas players in the first 10. Steele, of Leicestershire, with 30 wickets at 14.60, is a rather unexpected leader of the bowling list, where there are seven English players in the first 10 – more encouraging on the face of it, but two more overseas players immediately follow.

A cheerful note amidst the encircling gloom: July 6 was the 90th birthday of Andrew Sandham, England's oldest living Test cricketer, and one of the unluckiest. In most periods, he would have been a regular choice for England. As it was he played in only 14 Tests, only three times against Australia. (He made 325 against the West Indies at Kingston, though.) This was because he was an opening batsman, and coincided with Hobbs and Sutcliffe (Percy Holmes of Yorkshire suffered from the same complaint). Sandham, a small, smiling man, never let it depress him, and went on scoring piles of runs for Surrey. There must have been something about The Oval air in those days, despite all the tales of smog. Fender, 88 next month, and Hobbs, who lived to 81, are two examples that come to mind. Happy birthday!

## ROSE DOES WELL FOR ENGLAND
### WEEK ENDED JULY 18

ENGLAND did not do too badly in the Third Test. Although there was the familiar collapse in their first innings, they scored 400 in the second. The match lost the equivalent of nearly two days to the weather,

and was drawn. The most encouraging thing for England was the batting of Rose. I gather it was not so much the runs he made as the way he made them: though we must hesitate about acclaiming new England batsmen, for we have had some disappointments in the last few years.

## PROCTER v. BOTHAM AT SINGLE WICKET
### WEEK ENDED JULY 25

THE Benson and Hedges final, last Saturday, was washed out, as was much of the day's cricket, but the weather has improved since then, and play was possible on Monday. Northamptonshire won it, by six

### BENSON AND HEDGES FINAL SCOREBOARD

**NORTHAMPTONSHIRE**

| | | |
|---|---|---|
| G. Cook | c Gooch b Pont | 29 |
| W. Larkins | c Denness b Pont | 18 |
| R. G. Williams | c McEwan b Pont | 15 |
| A. J. Lamb | c Hardie b Phillip | 72 |
| P. Willey | c McEwan b Turner | 15 |
| T. J. Yardley | c Smith b Gooch | 0 |
| †G. Sharp | c Fletcher b Pont | 8 |
| *P. J. Watts | run out | 22 |
| Sarfraz Nawaz | not out | 10 |
| T. M. Lamb | lbw b Turner | 4 |
| B. J. Griffiths | b Turner | 0 |
| Extras (b 1, 1b 8, w 4, nb 3) | | 16 |
| Total (54.5 overs) | | 209 |

Fall: 36, 61, 78, 110, 110, 131, 190, 193, 209.
Bowling: Lever 11-3-38-0, Phillip 11-1-38-1, Turner 10-5-2-33-3, Pont 11-1-60-4, Gooch 11-0-24-1.

Gold Award: A. J. Lamb (Northants).

**ESSEX**

| | | |
|---|---|---|
| M. H. Denness | b Willey | 14 |
| G. A. Cooch | c A. J. Lamb | |
| | b T. M. Lamb | 60 |
| K. S. McEwan | b Willey | 38 |
| *K. W. R. Fletcher | b Sarfraz | 29 |
| B. R. Hardie | b Watts | 0 |
| K. R. Pont | b Williams | 2 |
| S. Turner | c Watts b Sarfraz | 16 |
| N. Phillip | not out | 32 |
| N. Smith | b Sarfraz | 2 |
| R. E. East | not out | 1 |
| Extras (b 1, lb 5, w 3) | | 9 |
| Total (55 overs) (8 wkts) | | 203 |

Did not bat: J. K. Lever.
Fall: 52, 112, 118, 121, 129, 160, 180, 198.
Bowling: Sarfraz 11-3-23-3, Griffiths 7-0-46-0, Watts 8-1-30-1, T. M. Lamb 11-0-42-1, Willey 11-1-34-2, Williams 7-0-19-1.
Umpires: B. J. Meyer and D. J. Constant.
*Captain. †Wicket-keeper.

runs, and Essex will feel that twice they threw it away. The decisive counter looked as if it would be played by Gooch, but Allan Lamb caught him off the bowling of Timothy Lamb. No relation, but quite a day for the flock.

On Tuesday I watched Procter play Botham at single wicket. Single wicket cricket has a long history. Indeed, it was the first aspect of the game to command large-scale public support. One of the drawbacks to the various modern attempts to provide a pepped-up version of single wicket has been that there are no standard rules. Procter and Botham, however, were meeting under the same ones as last year, when Procter narrowly won. Each had 20 overs to bat. Ten runs were deducted every time a batsman was out. Each bowled 10 overs, and the remaining overs were bowled by an agreed choice, Doshi of Warwickshire.

Procter was bowled first ball, so his score was minus ten, which baffled the scoreboard. He was out seven times, but after 70 had been deducted scored 112.

Botham was out nine times, and finished 27 runs behind. The man of the match was undoubtedly Doshi. It was a comical and cheerful occasion, not much resembling cricket, but a large crowd enjoyed it.

## BALLOON CATCH
### WEEK ENDED AUGUST 1

GLAMORGAN and Leicestershire are nestling side by side in the bottom six of the championship, though there have been times this season when both have looked better than that. On the first afternoon at Cardiff, I inadvertently nicked Wilfred Wooller's seat, quite enough to make up for some dullish cricket. There was another interesting moment when Cook, at mid-on, caught a balloon – I mean, your actual balloon. It must have drifted over from the Arms Park, where there were mighty celebrations to mark the centenary year of the Welsh Rugby Union.

The Gillette Cup semi-finalists are Middlesex, Surrey, Yorkshire and Sussex. The only close match was at Chelmsford, where Surrey won by losing fewer wickets in a tie. I saw Middlesex win at Worcester. The ground was almost full, the crowd, including many Middlesex supporters, confident to a man that their team is on the brink of the best season in its history. Worcestershire were all out for 126, and Middlesex won by 10 wickets. Daniel and Van der Bijl began with their usual containing spell, but the break-through came from a young man called Hughes. He is a fast-medium bowler, who will, I dare say, become faster, and has been at Durham University (whence Tyson came). He took three for 25, and 10 of those runs came in a nervous first over. Patel and Humphries made a stand for the sixth wicket, but three wickets fell in three overs after lunch, and the rest of the proceedings were formal. Going sadly away, Worcestershire supporters were saying that it had been a fatal mistake to bat first. But Middlesex were so much superior that it would have taken more than tactical decisions to change the result. They really are playing well.

The Oval Test (how odd it seems that it should not be the last) had moments of hope for England. At one time it seemed that they might make the West Indies follow-on, but there came the familiar batting collapse, this time in the second innings, and it was another draw.

Simon Hughes – an impressive spell for Middlesex.

## HOLT TROPHY BRINGS FRESH INTEREST
### WEEK ENDED AUGUST 8

TO Edgbaston, for the second day of the West Indies match. The weather was doubtful, but there was a big crowd. I have said it before, but I repeat that Holt Products, with their Trophy, have brought fresh interest to matches between the counties and the tourists – though I am sure they would agree that they have been fortunate in their touring team, this season. The West Indies only drew this match, but have won seven of their eleven against the counties. Warwickshire were saved from trouble by a partnership between Humpage and Oliver, and I heard several members reflect with satisfaction (since they feel they have had an overdose of imports in recent years) that Humpage was born in Birmingham, and Oliver just over the Staffordshire border in West Bromwich.

On Tuesday I was back at Cheltenham, to see Gloucestershire beat Hampshire by 197 runs. We have had many systems of deciding the County Championship, none of them, by the nature of the exercise, satisfactory; but the best have included some reward, direct or indirect, for saving a game. A drawn match has always been part of cricket, and often one of its excitements. The present system gives no incentive to a side with no chance of winning to fight it out. A good side would instinctively fight it out, but I am afraid Hampshire are not a good side just now. They were set to score 301 in 240 minutes, which gave them very little chance on a third day, against the Gloucestershire spinners at Cheltenham. But they had a fair chance of saving the match, if they put their minds to it, especially as there was always a chance of rain. Once they had lost some early wickets, they were like apparitions seen and gone.

## PROCTER'S WARM RECEPTION
### WEEK ENDED AUGUST 15

I was back at Cheltenham for the last match of the Festival, where Gloucestershire completed a trio of wins, which ensures them a respectable place in the final table. This one was against Middlesex, no less, and after they had been outplayed for two days. It was a captain's victory. After Brearley set them to score 270 in 285 minutes, I thought Titmus (a delight to see him again) would win Middlesex the match, even if the fast bowlers did not. Three wickets fell for 65. Sadiq was steadfast, and Procter began cautiously. "Putting the shutters up" somebody said, and there was a resigned air about the crowd.

*Titmus thus achieved the very rare feat of playing first-class cricket in five decades.*

But, when Procter means business, he likes to play himself in. I have known him play a couple of maiden overs in a Sunday League match, then score at the deuce of a rate and win it. Once he decided he knew what was going on, he became the master. The result meant a lot to him, because he had mistakenly put Middlesex in, and was conscious of the error. He drove and cut, choosing his angles so precisely that not even Brearley's constantly and carefully revised field-placings could cut off the strokes. When invited, which was not often, he hooked. I dare say it was an additional satisfaction to him that Brearley dropped him in the slips in his fifties. Gloucestershire won with an hour to spare. Not Grace, not Jessop, not Hammond ever came off the Cheltenham ground to warmer cheering. I think it was the best innings I have seen this season. I suppose Richards must have played several better, but I have not seen them.

The Gillette Cup finalists are the current championship leaders, Middlesex and Surrey. I cannot remember this happening before. Both semi-finals went into the second day. Middlesex beat Sussex, comfortably in the end, after scoring 180. Surrey secured a commanding position on the first day, putting Yorkshire in and bowling them out for 135, but found themselves struggling on the second.

The last Test at Headingley was drawn, so the West Indies won the rubber. It has not been a very happy series: too much rain, too many bouncers. John Woodcock, after paying tribute to the efficiency of this West Indies side, adds that "They have not smiled very much."

*I think they would have smiled more if the weather had been kinder. It was one of the least enjoyable Test series.*

# HAMSTRINGS TABOO IN RAWALPINDI
## WEEK ENDED AUGUST 22

O N Saturday at Taunton there was a beautiful innings by Gower. After his first few strokes a staunch Somerset supporter, a man who hates his side to lose, said "D'you know, I'd like to see him make 50." Gower quickly did, and I said "Well, you can start cheering for Somerset again," and he replied "No, I'd like to see him make a hundred." I was on the point of asking him whether he would settle for 150, and I am sure he would have said "Yes," when Gower was caught at the wicket for 94. His dismissal was greeted by the crowd with as much a sigh as a cheer. Brightness fell from the air. Such is the compelling effect which Gower has upon cricketers when he is going well.

I went to Hove, where Surrey kept a firm grip on second place in the championship, beating Sussex by 145 runs. Sussex were below strength, and Imran was unable to take a full part in the match because of a strained beefstring (my colleague from the *Telegraph*, an Indian gentleman, told me that if I used the word hamstring I would cop 10 lashes the next time I happened to be in Rawalpindi). All the same, they batted feebly in their first innings, only just saving the follow-on. They did better in the second, and I was

Paul Downton and Phil Edmonds watch Colin Wells while Clive Radley takes evasive action.

impressed again by young Wells, who has been having a good season. Buss, then the Sussex manager, said at the beginning of the season that he felt what the side needed was another class batsman: well, he has found one. But the best performance came from Knight, who batted and bowled admirably in both innings. We have always known the quality of his batting, but his bowling looks tighter, more aggressive this season than I have seen it before.

The Australians have arrived for their short tour, which will culminate in the Centenary Test, and England have won the first of the one-day matches without much difficulty.

## TO SUPPER WITH GENTLE JACK
### WEEK ENDED AUGUST 29

I HAVE seen very little cricket this week, partly because of the weather. I missed a visit to Nottingham to see the Australians, and a visit to Colchester, a place to which I always enjoy going. However, I had a day at Bristol for the Somerset match, still a West Country occasion. Procter scored some runs, and so did Graveney, Dredge the Demon of Frome took some wickets, and in the evening there was a pleasant little supper, at which one of the best of Gloucestershire batsmen and Test umpires, Jack Crapp, was guest of honour. Gentle Jack was in good spirits, glad to be out of the hurly-burly though he misses it. He came to supper on the strict understanding that he did not have to make a speech, and then made one, of the utmost grace and simplicity.

I then saw most of the Glamorgan match at Taunton. On the first two days, there was some good cricket, but no newspaper for which to write about it. On the third day, there was going to be a *Times* but there was no cricket. I did not expect any, as I passed through the drenched fields of Athelney, wondering, not for the first time, how Alfred ever managed to burn a cake there. Glamorgan scored 302, bowled out Somerset for 74 less, and were 147 for three in their second innings, well placed. On the last day, the umpires decided a start may be possible at four, but the weather grew worse, and so the poor newshound had none. I trailed away to the railway station, thinking of life's little ironies.

John Arlott says farewell from Lord's.

## ARLOTT'S LAST TEST BROADCAST
### WEEK ENDED SEPTEMBER 5

MIDDLESEX have won the championship, and Warwickshire the John Player League. The first has been predictable for some time, though Surrey clung on bravely, and made sure of second place. The Centenary Test was drawn, John Arlott broadcasting upon a Test for the last time, an occasion marked with appropriate celebrations (do not misunderstand me).

I was there when Middlesex made sure of it. There was no play on Saturday until a quarter past five, and Middlesex then lost three wickets. On Monday, Middlesex were all out for 163. When they were 127 for nine it did not look as if they would take a single batting point (they needed eight points for the championship). Then Van der Bijl had a thing or two to smite. What an acquisition he has been to them! I had my doubts whether, not young and unaccustomed to the championship grind, he would last till the end of the season, but he has confounded them. He has not only taken a lot of wickets, but often been a scourge to the opposition in the later batting, especially when runs were needed. Of course he is a strong, big man. Wilfred Wooler says he is considering an appeal under Law 42 – "to have a man that size *must* be unfair play." "Bidgie" and Daniel have been the foundation of the Middlesex success, although it has also made a big difference that they have had Brearley available regularly. Glamorgan fell behind after the first innings, and could not last out after the declaration.

The Centenary Test was spoilt by the weather, and some unhappy consequences of the weather. From the point of view of English cricket, the most encouraging thing was to see Gower making Test runs again. I was sorry that Athey, of whom, like many others, I have high hopes, did not do better. Botham's form is a worry, in more than one sense. He is not playing too well and, according to Alec Bedser, is too heavy. He first let it be known that he would drop the weight by some intensive football for Scunthorpe, and then, since this set off another alarm, said he had given up the idea of playing for Scunthorpe.

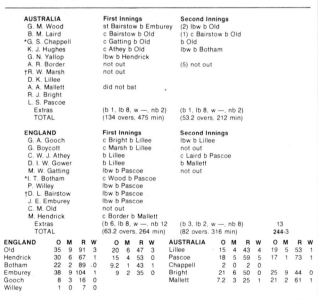

fashionably putting Surrey in. There was a handsome hundred by Knight, and some excellent bowling by Jackman and Intikhab. It was pleasant to see a leg-spinner (not, alas, an Englishman, and not young) having a long bowl, when the season has been so dominated by speed. Jackman, an unlucky but resilient cricketer, has taken more wickets than anybody. When he bowled Fowler, he bounced up the pitch and gathered the ball as it rebounded from the stumps, rolling over and appealing, just for fun, at the same time. It is this natural exuberance which makes everyone, not just the partisans at the Oval, like the Shoreditch Sparrow so much.

Then I had a day at Taunton, where Somerset collapsed rather dismally against Warwickshire, and lost by 10 wickets. Doshi, another spinner (also not English) reached his hundred wickets. The first-class season ended appropriately, with clouds scudding across the sky, and wind howling in the eaves.

Warwickshire with the John Player trophy. Left to right: Geoff Humpage, Andy Lloyd, David Smith, Bob Willis, David Brown (manager) and Dennis Amiss.

| AUSTRALIA | First Innings | Second Innings |
|---|---|---|
| G. M. Wood | st Bairstow b Emburey | (2) lbw b Old |
| B. M. Laird | c Bairstow b Old | (1) c Bairstow b Old |
| *G. S. Chappell | c Gatting b Old | b Old |
| K. J. Hughes | c Athey b Old | lbw b Botham |
| G. N. Yallop | lbw b Hendrick | |
| A. R. Border | not out | (5) not out |
| †R. W. Marsh | not out | |
| D. K. Lillee | | |
| A. A. Mallett | did not bat | |
| R. J. Bright | | |
| L. S. Pascoe | | |
| Extras | (b 1, lb 8, w —, nb 2) | (b 1, lb 8, w —, nb 2) |
| TOTAL | (134 overs, 475 min) | (53.2 overs, 212 min) |

| ENGLAND | First Innings | Second Innings | |
|---|---|---|---|
| G. A. Gooch | c Bright b Lillee | lbw b Lillee | |
| G. Boycott | c Marsh b Lillee | not out | |
| C. W. J. Athey | b Lillee | c Laird b Pascoe | |
| D. I. W. Gower | b Lillee | b Mallett | |
| M. W. Gatting | lbw b Pascoe | not out | |
| *I. T. Botham | c Wood b Pascoe | | |
| P. Willey | lbw b Pascoe | | |
| †D. L. Bairstow | lbw b Pascoe | | |
| J. E. Emburey | lbw b Pascoe | | |
| C. M. Old | not out | | |
| M. Hendrick | c Border b Mallett | | |
| Extras | (b 6, lb 8, w —, nb 12) | (b 3, lb 2, w —, nb 8) | 13 |
| TOTAL | (63.2 overs, 264 min) | (82 overs, 316 min) | 244-3 |

| ENGLAND | O | M | R | W | O | M | R | W | AUSTRALIA | O | M | R | W | O | M | R | W |
|---|---|---|---|---|---|---|---|---|---|---|---|---|---|---|---|---|---|
| Old | 35 | 9 | 91 | 3 | 20 | 6 | 47 | 3 | Lillee | 15 | 4 | 43 | 4 | 19 | 5 | 53 | 1 |
| Hendrick | 30 | 6 | 67 | 1 | 15 | 4 | 53 | 0 | Pascoe | 18 | 5 | 59 | 5 | 17 | 1 | 73 | 1 |
| Botham | 22 | 2 | 89 | .0 | 9.2 | 1 | 43 | 1 | Chappell | 2 | 0 | 2 | 0 | | | | |
| Emburey | 38 | 9 | 104 | 1 | 9 | 2 | 35 | 0 | Bright | 21 | 6 | 50 | 0 | 25 | 9 | 44 | 0 |
| Gooch | 8 | 3 | 16 | 0 | | | | | Mallett | 7.2 | 3 | 25 | 1 | 21 | 2 | 61 | 1 |
| Willey | 1 | 0 | 7 | 0 | | | | | | | | | | | | | |

I had a couple of days at The Oval, where Lancashire were beaten by an innings on the second evening, after

### MIDDLESEX v SURREY – 1980 GILLETTE CUP FINAL

| SURREY | Innings | Runs | MIDDLESEX | Innings | Runs |
|---|---|---|---|---|---|
| A. R. Butcher | b Selvey | 29 | *J. M. Brearley | not out | 96 |
| G. S. Clinton | c Radley b Selvey | 13 | †P. R. Downton | c Clarke b Knight | 13 |
| *R. D. V. Knight | c and b Emburey | 11 | C. T. Radley | c and b Thomas | 5 |
| D. M. Smith | c Van der Bijl b Daniel | 50 | M. W. Gatting | b Jackman | 24 |
| G. R. J. Roope | b Hughes | 35 | R. O. Butcher | not out | 50 |
| M. A. Lynch | c Gatting b Hughes | 3 | G. D. Barlow | | |
| Intikhab Alam | c Butcher b Van der Bijl | 34 | J. E. Emburey | | |
| D. J. Thomas | b Hughes | 4 | V. A. P. van der Bijl | did not bat | |
| R. D. Jackman | b Daniel | 5 | S. P. Hughes | | |
| S. T. Clarke | not out | 3 | M. W. W. Selvey | | |
| †C. J. Richards | run out (Hughes) | 0 | W. W. Daniel | | |
| Extras | (b 1, lb 5, w 1, nb 7) | 14 | Extras | (b 3, lb 11, w-, nb-) | 14 |
| TOTAL | (60 overs, 253 minutes) | 201 | TOTAL | (53.5 overs, 204 minutes) | 202-3 |

| MIDDLESEX | O | M | R | W | SURREY | O | M | R | W |
|---|---|---|---|---|---|---|---|---|---|
| Daniel | 12 | 3 | 33 | 2 | Jackman | 11 | 1 | 31 | 1 |
| Van der Bijl | 12 | 0 | 32 | 1 | Clarke | 8.5 | 1 | 29 | 0 |
| Selvey | 12 | 5 | 17 | 2 | Knight | 10 | 2 | 38 | 1 |
| Hughes | 11 | 0 | 60 | 3 | Thomas | 12 | 0 | 38 | 1 |
| Emburey | 12 | 2 | 34 | 1 | Intikhab | 12 | 0 | 52 | 0 |
| Gatting | 1 | 0 | 11 | 0 | | | | | |

Man of the Match: J. M. Brearley

# Final county table

| | P | W | L | D | Btg | Blg | Pts |
|---|---|---|---|---|---|---|---|
| Middlesex (13) | 22 | 10 | 2 | 10 | 58 | 80 | 258 |
| Surrey (3) | 22 | 10 | 4 | 8 | 51 | 74 | 245 |
| Nottinghamshire (9) | 22 | 6 | 5 | 11 | 42 | 64 | 178 |
| Sussex (4) | 22 | 4 | 3 | 15 | 60 | 60 | 168 |
| Somerset (8) | 22 | 3 | 5 | 14 | 56 | 70 | 168 |
| Yorkshire (7) | 22 | 4 | 3 | 15 | 51 | 64 | 163 |
| Gloucestershire (10) | 22 | 4 | 5 | 13 | 39 | 74 | 161 |
| Essex (1) | 22 | 4 | 3 | 15 | 47 | 62 | 157 |
| Derbyshire (16) | 22 | 4 | 3 | 15 | 47 | 62 | 157 |
| Leicestershire (6) | 22 | 4 | 2 | 16 | 45 | 58 | 157 |
| Worcestershire (2) | 22 | 3 | 7 | 12 | 54 | 61 | 151 |
| Northamptonshire (11) | 22 | 5 | 4 | 13 | 41 | 47 | 148 |
| Glamorgan (17) | 22 | 4 | 4 | 14 | 43 | 57 | 148 |
| Warwickshire (15) | 22 | 3 | 4 | 15 | 55 | 54 | 145 |
| Lancashire (13) | 22 | 4 | 3 | 15 | 26 | 58 | 145 |
| Kent (5) | 22 | 2 | 8 | 12 | 36 | 59 | 119 |
| Hampshire (12) | 22 | 1 | 10 | 11 | 34 | 56 | 102 |

Leicestershire and Somerset totals include six points in drawn matches when scores were level. 1979 positions in brackets.

## BATTING

(Qualification: 8 innings, average 10.00) *Not out

| | I | NO | R | HS | AV |
|---|---|---|---|---|---|
| A. J. Lamb | 39 | 12 | 1797 | 152 | 66.55 |
| J. Whitehouse | 19 | 8 | 725 | 197 | 65.90 |
| K. C. Wessels | 29 | 5 | 1562 | 254 | 65.08 |
| P. N. Kirsten | 36 | 6 | 1895 | 213* | 63.16 |
| G. M. Turner | 35 | 4 | 1817 | 228* | 58.61 |
| C. T. Radley | 34 | 8 | 1491 | 136* | 57.34 |
| Javed Miandad | 32 | 5 | 1460 | 181 | 54.07 |
| C. E. B. Rice | 36 | 9 | 1448 | 131* | 53.62 |
| G. Boycott | 28 | 4 | 1264 | 154* | 52.66 |
| J. H. Hampshire | 27 | 8 | 987 | 124 | 51.94 |
| I. V. A. Richards | 25 | 1 | 1217 | 170 | 50.70 |
| B. C. Rose | 26 | 4 | 1084 | 150* | 49.27 |
| J. G. Wright | 36 | 5 | 1504 | 166* | 48.51 |
| G. A. Gooch | 35 | 5 | 1437 | 205 | 47.90 |
| C. H. Lloyd | 15 | 2 | 621 | 116 | 47.76 |
| J. M. Brearley | 33 | 5 | 1335 | 134* | 47.67 |
| G. R. J. Roope | 30 | 9 | 996 | 101 | 47.42 |
| N. Russom | 13 | 8 | 235 | 79* | 47.00 |
| B. F. Davison | 32 | 4 | 1310 | 151 | 46.78 |
| J. A. Ormrod | 35 | 3 | 1495 | 131* | 46.71 |

## BOWLING

(Qualification: 10 wickets in 10 innings)

| | O | M | R | W | Av | BB |
|---|---|---|---|---|---|---|
| R. J. Hadlee | 222.1 | 82 | 410 | 29 | 14.13 | 5–32 |
| V. A. P. van der Bijl | 642.3 | 213 | 1252 | 85 | 14.72 | 6–47 |
| R. D. Jackman | 746.2 | 220 | 1864 | 121 | 15.40 | 8–58 |
| J. F. Steele | 347.5 | 139 | 704 | 40 | 17.60 | 7–29 |
| M. D. Marshall | 477.3 | 128 | 1170 | 66 | 17.72 | 7–56 |
| M. Hendrick | 444.5 | 128 | 980 | 55 | 17.81 | 7–19 |
| Imran Khan | 402.5 | 109 | 967 | 54 | 17.90 | 6–80 |
| M. J. Procter | 372.1 | 102 | 931 | 51 | 18.25 | 7–16 |
| W. G. Merry | 96 | 21 | 300 | 15 | 20.00 | 4–24 |
| J. E. Emburey | 739.2 | 248 | 1518 | 75 | 20.24 | 6–31 |
| P. J. W. Allott | 183 | 47 | 473 | 23 | 20.56 | 4–30 |
| P. J. Hacker | 379.2 | 99 | 1092 | 52 | 21.00 | 6–35 |
| C. M. Old | 503 | 160 | 1159 | 55 | 21.07 | 6–44 |
| S. T. Clarke | 605.3 | 139 | 1700 | 79 | 21.51 | 6–73 |
| W. W. Daniel | 492.5 | 112 | 1454 | 67 | 21.70 | 5–32 |
| W. Hogg | 340.1 | 69 | 1114 | 51 | 21.84 | 6–45 |
| Intikhab Alam | 277.2 | 77 | 792 | 36 | 22.00 | 5–83 |
| C. E. B. Rice | 329.4 | 80 | 859 | 39 | 22.02 | 5–25 |
| E. E. Hemmings | 622.5 | 171 | 1700 | 77 | 22.07 | 7–62 |
| D. S. Steele | 430 | 123 | 1221 | 54 | 22.61 | 7–133 |

The West Indies, by now the undisputed world champions of cricket, continued to assert their dominance after their wet summer in England. They went to Pakistan in November for a nine-week tour and, although winning only one Test, they were never in danger of losing one, even without two of their stalwarts, Holding and Greenidge, who were injured early on the tour. Holding's place was taken by Sylvester Clarke, who more than pulled his weight, whilst Malcolm Marshall proved a most able successor to Andy Roberts, who had not made the trip. Richards, as usual, was out on his own as the best batsman, though in Imran Khan he had a foeman worthy of his steel. Not that Imran had spectacular success; Pakistan's most successful bowlers were Mohammad Nazir Junior, an experienced off-spinner, and the left-arm orthodox Iqbal Qasim, both of whom have bobbed in and out of Pakistan sides over the years like migrating birds.

Back home the West Indies defeated England two-nil in a series reduced to four matches when the England team was forced to retire from Guyana in a hurry because of a political row. Bob Willis had been forced home early with a knee injury (it looked at the time rather like the end of his career) and his place was taken by Robin Jackman, an enthusiastic Surrey bowler whose belated chance to tour with an England side was begrudged by no-one. Jackman, however, had a South African wife and had many times been to the Republic to play. He was declared persona non grata by the Government of Guyana and the Second Test was cancelled.

Ian Botham, given the captaincy far too young, had a more or less impossible assignment, and lost much of his own devastating form; but he played the series in the sporting spirit which comes naturally to him and thanks to some outstanding batting by David Gower and Graham Gooch, both of whom proved that the West Indies fast bowling, on reliable pitches, was not unplayable, England's mainly young side did not leave the Caribbean in dishonour. They did so, however, in sadness, because the tragically early death of Ken Barrington during the Barbados Test had cast a general gloom over the team which was somehow appropriate.

A depressing story came out of the Australian season, too. In a one-day international during the triangular series with India and New Zealand, Australia's captain Greg Chappell caused an international furore when he instructed his brother Trevor to bowl an underarm sneak for the last ball to prevent New Zealand scoring a six which would have tied the match.

The older Chappell was soon expressing contrition as he found himself the object of a positive torrent of criticism, led by the Prime Ministers of the two countries concerned. In a nutshell, the action was "not cricket" and the reaction proved that people still cared about the spirit of the game.

Following yet another court hearing, the ABC won back the right to televise cricket in Australia, this time in simultaneous rivalry with Channel Nine.

In addition to Ken Barrington, it was a bad winter (and spring) for cricketing deaths: other great names in the game to pass into history included Jack Fingleton, George Geary, Dudley Nourse, Eric Hollies, "Nip" Pellew, Brian Sellers, Tim Wall and Arthur Wellard.

# — 1981 —

## *"WE PRAY AND BLESS THEE FOR THY BOUNTEOUS RAIN . . ."*
### *WEEK ENDING MAY 8*

I permitted myself at least one cheerful thought before the season began. The weather ought to be good. We have had four wet and often cold seasons. Back in 1976, you may remember, we suffered from intense heat and drought. Never in modern history were so many fervent prayers for rain uttered. There was once a Welsh preacher, famous for his power in prayer. He led his flock to the top of a neighbouring hill, in a time of drought. With his "Amen," the first drop of rain fell. Six months later it was still pelting down. Once more they went to the hilltop, though they had to travel most of the way by boat, so deep were the floods. "Lord," cried the preacher, "we praise and bless Thee for thy bounteous rain . . . but for St David's sake, Lord, have a bit of *common*." That is the prayer of cricketers just now.

But there is no sign just yet that it is being answered. I began, as usual, in the sodden Parks. Oxford scored 171, mostly on the Saturday. Over the weekend there were storms and snow; we had no power at High Littleton for a day and a half. In what play was possible on Monday and Tuesday the University took eight Glamorgan wickets for 107 runs. Against Somerset things were more normal, the University losing by an innings.

In the match between MCC and Middlesex, Gatting scored the first first-class century of the season, and it was much praised. A lot of people are hoping he will do well this year, after his disappointments in the West Indies. He is still young, and has the talent to become an England regular.

## *SURPRISE VICTORY FOR MINOR COUNTIES*
### *WEEK ENDING MAY 15*

THE weather has been rather better, and the early Benson & Hedges matches did not suffer too much. The surprise has been a victory for the Minor Counties

over Hampshire, their second win in the competition. Plumb, of Norfolk, scored 48 not out, and J. G. Tolchard, back with Devon after his spell with Leicestershire, 36. I was at Swansea, where Glamorgan had a comfortable win over Essex. Swansea was much as usual, the lovely ugly cricket ground. You have to be even more of a mountaineer to ascend to the press box, clambering among bricks and scaffolding. Although the swifts have come, the scoreboard still suffers from its winter rheumatics. The hospitality, however, is as good as ever, and Wilfred Wooller as good company. He ought once more to reach his 1,000 arguments in May without difficulty. Miandad played a lovely innings. Gooch and McEwan were both out early, and Essex were always struggling after that. One of the encouraging things for Glamorgan was the bowling of two of their local products, Barwick from Port Talbot, and Lloyd from Neath.

## *IT'S THE AUSTRALIANS – AGAIN*
### *WEEK ENDING MAY 22*

THE Australians are here, and have begun in miserable weather. There is not quite the excitement about an Australian tour that there used to be; Test matches are played too often. It will be the fifth

Early exercise for the Australian tourists before the opening game at Arundel.

time in seven years that we have seen them. The magic of my youth – when Australia came once every four years, and as soon as a tour was over we began discussing prospects for the next – has gone.

It has been a Benson & Hedges week. No less than five of the first set of matches had to be declared "no result." I went to Bristol, where not a ball was bowled.

In the second lot there were two "no results." I went to Derby, thinking it would be interesting to see Scotland. The umpires did not think the ground fit for play, but the captains decided to have a go. I suppose Swan, the Scottish captain, thought that if he won the toss he would have his best chance of getting Derbyshire on the run. But he lost it, Scotland were put in, and by the early afternoon were all out for 97. Derbyshire scored the runs without difficulty.

Scotland were invited to join the Benson & Hedges competition last season, on an experimental basis for two years. The experiment still hangs in the balance. I have never quite understood why Scottish cricket is relatively weak, they have produced some splendid players. Three of the heroes of my youth were Jardine (D.R.), Peebles (I.A.R.), and Gibb (P.A.). Denness (M.H.) was not too bad either. I saw Aitchison (Rev. J.) score 100 at Hamilton Crescent, in about six hours, against the 1956 Australians. He was a Church of Scotland minister – and I was never tempted to go and hear him preach – and I must not forget the deadliest of Scottish bowlers, who has flattened so many stumps, Hogman (A.).

But Brian Close, the Scottish coach, who was present, sporting a moustache like a sporran, need not give up hopes for his team. They did not have much luck. Scotsmen have not often had much luck at Derby. Prince Charlie spent the last happy night of his life there, and the most dejected morning.

## IN SEARCH OF PLAY
### WEEK ENDING MAY 29

I went to Taunton for the first day of the Australian match. It rained once more, not all the time but sufficiently to spoil the day. Hughes made a big hit into St. James's churchyard, without cracking a stained glass window on the bounce as Clive Lloyd once did. Botham bowled an impressive spell during the afternoon, encouraging to his supporters, who down here are numerous though a touch anxious.

Then to Cardiff. I was astonished, after two blank days, to find that there was any play on the third, so drenched was the land as I travelled up. However, there was a bit, and Kent lost five wickets for 44. The cricket might be described as good though gargly. I had a word

with Tom Cartwright, still looking remarkably fit though doleful. He asked me, "Have you ever known a worse May?"

*The more one reads these journals, the more one realises that May frequently tends to be the "worst ever"! This one, however, really was abysmal.*

My next assignment was at Worcester. The first two days were rained off, and there seemed very little chance of any play on the third, so I obtained permission to switch to Bristol, thinking it might be easier to watch the weather nearer home. It was a bad guess. There was no play at Bristol, sure enough, but at Worcester it cleared, and Lancashire won a one-day match, a young man called Fowler, one of the Durham University brood, apparently batting very well. The Australians at Swansea also had a blank day. So far they have lost 31 hours of play out of 54.

Graeme Fowler – a wicket-keeper/batsman.

## WOBBLING IN THE AFTERNOON
### WEEK ENDING JUNE 5

I usually enjoy myself at Basingstoke, and the bright sunshine helped to make the first day a happy one, though there was no rounders match to look at, over the wall, when the cricket grew dull. There was a splendid innings by Greenidge, who just failed to make his hundred. How glad Hampshire must be to have him back with them! The second day was miserable, although the players did their best. Hampshire saved the match on the third day, despite some wobbling in the afternoon. I was deeply impressed by the way David Shepherd gives batsmen out; his finger points to the heavens, unmistakably, his circumference swells nobly. He looks like Ajax defying the lightning. When he becomes a Test match umpire, as I have no doubt he will in time, and especially against the Australians, he may find (as Ajax did) that the lightning sometimes strikes back.

## YORKSHIRE LACK FIGHT
### WEEK ENDING JUNE 12

NO, the weather is not much better, though as it happened I had a fairly good week myself. I went to

Bristol to watch Yorkshire, the old xenophobia strong, but did not find much for comfort. They were beaten easily, after a promising start. What was disappointing was that they did not make a better fight for a draw on the third day. Old, as usual when he is fit and feeling like it, bowled a thoughtful length and line. Young Moxon failed, not surprisingly, since he was bearing the burden of a century in his first first-class match, just previously. Athey, in the first innings, was out to a bad, needless stroke. He is like the little girl with a curl in the middle of the forehead. I thought Whiteley, an off-spinner from Otley in his mid-twenties, looked as if he might have the right stuff in him.

Broad scored three fifties against Yorkshire in three days (counting the Sunday League). Physically, although he is left-handed, he reminds me of the philosopher Green (D.M., not T.H. – in fact I think D.M. is one up on his rival, because I don't know that T.H. ever wrote for *The Times*): a strong, heavy man who dislikes moving from his crease, though he has yet to acquire Green's aptitude for nudges and dabs. It is usually four, or nothing.

## ZAHEER SPECTACULAR
### WEEK ENDING JUNE 19

THE first match of the Bath Festival, which Somerset just saved against Gloucestershire, was notable for many good things, besides the jovial company. Zaheer scored a double century and a century. This was the sixth time he had scored two centuries in a match, and on each occasion – this is one of the more incredible statistics – one of the centuries has been a double. He is in spectacular form at present. I would not rate him as one of the world's greatest batsmen – looking back over history, I mean – for he has too many bad patches. He took a long time to grow accustomed to English pitches, and played a full season for Gloucestershire without winning his county cap. But when he is in form, even good bowlers (such as Botham) hardly dare to pitch the ball within his reach, and he has the Bradman-like touch of regarding the first hundred as no more than the necessary preliminary to the second. Somerset's hopes were kept alive in the first innings by Garner, who scored 90, not nearly so correctly; and on the last afternoon by their captain, Rose, who was

injured and limping, but went in at No. 10 and scored 85 not out. I felt this was the best game of cricket I had seen this season. It did not matter that it ended in a draw: a drawn match has always been a part of cricket.

I then went to Bristol to see the Sri Lankans, who were bowled out by Childs on the first day, but in the end achieved a respectable draw. Childs is a slow left-armer. I would say he is one to watch, save that slow left-armers are out of fashion. He turns the ball more than Graveney, though Graveney has the wily family head, and is still the better bowler for all occasions. Together they make a formidable combination, and a refreshing sight. It was the turn of Sadiq, the second apple-cheeked son of the West Country soil in the Gloucestershire side, to score the runs. When he had reached 185, it was his highest score in first-class cricket. A boy called Russell, hauled out of 'A' levels because of injuries to

Andy Brassington (far left) and Jack Russell competing for Gloucestershire's wicket-keeping role.

Gloucestershire's two senior wicket-keepers, did very well. He will be allowed to take the missing papers afterwards, and I wish him success in them. No doubt all his thoughts at present are on becoming a cricket professional, but he would be lucky to find such a career with Gloucestershire, for Brassington is just about the best – *qua* wicket-keeper – in the country, and looks set to command the position for a long time.

*Oh, the dangers of prophecy! Russell soon succeeded Brassington as the county's regular 'keeper.*

Dennis Lillee – still a threat to England's batsmen.

## THE BONE OF CAPTAINCY
### WEEK ENDING JUNE 26

SOMERSET, Surrey, Leicestershire and Kent are the Benson and Hedges semi-finalists. Yorkshire put up a good fight at Headingley, coming back into the game when they seemed to have no hope. Athey scored some runs, so did Hampshire. Many cricketers will tell you that Jack Hampshire was the best of all those English batsmen of the last 15 years, who never quite made it. I trust that Athey is not destined to follow his example. The Man of the Match, however, was Rose, who seems to be overcoming his eyesight difficulties, and is batting formidably well whenever I see him.

England have lost the First Test, chiefly because of dropped catches. No over of spin was bowled by either side throughout the match. I did not feel grieved over missing it, though it brings the question of the captaincy, that well-worn bone, once more to the interested dogs.

## BOTHAM BACK IN THE RUNS
### WEEK ENDING JULY 3

THE Second Test has started, Botham still captain. At the beginning of the week Sussex were leading the Championship; by the middle of it, when they came to Taunton, Surrey were. It does not count for much at this stage, with all the interruptions we have had. It would be nice to see Sussex win. Despite their distinguished history, and their gallery of great players, they never have. I hear very good reports of Greig, though rather disappointing ones of Wells, whom I thought a year ago would prove to be the better all-rounder. Of Parker, I have scarcely any doubt. He is bound to become an England player soon, provided he applies the touches of restraint at critical moments, and he has the intelligence to do that.

Botham got a century at Swansea, his first for 13 months. In the same match, Javed got two. Hampshire had an unexpected win at Old Trafford, and are also among the challengers. I can hardly see them as prospective champions, even with Greenidge and Marshall back, but they have shrugged off the disasters of last season, and Pocock has settled in as captain.

## BREARLEY RECALLED
### WEEK ENDING JULY 10

THE Second Test was a disappointing draw, especially from England's point of view. Botham has been dropped as captain, and Brearley recalled in his place. The appointment of Brearley was made on the basis that he was the likeliest man to save the series against Australia. This was, in principle, a correct decision, because beating Australia should be regarded as an end in itself, not a preparation for anything else. Even if none of your best eleven is going to make the following tour, they should still be chosen. Still, it does make you wonder about who is going to captain in India next winter. Brearley has repeated that he will not be available. I suppose Botham might be reappointed, if he recovers his form, though that cuts both ways for the poor chap. For if he does, there will be plenty to say, "Just shows how much better he is when he's not captain."

The Benson and Hedges finalists are Somerset and Surrey. I was at Taunton, where Somerset beat Kent, comfortably in the end, though they had some anxious moments, especially when Underwood was bowling. Botham's heart must have been warmed by the ovation when he took the ball in the second over. He bowled a long hop. Woolmer hooked it, and it looked a sure enough stroke, but it was caught by Popplewell, a running, falling catch, just inside the long-leg boundary. Popplewell batted, bowled and fielded admirably, and won the Gold Award. I think he is one of the coming men.

## GNAT WEST
### WEEK ENDING JULY 17

I began the week with a visit to Oxford, where the county played respectably against Glamorgan in the knock-out competition, which we are in future to know by this cacophonous name of the Nat West Trophy. There is nothing smooth and soothing about it, as there is with the name Gillette. Nat West suggests more to me the irritant midges which cop you when you are walking the dog on a summer evening in Somerset. The match was played on the Christ Church ground, partly because in the Parks no charge can be made. The county were

Ian Botham, happy to take instructions from Mike Brearley.

rewarded with a crowd of getting on for 2,000. Oxfordshire made a good start, but could not build on it, and Glamorgan, remembering one or two earlier embarrassments against Minor Counties, sensibly did not hurry.

Then I went to The Oval. The match was drawn, rather dully in the end, but there was some batting to remember. Amiss and Humpage both scored centuries. It was Humpage's fourth century in five innings. He is coming on famously as a batsman. As my colleague John Thicknesse observed, it is rather a pity that he is a wicket-keeper, because he is not nearly so good at that, and it distracts attention from his batting. I had another delay on the railway, nowhere near Didcot. I am afraid that the high speed trains, which have been a blessing to us in the west, are wearing out before their time – which you certainly could not say of Amiss or Intikhab and Jackman, the best Surrey bowlers. Small bowled well in the second innings, finishing with six for 76, the best figures of his career. The early editions of the evening paper had a banner headline, "GLADSTONE BAGS FIVE," which must have been the biggest publicity for the Grand Old Man since he was elected for three parliamentary seats simultaneously in 1880.

Gladstone Small in his second season for Warwickshire.

## THINGS ARE LOOKING UP
### WEEK ENDING JULY 24

THE season is cheering up. England's remarkable win in the Third Test has lifted spirits. The weather has improved – it is not consistent, but the drenched early weeks seem a long way away.

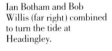
Ian Botham and Bob Willis (far right) combined to turn the tide at Headingley.

---

### England v. Australia
#### Third Test Match
Thursday, Friday, Saturday, Monday & Tuesday, 16th, 17th, 18th, 20th & 21st July 1981
**ENGLAND WON BY 18 RUNS**

15p · 15p

#### ENGLAND

| First Innings | | Second Innings | |
|---|---|---|---|
| 1—G. Boycott, b Lawson | 12 | lbw Alderman | 46 |
| 2—G. A. Gooch, lbw Alderman | 2 | c Alderman b Lillee | 0 |
| *3—J. M. Brearley, c Marsh b Alderman | 10 | c Alderman b Lillee | 14 |
| 4—D. I. Gower, c Marsh b Lawson | 24 | c Border b Alderman | 9 |
| 5—M. W. Gatting, lbw Lillee | 15 | lbw Alderman | 1 |
| 6—P. Willey, b Lawson | 8 | c Dyson b Lillee | 33 |
| 7—I. T. Botham, c Marsh b Lillee | 50 | not out | 149 |
| †8—R. W. Taylor, c Marsh b Lillee | 5 | c Bright b Alderman | 1 |
| 9—G. R. Dilley, c and b Lillee | 13 | b Alderman | 56 |
| 10—G. R. Dilley, c and b Lillee | 13 | b Alderman | 56 |
| 11—C. M. Old, c Border b Alderman | 0 | b Lawson | 29 |
| Extras | 34 | Extras | 16 |
| Total | 174 | Total | 356 |

**FALL OF WICKETS**
First Innings: 1-12 2-40 3-42 4-84 5-87 6-112 7-148 8-166 9-167
Second Innings: 1-0 2-18 3-37 4-41 5-105 6-133 7-135 8-252 9-319

| Bowlers | Overs | Mdns. | Runs | Wkts. | Bowlers | Overs | Mdns. | Runs | Wkts. |
|---|---|---|---|---|---|---|---|---|---|
| Lillee | 18.5 | 7 | 49 | 4 | Lillee | 25 | 6 | 94 | 3 |
| Alderman | 19 | 4 | 59 | 3 | Alderman | 35.3 | 6 | 135 | 6 |
| Lawson | 13 | 3 | 32 | 3 | Lawson | 23 | 4 | 96 | 1 |
| | | | | | Bright | 4 | 0 | 15 | 0 |

\* Denotes Captain   † Denotes Wicket Keeper   Umpires: B. J. Meyer and D. L. Evans
Scorers: E. I. Lester and D. Sherwood

#### AUSTRALIA

| First Innings | | Second Innings | |
|---|---|---|---|
| 1—J. Dyson, b Dilley | 102 | c Taylor b Willis | 34 |
| 2—G. M. Wood, lbw Botham | 34 | c Taylor b Botham | 10 |
| 3—T. M. Chappell, c Taylor b Willey | 27 | c Taylor b Willis | 8 |
| *4—K. J. Hughes, c and b Botham | 89 | c Botham b Willis | 0 |
| 5—G. N. Yallop, c Taylor b Botham | 58 | c Gatting b Willis | 0 |
| 6—A. R. Border, lbw Botham | 8 | b Old | 0 |
| †7—R. W. Marsh, b Botham | 28 | c Dilley b Willis | 4 |
| 8—R. J. Bright, b Dilley | 7 | b Willis | 19 |
| 9—D. K. Lillee, not out | 3 | c Gatting b Willis | 17 |
| 10—G. F. Lawson, c Taylor b Botham | 13 | c Taylor b Willis | 1 |
| 11—T. M. Alderman, not out | 0 | not out | 0 |
| Extras | 32 | Extras | 18 |
| Total (for 9 wickets declared) | 401 | Total | 111 |

**FALL OF WICKETS**
First Innings: 1-55 2-149 3-196 4-220 5-332 6-354 7-357 8-396 9-401
Second Innings: 1-13 2-56 3-58 4-58 5-65 6-68 7-74 8-75 9-110

| Bowlers | Overs | Mdns. | Runs | Wkts. | Bowlers | Overs | Mdns. | Runs | Wkts. |
|---|---|---|---|---|---|---|---|---|---|
| Willis | 20 | 8 | 72 | 0 | Botham | 7 | 3 | 14 | 1 |
| Old | 43 | 14 | 91 | 0 | Dilley | 2 | 0 | 11 | 0 |
| Dilley | 27 | 4 | 78 | 2 | Willis | 15.1 | 3 | 43 | 8 |
| Botham | 39.2 | 11 | 95 | 6 | Old | 9 | 1 | 21 | 1 |
| Willey | 13 | 2 | 31 | 1 | Willey | 3 | 1 | 4 | 0 |
| Boycott | 3 | 2 | 2 | 0 | | | | | |

---

The crowd at Taunton, however, was sparse. Somerset supporters are prone to extremes of emotion. At the beginning of the season you could not find one who was not confident of the Championship. Now that they are only sixth, they seem to have abandoned all hope: which is silly, because a couple of good wins would put them in strong contention again. The match against Derbyshire was a high-scoring draw. Derbyshire made 495 for seven, the highest total this season. Kirsten's 228 was the highest of his career, and his stand with Steele, 291, was a new county record for the third wicket. However, I did not see these latter events. I was present only on the Saturday, when Roebuck and Denning rescued Somerset after a poor start. Roebuck is a cultured batsman (and a cultured man as well, as readers of *The Cricketer* will know): one of the numerous Millfield products.

## OUR MAN IN BED
### WEEK ENDING JULY 31

A dismal week, for me, spent mostly in bed, and with the family away for the earlier part of it. I could not, for most of the time, summon up energy to go

County Championship
(as at August 4)

| | P | Pts |
|---|---|---|
| **1** Nottinghamshire | 16 | 187 |
| **2** Essex | 15 | 163 |
| **3** Surrey | 15 | 160 |
| **4** Sussex | 15 | 157 |

down our crooked staircase for food, let alone keep up with the cricket news. However, I can tell you that Somerset won the Benson and Hedges Cup, easily, as it always looks easy when Richards scores a hundred.

## EXTRAORDINARY THINGS GOING ON AT EDGBASTON
### *WEEK ENDING AUGUST 7*

I was glad to be back on the trail, especially as I began the week at Lord's. The weather was lovely. On the train up, I put aside *The Times*, yes, in the middle of the first leader, and lifted up mine eyes to see the countryside. The valleys laughed and sang. The barley rippled as properly brought up barley should. The cricket itself was not very exciting. There were three declarations, but a draw was always probable, after half a day had been lost on Saturday.

Still, the game had its moments. Bainbridge scored a century, full of beans after the recent award of his county cap. I had not realised he had such good cover drives and square cuts, though I dare say Brearley, who was of course away at the Test, might have found field-placings to frustrate them a little. Sadiq played a graceful innings. The "Little Smiler" has been enjoying something of a revival in the evening of his career.

Away from these comparatively pastoral proceedings, the most extraordinary things, of which you will have read, were going on at Edgbaston in the Test. After a rather dismal start, from an England point of view, it is building into a rubber the like of which has scarcely been seen here since 1902. Then on Wednesday we had the quarter-finals of the Nat West. Essex, Lancashire, Derbyshire and Northamptonshire were the winners. I suppose Nottinghamshire's defeat at Derby was surprising, and possibly Lancashire's win at Hove (though there are still few more dangerous opponents in a one-day match than Clive Lloyd).

## ENGLISHMEN NOT HIGH IN AVERAGES
### *WEEK ENDING AUGUST 14*

I have to remind myself from time to time to pause and look at the general scene. Both the batting and bowling averages are dominated by overseas players.

Sadiq Mohammad – "The Little Smiler".

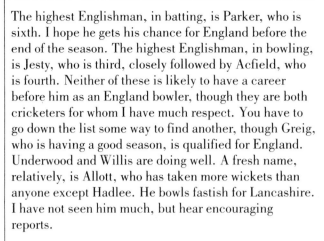

The highest Englishman, in batting, is Parker, who is sixth. I hope he gets his chance for England before the end of the season. The highest Englishman, in bowling, is Jesty, who is third, closely followed by Acfield, who is fourth. Neither of these is likely to have a career before him as an England bowler, though they are both cricketers for whom I have much respect. You have to go down the list some way to find another, though Greig, who is having a good season, is qualified for England. Underwood and Willis are doing well. A fresh name, relatively, is Allott, who has taken more wickets than anyone except Hadlee. He bowls fastish for Lancashire. I have not seen him much, but hear encouraging reports.

*Well, he did play for England – and before the season was out – but, sadly, only once during that series.*

The Championship is still a bit of a muddle. Nottinghamshire are ahead, but the next five counties not too far behind, and all with games in hand (in Hampshire's case three). Still, I cannot quite see Hampshire sustaining their effort, and points in hand are always better than games, especially when the weather, though it has improved, continues to have sudden lapses. Essex lead the John Player League, only by two points over Sussex, but Sussex have played a game more. Well, Essex, for all their recent successes, have never won the John Player, and Nottinghamshire have not won the Championship since 1929.

## FLURRY OF FLANNELS
### *WEEK ENDING AUGUST 21*

WELL, there it is. The rubber won, the Ashes retained, and the Fifth Test was, in its way, as good as the previous two, although this time it was the Australians, in the last innings, who provided most of the drama by nearly changing what had seemed to be the destined course of the match. It has been a joint triumph for Brearley and Botham. I have never been sure of the theory that it is dangerous to give your best player the captaincy, lest the extra responsibility will cause him to lose his form (there are too many examples to the contrary) but Botham's case will certainly be quoted every time the question arises in future.

England won the toss and elected to bat

**FIFTH TEST MATCH**
**OLD TRAFFORD**

Thursday 13th, August
Friday 14th, August
Saturday, 15th, August
  11.30 - 6.30 or '7.30'
Sunday 16th, August
  12.00 - 7.00 or '4.00'
Monday 17th, August
  11.00 - 5.30 or '.00

**FALL OF WICKETS**

| First Innings | | Second Innings | |
|---|---|---|---|
| 1 | - 19 | 1 | - 7 |
| 2 | - 25 | 2 | - 79 |
| 3 | - 57 | 3 | - 80 |
| 4 | - 62 | 4 | - 98 |
| 5 | -109 | 5 | -104 |
| 6 | -109 | 6 | -253 |
| 7 | -131 | 7 | -282 |
| 8 | -132 | 8 | -356 |
| 9 | -175 | 9 | -396 |

**FALL OF WICKETS**

| First Innings | | Second Innings | |
|---|---|---|---|
| 1 | - 20 | 1 | - 7 |
| 2 | - 24 | 2 | - 24 |
| 3 | - 24 | 3 | -119 |
| 4 | - 24 | 4 | -198 |
| 5 | - 58 | 5 | -206 |
| 6 | - 59 | 6 | -296 |
| 7 | -104 | 7 | -322 |
| 8 | -125 | 8 | -373 |
| 9 | -126 | 9 | -378 |

**Umpires:**
D. J. Constant, & K. E. Palmer.

England won by 103 runs
Price 15p.

## England v. Australia

**ENGLAND**

| | | First Innings | | Second Innings | |
|---|---|---|---|---|---|
| 1 | G. BOYCOTT | c Marsh b Alderman | 10 | lbw Alderman | 37 |
| 2 | G. A. GOOCH | lbw Lillee | 10 | b Alderman | 5 |
| 3 | C. J. TAVARE | c Alderman b Whitney | 69 | c Kent b Alderman | 78 |
| 4 | D. I. GOWER | c Yallop b Whitney | 23 | c Bright b Lillee | 1 |
| 5 | J. M. BREARLEY | lbw Alderman | 2 | c Marsh b Alderman | 3 |
| 6 | I. T. BOTHAM | c Bright b Lillee | 0 | c Marsh b Whitney | 118 |
| 7 | A. P. E. KNOTT | c Border b Alderman | 13 | c Dyson b Lillee | 59 |
| 8 | J. E. EMBUREY | c Border b Alderman | 1 | c Kent b Whitney | 57 |
| 9 | P. J. W. ALLOTT | not out | 52 | c Hughes b Bright | 14 |
| 10 | M. W. GATTING | c Border b Lillee | 32 | lbw Alderman | 11 |
| 11 | R. G. D. WILLIS | c Hughes b Lillee | 11 | not out | 5 |
| | | Ex. bs. 6 lb. 2 wds. | 8 | Ex. 1 bs. 12 lb. wds. 3 nb. | 16 |
| | | Total...... | 231 | Total...... | 404 |

| BOWLING ANALYSIS | O | M | R | W | Wds. | NBs. | O | M | R | W | Wds. | NBs. |
|---|---|---|---|---|---|---|---|---|---|---|---|---|
| Lillee | 24.1 | 8 | 55 | 4 | ... | ... | 46 | 13 | 137 | 2 | ... | 1 |
| Alderman | 29 | 5 | 88 | 4 | 2 | ... | 52 | 19 | 109 | 5 | ... | 2 |
| Whitney | 17 | 3 | 50 | 2 | ... | ... | 27 | 6 | 74 | 2 | ... | ... |
| Bright | 16 | 6 | 30 | 0 | ... | ... | 26.4 | 12 | 68 | 1 | ... | ... |

**AUSTRALIA**

| | | First Innings | | Second Innings | |
|---|---|---|---|---|---|
| 1 | G. WOOD | lbw Allott | 19 | c Knott b Allott | 6 |
| 2 | M. F. KENT | c Knott b Emburey | 4 | c Brearley b Emburey | 2 |
| 3 | K. J. HUGHES | lbw Willis | 4 | lbw Botham | 43 |
| 4 | G. N. YALLOP | c Botham b Willis | 0 | b Emburey | 114 |
| 5 | J. DYSON | c Botham b Willis | 0 | run out | 5 |
| 6 | A. R. BORDER | c Gower b Botham | 11 | not out | 123 |
| 7 | R. W. MARSH | c Botham b Willis | 1 | c Knott b Willis | 47 |
| 8 | R. J. BRIGHT | c Knott b Botham | 22 | c Knott b Willis | 5 |
| 9 | T. M. ALDERMAN | not out | 2 | lbw Botham | 0 |
| 10 | D. K. LILLEE | c Gooch b Botham | 13 | c Botham b Allott | 28 |
| 11 | M. R. WHITNEY | b Allott | 0 | c Gatting b Willis | 0 |
| 12 | T. M. CHAPPELL | Ex. bs. bs. wds. 6 nb. | 6 | Ex. bs. 9 lb. 2 wds. 18 nb. | 29 |
| | | Total...... | 130 | Total...... | 402 |

| BOWLING ANALYSIS | O | M | R | W | Wds. | NBs. | O | M | R | W | Wds. | NBs. |
|---|---|---|---|---|---|---|---|---|---|---|---|---|
| Willis | 14 | 0 | 63 | 4 | ... | 6 | 30.5 | 2 | 96 | 3 | ... | 15 |
| Allott | 6 | 1 | 17 | 2 | ... | ... | 17 | 3 | 71 | 2 | ... | ... |
| Botham | 6.2 | 1 | 28 | 3 | ... | ... | 36 | 16 | 86 | 2 | 2 | 1 |
| Emburey | 4 | 0 | 16 | 1 | ... | ... | 49 | 9 | 107 | 2 | ... | ... |
| Gatting | | | | | | | 3 | 1 | 13 | 0 | ... | 2 |

Mike Whitney – a surprise call to Test cricket.

There is a belief in Gloucestershire that the county always does well at Cheltenham. In 1980 they won all three matches. This year they won the first two, though they had to settle for a draw in the last. Against Hampshire, there was another good innings by "Little Smiler", though he strictly had no business to be playing at all. He was not among those originally chosen. However, Whitney, the young fast bowler who has a temporary arrangement with Gloucestershire, was summoned to join the Australians, and Sadiq, with Hampshire's agreement, was allowed to replace him, even though the match had begun. Had Whitney bowled or fielded, I doubt if a replacement would have been justified. Childs and Graveney bowled Hampshire out twice, as several more famous pairs of Gloucestershire spinners have done in the latter stages of a match at Cheltenham.

Kent won the toss, and had Underwood in the side. Kent made a solid start, chiefly due to Benson and Taylor, to whom I inadvertently referred in my report as Benson and Jedges. Zaheer scored an untroubled century, his ninth of the season, and became the first man to score 2,000 this season. As he did not receive a ball in May, this is a considerable feat. On the last day both sides seemed to have a chance of victory, first Gloucestershire, then Kent. It finished in a draw, but was a better match than many a slog-out.

## DEPRESSING EXPERIENCE FOR A YORKSHIREMAN
### WEEK ENDING AUGUST 28

I went to Lord's for the Yorkshire match. Both sides were keen to win, Middlesex because they still have an outside chance of the Championship (Nottinghamshire remain leaders), Yorkshire because they have been making a recovery from the unnameable disaster which threatened them a few weeks ago (they are now sixth from bottom). Yorkshire were captained by Hartley, who has yet to win his cap. I cannot think that this managerial decision has contributed to the harmony of the dressing-room.

There was an interesting passage of play on the first day. Yorkshire needed one run for their third batting point when the 100th over began. Edmonds bowled it. He is known as a great appealer, and he shouted, solitarily, for leg-before from the first two balls. "Now for the hat-trick!" cried a voice full of Sheffield sarcasm. It was an ill-omened comment. Hartley was bowled by the third, Carrick stumped off the fourth, Stevenson was nearly bowled by the fifth, and run out off the last.

Yorkshire were well in the match until nearly half way, but went to pieces in the face of a last-wicket stand by Tomlins and Daniel. There seemed to be eleven captains on the field, the placing dictated by the cursing distances; Sidebottom and Stevenson engaged in a private competition as to who could bowl most no-balls. Middlesex won easily in the end. It was a depressing experience for a Yorkshireman.

## RUMINATING IN THE WEST
### WEEK ENDING SEPTEMBER 4

THE Sixth Test was drawn, so England have won the rubber 3-1. It sounds conclusive, but I agree with John Woodcock that there was never very much between the sides. It was a pleasing touch that when England seemed in danger of defeat, Brearley played a good innings.

I was at Bristol for the Bank Holiday match against Somerset. Two interesting young cricketers were making their first-class debuts. Ollis batted patiently and skilfully. He comes from Keynsham. Everyone who

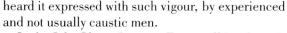

| County Championship (as at September 2) | P | Pts |
| --- | --- | --- |
| **1** Nottinghamshire | 21 | 283 |
| **2** Sussex | 20 | 255 |
| **3** Essex | 20 | 243 |
| **4** Somerset | 19 | 229 |

drives in the narrow lanes around Keynsham knows, fearfully, the vast Ollis lorries. He has their style, though not yet their weight. Doughty is a Yorkshireman, recommended to Gloucestershire by another Yorkshireman, Don Wilson, the coach at Lord's. He bowls at over medium-pace, and needs to smooth his run-up, but he is another who has the makings. Somerset were out for 147, but on a poor pitch it was enough. Garner and Dredge did most of the damage, indeed the amiable-looking Demon of Frome produced the best figures of his career. So did Childs, with nine for 56 in Somerset's second innings. I heard a comment by a disappointed Gloucestershire supporter, who has seen many matches against Somerset: "Well, s'pose we should ha' been cheering' *them*, 'cos they've still a chance, see, and we'm none, and 'tis all in west, like." And he took out his pipe, lit it ruminatively, and added "Still, I do like beating they . . . " I did not catch his last word, but it was plural and I am fairly sure it began with B.

## NOTTINGHAMSHIRE – NOT WITHOUT CONTROVERSY
### WEEK ENDING SEPTEMBER 11

NOTTINGHAMSHIRE are having to wait a bit while the others play their matches, but it now seems highly probable that they will win the Championship. Derbyshire have won (let me give it the dignified and proper title for once) the National Westminster Bank Trophy. It was an exciting match, won off the last ball, and I would have much enjoyed seeing it, even on television, but a different season has started, and I was watching Bath lose to Pontypool.

I am pleased that Derbyshire won, because it is the first time they have won anything since their single Championship of 1936; and I shall be moderately pleased if Nottinghamshire win, because they are one of the historic cricketing counties, one of those who made the game, and their last Championship was in 1929. I use the qualifying word "moderately" because there is a lot of feeling among cricketers that they have prepared their home pitches to suit them to an unfair degree. This kind of grumble has been heard before, notably when Surrey had their great run, and Laker and Lock were bowling everybody out at The Oval. But I have never

heard it expressed with such vigour, by experienced and not usually caustic men.

In the John Player League, Essex will be champions if they win their last match. If they lose, and Warwickshire win at Taunton, Warwickshire would be top. I have always maintained that Sunday cricket and Championship cricket are two quite different games, played with the same implements, and nothing illustrates it better than that Warwickshire are still in contention for the John Player League, and firmly at the bottom of the Championship.

## AU REVOIR, MY FRIENDS
### WEEK ENDING SEPTEMBER 18

EVERYTHING has gone much as expected. Nottinghamshire are champions, and Essex won the John Player. Sussex are second, maddeningly close. Sussex have never won the Championship, despite

Nottinghamshire – County Champions 1981. Back, left to right: Paul Johnson, Neil Weightman, Ian Pont, Kevin Saxelby, Roy Dexter, Tim Robinson, Mark Fell, Chris Scott. Middle: John Cope (development manager), Eddie Hemmings, Peter Hacker, John Birch, Bill Thornley (scorer), Kevin Cooper, Mike Bore, Bruce French, Graham Lyas (physio). Front: Paul Todd, Basharat Hassan, Richard Hadlee, Clive Rice (captain), Ken Taylor (manager), Mike Harris, Bob White, Derek Randall.

many marvellous players and several near-run things, especially in the early Thirties when they made repeated challenges to Yorkshire. Somerset have never won the Championship either. I hope Somerset win it next year, and Sussex the year after. No, I don't really. At heart I always have the hope that Yorkshire will win, but there is a double-devil of a row going on up there at the moment. I have suggested in print before that Yorkshiremen have much the same temperament as Latin Americans. No banana republic could do better than the latest efforts of the county broad as ten thousand beeves.

This is the fifth, and possibly the final, season that I have written this journal. At first I strained too much, trying to make sure that I had recorded every major

Bob Taylor and Barry Wood – partners in success at Lord's.

Ray East plus cigarette and celebratory drink – while the trophy is enough for Norbert Phillip.

cricketing event, whether I had seen it or not. This became very boring to me, and no doubt boring to you. Once I realised I was writing a journal, not a book of reference, it became easier to write, and I hope easier to read. You have favoured me with a considerable and kind correspondence, and it is interesting that your letters have mostly concerned, not Boycott and Brearley and Botham, but Didcot, the Shoreditch Sparrow, the Demon of Frome, Adam and Felicity and sundry other characters and places I have encountered.

## Schweppes County Championship Final Table

| | P | W | L | D | Bt | Bl | Pts |
|---|---|---|---|---|---|---|---|
| 1. Nottinghamshire (3) ..... | 22 | 11 | 4 | 7 | 56 | 72 | 304 |
| 2. Sussex (4 ) ..................... | 22 | 11 | 3 | 8 | 58 | 68 | 302 |
| 3. Somerset (5) ................. | 22 | 10 | 2 | 10 | 54 | 65 | 279 |
| 4. Middlesex (1) ................ | 22 | 9 | 3 | 10 | 49 | 64 | 257 |
| 5. Essex (8) ....................... | 22 | 8 | 4 | 10 | 62 | 64 | 254 |
| 6. Surrey (2) ..................... | 22 | 7 | 5 | 10 | 52 | 72 | 236 |
| 7. Hampshire (17) ............. | 22 | 6 | 7 | 9 | 45 | 65 | 206 |
| 8. Leicestershire (9) ......... | 22 | 6 | 6 | 10 | 45 | 58 | 199 |
| 9. Kent (16) ...................... | 22 | 5 | 7 | 10 | 51 | 58 | 189 |
| 10. Yorkshire (6) ............... | 22 | 5 | 9 | 8 | 41 | 66 | 187 |
| 11. Worcestershire (11) ...... | 22 | 5 | 9 | 8 | 44 | 52 | 172 |
| 12. Derbyshire (9) ............. | 22 | 4 | 7 | 11 | 51 | 57 | 172 |
| 13. Gloucestershire (7) ....... | 22 | 4 | 3 | 15 | 51 | 55 | 170 |
| 14. Glamorgan (13) ........... | 22 | 3 | 10 | 9 | 50 | 69 | 167 |
| 15. Northamptonshire (12).. | 22 | 3 | 6 | 13 | 51 | 67 | 166 |
| 16. Lancashire (15) ............ | 22 | 4 | 7 | 11 | 47 | 57 | 164 |
| 17. Warwickshire (14) ........ | 22 | 2 | 11 | 9 | 56 | 47 | 135 |

1980 positions in brackets.
Worcestershire and Lancashire totals include 12 points for wins in matches reduced to one innings.

| BATTING | | | | | | BOWLING | | | | | |
|---|---|---|---|---|---|---|---|---|---|---|---|
| Qualification: 8 innings | | | | | | Qualification: 10 wickets | | | | | |
| | I | NO | R | HS | Ave | | O | M | R | W | Ave |
| Zaheer Abbas | 36 | 10 | 2306 | 215* | 88.69 | R. Hadlee | 708.4 | 231 | 1564 | 105 | 14.89 |
| J. Miandad | 37 | 7 | 2083 | 200* | 69.43 | S. Clarke | 339.4 | 98 | 734 | 49 | 14.97 |
| A. Lamb | 43 | 9 | 2049 | 162 | 60.26 | J. Garner | 615.4 | 182 | 1349 | 88 | 15.32 |
| I. V. A. Richards | 33 | 3 | 1718 | 196 | 57.26 | A. N. Jones | .83 | 11 | 283 | 17 | 16.64 |
| C. Rice | 30 | 4 | 1462 | 172 | 56.23 | M. Holding | 271.1 | 75 | 715 | 40 | 17.87 |
| P. Kirsten | 35 | 6 | 1605 | 228 | 55.34 | I. Moseley | 355.4 | 88 | 842 | 52 | 18.11 |
| G. Turner | 42 | 4 | 2101 | 168 | 55.28 | A. Sidebottom | 305.5 | 88 | 899 | 47 | 19.12 |

*After retaining the Ashes with such dash, through Botham and his Svengali Brearley, England went to India under their new captain, Keith Fletcher. His Essex side had fared well again, despite losing the semi-final of the Nat West. Essex were defeated because they lost more wickets than Derbyshire, though the scores were level. Derbyshire won an enthralling final against Northamptonshire in exactly the same way.*

*Fletcher had little chance to engineer such exciting finishes in India. England, caught a little cold, lost the First Test, and the rest of the series was unbelievably turgid: five draws and a funereal over-rate by both sides, a fact which reflected badly on both the umpires and the two captains, Fletcher and Sunil Gavaskar. The latter*

*was as prolific as ever with the bat (500 runs in the six Tests) and it did not take a clairvoyant to guess that the Test record aggregate which Geoff Boycott achieved during the series would soon be broken again – by Gavaskar.*

*Boycott did not complete the tour, returning home because of "mental and physical tiredness." This hardly helped Fletcher, nor did the fact that throughout the trip many of his players were secretly planning to tour South Africa in March, against the wishes of the TCCB, for large sums of money put up by business interests in South Africa who were determined to end that country's long isolation from international cricket. Boycott, the main organiser of the touring party, had only been allowed into India in the first place after making a declaration against apartheid, in company with Geoff Cook, the Northants captain, who had also captained Eastern Province. Cook was not one of those who made the tour to South Africa; nor was Bob Willis, who withdrew from it at the eleventh hour, perhaps by then aware that he had a chance of assuming the greatest honour in English cricket. But those who went included many of the best players in the country, notably Graham Gooch who had been England's leading player overseas for the last two winters.*

*In order to continue playing against most of the other Test countries, the TCCB felt obliged to take a public stand against Gooch and his colleagues, banning them for three years. It was a sad echo of the Packer affair, this time with nasty political overtones.*

*The visitors to Australia were Pakistan, who lost the Test series two-one, and West Indies, who only drew their three-match series although, as usual, they won the one-day tournament.*

*Sri Lanka played Test cricket for the first time during this winter, losing to England (Emburey and Underwood to the fore) in their inaugural match at Colombo, and then losing two-nil on a short tour of Pakistan, though their leg-spinner Somachandra de Silva was the most successful bowler on either side.*

*Sri Lanka's appearance brought some badly needed variety to the international stage. The dullness of much of the winter's cricket was summed up by the final of the Ranji Trophy in which Delhi were declared winners on first innings at the end of a match lasting six days. The scores were Karnataka 705, Delhi 706 for eight!*

178

# — 1982 —

## WELL APPAREL'D APRIL IS FULL OF RUNS – FOR SOME
### *WEEK ENDING MAY 1*

ONE of my many main pleasures each winter is to read Alan Gibson's Journal of the Season. It is superb to pass an afternoon on North Curl Curl beach rummaging through the journal and remembering. Now it falls on me to relieve Alan and to place before you my jottings as the season develops. It is a task I undertake with mixed feelings, much as a stripper must fret if she is to follow Dolly Parton on stage. You see how the tone has already lowered!

It was quite inevitable, of course, that delaying the cricket season would bring the finest April for years. This was not "the cruellest month", but "well apparel'd April" treading on the heels of limping winter. Practice matches have been played beneath blue skies and in short sleeves.

Yes, we are underway again, with the champions playing MCC and cricket at the Parks and Fenners. Already Alan Jones, Allan Lamb, Peter Willey and Glenn Turner have scored centuries off university bowling. As far as I can see, views of university cricket divide into two camps – those who usually score a century, and those who don't!

To be fair, the universities have scored plenty of runs too. Pringle, Boyd-Moss, Cowan and Henderson, in particular, have attacked rusty county bowlers. Steve Henderson scored 209* against a full Middlesex team, an innings the more remarkable since Steve had not threatened to hit a century in any of his many innings for Worcestershire, who, as a consequence, released him at the end of last season.

April also brought to us our Cricket Association Annual General Meeting. Bob Willis brought a motion condemning dissent and asking for severe punishments for dissenters. I must say I do not agree that standards in county cricket have sunk so low in these last five years. Of course, there is much less walking and rather more appealing, but people do not claim catches which do not carry, and only one person has sworn at me in

Steven Henderson – no respect for the County Champions.

nine seasons (no, to be accurate, only one *opponent* has sworn at me).

Anyhow, I suspect the best way to improve behaviour is to search for strong umpires. With higher pay on offer, these last two years have seen the appearance in white coats of Jackie Birkenshaw, David Shepherd, Barry Leadbeater, and Billy Ibadulla amongst others – men who understand what happens on a cricket field. One can hardly harangue or stare at David Shepherd, he is much too cheerful and, moreover, much too much in charge.

Our meeting also raised the thorny issue of Geoff Boycott's tour to South Africa. Many cricketers feel that since the players were under contract to no one and were not being paid by anyone else, they could seek winter employment where they chose. They had no obligations. Others argued that the tourists had bitten the hand that fed them, in that they had knowingly imperilled the Pakistan and Indian tours to England without which professional cricket could not survive. In the end, the professional cricketers supported the three-year ban.

## AN EARLY PREDICTION: WATCH OUT FOR LANCASHIRE
### *WEEK ENDING MAY 8*

WITH the audacity of the young and the foolishness of the naive, I will plunge into some early predictions. Reading this, you can laugh or applaud. I won't care. I will be in Australia.

I suppose Middlesex, Essex, Somerset, Sussex and Nottinghamshire will do well, for they strike me as the strongest teams. I doubt if Nottinghamshire can repeat last season's superbly engineered triumph, though. They cannot win the toss so often, nor resist Test calls and injuries so successfully. Already, Cliff Rice is unable to bowl, and Derek Randall is threatening to recover his England place. They have signed Mike Hendrick, who will add to their ability to dismiss teams on green pitches. Hendrick's weakness, and perhaps this explains why he has never taken five wickets in a Test innings, is that his best deliveries are utterly unplayable. They are pitched short, and move so far that only Barry Richards can touch them.

I have a feeling Lancashire will do well too, under

Colin Croft – quietly hostile.

the leadership of Clive Lloyd. I know, if I have many more teams, I will be rivalling Hotspur's Twelve to Follow. Graeme Fowler scored lots of runs last year, and in Croft and Allott Lancashire are blessed with a penetrating attack, particularly with Lloyd's ability to inspire Croft. Croft hates batsmen. Whilst his West Indian partners are astonishingly meek off the field, Colin Croft is a loner, a Clint Eastwood of the Caribbean. He is reluctant to speak to opposing batsmen in lifts or at breakfast. One colleague says of him, "He doesn't like to give way at a roundabout!"

I do not want this journal to concentrate too much on Somerset (though Alan Gibson set a terrible example here!). But as one of our players broke a world record this week, I have to mention our game against Combined Universities, whilst modestly omitting to describe the ball with which I bowled Derek Pringle. Derek Taylor, our apparently ageless wicket-keeper, took eight catches in an innings to break the record for one-day matches. Derek has been a marvellous performer for Somerset, a reliable 'keeper who rises to brilliance when standing up to medium-pacers. If he does retire at the end of the season as he threatens (or is it promises?) we will miss his unobtrusive wicket-keeping and the periodic giggles which slip out as he lovingly studies his *Daily Telegraph* and discovers some particular hero of his to have performed some feat of staggering ineptitude or embarrassing skill.

## NO SUBSTITUTE FOR SPLIT TROUSERS
### WEEK ENDING MAY 15

Neil Williams – an impressive debut.

AT Lord's, Middlesex demolished Somerset; a young man named Neil Williams taking three valuable wickets in his first game. Williams, like Wilf Slack and Roland Butcher (and, I am told, a fast bowler called Cowans), is black. Already, Butcher has played for England, Gladstone Small of Warwickshire will, I think, within a year or two, and Slack has been mentioned in despatches. So our Test team could soon reflect the variety of races in the country.

As the season gathers its head, it has dawned even on we country folk that some of the rules have changed. My trousers tore in an embarrassing place at Lord's. Upon informing my captain, I received the news that I could

not have a substitute while I changed trousers. Some nit has passed a rule saying that players cannot have 12th men except for injury. So I ended up fielding at Lord's before a big crowd with split trousers. I only hope those who passed this rule had to sit and endure the resulting spectacle.

And we have the four-men-in-a-ring rule in Sunday League games too, now. This will change the game, in that it will be impossible to defend all corners of the boundary.

## AMBITIOUS TEAMS AND BAD WICKETS
### WEEK ENDING MAY 22

Norman Cowans – also eligible for England.

THIS week what have we? A two-day victory for Nottinghamshire over Hampshire at Trent Bridge. As usual, the pitch was reported. Many more pitches have been reported this year than ever before. A lot of nonsense is talked about the preparation of pitches. The groundsmen at Trent Bridge and Hove could prepare excellent pitches if they were so instructed. Last season, when Sussex visited Trent Bridge, John Barclay expected a wicket as green as an emerald. He inspected what he supposed to be the match wicket, only to discover an hour later the groundsman pitching stumps on a white bare surface 20 yards away! Nottinghamshire, you see, did not want to risk Imran and Le Roux on a greentop.

Sussex, by the way, have been known to prepare three separate pitches for the same match.

But with three-day cricket and 16 points for a win, it is inevitable that ambitious teams will prepare bad wickets. Last year, three teams were reported as having deliberately and consistently produced unreliable pitches. They were Nottinghamshire, Sussex and Somerset. Guess who came first, second and third in the Championship?

## ACROSS THE SEVERN – THREE TIMES IN TEN DAYS
### WEEK ENDING MAY 29

IT is not often that a trip to Wales is anticipated with pleasure. Cardiff has a ridge and several rugby fields, Swansea has empty stands, 72 steps, and Wilf Wooller.

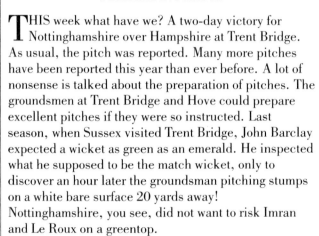

**Cheltenham**
Gloucestershire v.
Sri Lanka, August 1984.

**Arundel**
Duchess of Norfolk's XI v.
Australians, May 1985.

**Birtles Bowl**
Hudson's Hollywood XI v.
Cheshire, June 1985.

**Burton Court,
Chelsea**
Marlborough Blues v.
Old Wellingtonians,
The Cricketer Cup Final,
August 1980.

Alan Jones – over 30,000 runs for Glamorgan since 1957.

But Swansea is also blessed with the familiar, much-loved figure of Alan Jones.

I mention Alan because in April he was awarded a well-deserved MBE in recognition of his long and unstinting service in the cause of the Welsh. With his brother Eifion (he of the raucous appeals and ripping square-drives), Alan has stood fast in the dramas of Glamorgan cricket. He has survived the two imposters (no, I don't mean Javed and Majid), and remained the same self-effacing and reliable cricketer. In a pre-season friendly, Derek Taylor, who ought not to raise the subject of age, affected surprise to see Alan potter out to bat. He wondered aloud whether Alan might not retire soon. Jones simply stroked his fine crop of hair and peered mildly at Derek's hair, as threadbare as grass in the Australian outback.

Actually, owing to stunning organisation, we are due to cross the Severn Bridge three times in the space of ten days. Studying the fixture list I see that Nottinghamshire and Yorkshire must drive from Headingley to play in Somerset on the Sunday. And, of course, back after the game. No doubt other teams are making similarly hazardous journeys throughout the season. This is ridiculous, someone should do something about it before bleary-eyed cricketers die in a car crash.

Nor is Alan Jones the only senior batsman to be celebrated this week. One Glenn Maitland Turner has completed his 100 hundreds. For a fortnight he has been struggling to score that elusive ton, often being seen in the nets to the appalled consternation of bowlers, and once running around the Worcestershire ground in the not altogether demanding company of Younis Ahmed. Eventually, with yet another virtuoso performance, Turner collected his 100 against Warwickshire. Upon reaching 100 Billy Ibadulla (who brought Turner to England) took out a gin. Turner downed the drink and continued to amass 311*. To score 211* while under the affluence of incohol strikes me as a bit much, quite frankly.

*Ibadulla's generous act was made, I believe, to fulfil a longstanding promise.*

## WILLIS TO CAPTAIN AGAINST INDIA
### WEEK ENDING JUNE 5

THIS week brought us our first taste of international cricket. England's selectors invited Bob Willis to captain the team, a man already experienced at leading a county, and a faithful servant of England for a decade. Willis has taken 250 Test wickets for his country. He is still our best fast bowler. The sight of him roaring, no, charging, in to bowl in the Ashes series last year was not easily forgotten. Willis is one of those men well-liked by his team, yet a mystery to his opponents. With people he does not know, he can be abrupt, even cranky. I suppose it is shyness, either that or he is trying to frighten the living daylights out of you before the game.

Glenn Turner enjoys his gin and tonic surrounded by Warwickshire fielders (left to right) David Smith, Geoff Humpage, Asif Din, Simon Sutcliffe and Jim Cumbes.

Top level conference – Bob Willis with the selectors (left to right) Norman Gifford, Alan Smith, Peter May and Alec Bedser.

His team for the Prudential games included Allan Lamb and the Emperor, Barry Wood. In South Africa, Lamb is regarded more highly even than Wessels, Kirsten and McKewan. He is a robust, barrel-chested cricketer, with a simple approach to batting. He hits the ball very hard, very straight, and very often. Naturally (if you will forgive the pun) there is some debate as to whether someone born and raised in South Africa ought to be chosen by England. He will find it hard to overcome the feeling that he is not English. A few centuries would help.

As for Barry Wood's return to the England team, his record in one-day cricket speaks for itself. He has won endless Man of the Match awards, and is still a canny batsman and niggardly bowler. His appearances at Taunton provoke tremendous joy. His very smile, with the gap in his front teeth, causes uproar, and his vivid leap as he bowls brings whoops of joy from the crowd.

Willis's team was much too good for the Indians. At Headingley, England won by nine wickets (Wood 78*); at The Oval, England won by 99 runs. For India only the splendid Kapil Dev (60 and 47) defied England's superiority.

## PRINGLE JOINS WILLIS'S BAND
### WEEK ENDING JUNE 12

A N easy victory for England in the First Test despite Kapil Dev's heroics and Vengsarkar's fluent 157.

*Dilip Vengsarkar in command at Lord's.*

Kapil Dev took wickets with the new ball in both innings with his lively pace and control of swing, as well as striking 89 in 55 balls. He reminds me of a

musketeer. He is d'Artagnan. Flamboyantly, but politely, scything his way through republicans.

England chose an interesting team for the match. To open the batting, with Gooch, Boycott and Larkins not available, we found Tavaré and Cook. That does not yet have the convincing ring of Boycott and Edrich, or Simpson and Lawry. At present Tavaré and Cook sounds like two stand-up comedians thrown together and expected to work in harmony as well as Morecambe and Wise.

Ian Botham has been asked to bat at No 5, a shrewd idea. This will encourage Ian to show his majestic range of shots rather than his prodigious hitting. Another move of originality and imagination was the choice of Derek Pringle. His figures in county cricket are mediocre, but he has had a startling season with bat and ball for Cambridge.

*The choice of Pringle was original, certainly, but did the call come too early for him? The chances are that if he returns for England in the second half of the Eighties, he will be more effective.*

## WORLD CUP WEEK
### WEEK ENDING JUNE 19

IN the World Cup in Spain, Third World nations have made a surprising impression. Algeria, Kuwait and the Cameroons have played well. This permits the thought that cricket's World Cup could include more of the smaller countries.

As it happens, cricket's mini World Cup has begun this week too. Alas, only the team winning this long competition will be invited to play in the World Cup proper next season. This is a pity. Might it not be fun to see our friends from Papua New Guinea play the West Indies, or Bermuda play Australia? I suppose soccer is more of a team game in which well organised systems can restrain individual talent. Cricket is made up of a series of individual duels from which there is no escape. Papua New Guinea's openers might not yet be ready for Mr Holding or Mr Garner.

Meanwhile, back at Canterbury, Somerset defeated Kent to join Sussex, Lancashire and Nottinghamshire in the Benson & Hedges semi-finals. Lancashire's win at Lord's was quite easy in the end. Clive Lloyd hit 66. He must be nearing the end of his splendid career. Perhaps he can inspire his team to reach one more final, so that he can captain his county in a cup final at Lord's, a pitch he has graced so often with Lancashire and the West Indies.

## RETURN OF ILLINGWORTH AND THE GODFATHER
### WEEK ENDING JUNE 26

Ray Illingworth – back again with Yorkshire.

A SLIGHTLY startling week as news drifted down that Yorkshire had sacked Chris Old as captain and appointed 50-year-old Raymond Illingworth to this evidently slippery seat.

Those of us not involved in coups have enjoyed a pleasant few days, though (it being Bath Week) we have been deluged by rain. The Recreation Ground at Bath is in Avon these days. It used merely to be under the Avon. The ground is ringed by eight large tents, each full of businessmen sipping whisky or gin. The wicket has improved. No longer is it cut with a scythe for the first time a week before the Festival. In fact, the whole ground has the feeling of a business convention with a few dotty white figures rushing about in the middle to entertain industrialists.

Bath Week was brightened by a trip down the river, and by a visit from the Godfather, Brian Close.

Our boat trip was organised by Scyld Berry, and the cheerful party included Somerset players, Gloucestershire players, Dudley Doust, and the Indian touring team. We chatted jovially about Botham's left-handed sweep, which Doshi said he could play off any ball at any time. Dilip said he liked the shot, and that Botham was a genius. Is he setting a mysterious Oriental trap? Or is he overawed at bowling to someone he regards as a genius? As a clue to the subtleties of Dilip's mind, when a colleague remarked of someone, "He is a pain in the head", Dilip drily added, "I have a rather lower opinion of him". In the end, of course, an ex-England captain (not Peter May) threw a fairly willing Popplewell into the river, whereupon the current Indian captain suggested that Ravi Shastri might be the next victim. It is astonishing how popular Ian Botham is with opposing Test teams. He chatted with his Indian rivals as easily as he larked around with the West Indians.

During the cricket (there was a bit), Gloucestershire introduced their new signing, another huge West Indian, Franklyn Stephenson. There are now few counties without a large gentleman who bowls very quickly. Glamorgan have signed Winston Davis who, Viv Richards says, is "hasty". And he who Richards calls hasty . . . Probably Stephenson, with his superbly disguised slower ball, will win more games for Gloucestershire than Zaheer.

Franklyn Stephenson – new recruit for Gloucestershire.

🏏 *Stephenson proved to be a great talent due to waste his sweetness on the South African air – though they certainly appreciated him there, for all too brief a time.*

## OXFORD'S GENEROSITY A CULTURE SHOCK
### WEEK ENDING JULY 3

A BUSY week for cricket this was, with a Test match, a Varsity match and the Benson & Hedges semi-finals.

In the end the Manchester Test was spoilt by rain, but not before the Indians could stage a spirited

Winston Davis – the large gentleman at Glamorgan.

Gundappa Viswanath – fighting for India.

recovery led by Kirmani and Viswanath, and finished by Patil and Kapil. On Sunday, these men, the little 'uns and the big 'uns in partnerships, rushed India from 35 for three to 379 for seven, despite the perils of a dead pitch which from time to time produced a snorter or a shooter.

Kirmani, as bald as Yul Brynner, and the only Moslem in the party, had been reported as believing that the Indians had lost the First Test by being too defensive. This view emerges at Somerset sometimes, usually in the bath, pint in hand. Anyhow, Kirmani drove with panache, persuading Viswanath to unleash his cuts. After their loss, and the fall of Sharma to Edmonds (the only cricketer to read the *Financial Times*) Patil and Dev attacked with vigour. It is not often that cricket is blessed with the sight of two such eccentric stroke players in full flow together. They brought the series to life, and rejuvenated a depressed Indian team.

The Varsity match brought a victory for Cambridge after a generous declaration from Oxford. Apparently this is the first time Cambridge have won after a third innings declaration. Reading the paper with Vic Marks next morning, we suffered something of a culture shock. A generous declaration? What on earth was going on? You can't have generosity in a Varsity match, any more than you can in a Test or a Roses match. It strikes me as yet another concession to those misguided souls who believe cricket should be interesting or, worse, entertaining! Pith and nonsense, say I. The game should have ended in an incredibly dull draw, with Oxford batting all the last day to the fury of Cambridge, the journalists and both the people in the crowd.

Ian Botham's highest innings in Test cricket.

## FIRST VIEW OF THE PAKISTANIS
### WEEK ENDING JULY 10

AT Taunton I found myself umpiring a game between two Under-12 teams (again, I might add, of considerable drama, since one team, chasing a formidable 51 sank to 0 for two in one over, only to win seven overs later). In the nets beyond the boundary, practising 4½ hours, were the Pakistan touring team under the new leader, Imran Khan.

Under Imran and Intikhab, their ebullient manager, the Pakistanis appeared to be enthusiastic, determined and formidable. Previously, they had often appeared to be a talented bunch of egomaniacs. Perhaps at last they have found a captain who can forge a team from their latent ability.

Against Somerset, Mansoor played well for his 153. He has the wristy, fluent and relaxed style one associates with his countrymen, and his innings was full of nimble footwork and quick wit. Somehow or other he was able to drive Vic Marks' off-breaks pitching on leg through extra-cover. This reminded me of Zaheer's extraordinary ability to do just the same, and of the time in a run chase when we put a deep extra-cover for Marks and had Zaheer caught there!

I am afraid we did not see a great deal of the Pakistan batsmen apart from Mansoor and Mohsin, though Majid scored an aloof 48. We saw a good deal of leg-spinner Abdul Qadir, who has already dismissed 40 county batsmen. Qadir is a bouncy, effervescent man with a high arm. He fooled Richards with his first ball, a googly which missed Richards' off stump by a vindaloo. Abdul is one of those smiling leg-spinners, like Intikhab and Robin Hobbs. Evidently leg-spin attracts two sorts of men, the cheery and the grumpy. The grumpy ones are ferocious and tear their hair, curse, sweat, and glare at you. cheerful ones merely smile sadly as some clown of a batsman misreads a googly and Chinese cuts it.

A final word on the inspiring and doomed mini World Cup. It was won, easily in the end, by a resilient Zimbabwe team, out to establish themselves in international cricket. Bermuda were beaten in the final, Papua New Guinea came a splendid third, and Bangladesh fourth. I only hope all the players enjoyed themselves (didn't I hear that Gibraltar were "only here

Abdul Qadir – a flurry of activity.

County Championship (as at July 6)

| | P | Pts |
|---|---|---|
| 1 Middlesex | 9 | 132 |
| 2 Sussex | 9 | 113 |
| 3 Nottinghamshire | 8 | 99 |
| 4 Hampshire | 9 | 93 |

**20p**    England v. India    13-7-82

### THIRD TEST

**at The Oval, Thursday, Friday, Saturday, Monday & Tuesday, 8, 9, 10, 12 & 13 July 1982**

Any alterations to teams will be announced over the public address system.

| ENGLAND | First Innings | | Second Innings | |
|---|---|---|---|---|
| 1 Geoff Cook (Northamptonshire) | c Shastri b Patil | 50 | c Yashpal b Kapil Dev | 8 |
| 2 Chris Tavaré (Kent) | b Kapil Dev | 39 | | |
| 3 Allan Lamb (Northamptonshire) | run out | 107 | | |
| 4 David Gower (Leicestershire) | c Kirmani b Shastri | 47 | | |
| 5 Ian Botham (Somerset) | c Viswanath b Doshi | 208 | | |
| 6 Derek Randall (Nottinghamshire) | st. Kirmani b Shastri | 95 | | |
| 7 Derek Pringle (Essex) | st. Kirmani b Doshi | 9 | | |
| 8 Phil Edmonds (Middlesex) | c sub (Parkar) b Doshi | 14 | | |
| † 9 Bob Taylor (Derbyshire) | lbw b Shastri | 3 | | |
| 10 Paul Allott (Lancashire) | c Yashpal b Doshi | 3 | | |
| *11 Bob Willis (Warwickshire) | not out | 1 | | |
| | B3, l-b5, w, n-b10 | 18 | B, l-b, w, n-b | |
| | Total (173.3 overs) | 594 | Total | |

Fall of wickets—First Innings   1—96 ... 2—96 ... 3—185 ... 4—361 ... 5—512 ... 6—534 ... 7—562 ... 8—569 ... 9—582 ... 10—
Second Innings   1—12 ... 2— ... 4— ... 5— ... 6— ... 8— ... 9—

O.    M.    N.b.   2nd. Innings   O.   M

for the beer"?), and that they saw more of England than Birmingham and its surround.

## YORKSHIRE'S OUTSTANDING VICTORY
### WEEK ENDING JULY 17

FINALLY the Indian Test Series has stumbled to its dull end, not deeply mourned. I wonder when a touring team in England for the first half of the season last emerged victorious.

*Since "double-header" Test series were first introduced in the summer of 1965, England have never lost a single match in the opening series.*

Imran's Pakistanis continue to storm round England thrashing weak county teams and complaining that they are not facing any good bowlers. I wonder how often Imran himself has played for Sussex against tourists?

In the second round of the NatWest, Yorkshire's victory was much the most remarkable. Chasing Worcestershire's 286, they were 40 for four overnight, having lost their four top batsmen to Inchmore's inswingers. The morning papers were full of news of further disasters at Yorkshire. As it turned out, these reports were as premature as American newspaper reports of Dewey's defeat of Truman. Bairstow hit 92, Hartley 58, Chris Old 55*, and Graham Stevenson 28*, to bring an outstanding victory.

## MOSES HITS THE BIG TIME
### WEEK ENDING JULY 24

VERY hard to think of anything to write about this week. I have scratched about for inspiration. I have walked along cliffs with pen, paper, and can of Heineken, but the muse has remained silent. Therefore it is with reluctance (the degree of which you must judge) that I will dwell upon Somerset's victory in the Benson & Hedges Final.

As a match, the final was disappointing. Nottinghamshire had hit a bad patch, weakened by injuries to Hadlee and Hendrick, and by Test calls to Hemmings and Randall. They came to their first Lord's final having lost a series of games, and low on confidence, just as Somerset did in 1978.

By contrast, Somerset had gathered momentum for the final by a narrow victory at Colditz (The Oval, I mean). This raised spirits, and our team dinner was a cheerful if somewhat disreputable occasion.

Everyone at Somerset was delighted that at last Hallam Moseley had appeared at a Lord's final. Moses had missed, for various reasons, each of the previous three finals, despite giving Somerset 13 years' willing service. In his first final Hallam was as nervous as the Nottinghamshire players. Upon being summoned to bowl, Hallam was a bag of jitters. I advised him to relax, and he replied, "Don't worry, Herbie," which was not promising! Of course, in the end, helped by Superman's beer, he bowled very well.

Apart from the final it has been a quiet week. Greenidge scored yet another 100 against Glamorgan, Hemmings hit 127* at Headingley, and Gower's 176* against Pakistan protected his Test place, which for no apparent reason appears to be under threat again. The most cheering performance, though, was that of Paul Romaines, who hit 186 against Warwickshire. Paul has been trying to break into county cricket for years. He must have despaired at times of his ability to demonstrate his quality at the right time. He joined Gloucestershire from Northants; at last his chance has come. I expect he will enjoy success all the more for having to wait so long.

## TURNAROUND AT SOUTHPORT, TO AND FRO AT EDGBASTON
### WEEK ENDING JULY 31

ECHOING around the timbers at Southport is that lament of all cricketers, "You see, captain, you shouldn't have declared". Besides believing that their captain loses two out of three tosses (more, on a sunny day) teams see their skipper as a wild, romantic character roaming around wanting to declare. No ordinary team man ever thinks a declaration necessary, never mind advisable.

Warwickshire, you see, had declared their first innings with only four men out and had been dismissed cheaply in their second innings to enable Lancashire to win by 10 wickets. The culprit of this reckless behaviour was the wise and careful Dennis Amiss. In his defence, I ought perhaps to mention that his team were 523 for four at the time.

I wonder if many games have been lost from so apparently impregnable a position? During this extraordinary match, Humpage scored 254, Kallicharran 230* (his third double century of the season), and Fowler a century in both Lancashire innings (with a runner both times).

Everything else pales into insignificance beside Southport, but there is a tense Test match being fought out at Edgbaston. As I write, Pakistan need 313 in their second innings to win a match that is swinging first this way and then that. Imran (surely the strongest of all fast bowlers) took seven for 52 in England's first innings to give his side an advantage then immediately lost by poor batting. It must have been frustrating for Imran to see the batsmen who have swept all before them in recent weeks fall so easily in a Test match.

For England, Tavaré has been invaluably stubborn, Randall has scored a century as an opener (defying those who suspect that he who is promoted to open is soon for the chop), and Gower played with diffident elegance. Spice was added to the end of England's second innings by an encouraging last wicket stand between Taylor and Willis, two stout campaigners, who added 79. All of the Englishmen were troubled by the mysteries of Abdul Qadir, though both Randall and Taylor invented an effective sweep shot which was played irrespective of the spin of the ball when Abdul tossed one up.

*Alas, Tavaré took his reputation for stubbornness too seriously and by the mid-Eighties had not achieved quite what he was capable of. Yet should he have gone to the West Indies in 1985 – 86?*

England have two debutants in this match. Ian Greig replaced the injured Pringle, and took four for 53; astonishingly, exactly the figures produced by brother Tony in his first Test. Eddie Hemmings bowled well on his debut, taking three wickets and exploding my theory that Pakistanis devour off-spinners as mice devour cheese. Hemmings has developed a curl in his bowling so that the ball drifts away from the batsman before spinning back. Unless, of course, it is a top-spinner (a ball, like the leg-cutter, bowled far more often when

Ian Greig on his debut for England.

Richie Benaud is commentating than when he is not!).

Can Pakistan score 313 to win the Test? As a footnote I will observe that Botham has a broken toe (forgive the pun), a badly bruised hand, and a thigh strain. Worse, he has scored 0 and two in the game, and been punished with the ball. It is rare that a Test goes by without Botham at some stage taking it by the scruff of the neck.

## A WIN FOR ENGLAND AND A MASTERPIECE FROM KALLICHARRAN
### WEEK ENDING AUGUST 7

WE won. Botham thundered down 21 overs taking four wickets to thrust defeat upon the Pakistanis. Only Imran with 65 matched Botham's muscular effort.

Back at Taunton a few days later, Botham plundered 85 in Somerset's NatWest quarter-final against Warwickshire. It was not sufficient to bring victory. Although Somerset reached 259, they suffered at the hands of an innings of extraordinary brilliance by the elf-like Kallicharran.

Warwickshire deserve their victory. They have been plagued by injury throughout the season, so that the team has been as empty in its middle as an Italian election campaign. But the return of Willis and Anton Ferreira has given the team a bit of life. Ferreira is one of those men much appreciated by captains for their cheerful competitiveness and irrational optimism. With his rumbling demeanour he can lift a jaded dressing-room with a joke or a song.

One interesting move made by Warwickshire is to open with Lloyd (also a chirpy character) and Smith, leaving Dennis Amiss to bolster the middle order. Previously, if you could dismiss Amiss early, you might hope to skittle Warwickshire. With him at No 4, their line-up (Lloyd, Smith, Kallicharran, Amiss, Humpage) has a looming threat about it.

## IT'S FESTIVAL WEEK – AND VIV GETS "SERIOUS"
### WEEK ENDING AUGUST 14

AS tents spring up mushroom-like in improbable fields which have hitherto caused no one any

Eddie Hemmings – a first Test appearance in his 17th season of first class cricket.

County Championship (as at August 4)

| | | P | Pts |
|---|---|---|---|
| **1** | Middlesex | 14 | 194 |
| **2** | Leicestershire | 13 | 168 |
| **3** | Essex | 14 | 165 |
| **4** | Hampshire | 13 | 161 |

offence, let alone injury, as scaffolding is erected for stands, as damp decrepit pavilions are coated with paint, you can be sure of one thing: it's festival time again. At Weston, Cheltenham, and Eastbourne, cricketers have been striding to the square to see what Festival Week holds in store for them. It is an inspection filled with trepidation, for cricketers do not necessarily view festival cricket as a pleasant interlude before a crowd basking in bright sunshine with the promise of wine and cheese in the evening. It all depends upon the pitch. If it is bumpy, the week could bring broken fingers and cracked ribs. If it is flat, the week will be fun.

I ought to add that bowlers take the opposite view.

Middlesex arrived at Weston led by their Grey Eminence, their Merlin, at the head of the Championship. They left with a bigger lead. Somerset lost by a mile, hustled to defeat by Cowans and Hughes, who dismissed Somerset for 57. Most of us fell trying to avoid Harriers (work that one out for yourself!).

Your correspondent fell to a decision of doubtful accuracy, but his disappointment was brief since the next ball skimmed Richards's cap. Viv Richards described this ball as the most "serious" he had faced since Thomson in 1975. Viv uses that word "serious" to convey a dangerous, even sinister force. The Mafia are serious. The Ghurkas are serious. Mr Cowans, evidently, is serious.

Phillippe Edmonds bowled well too, leaving many baffled as to why he is not settled in the England team. Possibly his air of benign superiority upsets too many people.

Up to the road at Cheltenham School where draws are rare, Gloucestershire entertained Nottinghamshire (to whom they lost), and Middlesex (who were frustrated by rain). Here it was the pitch which imperilled life and limb. John Childs was hit on the chin fielding at cover! Weston can be like that.

## *MOHSIN KHAN'S DOUBLE CENTURY*
### *WEEK ENDING AUGUST 21*

AT Lord's, Pakistan levelled the series with a 10-wicket win, narrowly thwarting the rain's efforts to save England. Their victory was comprehensive, and

England badly missed Bob Willis, absent with a neck injury. David Gower led his country for the first time and was unfortunate to lose the toss and be saddled with too military an attack for so slow a pitch. There was not much Gower could do to avoid defeat.

For Pakistan, Mohsin Khan scored 200, only the sixth double century in Test matches at Lord's. Mohsin

Mohsin Khan during his memorable innings.

 **LORD'S**  **GROUND**

## CORNHILL INSURANCE TEST SERIES
# ENGLAND  v.  PAKISTAN

THURS., FRI., SAT., SUN. & MON., AUGUST 12, 13, 14, 15 & 16, 1982    (5-day Match)

| PAKISTAN | | First Innings | | Second Innings |
|---|---|---|---|---|
| 1 Mudassar Nazar | ...United Bank | c Taylor b Jackman | ... 20 | |
| 2 Mohsin Khan | .........Habib Bank | c Tavare b Jackman | ...200 | |
| 3 Mansoor Akhtar | ...United Bank | c Lamb b Botham | ...... 57 | |
| 4 Javed Miandad | ......Habib Bank | run out | ........ 6 | |
| 5 Zaheer Abbas | ................P.I.A. | b Jackman | ......... 75 | |
| 6 Haroon Rashid | ......United Bank | l b w b Botham | ........ 1 | ......... |
| †7 Imran Khan | .................Lahore | c Taylor b Botham | ...... 19 | |
| ~~8 Tahir Naqqash~~ | ................M.C.B | c Gatting b Jackman | | |

has had a tremendous tour. His average is over 100. Apart from him, Pakistan's main scorer was Zaheer, though Javed made up for his second run-out by helping Mohsin rush Pakistan to victory as time slipped by. It is interesting that of all the fine Pakistan batsmen of this decade, Javed has much the best record in Test cricket. Whilst Zaheer, Majid, Asif and Mushtaq all average around 40, Javed's average is 54. Of the others, Zaheer has played some huge innings, particularly against India, and Majid has an excellent record against the West Indies and Australia.

But Mohsin's innings could not have won the game for his country had England batted well. As it was, England gradually subsided to Sarfraz, Imran and Qadir, failed to avoid the follow-on and in the second innings were bowled out by Mudassar.

For the first time this century a three-match series stands one all. Headingley will decide the issue.

Meanwhile, at Edgbaston, Warwickshire, conquerors of Somerset, beat Yorkshire to reach the NatWest final. David Smith scored a century with his ramrod straight bat. Meeting Warwickshire in the final will be Surrey, who overcame the loss of the toss and Middlesex to enter their fourth final of the last few seasons. This time I suspect they will be lucky, if only because they deserve a change of fortune.

## LEICESTERSHIRE STEP UP THE CHASE
### WEEK ENDING AUGUST 28

AS August pressed towards September, things begin to settle. Sussex need to win but one of their last three Sunday League games to be champions, a trophy they have been hunting with immense enthusiasm for four years. And either Middlesex or Leicestershire will win the Championship, much the most coveted of the trophies.

Leicestershire have come with a late run (like Brian Close's horses) to challenge Middlesex. It is probably too late (the resemblance is uncanny). Nevertheless, this week they won both their Championship games, while Middlesex could win only one.

At Taunton, Leicestershire played well. David Gower, who if he were a Muppet would be called Molly, scored 111. Briers and Balderstone attacked with vigour too. I do not know how Leicestershire have managed it, but these days they seem able to play Davison, Roberts and Clift. Presumably two of these are English. I suspect Roberts is not one of them, in which case, can someone explain why Davison is not in the Test team?

It was Nick Cook who bowled Somerset to defeat, his flighted spinners contrasting with John Steele's insidious deliveries. Cook has taken over 70 wickets already this season, and must be close to a tour place. By some masterpiece of the computer, Leicestershire

drove from Taunton to Colchester to face Essex, who play their game in an assortment of pleasantly situated places. If memory serves me well, Colchester is one of these places where you change by rota, the rooms being too tiny to tolerate 11 cricketers and their "coffins".

While Leicestershire were defeating Essex, Middlesex managed to beat Surrey at Lord's.

One surprise (and surprised) member of the Middlesex team was F. J. Titmus. Apparently he strolled out into the home dressing-room 20 minutes before the start to say hello, and was hailed by Mike Brearley with the news that Hughes had broken down and the sub-post office would have to wait. Titmus took three wickets, Emburey four, and Edmonds three, as Surrey collapsed in pursuit of Brearley's typically creative declaration.

One absentee from the Surrey team was Pat Pocock, who has been seriously ill for a month. Happily, he is well now, and may yet find a place in Surrey's team for Saturday's NatWest Final. Less happy news is hidden in the lists of cricketers not retained by their counties. Less money will be available from the TCCB this year, and counties are feeling the pinch. Already, Todd, Kennedy, Roope, Reidy, Hemsley, Gifford, Alleyne, Lee and Wilson have been released. Doesn't sound such a bad team, does it?

## TEST DISAPPOINTMENT FOR IMRAN BUT SUSSEX TAKE THE JPL
### WEEK ENDING SEPTEMBER 2

A NARROW and dramatic victory for England at Headingley gave Willis's team the series. Imran must have been terribly disappointed to lose. For once again he led his team with immense courage. Quite rightly he was made Man of the Match and of the Series. Sadly, some of his colleagues did not play well; Zaheer, Mohsin and Mansoor, in particular, falling to poor shots. Imran would also reflect upon the injuries to Sarfraz and Tahir, which prevented either playing on the ground where he might have been most valuable.

For England the best innings was played by Graeme Fowler, an inspired selection. Fowler scored 86 in England's winning 221 for seven. Graeme has had a second good season for Lancashire, and what's more, is a perky left-hander and an ideal compliment to Tavaré's stern resistance. As we discovered at Leicestershire, Fowler is "a bit of a card" (to use Vic Marks's phrase). He is a restless, chattering and likeable man. He will be an asset in Australia as long as he doesn't room with Derek Randall.

England's other debutant was my friend Vic Marks. Vic is probably not as lethal a bowler as Hemmings on a crumbling pitch (though apart from Chandrasekhar and Underwood, who was the last spinner to win a Test for his team in England?), but a hard winter in Perth and long spells for Somerset have helped him to develop a control of flight which lures batsmen to their doom on good pitches. Also, Vic, with his technique grown in the back yard of his father's farm, is a fast scoring batsman when in touch. He is a good man to have around in a crisis, and he found a staunch partner in Bob Taylor to guide England home.

Imran's disappointment with Pakistan will have been assuaged a little by the pleasure he must feel at Sussex's remarkably easy win of the Sunday League. With two games to go, their lead is unassailable. It has been a long and winding road for Barclay's team, and they have deserved their eventual triumph. They are a team who rely no less upon the timely contributions of Barclay, Phillipson and Gould than on the sudden inspirations of Le Roux, Mendis, Parker and Greig.

Sussex captain John Barclay with a well-deserved trophy.

## SURREY DESERVE THEIR VICTORY
### WEEK ENDING SEPTEMBER 11

IN the second NatWest final at Lord's, Surrey easily defeated Warwickshire. It was the second poorly contested final of the summer. We could not expect last year's heroics every season. Warwickshire, the less experienced team, lost the toss and had to bat at 10 a.m. By 11.30 a.m. the game was effectively over. Clarke, Jackman, Knight and Thomas had exploited a slightly damp pitch and the batsmen's doubts to the full and Warwickshire had sunk to 80 for eight. Clarke, with his freakish action and whirl of arms, is not easy to follow. More, his changes of pace are dramatic! With bowlers of classical style, Holding and Imran say, the batsman can pick up the ball and avoid it. Clarke and Croft hurt batsmen more often because they are ungainly and unpredictable.

Surrey needed but three men to pass Warwickshire.

A word of warning for Bob Willis from bowler Robin Jackman during the NatWest final.

Butcher batted as well as ever off the back foot. As before, Alan has had a topsy-turvy season, ending on a high note after a depressing start. Smith played with vigour and it was a pity Lynch did not bat, for he too is a belligerent stroke player.

Surrey deserved this victory (especially those men who have suffered in all three of their recent defeats in finals). I was only sorry to see Dennis Amiss fall for a duck. He had the bad luck to reach Lord's out of form and despite long nets in Taunton immediately before the final could not recover his full confidence. It is intriguing and comforting to the rest of us that so apparently authoritative a batsman, such a skilful player could feel so very vulnerable.

## A FITTING FINAL WEEK FOR MIDDLESEX AND BREARLEY
### WEEK ENDING SEPTEMBER 18

MIDDLESEX are champions and a fitting end to Mike Brearley's career. He led his county to four Championships and was a tough and imaginative leader. If there were times when opponents wondered what the grey eminence was doing playing cricket, these were outnumbered by the times batsmen wished he were not. Brearley had the ability to do exactly what a batsman least wanted him to do. If the fellow could not play left-arm spin, Edmonds was soon on. If he played too early a swing bowler would be introduced. Besides his quick understanding of batsmen, Brearley was a ruthless captain. On the field he could be brusque (at Weston he told Simon Hughes to "go where I damn well put you") and I expect he needed to be to retain charge of a team so strong in character.

Cricket will miss Mike Brearley's games of chess

Mike Brearley retires from first-class cricket after leading Middlesex to victory at Worcester. Worcester players (left to right) Patel, Neale, Warner, Humphries, Illingworth and Curtis applaud as Brearley leaves the field.

with human beings. We'll miss Lloyd Budd too, an umpire of much gentleness and mild toleration. Lloyd was a highly respected umpire, though cricketers like to tease him about his determination that play should continue in all conditions by feigning torches and umbrellas. Not all umpires share Lloyd Budd's devotion; quite a few rather enjoy a quiet puff and a pot of tea when rain falls.

Finally, my apologies to all those people I should have mentioned in this journal but did not (did I tell you about Neil Taylor's Benson & Hedges innings? Or about Roberts's efforts? Or Richards? Or the Steeles whose careers run so parallel except that David bowls more no-balls?). Let me end with the cry of a Somerset supporter (in the hope that it is not true) who, upon seeing me hit a six, called out, "Well I'm damned, I've seen it all now!"

*The South Africans spread their net a bit wider during the winter, inviting – or beguiling – teams from the fledgling Test country, Sri Lanka, who could afford to lose none of their small band of players; and West Indies, who were able to provide a strong team from those prepared to risk lifetime bans. This still left the official West Indies side with plenty of high-class cricketers and they duly defeated India at home in a series notable mainly for the return to matchwinning form of Andy Roberts (24 wickets at 22 each) and the courageous batting of Mohinder Amarnath, who scored 598 runs in nine Test innings.*

*England, less able to absorb the loss of good players to South African bans, lost the Ashes in Australia, despite an enthralling three-run victory at Melbourne; brave bowling by Willis; and solid batting from Gower, Randall and the South African-born Lamb.*

*Greg Chappell achieved a lifetime's ambition in winning back the urn, contributing runs himself at vital times and making the most of his bowling resources despite the absence for most of the season of the great Lillee, one of whose knees had failed him. In his absence, the great trier Jeff Thomson returned to the limelight and Geoff Lawson had his best series for his country with 34 wickets. The spirited off-spinner Bruce Yardley also showed that England (who had picked three bowlers of this type) did not have a monopoly when it came to finger-spin.*

*In the limited-overs internationals which followed the Tests England came a poor third to Australia and New Zealand. It was not a good omen for the third World Cup, due in England in June.*

## SCHWEPPES COUNTY CHAMPIONSHIP

|  | P | W | L | D | Bt | Bl | Pts |
|---|---|---|---|---|---|---|---|
| Middlesex (4) | 22 | 12 | 2 | 8 | 59 | 74 | 325 |
| Leicestershire (8) | 22 | 10 | 4 | 8 | 57 | 69 | 286 |
| Hampshire (7) | 22 | 8 | 6 | 8 | 48 | 74 | 250 |
| Nottinghamshire (1) | 22 | 7 | 7 | 8 | 44 | 65 | 221 |
| Surrey (6) | 22 | 6 | 6 | 10 | 56 | 62 | 214 |
| Somerset (3) | 22 | 6 | 6 | 10 | 51 | 66 | 213 |
| Essex (5) | 22 | 5 | 5 | 12 | 57 | 75 | 212 |
| Sussex (2) | 22 | 6 | 7 | 9 | 43 | 68 | 207 |
| Northamptonshire (15) | 22 | 5 | 3 | 14 | 61 | 54 | 195 |
| Yorkshire (10) | 22 | 5 | 1 | 16 | 48 | 51 | 179 |
| Derbyshire (12) | 22 | 4 | 3 | 15 | 45 | 64 | 173 |
| Lancashire (16) | 22 | 4 | 3 | 15 | 48 | 55 | 167 |
| Kent (9) | 22 | 3 | 4 | 15 | 55 | 63 | 166 |
| Worcestershire (11) | 22 | 3 | 5 | 14 | 43 | 54 | 141 |
| Gloucestershire (13) | 22 | 2 | 9 | 11 | 46 | 55 | 133 |
| Glamorgan (14) | 22 | 1 | 8 | 13 | 43 | 60 | 119 |
| Warwickshire (17) | 22 | 0 | 8 | 14 | 58 | 53 | 111 |

Worcestershire total includes 12pts from match reduced to 1 innings.
1981 positions in brackets.

## FIRST CLASS AVERAGES

### BATTING
(Qualifications: 8 innings, average 10.00)

| | M | I | NO | HS | R | Avge | 100 | 50 |
|---|---|---|---|---|---|---|---|---|
| G. M. Turner | 9 | 16 | 3 | 311* | 1171 | 90.07 | 5 | 3 |
| Zaheer Abbas | 16 | 25 | 4 | 162* | 1475 | 70.23 | 5 | 8 |
| A. I. Kallicharran | 23 | 37 | 5 | 235 | 2120 | 66.25 | 8 | 5 |
| P. N. Kirsten | 21 | 37 | 7 | 164* | 1941 | 64.70 | 8 | 6 |
| G. Boycott | 21 | 37 | 6 | 159 | 1913 | 61.70 | 6 | 10 |
| M. W. Gatting | 23 | 34 | 6 | 192 | 1651 | 58.96 | 6 | 5 |
| T. E. Jesty | 22 | 36 | 8 | 164* | 1645 | 58.75 | 8 | 4 |
| J. G. Wright | 21 | 39 | 6 | 190 | 1830 | 55.45 | 7 | 5 |
| B. F. Davison | 22 | 37 | 4 | 172 | 1800 | 54.54 | 7 | 8 |
| Younis Ahmed | 18 | 29 | 6 | 122 | 1247 | 54.21 | 4 | 7 |
| J. Simmons | 18 | 21 | 12 | 79* | 487 | 54.11 | — | 4 |
| P. Willey | 23 | 41 | 6 | 145 | 1783 | 50.94 | 5 | 8 |
| D. M. Smith (Sy) | 14 | 25 | 4 | 160 | 1065 | 50.71 | 3 | 5 |
| Javed Miandad | 18 | 29 | 8 | 105* | 1051 | 50.04 | 1 | 9 |
| D. P. Hughes | 23 | 36 | 9 | 126* | 1303 | 48.25 | 3 | 6 |
| C. J. Tavaré | 20 | 36 | 4 | 168* | 1522 | 47.56 | 3 | 10 |
| D. W. Randall | 20 | 33 | 4 | 130* | 1369 | 47.20 | 4 | 8 |
| J. M. Brearley | 20 | 32 | 9 | 165 | 1083 | 47.08 | 3 | 4 |
| S. J. O'Shaughnessy | 11 | 19 | 7 | 62 | 560 | 46.66 | — | 7 |
| A. J. Lamb | 18 | 30 | 2 | 140 | 1302 | 46.50 | 5 | 4 |
| D. I. Gower | 20 | 35 | 2 | 176* | 1530 | 46.36 | 5 | 12 |
| C. G. Greenidge | 21 | 41 | 8 | 183* | 1526 | 46.24 | 3 | 4 |
| I. V. A. Richards | 20 | 31 | 2 | 181* | 1324 | 45.65 | 4 | 5 |
| W. Larkins | 24 | 44 | 3 | 186 | 1863 | 45.43 | 5 | 9 |
| B. C. Rose | 21 | 32 | 8 | 173* | 1090 | 45.41 | 2 | 5 |
| Imran Khan | 16 | 20 | 7 | 85 | 588 | 45.23 | — | 3 |
| R. J. Boyd-Moss | 23 | 41 | 5 | 137 | 1602 | 44.50 | 5 | 10 |
| R. S. Cowan | 8 | 16 | 4 | 143* | 533 | 44.41 | 2 | 2 |
| I. T. Botham | 17 | 29 | 1 | 208 | 1241 | 44.32 | 3 | 7 |
| G. A. Gooch | 23 | 38 | 1 | 149 | 1632 | 44.10 | 3 | 12 |
| W. N. Slack | 25 | 40 | 6 | 203* | 1499 | 44.08 | 2 | 10 |

### BOWLING
(Qualification: 10 wickets in 10 innings)

| | O | M | R | W | Ave | Best | 5wI |
|---|---|---|---|---|---|---|---|
| R. J. Hadlee | 403.5 | 122 | 889 | 61 | 14.57 | 7-25 | 4 |
| M. D. Marshall | 822 | 225 | 2108 | 134 | 15.73 | 8-71 | 12 |
| M. W. Gatting | 135 | 40 | 343 | 21 | 16.33 | 5-34 | 1 |
| Imran Khan | 484.4 | 134 | 1079 | 64 | 16.85 | 7-52 | 2 |
| W. W. Daniel | 469.4 | 107 | 1245 | 71 | 17.53 | 9-61 | 5 |
| J. Garner | 259.1 | 76 | 583 | 33 | 17.66 | 6-23 | 4 |
| M. Hendrick | 244.2 | 86 | 473 | 26 | 18.19 | 5-21 | 1 |
| G. S. le Roux | 467 | 116 | 1210 | 65 | 18.61 | 5-15 | 3 |
| A. M. E. Roberts | 428.2 | 114 | 1081 | 55 | 19.65 | 8-56 | 5 |
| F. D. Stephenson | 197.3 | 40 | 632 | 32 | 19.75 | 6-63 | 1 |
| S. T. Clarke | 659.3 | 162 | 1696 | 85 | 19.95 | 6-63 | 6 |
| J. F. Steele | 470.2 | 134 | 1075 | 52 | 20.67 | 5-4 | 3 |
| T. E. Jesty | 288.1 | 89 | 750 | 35 | 21.42 | 6-71 | 1 |
| K. Saxelby | 291.4 | 68 | 799 | 37 | 21.59 | 4-18 | — |
| M. K. Bore | 279.1 | 104 | 609 | 28 | 21.75 | 6-134 | 1 |
| N. G. Cowans | 222.3 | 50 | 721 | 33 | 21.84 | 5-28 | 2 |
| L. B. Taylor | 582.1 | 153 | 1465 | 67 | 21.86 | 5-24 | 3 |
| P. H. Edmonds | 789 | 242 | 1768 | 80 | 22.10 | 8-80 | 3 |
| D. L. Underwood | 690.4 | 223 | 1751 | 78 | 22.44 | 7-79 | 5 |
| N. Phillip | 584.1 | 107 | 1842 | 82 | 22.46 | 6-50 | 5 |
| W. N. Slack | 81 | 18 | 225 | 10 | 22.50 | 3-17 | — |
| S. J. Malone | 150.5 | 35 | 505 | 22 | 22.95 | 7-55 | 2 |
| I. T. Botham | 491.4 | 114 | 1517 | 66 | 22.98 | 5-46 | 4 |
| J. E. Emburey | 764.5 | 198 | 1787 | 77 | 23.20 | 5-50 | 2 |
| N. G. B. Cook | 847.1 | 257 | 2093 | 90 | 23.25 | 7-63 | 6 |
| J. G. Thomas | 140 | 25 | 514 | 22 | 23.36 | 5-61 | 1 |
| J. K. Lever | 543.5 | 112 | 1683 | 72 | 23.37 | 6-48 | 5 |
| D. R. Pringle | 433.1 | 122 | 1087 | 46 | 23.63 | 6-33 | 2 |
| K. St J. D. Emery | 659 | 152 | 1969 | 83 | 23.72 | 6-51 | 3 |
| J. W. Southern | 439.5 | 118 | 1314 | 55 | 23.89 | 5-51 | 2 |
| T. M. Tremlett | 353.3 | 114 | 766 | 32 | 23.93 | 5-59 | 1 |

# — 1983 —

## *ESSEX FOR THE CHAMPIONSHIP?*
### *WEEK ENDING MAY 1*

APPARENTLY this has been the wettest April since before *Wisden*, and apparently an unforeseen Mexican volcanic eruption is to blame. I gather it has produced a haze between sun and earth. And they want to stage football's next World Cup!

If it is to be a wet summer we can assume that Essex will win the Championship. Evidence indicates that rain interferes with fewer games in the East than in the West and that it will be more difficult for Gloucestershire. Glamorgan, Lancashire and Somerset in particular to win the Championship if it is to rain all the time.

In any event, one bearded rumbustious character from Essex has already hit a century. There must have been times during the winter when England's selectors regretted the absence of Graham Gooch, and he will be sorely missed in the World Cup. Had he, Willey, Emburey and Edmonds (who *was* available) been around in Australia the Aussies might not have taken the Ashes.

## *OPPONENTS WILT IN THE GLARE OF RICHARDS*
### *WEEK ENDING MAY 8*

AT about 11.40 on Wednesday, Sussex's score stood at 19 for eight. Hadlee and Hendrick had taken the wickets on a damp Hove pitch. Unfortunately Sussex fought back to pass 100 with Pigott and Phillipson adding 90. But 19 for eight is quite something in a first-class game. Sussex lost by an innings despite some typical Troutbeck obduracy. (Barclay is apt to ask "Am I being frightfully boring?" but he is a stubborn man in a crisis which, like Bailey, he sometimes seems to create.)

Hadlee took the wickets and scored a century. He has a silent, lean menace about him and a brooding intensity which suggests New Zealand might be an interesting outside bet for the World Cup.

Nor did Sussex find much encouragement at Taunton, continuing their sluggish start to the season. Surrey have started poorly too which is surprising since these two counties spent their pre-seasons in the sunshine of Spain and were able to practise more than anyone else. Sussex met Vivian Richards in fiercely run-hungry mood. Two evenings before he'd returned from Antigua and had a net. Though the county game was over, every Somerset player lingered in the dressing room to watch him, a tribute rarely paid by cricketers to each other. Richards is at his formidable best at the moment, sharpening his technique for the World Cup. In this mood he stares down bowlers, like Hagler and Holmes do, never blinking and never taking a backward step. He imposes his mastery upon his opponents by the way he walks to the crease head upright. He has learned from his enjoyment of boxing that champions must not have, let alone show, a touch of doubt.

Ole Mortensen – Derbyshire's new acquisition from Denmark.

## *DILLEY FIRING IN THE SODDEN EAST*
### *WEEK ENDING MAY 14*

DR JOHNSON said that the period between Easter and Whitsun (May 22 this year) is propitious to study for it is ever wet and one might learn the "low Dutch language". If it was wet then and it is wet now I wonder if there will ever come a time when the English cricket season at its top level will begin in June and end in September? Is not four months intense cricket enough? Might not cricketers be better able to find winter jobs if summer were rather less long? It is not as if anyone seems to watch cricket in April or May anyway.

Our theory, developed a fortnight back, that the Western belt counties suffer more from rain than their rivals has not worn well. The Middlesex Secretary has said that Middlesex are at a grave disadvantage because all their early games are at Lord's where the winds don't blow and the drains don't drain. A little later Ray Illingworth explained that Yorkshire couldn't win the Championship either because it rains so much more in the North than anywhere else. Considering this, one is almost lost in admiration for Yorkshire's achievement in winning the title 31 times and for Middlesex who have won it eight times.

What cricket has been played this week has been in the East. At Chelmsford, a bustling and amusing ground as chirpy as a bird sanctuary, Essex lost to Tavaré's Kent in a one-innings Championship game and then defeated Somerset in the Benson and Hedges Cup. Keith Fletcher is the only captain of 1977 vintage still leading his county. An achievement all the more remarkable since he appears to be leading the nuttiest team. In the dressing room he must feel as staunchly righteous as a lighthouse but he has been very lucky in the characters of his senior players: Lever, Acfield, Turner and East in particular have been serving loyally for decades and if they are a shade fruity off the field they are ruthlessly competitive on it.

Chris Tavaré played the major innings in Kent's victory at Chelmsford: he scored 94 to follow his crisp 82 in 15 overs against Surrey last Sunday. Already Tavaré is surprising some with his tough determination. Under his leadership I suspect Kent will do very well. They are a young and capable team with a local captain to lead them. They will depend a lot though on their most penetrating bowler, Graham Dilley. Dilley has suffered sufficient setbacks for the last two years to finish a lesser man. His gentle, honest personality belies those mountainous limbs and the blond hair of a Saxon invader. He cannot easily have endured those unkind cuts. He's not one who can down a pint and laugh the whole thing off. That he has returned with, word has it, more pace than ever, is a tribute to his courage. At Chelmsford he bowled Gooch first ball with a scorcher and took five for 70. Apparently he is running in smoothly, shoulders rolling, head upright like Michael Holding, and bowling very fast. People overseas are always asking "What's happened to Dilley?" I think they'll find out soon enough.

Middlesex are being led by Michael Gatting who will be a cheerful successor to that grey-haired fellow in turned-up whites. Glamorgan have a new skipper too. At first sight it appeared as if Mr Wooller had in desperation turned to Dr Who, so abundant were scarves, trenchcoats and hair but it turned out to be Mike Selvey who has joined the unequal struggle.

*Gatting has remained cheerful, and, in a very different way from Brearley, also a highly effective captain of a very powerful county team.*

It will be interesting to see whether these new captains can add sparkle to their teams. It is becoming harder for professional captains with so much more at stake and so many cricketers on their staffs. In former times the skipper could pin the names of his 11 senior players on the board and leave them to it. Now more immediate form is required and if an established cricketer is out of sorts he must be dropped. Not an easy task for a professional amongst his peers. Possibly the idea of cricket managers will spread, or possibly the trend towards captains who would have played years ago as amateurs (Knight, Selvey, Tavaré, Barclay, Pocock) will grow.

## GLOUCESTER STOOP IN ABERDEEN
### WEEK ENDING MAY 22

IT has been another wet week. Even cricketers who have long held the view that rain is a blessed relief from having to bat or bowl think it is a bit much for it to rain all the time. Ironically one of the few places where cricket was played was in Aberdeen where Gloucestershire stooped to 45 for six before passing Scotland's 93. Scotland have yet to win a Benson and Hedges game and Ireland haven't yet won in the NatWest cup, but it adds spice (well haggis and stew anyhow) to have these emerging national teams playing in our domestic cricket. I wonder if they cannot be persuaded to enter teams in the County Championship, perhaps on a part-time basis rather like Tasmania used to do in the Sheffield Shield? I doubt if they would embarrass themselves, certainly no more than other teams have done in their formative years in first-class cricket.

## COMMON SENSE IN SHORT SUPPLY
### WEEK ENDING MAY 29

YES, it has been a wet week again. Were a girl to be asked "Shall I compare thee to a summer's day," she'd reply "Well, actually, no thanks".

An unfamiliar yellow object did appear on Wednesday enabling the County Championship games to begin. Most of the best performances in these games came from wily old professionals who'd seen a thing or two and realised that fancy shots are not the thing for a wet May. Alan Jones hit 57, Dennis Amiss 142 and Chris Balderstone led Leicester to victory over Essex with 82 and 97 not out.

For his adopted county Gloucestershire at Edgbaston, John Shepherd took seven for 50 and then led his team's recovery from 83 for six by smiting 168. It was an astonishing effort by an immensely popular, skilful cricketer.

If Shepherd is the cricketer of the moment, Hampshire are the team. They are joint top of the Sunday League with Yorkshire and Somerset, lead the Championship and have reached the Benson and Hedges quarter-finals. Hampshire, like Leicestershire, quickly realised the value of transforming overseas players into Englishmen. Chris Smith and his brother Robin have been on their staff for years. A shrewd investment, for Chris is now English and can play in the same team as Greenidge and Marshall. Robin will be English in 1985. I suppose Chris Smith could easily be picked for England and he wouldn't let them down. Yet it doesn't seem quite right somehow that men like Smith and Davison, Clift and Shepherd and Hallam Moseley are available for selection by England. I wonder if a third category of cricketer could be created for men who whilst not overseas players for the purposes of domestic cricket are nevertheless unavailable for international selection?

The South African issue has returned to our front pages. The West Indies cancelled a charity friendly against Yorkshire because Boycott and Sidebottom were in the opposition and they had toured South Africa. However much one is appalled by the South African regime, however much one supports the boycott of South Africa (and I do support it, not withstanding the hypocrisy of successive governments, because cricket relations with South Africa help secure a regime which believes that Dredge, Roebuck and Popplewell are superior at birth to Richards, Garner and Moseley) it does seem ridiculous to postpone a charity game because of an offence for which the two players had already been punished by Test bans. We are nearing a stage where white nations and black nations cannot play cricket against each other and it will need a great deal of common sense if this situation is to be avoided. There

Robin Smith (top) and his elder brother Chris – qualifying with Hampshire to become English.

is not a lot of common sense about at the moment.

## SURREY HIT FOURTEEN
### WEEK ENDING JUNE 5

WHAT a bewildering game cricket can be! Every once in a while it throws at you something so outrageous as to confound the supposed range of apparent possibilities. For spectators there is always that slight chance that it will be today that will bring some astonishing piece of cricket. It might be a chilling Monday or a shining Saturday, it doesn't matter, extraordinary days come at their own leisure.

When Fletcher declared an hour before the close of play on the second day at Chelmsford I doubt if he expected much more than to pick up two or three wickets as the game meandered towards a draw. After all, he scored 110 out of 287 and the pitch was good. As it turned out Surrey were bowled out for 14.

It must have been one of those days, when batsmen if they do not middle the ball, edge it or are bowled by it. Surrey lost five wickets with their score on eight and only avoided the lowest ever score (12) by an edge through the slips and a wild swipe to cow corner. Till then no one had thought such a collapse was possible; not on dry pitches and in these days when even tail-enders can bat. We should not so have underestimated cricket nor the frailty of its players.

Roger Knight observed that "we didn't bat very well" and put matters right with a brave match-saving century in the second innings. Of course, the papers and cameras were there for the final day but few actually saw the collapse (though I dare say it will be hard to find anyone in Essex for a year or two who wasn't there). Naturally Henry Blofeld was at the scene of disaster.

Our sympathies this week must go to Gloucestershire who, plagued by financial crisis, find themselves knocked out of the Benson and Hedges Cup without losing a game in this or any other competition. David Graveney, with the wise support of John Shepherd, has gradually built Gloucestershire into a happy, determined and capable team who are short of one penetrating bowler to win trophies. Their quarter-final with Middlesex had to be decided on the toss of a coin after three days sitting watching the rains fall. As so often in these matters the team which most needed to win the toss lost it. It was appalling bad luck. David Graveney's comment that he hoped he hadn't been responsible for the end of Gloucestershire cricket cast a dark shadow.

As the domestic season ploughs on with the left-handers scoring centuries – Fowler, Andy Lloyd and Kallicharran amongst them (will somebody do a study on the proportion of first-class centuries scored by left-handers compared to the number of left-handers in the society?) – the international teams are gathering for the World Cup. Sadly we will miss Imran Khan's formidable bowling and Greg Chappell's haughty skills but despite their absence it will be a dramatic contest. In recent times India have defeated the West Indies, Sri Lanka have beaten Australia and England have lost time and again to New Zealand. Add to that the unknown quantities of Zimbabwe and the batting of Pakistan and we could be in for the most open World Cup so far.

*So it proved: West Indies did not win it, and Zimbabwe had a memorable encounter with Australia – head on!*

## WHO WANTS TO BE IN CHARGE?
### WEEK ENDING JUNE 11

CAPTAINCY is not what it's cracked up to be! I discovered this at 11.45 on Wednesday when I looked up at Bristol's large unsympathetic scoreboard to see Gloucestershire's score of 84 for no wicket in 13 overs.

It was my first-ever game as Somerset captain. A week before I'd been seventh in line of succession and about as likely to succeed as Princess Anne's second niece. Injuries and World Cup selections had caused me to be plucked from my peers as is a Speaker (except he's dragged from his Commons).

It was the helicopter's fault. I'd lost the toss. (Somerset captains always lose the toss because they always call tails and science has revealed that 10p coins are weighted to fall heads more often than not.) The helicopter hit up 84 in what seemed like 15 minutes but can't have been. The helicopter, if you haven't guessed, is the name Gloucester players are calling Andy Stovold, a comment upon his whirling arms causing mayhem to his immediate surroundings.

Stovold's approach to batting this June is simple. If it's up he whacks it. If it's short he whacks it. If it's wide he whacks it. If it's straight he whacks it.

We drew the game in the end, a predictable result with two ex-Millfield captains.

In quieter pastures the World Cup began. Already it has been blessed with dry weather and interesting cricket. Zimbabwe fought back from 94 for five to reach 239 for six and defeated Australia who could score no more than 226 though Wessels, who stands with his back to the bowler as McEnroe does when he's serving, scored 76. Duncan Fletcher, leading a resilient team with much tenacity, hit 69 not out and took four wickets.

Nor were Australia the only favourites to fall. India, who lost a practice game to the Minor Counties, beat the West Indies, the first defeat suffered by Clive Lloyd's

# Zimbabwe defeat Australia by 13

### By NEIL HALLAM at Trent Bridge

ZIMBABWE, the "junior" competitors in the Prudential World Cup, emphatically demonstrated their right to keep company with the major Test-playing nations with a remarkable 13-run victory *The score* *r Australia*

team in three World Cups. For India Yashpal Sharma scored 89 and most of the others contributed something towards their total of 262. The West Indies collapsed ignominiously to 157 for nine only for Garner and Roberts to stage a remarkable last wicket partnership. Roberts is known for his doughty innings but "Big Bird" Garner has slipped down the orders of Somerset and the West Indies, humbly batting below Croft and Hallam Moseley at times. This fall has been caused by a predilection for "swiping". During the winter Garner announced to the West Indies that he was "done swiping". India dismissed him not once in the Test series though he didn't score many runs because as soon as he came in his partners took it into their heads to "pelt a lash". This time Roberts stayed with Garner and they added 71 runs, causing much head-rolling amongst the Indians before Kapil recalled his left-arm spinner, Shastri, who had Joel stumped with the West Indies 34 adrift.

Not all the games went to the outsiders. Pakistan scored 338 against Sri Lanka, who replied with a spirited score of 288 for nine, and at The Oval England put behind them their persistent defeats of the winter by trouncing New Zealand by 106 runs.

## D'ARTAGNAN SORTS OUT ZIMBABWE
### *WEEK ENDING JUNE 18*

THIS World Cup has been fought out in fresh places where cricket is eagerly followed but where the grounds do not lend themselves to Test matches. Possibly the two best games of the week were played in smiling sunshine beneath the steeples and Quantocks of Taunton and the tents and rhododendrons at Tunbridge Wells.

At Taunton a hearty crowd added colour and noise to England's match against Sri Lanka. Though the locals Botham and Marks were run out for nought and five, the spectators enjoyed the day and cheered the game Sri Lankans as they chased England's 339 in 60 overs. David Gower in a memorable display glided to 130, hitting five sixes into the car park without ever appearing violent.

At Tunbridge Wells India's hopes tottered when they fell 17 for five against Zimbabwe. An early plane back to Bombay awaited them. In strode their musketeer of a captain (*The Cricketer* christened him the Haryana Hurricane a while back but he is more D'Artagnan to me) to sort things out. With Binny, Madan Lal and Kirmani, Kapil Dev transformed the innings so that India reached 266 for eight in 60 overs. Kapil scored 175 not out, a captain's innings. This Indian team bat a long way down – Kirmani came in at No 10 – and under Kapil they are playing with spirit and unity.

On the domestic front (is it a front?) county cricketers are rushing up and down motorways playing our games. For obscure reasons Lord's has packed as much county cricket as possible into the World Cup period. Somerset have been playing for the last 25 days (my figures may not be accurate, but they feel accurate), days untroubled by cloud or rain. With eight county games,

two University friendlies and four World Cup matches on at the same time, the resources of Lord's have been stretched. While counties are searching for bodies to put upon the field, Lord's has been searching for umpires.

## DEFEAT WITH DIGNITY FOR LLOYD AND HIS LIEUTENANTS
### *WEEK ENDING JUNE 25*

IN a splendid final at Lord's India deservedly won the World Cup when the West Indies failed to chase a meagre 183. It had seemed such a miserable total to present to that formidable batting line up and yet perhaps it made little difference what it was the West

Almost there – Indians celebrate the fall of Marshall's wicket.

Indies chased. If they played well they would reach whatever target was set them. If they played badly they would beat themselves almost however small the opposition's total. At Lord's India fielded like tigers and bowled with accuracy and swing. Once the mighty Richards fell and with Clive Lloyd already hobbling after pulling a muscle there was no one to "hole up de side." Hard though Dujon, Marshall and Garner fought, the wickets kept tumbling and catches kept going to hand. It was India's day and they rejoiced in it. Amarnath was Man of the Match for the second time in a week, scoring valuable runs and picking up three good wickets.

## SPIN TWINS KEEP MIDDLESEX AHEAD
### *WEEK ENDING JULY 2*

AS attention returns to county cricket it is cheering to report that it has been a stirring week in the

Championship. There were victories for Middlesex, Leicestershire, Essex and Warwickshire (their fifth in a row) as well as more lowly Nottinghamshire.

Middlesex, with their spin twins fast approaching 100 wickets each (I wonder when this was last achieved by two spinners in the same team?) and Roland Butcher heading the catching list, including wicket-keepers, are still well ahead of the table but they are being hotly pursued by Essex and Leicestershire who unleashed Ferris at us during the World Cup. Ferris is a strapping 19-year-old who could qualify either for England or the West Indies. That he chose the West Indies suggests that he is "a serious man" which will cause the old pros amongst us to sigh wearily once again and to mutter "Oh no, not another one."

The Varsity match was, quite properly, drawn. As usual it was the batsmen's match with Boyd-Moss scoring two centuries in the game. For Cambridge, Pathmanathan hit 50, having returned from Sri Lanka for a second degree. If memory serves me well, he was at Oxford last time. Perhaps he is learning from A. R. Wingfield-Digby who discovered that if you change courses often enough (though in his case it must, I suppose, have been religions) you could spend several decades amiably rolling down a few overs, clouting a few fours and repairing to Vincents for a pint. It was Pathmanathan, you may recall, who hit Old for 36 in four overs to speed the Universities to a hugely enjoyable Benson and Hedges victory at Barnsley, after which Boycott appeared in our dressing room to observe that when he wished us luck before the game he hadn't meant "that much bloody luck".

George Ferris – a serious threat to Leicestershire's opponents.

## TOURIST MATCHES A DEAD WEIGHT
### *WEEK ENDING JULY 11*

THE New Zealanders have started their tour in the West and drew at Taunton scoring 544 for nine with no-one scoring a century. It was a game played before sparse crowds and against a weakened county keen to rest its better players in their only non-competitive game of the season. I'm afraid that's what tourist matches have come to. They are, quite frankly, a nuisance. David Graveney has suggested that tourists should play four-day matches against regional teams

selected by the Test selectors. This seems a good idea to bring fresh life to what is at the moment a dead weight. Elsewhere, the Benson and Hedges semi-finals were disappointing with the two weaker teams, Kent and Lancashire, losing the toss and the match on a humid morning. Middlesex and Essex will be, I suspect, excellent opponents in the final.

## NAUGHTY RANDALL RESISTS THE SEVERE MR HADLEE
### *WEEK ENDING JULY 18*

ON Wednesday MCC members decisively supported their Committee's refusal to send a touring team to South Africa. At present the ICC countries are holding firm even if some of their best players are accepting the "blood money" as some of the more formidable West Indian cricketers call it. This will not last for ever; sooner or later South African money will break the boycott, a boycott already weakened by the stunning hypocrisy of successive Governments. And, when that happens, I wonder if we will have to endure separate black and white international cricket groups. It would be richly ironic, would it not, if cricket were then to have its own apartheid!

At The Oval a new Test series has begun, with England selecting Phil Edmonds and Derek Randall as well as Neil Foster of Essex, who was made twelfth man. Randall, in John Arlott's words, "reminds spectators of their own mortality". One imagines him as a schoolboy jumping up and down in his seat, probably with one leg behind his head, a fellow of good intensions, who occasionally spills ink over everyone and might be seen to throw the odd paper dart. In England's meagre first innings Randall scored 75 not out, resisting with skill and fortitude the varied threats of Richard Hadlee. Hadlee saved his team with the bat too, scoring 84 to take his team up to England's total from the dire straits of 41 for five.

Hadlee has the appearance of a rickety church steeple and a severe manner which suggests that women are not likely to be ordained just yet. The battle between Hadlee and the Englishmen had a gaunt unrelenting atmosphere as if their respect for each other exceeded their affection. In England's second innings Fowler and Tavaré cemented their team's advantage

Richard Hadlee – an all-round assault on England.

with centuries and on Saturday England ploughed on adding 184 runs and giving New Zealand cause to regret their failure to seize the initiative. It was a dull day of cricket for the big Saturday crowd but I suspect the enemy of Test cricket is not so much slow scoring as mediocre players.

## DESPERATE EXCITEMENT IN B&H FINAL
### WEEK ENDING JULY 25

I'M afraid I spent most of Saturday at my sister's wedding and it is only by the merest chance that I am able to describe the thrilling finale to this season's Benson and Hedges Cup final. It was 8.15 p.m. when I arrived home and seeking solace from the dramas of the day I turned on my television expecting to see Bernard Levin interview Henry Moore. The cricket was still on and the interview cancelled, a misfortune for *The Times* reporter who nevertheless managed to review it for Monday's paper.

And so it was that I shared with tens of thousands at the game and millions on television the traumatic final few overs bowled in the gloom of a Lord's evening. Radley had scored a typically rigorous 81 not out to help Middlesex to 196, and in reply Essex had galloped away led by Gooch from Leytonstone and Hardie from Stenhousemuir. They reached 84 in the 14th over when Gooch was caught by Downton, whereupon Fletcher's team lost their way. The gnome himself fell cheaply, caught at silly point off Edmonds. So often it is Fletcher

upon whom Essex rely to survive their anxious moments. Without him, they sometimes resemble a group of hikers on Exmoor who have lost their maps.

Middlesex huddled around the bat, dashing in to prevent singles. Essex needed only 24 in seven overs with five wickets left. Daniel was summoned. His first spell had been poor, his mighty frame had been stiff and without rhythm. This evening he hurled himself at the batsman, faster still after being denied an lbw and called for a wide. Pringle fell and Ray East ran himself out. Turner lofted Cowans, only to be neatly caught by deep mid-on, who wasn't even playing. In fact, he'd had to ask his dad whether being cup-tied meant he couldn't be twelfth man. It didn't, so there we were, Turner, caught Carr bowled Cowans. I doubt if John Carr felt quite as calm as he looked. An odd run was scrambled here and there and then Cowans bowled a short ball which was hooked by David East. I think it was David East, though the flurry and scurry of events defies accurate recollection. Finally Cowans bowled to Foster with a handful needed in the last over. He pitched up, the ball came back down the slope and uprooted Foster's off stump. Middlesex had pinched an extraordinary victory in an exhilarating final. The game ended in fading light about ten to nine and it was won by the more tenacious team, though not necessarily the more gifted.

*To add a prediction to a comment, I am sure we will hear more, in coming years, of John Carr.*

It was exhausting to watch that final half hour. What on earth players and spectators must have suffered who were there all day I cannot say. One-day games throw at their followers so many highs and lows heaping upon each other like some grand game of snakes and ladders. The moment you relax content that things are going your way is the moment some idiot loses his wicket or lets one through his legs. The balance is fine and easily disturbed. When I retire (and if I have to play or watch any more of these desperate final few overs this will not be long delayed) I vow only to watch dull cricket games meandering to an entirely satisfactory draw. Then I can chat to my neighbours, attempt a crossword, bite a cheese sandwich without forever cursing a man for his incompetence or trying to work out who is ahead on run rate.

Mike Gatting lies at the feet of Derek Pringle and wicket-keeper David East as the finger of umpire Bird rules him out.

Everything else this week was dwarfed by this stirring contest. Still Edmonds and Marks slowly spun England to victory in the First Test match despite Wright's skilful 88. And Zaheer's brillance outshone Gower at Leicester, helping Gloucestershire's successful chase for 303 to win. Essex lost the second tight game to Tavaré's fighting Kent team and Somerset defied a pitch resembling a group of saucers to overcome Lancashire at Old Trafford and to reach the NatWest Cup quarter-final with Northamptonshire, Warwickshire and Sussex.

## NZ ON BRINK OF FAMOUS WIN
### WEEK ENDING AUGUST 1

NEW Zealand are poised to win a Test match in England for the first time. Although their cricket history is proudly littered with staunch, craggy cricketers like Bevan Congdon and superbly gifted men like Martin Donnelly, New Zealand have not yet won a Test in this land where the game began. Howarth's team is a collection of travelled professionals and local cricketers. They may appear to rely heavily upon Howarth, Wright and Hadlee but some of the lesser-known men are seasoned campaigners with a tough resilience about them. Bruce Edgar has a stoicism and a style similar to John Edrich's and Lance Cairns would scoff at the idea of carrying a sheep under each arm. A mere sheep? At Headingley Edgar struck a typically trenchant 84 and Cairns's mild in-swingers brought a handful of wickets. Remarkably Hadlee took not one wicket in this Test match which is not to say he bowled less than magnificently.

Bob Taylor – probably the best in the world.

## DR WHO PULLS OFF TWO
### WEEK ENDING AUGUST 8

NEW Zealand won the Second Test by five wickets despite Willis's bounding aggression and Gower's polite century. These two men, with Botham and Taylor, might very well be included in any world team. Bob Taylor, as ever, is keeping wicket so well that you hardly notice him at all.

I must mention Dr Who. He has led Glamorgan to two Championship wins in a row, and Jack Simmons – who represents most of what is best about cricket – has

A shower of champagne for New Zealand after their historic win at Headingley.

County Championship (as at August 3)

| | | P | Pts |
|---|---|---|---|
| **1** | Middlesex | 15 | 247 |
| **2** | Essex | 16 | 222 |
| **3** | Leicestershire | 16 | 180 |
| **4** | Hampshire | 17 | 179 |

bowled Lancashire to two victories. I wonder if there is something about off-spinning which attracts reliable, beery, cheerful fellows? Studying the list of county off-spinners I discover Cowley, Simmons, Marks, Willey, Miller, Emburey, all of them fellows with seasoned senses of humour. Compare this to the left-arm spinners who mostly live on the edge of their nerves and share my wonder. Perhaps those who turn the ball into the bat feel a measure of generosity while those who turn it away suffer a life full of missed edges.

## CRICKET'S CROCKS
### WEEK ENDING AUGUST 14

THERE was a time during this week when it began to appear if war had been declared. Men were being called up left, right and centre. Men were being plucked from cosy county games and men were being sent home unfit for service. One man ricked his back emerging from his car, another hit 75 only to be told he was unfit for England. Edmonds and Fowler did not play, Dilley was not considered. Andy Lloyd was sent for and then sent back rather like one of John Wright's partners. Smith, Cook and Foster were summoned and made their Test debuts.

These three men enjoyed varying fortunes. Chris Smith fell to his first ball in Test cricket, a straight ball which he simply missed. But he scored 43 good runs in the second innings. Nick Cook's debut was a huge success, though chillingly reminiscent of Phil Edmonds's. In his first spell of bowling he took four for 28 in 20 overs. Cook has plied his trade with patience and perseverence in the sombre surroundings of

**LORD'S GROUND**

CORNHILL INSURANCE TEST SERIES

## ENGLAND v. NEW ZEALAND

THURS., FRI., SAT., MON. & TUES., AUGUST 11, 12, 13, 15 & 16, 1983    (5-day Match)

### ENGLAND

| | | First Innings | | Second Innings | |
|---|---|---|---|---|---|
| 1 C. J. Tavare | Kent | b Crowe | 51 | c Crowe b Hadlee | 16 |
| 2 C. L. Smith | Hampshire | l b w b Hadlee | 0 | c Coney b Hadlee | 43 |
| 3 D. I. Gower | Leicestershire | l b w b Crowe | 108 | c Crowe b Gray | 34 |
| 4 A. J. Lamb | Northamptonshire | c sub b Chatfield | 17 | c Hadlee b Gray | 4 |
| 5 M. W. Gatting | Middlesex | c Wright b Hadlee | 81 | b Gray | 16 |
| 6 I. T. Botham | Somerset | l b w b Cairns | 8 | c Coney b Chatfield | 61 |
| *7 R. W. Taylor | Derbyshire | b Hadlee | 16 | c and b Coney | 7 |
| 8 N. A. Foster | Essex | c Smith b Hadlee | 10 | c Wright b Hadlee | 3 |
| 9 N. G. B. Cook | Leicestershire | b Chatfield | 16 | c Bracewell b Chatfield | 5 |
| †10 R. G. D. Willis | Warwickshire | c Smith b Hadlee | 7 | not out | 2 |
| 11 N. G. Cowans | Middlesex | not out | 1 | c Smith b Chatfield | 1 |
| | | B 3, l-b 2, w 2, n-b 3, | 11 | B 5, l-b 6, w 0, n-b , | 20 |
| | | **Total** | **326** | **Total** | **211** |

#### FALL OF THE WICKETS
1—3   2—152   3—174   4—191   5—218   6—288   7—290   8—303   9—318   10—326
1—26   2—79   3—87   4—119   5—147   6—195   7—199   8—208   9—210   10—211

ANALYSIS OF BOWLING

| | 1st Innings | | | | | | 2nd Innings | | | | | |
|---|---|---|---|---|---|---|---|---|---|---|---|---|
| Name | O. | M. | R. | W. | Wd. | N-b | O. | M. | R. | W. | Wd. | N-b |
| Hadlee | 40 | 15 | 93 | 5 | 1 | 3 | 26 | 7 | 42 | 3 | 0 | ... |
| Cairns | 23 | 8 | 65 | 1 | ... | ... | 3 | 0 | 9 | 0 | ... | ... |
| Chatfield | 36.3 | 8 | 116 | 2 | ... | 1 | 13.3 | 4 | 29 | 3 | ... | ... |
| Crowe | 13 | 1 | 36 | 2 | 1 | ... | ... | ... | ... | ... | ... | ... |
| Coney | 8 | 7 | 6 | 0 | ... | ... | 6 | 4 | 9 | 1 | ... | ... |
| Bracewell | ... | ... | ... | ... | ... | ... | 11 | 4 | 20 | 0 | ... | ... |
| Gray | ... | ... | ... | ... | ... | ... | 30 | 8 | 73 | 3 | ... | ... |

### NEW ZEALAND

| | | First Innings | | Second Innings | |
|---|---|---|---|---|---|
| 1 B. A. Edgar | Wellington | c Willis b Cook | 70 | c Lamb b Cowans | 27 |
| 2 J. G. Wright | Northern Districts | c Lamb b Willis | 11 | c Taylor b Botham | 12 |
| †3 G. P. Howarth | Northern Districts | b Cook | 26 | c Taylor b Willie | 0 |
| 4 M. D. Crowe | Auckland | b Botham | 48 | c Foster b Cowans | 12 |
| 5 J. V. Coney | Wellington | b Cook | 7 | c Gatting b Foster | 68 |
| 6 E. J. Gray | Wellington | c Lamb b Botham | 11 | c Lamb b Cook | 17 |
| 7 J. G. Bracewell | Auckland | c Gower b Cook | 0 | l b w b Willis | 4 |
| 8 R. J. Hadlee | Canterbury | c Botham b Cook | 0 | b Willis | 28 |
| 9 B. L. Cairns | Northern Districts | c Lamb b Botham | 5 | b Cook | 16 |
| *10 I. D. S. Smith | Central Districts | c Lamb b Botham | 3 | not out | 17 |
| 11 E. J. Chatfield | Wellington | not out | 5 | c and b Cook | 2 |
| | | B , l-b 5, w , n-b 3, | 8 | B 3, l-b 4, w , n-b 7, | 14 |
| | | **Total** | **191** | **Total** | **219** |

#### FALL OF THE WICKETS
1—18   2—49   3—147   4—159   5—176   6—176   7—176   8—183   9—184   10—191
1—15   2—17   3—57   4—61   5—108   6—154   7—158   8—190   9—206   10—219

ANALYSIS OF BOWLING

| | 1st Innings | | | | | | 2nd Innings | | | | | |
|---|---|---|---|---|---|---|---|---|---|---|---|---|
| Name | O. | M. | R. | W. | Wd. | N-b | O. | M. | R. | W. | Wd. | N-b |
| Willis | 13 | 6 | 28 | 1 | ... | 3 | 12 | 5 | 24 | 3 | ... | 7 |
| Foster | 16 | 5 | 40 | 0 | ... | ... | 12 | 0 | 35 | 1 | ... | ... |
| Cowans | 9 | 1 | 30 | 0 | ... | ... | 11 | 1 | 36 | 2 | ... | ... |
| Botham | 20.4 | 6 | 50 | 4 | ... | ... | 7 | 2 | 20 | 1 | ... | ... |
| Cook | 26 | 11 | 35 | 5 | ... | ... | 27.2 | 9 | 90 | 3 | ... | ... |

Umpires—D. J. Constant & D. G. L. Evans       Scorers—E. Solomon & J. O'Sullivan

† Captain       * Wicket-keeper

Play begins each day at 11.00

Luncheon Interval each day 1.00—1.40

Tea Interval each day 3.40—4.00, or when 35 overs remain to be bowled, if later.
Stumps drawn each day at 6.00, or after 96 overs have been bowled, whichever is the
later.   In the event of play being suspended, for any reason, for one hour or more on
any of the first four days, play may continue on that day until 7.00.
(Timings may be varied according to state of game)

**New Zealand won the toss and elected to field**

**England won by 127 runs**

Leicester and his rigorous grounding will hold him in good stead.

As for Neil Foster, well he'll be realising with Cairns that cricket is a rum old game. Foster bowled well, took a wicket and enjoyed himself. A day later he returned to Essex to discover that he couldn't play again this season because of problems with his back. Apparently he has an injury somewhat similar to those suffered by Lillee and Thomson years ago. Hopefully he can match their courage and bounce back to give the West Indians a little of their own medicine next year. Cairns, by the way, had an agonising game. England's victory was due largely to Gower's century on the first day. Cairns dropped him twice, one of them a dolly to square leg. He was a hero last week and he's a villain this one.

Neil Foster – Test debut then injury.

## BAPTISTE PROVES A POINT
### WEEK ENDING AUGUST 20

IT has been Botham's week. His cricketing life seems to lurch from triumph to disaster. There doesn't appear to be much in between. At Lord's he scored 61 runs and took four for 50 for England and then played a captain's innings of 96 not out to steer Somerset past Middlesex and into the NatWest final. This was an innings of intense effort, a disciplined, responsible knock which reminded those of us who grew up with him that his greatest talent has always been his immense competitive instinct. As a youngster Botham always wanted to bowl or to bat, at any rate to be involved. When cricket inspires him in his adulthood, which is not always, he remains a cricketer to dominate his age.

Kent beat Hampshire in the other semi-final by 71 runs with Eldine Baptiste winning Man of the Match with his five for 20. Hampshire alone amongst the counties have never reached a final at Lord's and Cowdrey and Baptiste exploited nervous batsmen. Pocock's team must lay aside the demon quickly lest it pursue them in every semi-final to come.

As a cricketer Baptiste resembles Kapil Dev with his flashing blade and fast-medium swingers. As a man he is an Antiguan, with the proud privacy that entails. Vivian Richards has been his inspiration, forcing him to scorn fortune when most she offers blows. It has not been easy for Baptiste at Kent, he's had to fight his way into the team against a background of people who'd like to make Kent a second Yorkshire. But with Richards's encouragement he stuck to his task and his reward is not only a final at Lord's but a winter tour with the West Indies.

## ESSEX v. MIDDLESEX – THE EPIC CONTINUES
### WEEK ENDING AUGUST 27

AS the Championship season totters towards its close Middlesex and Essex are slugging away at each other like two punch-drunk fighters in the 15th round. Essex are 13 points ahead and have played one more game, and Middlesex are beginning to look the more tired. Two extra three-day games were added to our fixture list this season and I suspect all professional cricketers are more drained of mental energy than ever before this year. It takes only a pint and a pasty to restore physical health but minds numbed by incessant pressure need longer periods of rest.

In the final Test Botham hit 100 off 99 balls and, with Randall batting with panache, England ended the first day 363 for seven. These two were particularly severe on a second new ball, a fact to delight David Lloyd of Lancashire. I say this because Lloyd holds a theory that it is a batsman's duty to hit a new ball on to some concrete to ruin its shine. Lloyd has a list of grounds where concrete is readily available. Once when Clive Lloyd hit a towering six and the ball soared behind Hove into some flats David Lloyd stood up, joined in the applause and said "By golly, that's the best concrete shot I've seen in years."

Nick Cook is bowling England to victory in a steady and unassuming way. He is giving Phillippe Henri Edmonds good cause to regret that back injury.

## WE WIN THE CUP, WITH HELP FROM OUR LOYAL HORDES
### WEEK ENDING SEPTEMBER 4

ON a cold, dark day at Lord's Somerset won the third NatWest Cup final, beating Kent by 24 runs. It was a nervous, tight game in which Somerset's disadvantage in batting first on a damp pitch was balanced by Kent having to face "Big Bird" Garner in fading light towards the end of the day.

Anglo-Caribbean joy in the Somerset camp as Joel Garner collects another wicket.

It was a bowler's match and only Richards and Tavaré were able to dominate for any length of time. As a low scoring game, it was a contest which frayed rather than excited spectators. It was not a match to send off

the season in style but it was a game in which the struggling teams were rarely far apart. Even at the end, with Ellison and Dilley swinging lustily, it seemed possible for Kent to win. They needed only 42 in eight overs, but four of these would be bowled from the gloomy end by Joel Garner. As it was, Ellison and Dilley swung once too often and Somerset had won a cup final for the fourth time in five years.

Our day at Lord's was slightly spoiled by newspaper comments that Kent deserved to win because they have a local team where Somerset rely heavily on two overseas stars and, moreover, that our supporters would ruin the whole day.

I suppose Kent have only one overseas star, the other ten men are local; but then so are eight of the Somerset side. Out of 21 players on our staff only five learned their cricket outside the county. As for our supporters, well they did sing a few songs and one or two were rather rude but mostly they added to the festivities with good humour. When, on Sunday, these same supporters turned up in their thousands at Worcester their hosts were pleased enough to see them. It put an extra £5,000 on the gate which meant that Worcester could keep one more cricketer on their staff next year.

## FITTING FAREWELL FOR RAY EAST
### WEEK ENDING SEPTEMBER 12

ESSEX won their second Championship and in lifting the Sunday League Yorkshire secured their first trophy win since 1969.

Fletcher's team could not win their last match. They were thwarted by the resistance of Boycott and Moxon. But a draw was enough to take the title, as Middlesex were frustrated by Nottinghamshire. It was a well-deserved triumph for Essex, rewarding a staunch team effort that lasted all season. They are an excellent, experienced team who have hardly changed in ten years, though during this campaign Fletcher took his chance to give Gladwin a run of games and of course Foster burst into England's XI. But it is the old stagers who deserve most of the praise; Lever bravely fought back from a nasty stomach operation to take 100 wickets in 17 matches – what a marvellous, hard-working cricketer he is – and Ken McEwan scored

| County Championship (as at September 1) | P | Pts |
|---|---|---|
| **1** Essex | 22 | 311 |
| **2** Middlesex | 21 | 294 |
| **3** Hampshire | 22 | 277 |
| **4** Warwickshire | 21 | 248 |

over 2,000 runs. McEwan was voted cricketer of the year by the players, a suitable accolade for a modest man who enjoyed a scintillating summer. These two in particular were responsible for Essex being able to fulfil both the ingredients for Championship success, scoring your runs quickly and dismissing the opposition twice.

Incidentally, I gather that Raymond East may be absent from our ranks next year. Just in case this is true may I farewell him with my favourite East story (there are plenty more in the bag if he doesn't retire). Apparently East was grimly walking out to bat against Lancashire on a wet, flying pitch. People were being hit in the teeth left, right and centre. East decided this wasn't for him and whispered to Shuttleworth that if he would be so kind as to pitch the last ball up and straight he, Raymond East, would miss it so departing the scene in one piece. Shuttleworth steamed in, bowled a straight half volley which East swung mightily for six. Shuttleworth spoke some words and stormed back to his mark. Next ball he moved in and as he bowled, East hurled aside his bat, dived to the ground and lay flat on his stomach, watching as the bouncer flew far over his head! We will miss him.

I am afraid Somerset and Gloucestershire finished well down the table. Perhaps C. B. Fry had us worked out years ago when, watching a game at Lord's, he observed: "There! You see? It's always like that with these West Countrymen: they bowl superbly for an hour or so and then begin to think about apples."

I will end with my two most stark memories of the season. One was the sight of seven Somerset cricketers sound asleep on the floor of our dressing room in Derby while a county match was in progress. We play far too much tense cricket, and at times this reduces our performances to a chore. No other game expects its players to stay at their peak for such a long time. Can we not persuade Northumberland, Durham and Scotland to join the County Championship? Can we not play at most 20 games a year, with the NatWest Cup Final on the last day of the season?

Finally at Leicester dear old Sam Cook, a most popular umpire, had to leave Somerset's match suddenly. He was replaced by Leicestershire's coach Ken Higgs. There cannot be much wrong with a game in which both teams are entirely happy that one team's coach should act as a neutral referee.

Ray East – always the joker.

### SCHWEPPES COUNTY CHAMPIONSHIP

| | P | W | L | D | Bt | Bl | Pts |
|---|---|---|---|---|---|---|---|
| Essex (7) | 24 | 11 | 5 | 8 | 69 | 79 | 324 |
| Middlesex (1) | 24 | 11 | 4 | 9 | 60 | 72 | 308 |
| Hampshire (3) | 24 | 10 | 2 | 12 | 62 | 71 | 289 |
| Leicestershire (2) | 24 | 9 | 3 | 12 | 52 | 81 | 277 |
| Warwickshire (17) | 24 | 10 | 3 | 11 | 52 | 64 | 276 |
| Northamptonshire (9) | 24 | 7 | 4 | 13 | 63 | 77 | 252 |
| Kent (13) | 24 | 7 | 4 | 13 | 68 | 70 | 250 |
| Surrey (5) | 24 | 7 | 4 | 13 | 65 | 70 | 247 |
| Derbyshire (11) | 24 | 7 | 5 | 12 | 46 | 65 | 219 |
| Somerset (6) | 24 | 3 | 7 | 14 | 57 | 75 | 180 |
| Sussex (8) | 24 | 3 | 10 | 11 | 50 | 72 | 170 |
| Gloucestershire (15) | 24 | 3 | 8 | 13 | 56 | 61 | 165 |
| Lancashire (12) | 24 | 3 | 4 | 17 | 56 | 61 | 165 |
| Nottinghamshire (4) | 24 | 3 | 10 | 11 | 39 | 62 | 149 |
| Glamorgan (16) | 24 | 2 | 10 | 12 | 45 | 64 | 141 |
| Worcestershire (14) | 24 | 2 | 11 | 11 | 43 | 54 | 129 |
| Yorkshire (10) | 24 | 1 | 5 | 18 | 45 | 64 | 125 |

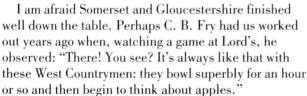 *For supporters of England, the winter of 1983-84 was an almost uniformly depressing one. For the first time an England side lost Test series to both New Zealand and Pakistan and in both cases they deserved to do so, Richard Hadlee proving the main matchwinner for New Zealand and Abdul Qadir for Pakistan. Some members of Willis's team were alleged by a Sunday newspaper to have taken drugs while in New Zealand. The Test and County Cricket Board's subsequent inquiry cleared them of doing anything which might have affected their performance on the field.*

*Towards the end of the tour, Willis returned home from Pakistan with a virus and Botham with a knee injury. The result of losing the team's most effective Test bowlers was to bring out the best in those who remained. David Gower, taking over as captain, scored 152 at Faisalabad and 9 and 173 not at Lahore, two games in which England regained at least some honour.*

*New Zealand, greatly toughened up by all the increased activity in Test and international cricket in recent years, had a good winter, comfortably disposing of Sri Lanka in the first major tour to that country. But the team of the season were again the West Indies who defeated India three-nil in a six-Test series in India with Marshall and Holding taking 33 and 30 wickets respectively and Lloyd making use of all his experience to score 496 runs at an average of 82.*

*Returning home in the early months of 1984, the West Indies swept away a meek challenge from Australia, who had just beaten Pakistan on their own pitches. The first two Tests were drawn, but West Indies reeled off savage victories in the last three games as they began the longest run of Test victories in the game's history.*

# ╺ 1984 ╺

## LETTUCE TIME AGAIN
### *WEEK ENDING APRIL 29*

WELL I, at any rate, enjoyed my winter. Tortoises, I suspect, enjoy the sanctuary of their shells during the dark months and regret the brighter mornings when it occurs to them that it is time once more to munch lettuce.

I was in Sydney, by the way, gazing at the waves I could never quite catch. The months idled by in a blur of harvesting wheat (some of it good enough for animal feed, the rest sent off for the Americans) and cricket scores in the papers recording another Test match in progress. This round of Test matches is beginning to resemble a soap opera churned out day after day. Tests are supposed to be invigorating, a rare challenge to fresh spirits. I can scarcely remember who played whom this winter, let alone which team won.

If the routine of the Tests dulled interest, there were always Yorkshire's troubles to entertain cricket followers. Few institutions can be so solemn or so littered with intrigue. In this episode Illingworth departed, one committee resigned and was replaced by another, and Boycott outstared even Trueman's rusty comment that golf might have been his game. Athey, in his Bristol home, must have contemplated this squabble with a broad grin.

 **LORD'S**  **GROUND** (15p) (15p)

### M.C.C. v. ESSEX

Wednesday, Thursday & Friday, April 25, 26 & 27, 1984     (3-day Match)

| M.C.C. | | First Innings | | Second Innings |
|---|---|---|---|---|
| 1 C. L. Smith | Hampshire | c Gooch b Lever | 43 | |
| 2 T. A. Lloyd | Warwickshire | c Fletcher b Pringle | 60 | |
| 3 M. C. J. Nicholas | Hampshire | | | |
| †4 D. I. Gower | Leicestershire | c Hardie b Lever | 1 | |
| 5 M. W. Gatting | Middlesex | c East b Lever | 2 | |
| 6 C. S. Cowdrey | Kent | c Gooch b Foster | 14 | |
| 7 R. G. Williams | Northants | b Gooch | 23 | |
| *8 P. R. Downton | Middlesex | | | |
| 9 N. F. Williams | Middlesex | | | |
| 10 N. G. B. Cook | Leicestershire | | | |
| 11 N. G. Cowans | Middlesex | | | |
| | | B , l-b , w , n-b | | |

## MANNERS STILL MAKETH THE CRICKETER
### *WEEK ENDING MAY 5*

STILL the sun shines (it was a blazing April – I forgot to mention that). There is dust on the umbrellas, and already the sheep are wondering where their shearers are. This is, of course, absolutely disastrous. A superb spring will bring forth a saturating summer, no-one in England expects anything else, except Vic Marks who says there is a shortage of hay, and the sun will shine to help the crop. He takes the view that God is a farmer, and keeps an eye on these things.

It's even been sunny in Manchester, where Geoff Miller scored his first 100 in top class cricket. It is not easy to unravel the block that has prevented him scoring a hundred earlier in his career, perhaps it is that on the brink of realising his superb gifts of touch and originality, he retreats into orthodox professionalism for which, perhaps, his respect is too profound.

Everyone in cricket will celebrate with Miller for cricket has not lost its manners. We still applaud our opponents when they reach fifty, fieldsmen still wait for the batsmen to leave the field, and umpires are rarely defied in public and never abused (let McEnroe try his curses on Bill Alley!). Cricketers have not, I suspect, changed much over the years.

Geoff Miller – a century at last.

## OVERS BOWLED THE KEY TO TEA
### *WEEK ENDING MAY 12*

IT is not, in cricket, always a simple matter to distinguish the bizarre from the orthodox. On Tuesday Somerset played a friendly on Lord Tim's bumpy country pitch to a background of banjos and brass bands and it was certainly an unusual experience.

It was, by the way, a benefit game. Benefits have stretched far beyond a reward to a county stalwart. They are businesses and if the beneficiary is famous they resemble national Oxfam appeals. Perhaps the system should be reviewed. I'd suggest 1990 as an appropriate year for change.

I may not last that long. If I do I'll be a veteran, like Brian Rose who says he cannot be expected to chase a ball in the field now that he is 33.

There are four stages in a professional career. He starts with the ill-advised enthusiasm of a daffodil in April and a brilliant career appears certain. But (it is the way of all flesh) soon he slips into his second stage. People realise that he hasn't actually achieved anything in four years, whereupon they condemn him as another who failed to fulfill his potential, another broken light-bulb. Eventually, after several traumatic years, he emerges as a wily old pro. This is the pinnacle of his career, and he learns to inspect the pitch to telling effect. Finally he is a veteran, as his mistresses abandon him for Barry Manilow records. This is Rose's stage (I speak metaphorically you understand). I am, I think, a wily old pro still.

One more thing. It emerged this week that no-one knew when to take tea. It matters not how the clock stands, nor whether there is honey for the sandwiches, what matters is how many bloody overs have been bowled.

## GOWER TO SUCCEED TO THE PURPLE
### WEEK ENDING MAY 19

IT is as if I were a doctor who, having pronounced death, hears a burp from the body. Not content with alarming Surrey, the Combined Universities this week defeated Gloucestershire in the Benson and Hedges Cup. Miller followed his 91 at The Oval with a century (he scored a pair against Somerset, and is having an interesting season) and John Carr hit 66 and took the last few wickets having been saved from this purpose by his evidently courageous captain. This is Oxbridge's first win since the cherished triumph at Barnsley in 1977 when A. R. Wingfield-Digby and R. le Q. Savage shocked the loudspeaker man and surprised Yorkshire.

*Andrew Miller went on to score 128 not out in the 1984 Varsity match, captained Oxford in 1985 and has played some useful innings on his occasional appearances for Middlesex.*

Middlesex, Kent and Leicestershire were eliminated (if that does not sound too Russian a word) so that the three main rivals for the England captaincy were denied the opportunity to lead their teams in the Benson and

Hedges quarter-finals. Gatting, Tavaré and Gower would, I think, make excellent captains for they have the mixture of diplomacy and determination that would help them to ignore the critics and the advisors without being too obvious about it. Willis and Botham have dominated England's cricket since Brearley and perhaps it is time for a fresh spirit to guide the team.

It is to David Gower that Willis's mantle will probably fall, and it could not fall into more deserving hands. In Pakistan Gower's hidden strength and inventiveness flowered after Willis and Botham returned to England and if, after those magnificent innings and inspired declarations, there are still people who imagine he is too casual we can only observe that they said much the same of Sir Frank Worrell. Gower moves with the ease of water flowing down a slope, but he has the resolution required in great batsmen and national captains.

Not that he will win his first series. The West Indies, you will understand, have arrived.

*Not even Peter Roebuck would have forseen the punishment that the West Indies were to heap on the luckless Gower.*

David Gower – looking ahead to a daunting task.

## WEST INDIANS FORMIDABLY STRONG
### WEEK ENDING MAY 26

IT was when Marshall's third ball flew over Dujon's head for four byes that Somerset's batsmen realised that it was not going to be an enjoyable match. These days there seem to be more wickets with uneven bounce (I've noticed, too, that the country at large is falling to pieces). In recent years efforts to add pace to pitches have spoilt several batsmen's paradises – in particular at Edgbaston, Trent Bridge, Chelmsford and now, it appears, at Taunton.

We are, of course, used to the idea of West Indian cricket as a hard, unrelenting attack upon the batsmen. Lloyd has guided his team from the calypso years to a new toughness symbolised by the tight, taut lines of reggae. They are formidably strong. Haynes is back in form, Lloyd has returned to his magnificent best, Richards appears to be relishing his cricket more than for years, and in Dujon, Baptiste and Harper the West

Indies have at their command a group of intelligent, calm men who will add mettle to this proud team. Harper, in particular, is an intriguing cricketer. It will not encourage batsmen that the West Indian spinner stands at 6ft 5in, but they will not be surprised to learn that he is intensely serious and very able.

## RICHARDS RULES THE SCORECARD
### WEEK ENDING JUNE 2

RICHARDS destroys with a brutal majesty which brooks no argument. His every movement, his very stare, is poised and menacing, a statement of his superiority. He asserts his authority with sudden bursts of savagery during which enemies are torn to pieces, and yet never drops that haughty demeanour unless it is to smile at some passing fancy.

At Old Trafford this week Richards indicated that he remained the best and, what's more, intended to keep things that way. The scorecard of the West Indies innings bears reproduction . . .

**FIRST MATCH: Old Trafford, May 31**

**WEST INDIES**

| | | |
|---|---|---|
| C. G. Greenidge | c Bairstow b Botham | 9 |
| D. L. Haynes | run out | 1 |
| R. B. Richardson | c and b Willis | 6 |
| I. V. A. Richards | not out | 189 |
| H. A. Gomes | b Miller | 4 |
| *C. H. Lloyd | c Pringle b Miller | 8 |
| †P. J. Dujon | c Gatting b Miller | 0 |
| M. D. Marshall | run out | 4 |
| E. A. E. Baptiste | c Bairstow b Botham | 26 |
| J. Garner | c and b Foster | 3 |
| M. A. Holding | not out | 12 |
| | Extras (b 4, lb 2, w 1, nb 3) | 10 |
| | Total (for 9, 55 overs) | 272 |

Fall of wickets: 5, 11, 43, 63, 89, 98, 102, 161, 166.
Bowling: Willis 11-2-38-1, Botham 11-0-67-2, Foster 11-0-61-1, Miller 11-1-32-3, Pringle 11-0-64-0.

**ENGLAND**

| | | |
|---|---|---|
| G. Fowler | c Lloyd b Garner | 1 |
| T. A. Lloyd | c Dujon b Holding | 15 |
| M. W. Gatting | lbw b Garner | 0 |
| *D. I. Gower | c Greenidge b Marshall | 15 |
| A. J. Lamb | c Richardson b Gomes | 75 |
| I. T. Botham | c Richardson b Baptiste | 2 |
| †D. L. Bairstow | c Garner b Richards | 13 |
| G. Miller | b Richards | 7 |
| D. R. Pringle | c Garner b Holding | 6 |
| N. A. Foster | b Garner | 24 |
| R. G. D. Willis | not out | 1 |
| | Extras (lb 6, nb 3) | 9 |
| | Total | 168 |

Fall of wickets: 7, 8, 33, 48, 80, 100, 115, 162.
Bowling: Garner 8-0-18-3, Holding 11-2-23-2, Baptiste 11-0-38-1, Marshall 6-1-20-1, Richards 11-1-45-2, Gomes 3-0-15-1.

Umpires: D. J. Constant and D. R. Shepherd.
Man of the Match: I. V. A. Richards

**WEST INDIES WON BY 104 RUNS**

**SECOND MATCH: Trent Bridge, June 2**

**WEST INDIES**

| | | |
|---|---|---|
| C. G. Greenidge | c Botham b Pringle | 20 |
| D. L. Haynes | lbw b Willis | 4 |
| R. B. Richardson | c Gower b Pringle | 10 |
| I. V. A. Richards | c Pringle b Miller | 3 |
| H. A. Gomes | b Pringle | 15 |
| *C. H. Lloyd | c Pringle b Miller | 52 |
| †P. J. Dujon | run out | 21 |
| M. D. Marshall | run out | 20 |
| E. A. E. Baptiste | lbw Willis | 19 |
| M. A. Holding | b Botham | 0 |
| J. Garner | not out | 6 |
| | Extras (7 lb, 2 nb) | 9 |
| | Total | 179 |

Fall of wickets: 24, 38, 39, 43, 75, 128, 148, 160, 161
Bowling: Willis 9.3-0-26-2, Botham 9-1-33-1, Pringle 10-3-21-3, Miller 10-2-44-2, Foster 10-0-46-0.

**ENGLAND**

| | | |
|---|---|---|
| G. Fowler | b Baptiste | 25 |
| T. A. Lloyd | c Dujon b Baptiste | 49 |
| *D. I. Gower | lbw Marshall | 36 |
| A. J. Lamb | b Gomes | 11 |
| I. T. Botham | c Gomes b Holding | 15 |
| M. W. Gatting | b Garner | 6 |
| †D. L. Bairstow | b Holding | 9 |
| G. Miller | not out | 3 |
| D. R. Pringle | not out | 2 |
| N. A. Foster | did not bat | |
| R. G. D. Willis | did not bat | |
| | Extras (4 b, 14 lb, 6 nb) | 24 |
| | Total | 180 |

Fall of wickets: 75, 103, 131, 145, 157, 173, 177.
Bowling: Garner 9-1-22-1, Holding 8.5-1-29-2, Marshall 10-1- 30-1, Baptiste 10-2-31-2, Richards 5-0-23-0, Gomes 5-0-21-1.

Umpires: H. D. Bird and D. O. Oslear.
Man of the Match: D. R. Pringle

**ENGLAND WON BY 3 WICKETS**

Richards's domination was absolute; with Holding he added 104 in the last 14 overs of the innings. Whilst his team mates struggled Richards brutally demolished the bowlers, by the end disclaiming easy runs so that he

could secure the strike. It was a *tour de force*, a statement of mastery rarely rivalled in this difficult game.

England fought back tenaciously to level the series at Trent Bridge, where Gower owed much to Willis's flailing excellence and Pringle's flourish.

Incidentally most of England's runs have been scored by the left-handers, Fowler, Lloyd and Gower. There is a theory about that Garner in particular dislikes bowling to left-handers, the evidence being that Border and Phillips scored most of Australia's runs in March. There may be something in it. We shall see. I've always maintained it's easier for left-handers anyway.

## ROSES REVIVED
### WEEK ENDING JUNE 9

AFTER the Benson and Hedges quarter-finals there is a chance we will have our first Roses Final (well, the first since Bosworth at any rate). These last few years have seen the cups in the North run almost dry, a turn of events endured with more stoicism in Manchester than in Leeds, and many people will hope that the wheel has turned again.

It was, of course, Richards who won the one-day series for the West Indies. He strolled to the wickets as if he were MacArthur returning to Singapore, every movement poised, each stare imperious. Once again he was especially merciless with Widow Twankey who has incidentally announced that he will retire from first-class cricket at the season's end. Willis has served England extraordinarily well and his too vigorous campaign against World Series Cricket and its players can be explained as the conduct of a man loyal to his game and its established order.

## VIC'S TALES OF THE UNEXPECTED
### WEEK ENDING JUNE 16

IN his *Somerset Scrapbook* Vic Marks observes that our cricket is noted for its "unpredictability, its larger than life characters." He hinted that this reputation was less deserved these days. What he did not mention was that he intended to restore it.

This week he first refused to declare against Middlesex, condemning the game to a stalemate which

County Championship (as at June 2)

| | | P | Pts |
|---|---|---|---|
| 1 | Leicestershire | 6 | 80 |
| 2 | Kent | 5 | 67 |
| 3 | Essex | 6 | 63 |
| 4 | Nottinghamshire | 6 | 61 |

might have confused Americans who'd find it hard to imagine why all those players and officials bothered to turn up if neither side wanted to win. Our match resembled one of those yawning Italian goalless draws though the crowd seemed happy enough with their coffee and crosswords. In these parts they take the view that if the smart alecs from London bat all one day our upstanding young men are entitled to bat the next two.

Hard upon this, Vic and the Somerset cricket committee met at the front of our barge as we floated down the Avon. I doubt if the Yorkshire committee meet on a boat (they'd need Cleopatra's "burnished throne"). Whether the tranquillity of the evening affected their decisions I cannot say but within two days Brian Langford had appeared as twelfth man and a garage mechanic I had not previously met had made his Somerset debut. When Murray Turner walked into our pavilion at Bath I assumed he was either a punk (a group to whom my feelings are of the utmost cordiality) or an opposing player. Upon being introduced it emerged that Murray was Vic's Harold Gimblett and that we were off once more on our Tales of the Unexpected.

Essex – that other bastion of the improbable – defeated Warwickshire despite following on, and evidently do not intend easily to let slip their Championship. McEwan and Lever performed as nobly as ever and Pringle took four for 13 without ever appearing quite awake.

## LANCASHIRE REVIVE MEMORIES OF BOND
### WEEK ENDING JUNE 23

I MISSED most of the Benson and Hedges semi-finals because I was on the golf course with Marks (who played the outward nine poorly but was not quite so successful when we turned for home). I did catch the last few overs of the Warwickshire and Yorkshire match and could share the poignant sorrow of the crowd when Yorkshire's brave chase failed by three runs. They have not reached a cup final since 1965, the year Boycott graced the final with the innings for which he will be most fondly – and regretfully – remembered. He scored 146 that day in an innings as full of panache and nerve as any seen at Lord's. Yorkshire scored 317 for four and

word has it that, under the impression that the ground was hopelessly waterlogged, they'd spent much of the previous night in the more eventful areas of London.

Warwickshire deserve their place in the final, and it offers them a chance to erase memories of their timid effort last year. This time, with Kallicharran sparkling like a cracker on a clear November night, and with Andy Lloyd returned from his injury (more on that in a minute) they will want to give a good account of themselves.

Willis's team meet Lancashire in the final. I am slowly retreating from my view that Lancashire cannot possibly win anything. They are high in the Sunday league too and on Wednesday they beat Nottinghamshire with time to spare. Chadwick scored 83, and Abrahams guided his team home. If they field with the spirit of Jackie Bond they may yet surprise us. Bond's catch to dismiss Asif in a Lord's final lingers in the memory; he could not possibly climb so high. It was sheer will-power.

At Edgbaston the West Indies won the First Test match by an innings which was disappointing after England's efforts in the one-day series. Andy Lloyd suffered a nasty blow on the head as he ducked into a bumper, and will miss a month's cricket. He was wearing a helmet which was just as well except that it is obvious that these helmets are not strong enough.

It is usual for England selectors to explore the depth of their talent during a series against the West Indies. Already there is talk of searching for men as resilient as Edrich, Close and Steele who were called upon to withstand the storms in 1976. Perhaps this might rather be the time to expose younger men of talent – Whitaker, Patel, Terry and Benson spring to mind (though the latter is injured) – after all sometimes great men can be weaned amidst wolves.

In the Championship Boycott is top of the batting averages and Underwood leads the bowling. It could easily be 1964.

## ENGLAND CHANGE THE GUARD
### WEEK ENDING JUNE 30

THE England selectors are changing the guard. Odds were offered early in the season to any man who thought he could predict England's openers for the Fifth

Andy Lloyd becomes the first casualty of the series.

Test. At any rate Fowler, Lloyd, Moxon and Broad have already been chosen and Robinson, Whitaker and Terry tipped. But Broad and Fowler added 101 so perhaps they will survive.

Finally, sadly, Bob Woolmer has been forced to retire from the game because of a back injury. With his departure, cricket loses one of its most phlegmatic characters and gifted timers of the ball who ought really to have played in more elegant times.

## THE LEG-SPINNER RETURNS
### WEEK ENDING JULY 7

AN artist friend of mine yearns for the return of the leg-spinner as Compton Mackenzie's monarch of the glen yearned for the rising of the clans. He has had a good week, for Derbyshire's Kim Barnett took six for 24 and in Shropshire's triumph over Yorkshire Mushtaq snared three for 38 with his cheerful wiles. Mushtaq, that fine Shropshire lad, did not dismiss Boycott which may well have been because the maestro alone could detect his googly. There is a story about that one English Test batsman eventually discovered the trick of reading Gleeson. He mentioned this to Boycott and was told. "Aye, ah've been able t'read 'im for a month. Don't tell t'others, will you?"

In Hastings, where all has been quiet these 918 years, Derek Underwood carved his first century as Kent tied with Sussex. It was a low-scoring game and Underwood had entered the fray as nightwatchman. He defied le Roux and the rest till tea and will treasure this ton above almost everything else. By the way, he finally took his 300th John Player League wicket on Sunday. He'd been stranded for three months on 298 like some darts player unable to hit double top.

I have left the Test match until the end because, after England had held Lloyd's team for four days, the West Indies first thrashed then sauntered their way to victory. Gower had invited them to score 341 in five hours and they won at their leisure with Greenidge 214 not out and Gomes 92 not out. This loss must have damaged the morale of England who had played so well for so long. Of course, people are saying Gower ought not to have declared but whenever a chance of defeating the West Indies appears, risks must be taken. And Gower was not to be blamed for the inaccuracy of his bowlers. It

Derek Underwood – a purposeful batsman.

Larry Gomes and Gordon Greenidge at a canter.

must have been a shattering experience, and a sad one.

The moment of victory for the West Indies.

## GOMES THE QUIET COLLECTOR
### WEEK ENDING JULY 14

ANOTHER Test match has started, heralded by Brian Close's announcement that "we haven't a cat in hell's chance". This Test is being played at Headingley on a pitch as reliable as Puckoon's clock. Only Larry Gomes has batted with a sense of security. At the crease he appears rather dozy, as if he might at any moment nod off. He scarcely seems to move at all and yet he collects his runs with serene politeness. Either he has a good bat or an acute gift of timing (I thought I'd timed one stroke rather well at Northampton on Monday until I heard David Steele growl "Bloddy hell, that's a good bat isn't it." Marshall has broken his thumb and is batting one-handed, as well as bowling one-handed which is not quite so unusual.

Four runs with one hand – Malcolm Marshall takes a boundary off Paul Allott.

## WATCHING THE CROWE FLY
### WEEK ENDING JULY 21

IN this month's Trent Bridge newspaper Clive Rice asserts that we play far too much cricket. He argues that the wear and tear of continuous county cricket forces players to pace themselves as if they were boxers in a title fight. He adds that fast bowlers in particular reduce their pace as well as being denied time to recover from the little strains and niggles of their trade. I must echo these sentiments. Overseas domestic cricket has a harder edge because teams prepare for each match and play with the utmost vigour, whereas in England we rumble along from match to match without a chance to freshen our spirits.

Martin Crowe – settling in at Somerset.

In the Nat West Trophy second round there were centuries by Fowler, Dyer (as Warwickshire beat Shropshire) and Gower. Middlesex, who are reviving, scrambled home against Nottinghamshire in the match of the day, Northants beat Worcester and Somerset won at Hove. Martin Crowe was the fourth centurion on the day, and his was a magnificent innings. He started poorly this season, possibly daunted by replacing Richards, but in the last two months has shown himself to be a batsman of the highest calibre.

After forecasting a wet summer (as I write I gaze upon a brown garden and wilting flowers) I am wary of predictions and so I will merely advise you to catch Crowe if he is ever in your area. He is very, very good.

## "FLAT JACK" FRUSTRATES WARWICKS
### WEEK ENDING JULY 28

WELL, of course, Lancashire won the Benson and Hedges Cup. They dismissed Warwickshire for 139 and passed that score with six wickets in hand. Warwickshire depended upon Kallicharran and Amiss to score their runs and shortly before lunch, their score on 106 for two, these men were in command. But "Flat Jack" Simmons bowled a miserly spell, frustrated even these two resounding batsmen and forced them to take liberties at the other end. When Amiss was out, Kallicharran disappeared into a shell of responsibility realising he had to carry the burden of the batting.

Lancashire's runs were scored, not by Fowler's irreverence nor by Ormrod's durability (he reminds me of that battery which keeps going a little longer than its rivals) but by Neil Fairbrother whose innings was full of perky strokes. He is a bouncy fellow and highly regarded by the sages around him.

Meanwhile back in Manchester England are playing the West Indies. I have a theory (this may not surprise you) that England ought to play Lloyd's fast bowlers on a more bouncy pitch upon which they could safely play back to almost every ball. This Old Trafford wicket was so low that back foot play was risky. To survive, our batsmen had to try to reach forward to these fast bowlers, which meant they were ill prepared for any ball which bounced steeply. If we played on pitches of a high uniform bounce our batsmen would find survival

Jack Simmons – always in control.

rather easier than they have done this year.

Sadly, Paul Terry could not avoid a bouncer from Winston Davis and his arm was broken. He will miss the rest of the season and, I suppose, will not represent his county for some time to come. He is a brave player who scored a hundred earlier in the season against Sylvester Clarke at his most lethal.

And so England slipped to defeat with Greenidge and Dujon striking centuries and only Lamb able to reply in kind for England. Our only crumb lay in the rediscovery of the excellent Pat Pocock, who whirled down his cunning off-breaks to take four wickets. In April his revival had seemed improbable – rather as if Val Doonican were suddenly to hit the top of the charts – but this week has been one for tried and trusted spinners.

Paul Terry – reluctant to give in on his Test debut.

*Pocock was to earn a second visit to India that winter but the return of John Emburey in 1985 must surely have spelt the end of Pat's Test career which started in 1968 and which included 19 matches overseas but only six at home.*

## MINOR FOLLIES
### WEEK ENDING AUGUST 4

I MUST mention an article hidden on the racing pages of *The Times* in which Michael Berry reports upon the past week in Minor County cricket. It appears that:
1. Lightning struck the pitch during a match between Staffordshire and Norfolk.
2. Herts deliberately presented Suffolk with 55 extras in the penultimate over of a dying game to try to persuade them to revive their risky run-chase.
3. Parry was given leg-before but recalled from the pavilion when everyone remembered that this year you cannot be leg-before if the ball has bounced twice.
4. Edrich and Clements of Suffolk were disciplined but no-one knew why.
5. Mushtaq left his team's game at a crucial stage to fulfill a club commitment.

That was the week that was.

## LIFTING UP THEIR HEARTS
### WEEK ENDING AUGUST 11

IT is Weston week. I cannot tell a lie. Weston week is not dear to my heart. It has deck chairs, pine trees, tarts and ice-creams. People wear sandals. Where are the forbidding stands and the distant, mournful spectators? Where are the solemn rituals and the distant struggles? Where the drizzle and the delays? Weston is for donkeys, Punch and Judy shows and beach cricket. (If you can tolerate that sort of thing.) I never get any runs at Weston.

Our visitors this week included Surrey who were, I daresay, pleased to leave the echoing caverns of The Oval. Surrey are managed by Mickey Stewart, one of a group of men (including Jackie Bond, David Brown and Brian Luckhurst) appointed to organise and discipline the cricket of their county teams. At Sussex John Barclay has asked a chaplain to help his players to their fulfilment and our old friend Wingfield-Digby (who took eight wickets for Dorset the other day) is to direct the Christians In Sport movement. These developments recognise the ever harsher tensions of a cricket season and the need to guide players emotionally as well as technically.

And, as the Fifth Test begins on an ominously bouncing Oval pitch, Sri Lanka have arrived. They are to play a Test at Lord's and are at present engaged in county games. They are delighting spectators with their entertaining, sometimes impetuous strokes and their legspinner. They play their cricket without inhibition and with a warmth not altogether suited to the age. If this Test series has taught anything, it is that heavy artillery is more valuable than light rifles, however heroically handled.

## RICE'S RECIPE FOR SUCCESS
### WEEK ENDING AUGUST 18

RICHARD Hadlee struck 210 not out as Notts recovered from 17 for four to reach 344 and to defeat Middlesex by an innings. Apparently, the pitch was lively and Daniel bowling as if the thorn were in *his* foot. Our "rickety church steeple" has the reputation of fearing fast bowling, and is supposed to be without a solid technique. It is said he relies upon clean hitting as does Kapil Dev rather than massive presence as does Botham. With his innings at Lord's Hadlee has stamped his authority on the crease and his stature as an all-rounder brooks no argument.

Notts are closing on Essex, and continue to defy

those who say Middlesex, Sussex, Leicester and Essex are stronger teams. Their recipe is, I think, an old one. Their batsmen build innings – Robinson, dour yet crisp (like lettuce), Randall who "reminds us of our mortality", the amply bottomed Broad, Rice as upright as a lay preacher and, latterly, Johnson, an impish player deft on his feet. They are all in the averages, that list of our sins collected not by St. Peter but by Bill Frindall. And their bowlers are capable of dismissing teams. It was Cooper who bowled out Middlesex, and Hemmings and Such have taken their wickets cheaply. They are denied the services of Hendrick and Rice, two vital parts of their artillery, so their high place in the table is deserved. Incidentally, Nottingham's victory was in London not at Trent Bridge. They do not entirely rely upon the second great doctor of cricket, the one who prepares their pitches.

Middlesex, who are beyond redemption in every other competition, have reached the Nat West Final. Gatting and Slack scored their runs and for Northants only Bailey and Larkins shone. Kent are the other finalists, having defeated Warwickshire who were without Willis who is ill. Kallicharran, with his darting strokes, reached 86 but his partners failed. Tavaré (who really ought to be a monk), Ellison and Benson took Kent to Lord's. Benson has missed most of the season but is scoring well this month with his sturdy simplicity.

England lost the Test series five nil in the end, with Haynes hitting a hundred and Holding streaming in off his full run for the first time this season. It was as if Nijinsky (the horse I mean) had interrupted his grazing to unleash one last magnificent burst. The series had an air of inevitability about it since that first morning at Edgbaston when Gower was forced to play two spinners (of all the irrelevancies) and to bat first (of all the idiocies).

## SRI LANKANS CARVE THE ENGLISH PORK PIE
### WEEK ENDING AUGUST 25

IN *The Guardian*, Matthew Engel observed that "Nothing in this year of cricketing disasters had provided a preparation for the astonishing business now going on at Lord's." The business referred to in these chillingly Churchillian phrases was the demolition of England's best bowlers by the wrists of Wettimuny and

Sidath Wettimuny – a massive innings of 190 on his first appearance at Lord's.

Duleep Mendis, the Sri Lankan captain on his way to a breathtaking century, to be followed by 94 in the second innings.

the dash of Duleep Mendis. The Sri Lankans were astonished by the infertility of the English game, by its wooden wrists and guileless bowling.

For the Sri Lankans, it was a thrilling challenge to wit and sinew, to the English it was one more match at the end of a gruelling season. Nevertheless, the Sri Lankans were wonderfully entertaining, especially in the fluency of their strokes and the correctness of their footwork. They batted like public schoolboys, or as I imagine men used to before fast bowlers dominated the game. They reminded us of a time when off-drives and delicate late-cuts were to the fore, of a time of chivalry and swords before the artillery.

*As the England "B" team found to their cost, the Sri Lankan "public schoolboys" tradition is being carried with gusto by the likes of Gurushinghe, Mahanama and Samarasekera.*

Allan Lamb congratulates Pat Pocock on his first run for England in eight years – scored against the Sri Lankans at Lord's.

## RADLEY AND EMBUREY LIFT THE CUP
### WEEK ENDING SEPTEMBER 1

I WENT to Lord's for the cup final, rising early to catch a train, meeting Scyld Berry at Paddington and strolling to the game along a canal lined by barges. I had not realised a final was such a social event. With people picnicking on the grass behind Lord's and bumping into old friends around the ground. The Long Room was as daunting as it was silent and the Press Box was full of men sipping coffee (it was early in the day) wondering who would emerge as their hero.

Middlesex won in the end off the last ball. Had Emburey missed it rather than cracking it to the boundary Tavaré would have lifted a cup rather than tasting defeat a second time. These things hang by a thread. It was a day of gritty cricket with Underwood ploughing in over upon over; Radley chipping runs, his expression as full of tales as the North face of the Eiger; Daniel stamping in; Edmonds as lofty as a mountain in a range of hills and Gatting as ebullient as a farmer and yet haunted by an elusive insecurity. In the end the game was won by Radley's craggy persistence and Emburey's pragmatism. He is the Gilbert to Edmonds's Sullivan.

Clive Radley pacing the Middlesex challenge.

## NatWest Bank Trophy Final

**15p**     ### KENT v. MIDDLESEX     **15p**

#### at Lord's Ground, †Saturday, September 1st, 1984

| KENT | | |
|---|---|---|
| 1 N. R. Taylor | b Slack | 49 |
| 2 M. R. Benson | st Downton b Emburey | 37 |
| ‡3 C. J. Tavare | c Downton b Daniel | 28 |
| 4 D. G. Aslett | run out | 11 |
| 5 C. S. Cowdrey | c Radley b Daniel | 58 |
| 6 R. M. Ellison | not out | 23 |
| 7 G. W. Johnson | run out | 0 |
| *8 S. N. V. Waterton | not out | 4 |
| 9 D. L. Underwood | | |
| 10 T. M. Alderman | | |
| 11 K. B. S. Jarvis | | |

B 10, l-b 8, w 3, n-b 1, ... 22

Total... 232

#### FALL OF THE WICKETS
1...96 2...98 3...135 4...163 5...217 6...217 7... 8... 9... 10...

| Bowling Analysis | O. | M. | R. | W. | Wd. | N-b |
|---|---|---|---|---|---|---|
| Cowans | 9 | 2 | 24 | 0 | ... | ... |
| Daniel | 12 | 1 | 41 | 2 | 1 | ... |
| Hughes | 10 | 0 | 52 | 0 | 1 | ... |
| Edmonds | 5 | 0 | 33 | 0 | ... | ... |
| Slack | 12 | 2 | 33 | 1 | 1 | 1 |
| Emburey | 12 | 1 | 27 | 1 | ... | ... |

| MIDDLESEX | | |
|---|---|---|
| 1 G. D. Barlow | c Waterton b Jarvis | 25 |
| 2 W. N. Slack | b Ellison | 20 |
| ‡3 M. W. Gatting | c Tavare b Jarvis | 37 |
| 4 R. O. Butcher | b Underwood | 15 |
| 5 C. T. Radley | c Tavare b Ellison | 67 |
| *6 P. R. Downton | c Cowdrey b Jarvis | 40 |
| 7 J. E. Emburey | not out | 17 |
| 8 P. H. Edmonds | not out | 5 |
| 9 S. P. Hughes | | |
| 10 N. G. Cowans | | |
| 11 W. W. Daniel | | |

B , l-b 7, w 1, n-b 2, ... 10

Total... 236

#### FALL OF THE WICKETS
1...39 2...60 3...88 4...124 5...211 6...217 7... 8... 9... 10...

| Bowling Analysis | O. | M. | R. | W. | Wd. | N-b |
|---|---|---|---|---|---|---|
| Alderman | 12 | 0 | 53 | 0 | ... | ... |
| Jarvis | 12 | 1 | 47 | 3 | ... | ... |
| Ellison | 12 | 2 | 53 | 2 | ... | ... |
| Cowdrey | 12 | 1 | 48 | 0 | 1 | ... |
| Underwood | 12 | 2 | 25 | 1 | ... | 2 |

## FLETCHER'S CUSSED WILL
### SEASON ENDING SEPTEMBER 12

E SSEX are the champions. With one ball of the season left, Mike Bore was caught at long-off as he tried to strike the boundary which would have given Notts the title. It was a dramatic end and an emotional one; for Rice had lifted his team to the very edge of victory with a brave 98. Four boundary catches were taken, four other men were stumped and finally

Clive Rice shows his disappointment at being caught out within sight of the Championship.

Nottinghamshire were beaten. They were game to the end and, though Rice made no excuses, he must have regretted the injuries to Such, Saxelby and Hendrick and the feebleness of Essex's opponents in August.

Nevertheless, it was a magnificent scrap and Essex are worthy champions. They owe much to Lever's persistence, to Gooch's buccaneering innings and to Fletcher's cussed will. His team won both leagues, the first time this double has been achieved, a testimony to the consistency of a team which had for years seemed doomed to wrestle with its brittle brilliance.

## FINAL BRITANNIC ASSURANCE CHAMPIONSHIP TABLE

| | P | W | L | D | Tie | Bt | Bg | Pts |
|---|---|---|---|---|---|---|---|---|
| Essex (1) | 24 | 13 | 3 | 8 | 0 | 64 | 83 | 355 |
| Nottinghamshire (14) | 24 | 12 | 3 | 9 | 0 | 68 | 81 | 341 |
| Middlesex (2) | 24 | 8 | 7 | 9 | 0 | 63 | 78 | 269 |
| Leicestershire (4) | 24 | 8 | 2 | 14 | 0 | 60 | 78 | 266 |
| Kent (7) | 24 | 8 | 3 | 11 | 2 | 45 | 65 | 254 |
| Sussex (11) | 24 | 7 | 6 | 10 | 1 | 54 | 79 | 249 |
| Somerset (10) | 24 | 6 | 7 | 11 | 0 | 60 | 78 | 234 |
| Surrey (8) | 24 | 6 | 6 | 12 | 0 | 62 | 72 | 230 |
| Warwickshire (5) | 24 | 6 | 7 | 11 | 0 | 71 | 60 | 227 |
| Worcestershire (16) | 24 | 5 | 5 | 14 | 0 | 66 | 74 | 220 |
| Derbyshire (9) | 24 | 4 | 6 | 14 | 0 | 72 | 66 | 202 |
| Northamptonshire (6) | 24 | 5 | 9 | 9 | 1 | 58 | 56 | 202 |
| Glamorgan (15) | 24 | 4 | 2 | 18 | 0 | 65 | 71 | 200 |
| Yorkshire (17) | 24 | 5 | 4 | 15 | 0 | 59 | 55 | 194 |
| Hampshire (3) | 24 | 3 | 13 | 8 | 0 | 58 | 62 | 168 |
| Lancashire (13) | 24 | 1 | 9 | 14 | 0 | 49 | 72 | 137 |
| Gloucestershire (12) | 24 | 1 | 10 | 13 | 0 | 56 | 61 | 133 |

Sussex total includes 12 pts for a win in a match reduced to one innings.
PRIZE MONEY: Essex £15,000; Notts £7,500; Middlesex £3,500; Leicestershire £1,750.

## FIRST CLASS AVERAGES

### BATTING
(Qualifications: 8 innings, average 10.00)
* not out

| | M | INO | HS | R | Avge | 100 | 50 |
|---|---|---|---|---|---|---|---|
| M. W. Gatting | 24 | 43 | 10 | 258 | 2257 | 68.39 | 8 | 10 |
| P. W. Denning | 5 | 8 | 3 | 90 | 338 | 67.60 | — | 3 |
| G. A. Gooch | 26 | 45 | 7 | 227 | 2559 | 67.34 | 8 | 13 |
| Javed Miandad | 8 | 15 | 2 | 212* | 832 | 64.00 | 2 | 3 |
| G. Boycott | 20 | 35 | 10 | 153* | 1567 | 62.68 | 4 | 9 |
| J. G. Wright | 12 | 21 | 1 | 177 | 1201 | 60.05 | 2 | 9 |
| D. L. Amiss | 26 | 50 | 10 | 122 | 2239 | 55.97 | 6 | 14 |
| M. D. Crowe | 25 | 41 | 6 | 190 | 1870 | 53.42 | 6 | 11 |
| V. J. Marks | 24 | 34 | 10 | 134 | 1262 | 52.58 | 3 | 6 |
| A. I. Kallicharran | 26 | 50 | 6 | 200* | 2301 | 52.29 | 9 | 7 |
| R. J. Hadlee | 24 | 31 | 8 | 210* | 1179 | 51.26 | 2 | 7 |
| R. T. Robinson | 27 | 47 | 7 | 171 | 2032 | 50.80 | 5 | 11 |
| P. Johnson | 10 | 14 | 1 | 133 | 647 | 49.76 | 2 | 3 |
| T. A. Lloyd | 8 | 14 | 2 | 110 | 590 | 49.16 | 2 | 4 |
| C. E. B. Rice | 24 | 39 | 7 | 152* | 1553 | 48.53 | 3 | 6 |
| G. W. Humpage | 26 | 47 | 8 | 205 | 1891 | 48.48 | 5 | 9 |
| V. P. Terry | 16 | 28 | 3 | 175* | 1208 | 48.32 | 5 | 6 |
| R. A. Smith | 7 | 13 | 3 | 132 | 483 | 48.30 | 1 | 2 |
| P. A. Neale | 25 | 43 | 7 | 143 | 1706 | 47.38 | 2 | 11 |
| P. M. Roebuck | 24 | 37 | 1 | 159 | 1702 | 47.27 | 7 | 4 |
| P. W. G. Parker | 26 | 40 | 4 | 181 | 1692 | 47.00 | 6 | 6 |
| K. S. McEwan | 27 | 44 | 6 | 142* | 1755 | 46.18 | 4 | 10 |
| K. J. Barnett | 24 | 41 | 3 | 144 | 1734 | 45.63 | 6 | 9 |
| B. C. Broad | 23 | 40 | 5 | 108* | 1549 | 44.25 | 1 | 13 |
| Younis Ahmed | 21 | 35 | 4 | 158* | 1369 | 44.16 | 2 | 9 |
| J. Derrick | 10 | 15 | 7 | 69* | 351 | 43.87 | — | 3 |
| D. L. Haynes | 13 | 18 | 1 | 125 | 743 | 43.70 | 2 | 5 |
| C. M. Wells | 26 | 39 | 7 | 203 | 1389 | 43.40 | 5 | 4 |
| G. S. Clinton | 19 | 28 | 6 | 192 | 948 | 43.09 | 2 | 5 |
| W. N. Slack | 25 | 46 | 8 | 145 | 1631 | 42.92 | 4 | 6 |
| Kapil Dev | 12 | 19 | 4 | 95 | 640 | 42.66 | — | 6 |
| T. S. Curtis | 22 | 36 | 3 | 129 | 1405 | 42.57 | 3 | 8 |
| D. M. Smith | 17 | 31 | 5 | 189* | 1093 | 42.03 | 2 | 5 |
| D. R. Turner | 20 | 37 | 4 | 153 | 1365 | 41.36 | 3 | 7 |
| D. W. Randall | 25 | 40 | 3 | 136 | 1528 | 41.29 | 3 | 12 |
| T. E. Jesty | 25 | 44 | 4 | 248 | 1625 | 40.62 | 5 | 4 |
| J. W. Lloyds | 20 | 30 | 10 | 113* | 812 | 40.60 | 1 | 5 |
| A. J. Lamb | 18 | 34 | 4 | 133* | 1209 | 40.30 | 5 | 5 |
| R. O. Butcher | 23 | 40 | 7 | 116 | 1326 | 40.18 | 2 | 10 |
| P. E. Robinson | 15 | 24 | 5 | 92 | 756 | 39.78 | — | 4 |
| T. J. Boon | 21 | 37 | 6 | 144 | 1233 | 39.77 | 4 | 4 |
| G. Cook | 22 | 43 | 4 | 102 | 1539 | 39.46 | 2 | 9 |
| R. D. V. Knight | 21 | 35 | 3 | 142 | 1254 | 39.18 | 3 | 4 |
| K. Sharp | 24 | 39 | 2 | 173 | 1445 | 39.05 | 3 | 8 |
| R. A. Woolmer | 8 | 14 | 3 | 153 | 427 | 38.81 | 1 | 2 |
| M. A. Lynch | 25 | 41 | 1 | 144 | 1546 | 38.65 | 4 | 8 |

### BOWLING
(Qualification: 10 wickets in 10 innings)

| | O | M | R | W | Avge | Best | 5wI |
|---|---|---|---|---|---|---|---|
| R. J. Hadlee | 772.2 | 245 | 1645 | 117 | 14.05 | 7-35 | 6 |
| R. A. Harper | 314.1 | 109 | 676 | 37 | 18.27 | 6-57 | 3 |
| P. J. W. Allott | 604.5 | 171 | 1496 | 79 | 18.93 | 7-72 | 6 |
| D. L. Underwood | 676.4 | 250 | 1511 | 77 | 19.62 | 8-87 | 2 |
| T. M. Tremlett | 669.5 | 209 | 1444 | 71 | 20.33 | 5-48 | 2 |
| A. Sidebottom | 488.1 | 105 | 1292 | 63 | 20.50 | 6-41 | 3 |
| G. S. le Roux | 604.2 | 154 | 1647 | 78 | 21.11 | 6-57 | 2 |
| S. T. Clarke | 651.1 | 165 | 1687 | 78 | 21.62 | 6-62 | 2 |
| N. G. Cowans | 693.1 | 76 | 1593 | 73 | 21.82 | 6-64 | 2 |
| J. K. Lever | 874.5 | 195 | 2550 | 116 | 21.98 | 8-37 | 8 |
| N. E. Briers | 109 | 24 | 264 | 12 | 22.00 | 3-48 | — |
| P. M. Such | 386.5 | 122 | 937 | 42 | 22.30 | 5-34 | 2 |
| G. A. Gooch | 321.1 | 75 | 850 | 38 | 22.36 | 4-54 | — |
| R. M. Ellison | 535.5 | 142 | 1323 | 59 | 22.42 | 5-27 | 1 |
| M. J. Weston | 123.4 | 49 | 315 | 14 | 22.50 | 4-44 | — |
| T. M. Alderman | 559.4 | 149 | 1725 | 76 | 22.69 | 5-25 | 3 |
| A. M. E. Roberts | 265 | 70 | 769 | 33 | 23.30 | 7-74 | 3 |
| Kapil Dev | 296.3 | 75 | 819 | 35 | 23.40 | 5-30 | 2 |
| E. E. Hemmings | 797.5 | 234 | 2220 | 94 | 23.61 | 7-47 | 7 |
| C. M. Wells | 497.2 | 146 | 1396 | 59 | 23.66 | 5-25 | 2 |
| M. R. Davis | 500.4 | 108 | 1569 | 66 | 23.77 | 7-55 | 4 |
| N. A. Foster | 687.1 | 148 | 2098 | 87 | 24.11 | 6-79 | 4 |
| R. M. Ellcock | 221.2 | 32 | 714 | 29 | 24.62 | 4-34 | — |
| K. B. S. Jarvis | 570.5 | 128 | 1788 | 72 | 24.83 | 5-30 | 2 |
| A. N. Jones | 208.1 | 44 | 636 | 25 | 25.44 | 5-29 | 1 |
| C. E. Waller | 610.3 | 221 | 1349 | 53 | 25.45 | 6-75 | 1 |
| G. Monkhouse | 459.5 | 120 | 1273 | 50 | 25.46 | 4-41 | — |
| P. B. Clift | 620.1 | 165 | 1608 | 63 | 25.52 | 8-26 | 2 |
| G. Miller | 897.2 | 257 | 2236 | 87 | 25.70 | 6-30 | 6 |
| P. I. Pocock | 638.5 | 169 | 1621 | 63 | 25.73 | 7-74 | 3 |
| D. A. Reeve | 572.4 | 175 | 1420 | 55 | 25.81 | 5-22 | 1 |
| V. J. Marks | 808 | 226 | 2233 | 86 | 25.96 | 8-141 | 5 |
| J. Simmons | 619.4 | 177 | 1644 | 63 | 26.09 | 7-176 | 7 |
| S. R. Barwick | 477.4 | 128 | 1314 | 50 | 26.28 | 7-38 | 2 |
| I. T. Botham | 449.4 | 93 | 1562 | 59 | 26.47 | 8-103 | 4 |
| K. E. Cooper | 623.2 | 217 | 1364 | 51 | 26.74 | 8-44 | 1 |
| N. Phillip | 275.2 | 48 | 911 | 34 | 26.79 | 5-48 | 1 |
| W. W. Daniel | 462 | 86 | 1463 | 54 | 27.09 | 4-53 | — |
| P. H. Edmonds | 823.3 | 233 | 2096 | 77 | 27.22 | 8-53 | 2 |
| J. F. Steele | 673 | 175 | 1867 | 68 | 27.45 | 5-42 | 4 |
| J. E. Emburey | 865.3 | 255 | 1978 | 72 | 27.47 | 5-94 | 1 |
| D. J. Thomas | 505.4 | 114 | 1654 | 60 | 27.56 | 6-36 | 2 |
| W. W. Davis | 547.5 | 118 | 1725 | 62 | 27.82 | 5-32 | 4 |
| D. R. Pringle | 580.1 | 127 | 1784 | 64 | 27.87 | 7-53 | 3 |
| A. M. Ferreira | 772.1 | 156 | 2208 | 79 | 27.94 | 6-70 | 1 |
| L. L. McFarlane | 272.5 | 45 | 875 | 31 | 28.22 | 4-65 | — |
| J. R. T. Barclay | 417 | 117 | 1023 | 36 | 28.41 | 4-32 | — |

*England did indeed begin afresh. Their tour of India could not have started more miserably, with India's President, Mrs Gandhi, assassinated in Delhi a few hours after their arrival in the Indian capital and the British High Commissioner also assassinated, in a totally unrelated yet bizarre incident, on the eve of the First Test in Bombay. That match was lost but David Gower's side put the run of defeats behind them with a victory at Delhi and went on to take the series by two matches to one. In Madras, indeed, they won with a real flourish: a pitch with a rare amount of reliable bounce (rare, that is, by the standards of modern Test pitches all round the world) brought out the best in Fowler and Gatting, who both made double hundreds, while Neil Foster excelled himself with 11 wickets.*

*Part of England's success was due to personality. Gower was able to settle down as captain without the outsize shadow of Ian Botham hanging over him and Mike Gatting emerged for the first time in England colours as the dominating batsman all knew him to be. On the other side, India did not play to their full potential, Kapil Dev and Patil at one stage being dropped for a less than responsible attitude and Gavaskar clearly wearying of the internal politics of the game. Yet he recovered enough to lead his men to a most convincing victory in the spurious "World Championship of Cricket" held in Melbourne and Sydney to celebrate the 150th anniversary of the State of Victoria. It is not denigrating India's achievement to wonder what will be the next reason for a World Championship in Australia – the anniversary of the planting of the first tree in the Nullarbor Plain?*

*New Zealand had the busiest winter of all. First they journeyed to Pakistan and lost an ill-tempered series two-nil, without their great all-rounder, Richard Hadlee. Then, at home, they turned the tables with a two-nil victory over the same opposition. Pausing to play in the so-called World Championship, they then travelled to West Indies and, predictably enough, were well beaten. The novelty here, however, was that Clive Lloyd had finally retired from Test cricket, leaving Viv Richards to assume the purple. His Empire was still the strongest, world championships or not.*

# — 1985 —

*Alan Gibson was to have returned as diarist for 1985 but intermittent illness throughout the summer prevented him from maintaining the necessary flow. Peter Roebuck returned to fill the breach with his memories of the season supplemented by a summary of the 1985 highlights.*

JUMPING out of the bath to answer the telephone, hearing our beloved editor asking for a quick piece about the season. Jumping back into the bath, terrific washing of hair (time, though, for conditioner – did Albert Lightfoot condition his hair?) and then pencil and paper. Memories of 1985? They do not rush down the hill, charging over the stones, driving the writer to remember. We won the Ashes, it is true, but I was not involved in that, did not see a ball bowled except on television and then usually on the news. Can Australia really have bowled so many half-volleys on leg-stump? People say there are many more bad balls bowled these days. Why are none of them bowled to me? Heavens, I stay in long enough. Batted for 70 hours this season. Faced 747 balls against Worcestershire. Hardly a half-volley on leg-stump among them. Or is it something we are doing wrong?

First memory is of sitting up until four in the morning watching Bob Geldof's rock concert, waiting for Mick Jagger and Bob Dylan. Opened the batting next day, hardly able to pick the bat up. Turned out to be one of Viv's. Swopped bats but it made no difference. Out cheaply, and then it rained. Most of the time it rained, leaving in the cricketer the nagging question "And shall I have to bat?"

Second memory is of Derek Randall, facing Pringle and the match lost. Eighteen needed in one over. I'd been reading all day – something about Robespierre – and had avoided the drama. Turned on the television and there it was, 45 needed in four overs. Then 18 in six balls. Well, it's all over now. Fletcher is too straight at mid-off. Wham, boundary to his left. Randall is an off-side player, yet every one is deep and to leg. Pringle, a lovely fellow but as difficult to rouse as a slumbering lion, angles the ball into the pads, Randall steps back and guides it to the Tavern. Hope renewed.

Suddenly the game is in the bag. Last ball, two to win. Last ball; two to win? Same thing in 1984, for the Championship that time, Fletcher chats to Pringle. Is he saying "Don't bowl a no-ball" in the manner of Sir Frank Worrell? Is he changing tactics or saying "at the toes" once more? Maybe he's telling Pringle he'll have to marry if Essex lose. Pringle fires to leg. Randall, unswerving, backs away and finds the ball on his pads and, in a tangle, pops it to Prichard at mid-wicket. Another extraordinary final at Lord's, another great victory for Essex. How do they manage it with all those old faithfuls?

*Someone up there must have an account with the NatWest – this was the third last-ball victory in five years under their sponsorship.*

## IMPRESSIVE AUSTRALIANS

ANOTHER memory, the Australians at Taunton. Lawson, Thomson and McDermott were very impressive, very fast. Hilditch was caught at long-leg, and cursed as he played the shot. Border off the mark with a six into the graveyard. At Lord's, the game in the balance, with Botham walking around reminding

Craig McDermott (far left) – new spearhead of the Australian attack, and Ian Botham – at his most aggressive against the Australians.

everyone of 1981, it was Border who saw his team to victory. He's had two hard series, this staunch captain. His bowlers lacked variety and his batsmen lost their wickets too easily. Gower purred like a cat sipping a bowl of milk, Botham raged, goading every game into life. Edmonds, aristocratically amused by the whole thing, baited Border into a wild swipe. Emburey, arm pulling past his ear, grafting for his wickets.

And Graham Gooch, moustache bristling, not bumbling around but striding purposefully, striking the ball as if it contained the hypocrisies of the world. Gooch was a favourite. At Taunton he thumped 173*, seizing the game for his team, thrashing Botham's bumpers. Then, on a rare sunlit evening, his voice pitched as high as W. G.'s, he talked about his technique. He hits through the ball, and recognises his vulnerability on seaming pitches. He believes this method will bring him most runs, especially in the West Indies.

Can't sit on the splice there. Boycott used to defend magnificently for 90 minutes and then be caught at fourth slip for nine. Can't see any point in that. Might not go to the West Indies. Not necessarily a terrible blow. Lots of fast bowlers out there. Could sit in front of a fire, toasting toes.

## MARSHALL'S FINGER-CRUSHER

I broke a finger this season. Never done that before. Bumper from Malcolm Marshall crushed this finger. Trainer ran on, said it was dislocated, snapped it back and asked if I was okay. Carried on until Tremlett hit the off-stump. Then off to Dr Cutting for an x-ray. Broken. Out for a month. Slept in next morning, pottered to the ground, cup of coffee, leisurely lunch, good luck lads. Followed the scores on the radio. Went to see some friends in Athens. Bought a *Telegraph* every night at a kiosk down the road. Opened it immediately to see how Somerset were going on. Disturbed by the number of high scoring games I was missing. And what was the story behind those cold figures? Had Paul's lbw been out? How was Mark bowling? Better get back. "When are you going to be fit then?" Maybe I should have stayed.

Lovely chap, John Inchmore. In the bar we sat, two old-timers really, and he said he couldn't understand why I wasn't going to be picked for any of these tours. Scored 100 next day. Facing Inchmore, in he runs, thought passes: "This chap thinks I should be going to Bangladesh this winter."

Worcestershire had another fellow, Neal Radford, marvellous bowler. Top wicket-taker in the country. Not

at all surprised. Best new-ball bowler in the country on this year's form. Only chap to hurt me this year, hit on the arm by a bouncer. Still sore a week later. He hit Richards too. Richards strolled down the pitch, said he'd been hurt, said he wasn't going to show it and said he felt like giving a bit back in return; which he did.

I didn't play against "Syd" Lawrence but they say he's very fast. So is Gregory Thomas. He caught Botham one-handed in front of the river stand. So he's a cricketer too.

Two of England's fastest – David (Syd) Lawrence of Gloucestershire (far left) and Greg Thomas of Glamorgan.

Lovely September, after another cold spring. We're in The Parks again next April, muffled under sweaters, and yet October arrives and still the sun shines. Down the road two village teams are going to carry on playing each other until the weather turns. They've had so few warm days.

In our pub stands a trophy, for our team was runner-up in . . . well, no one quite knows what cup it was but the day had a Pickwickian feel to it for those who were there. I was in Manchester.

Lots of memories, despite the rain. Allan Border embracing David Gower as they left the field, with a century to his name. He meant it, too.

A few tragedies as well. Those dreadful days in Belgium and Bradford, sitting and hoping it never happens in cricket. A month later, a tense, bitter struggle at Taunton between Hampshire and Somerset, the very stuff of cricket. Crowd, packed into a small ground, cramped in their stands and shouting nastily. No, not the crowd, a dozen or so near the pavilion, who cared more about the result than the players. A little frightening, as play ended to see these dozen people jostle the umpires and groundsman.

And so it ends; McEwan and Popplewell have departed. A quiet season is over. Hampshire gave their all, playing with the hunger of the unfulfilled. Essex battled on, determined beneath their laughter. Somerset, for whom the score stood so often at 10 for two, rescued by Richards, who reached a fresh magnificence. We bowled our overs and scored more quickly than anyone else and still finished bottom. Middlesex took the Championship, and deservedly so for they missed half their men for most of the season. In

Viv Richards (far right) – yet more runs, and David Smith – promising power and aggression.

the West, Gloucestershire, cleverly collecting players, fought an outstanding campaign and Worcestershire improved sharply, too. They say that David Smith has thumped an opponent and a captain. He's just the sort of fellow we'll need in the West Indies. Anyone who cares that much, anyone who is that brave it's best to have in our side.

Finally, there were the wise words of R. E. S. Wyatt. He says: "The trick is to think you're not quite as good as you are." After all these years he has not forgotten.

### REVIEW OF THE SEASON
### APRIL

○ Channel Nine announce a scaling down of their plans for spectacular coverage of the Ashes series.

○ Laxman Sivaramakrishnan, man of the series for India against England, signs to play for Whalley in the Ribblesdale League.

○ Trevor Jesty joins Surrey from Hampshire.

○ Australia are forced to drop three players chosen to tour England because of their involvement with the unofficial tour to South Africa.

○ Sylvester Clark returns to The Oval from South Africa

Laxman Sivaramakrishnan – getting used to English conditions.

with a serious back complaint: Surrey begin negotiations to sign Anthony Gray from Trinidad.

○ Chris Tavaré hits three sixes in four balls in the course of a Britannic Championship century against Hampshire.

○ Alan Butcher hits the first Championship 100 of the season but Glamorgan beat Surrey to take an early lead in the table.

○ Norman Cowans takes six for 68 and Mark Nicholas and Martyn Moxon both make 100s for MCC against the champion county, Essex, at Lord's.

○ Yorkshire's members vote to make it impossible in future for a contracted player to be simultaneously a member of the committee.

### MAY

○ Viv Richards leads West Indies to success against New Zealand.

○ J. G. W. Davies is nominated by F. G. Mann as the next President of MCC.

○ Glamorgan are team of the month in the Championship and Paul Allott wins back his England place with 25 wickets in May.

○ The GLC criticise fire and safety precautions at Lord's and The Oval; Somerset close their old Pavilion at Taunton because it is deemed a fire hazard.

○ Graham Gooch hits 202 out of 297 for five in Essex's second innings against Nottinghamshire at Trent Bridge.

○ Chris Cowdrey scores a career-best 159 for Kent against Surrey.

○ Sussex bowl Glamorgan out for 58 (Imran Khan four wickets, Dermot Reeve five) and win despite a second innings 447 by Glamorgan with centuries by Steve Henderson and Rodney Ontong.

○ Tim Tremlett (102) and Kevan James (124) put on record 227 for Hampshire's eighth wicket against Somerset, who lose despite Ian Botham's 149 out of 193 with six sixes and 20 fours.

○ Essex, Derbyshire, Northants, Kent, Leicestershire, Hampshire, Worcestershire and Middlesex qualify for the quarter-finals of the Benson and Hedges Cup.

○ Allan Border hits four consecutive centuries in first-class matches.

○ Surrey and Warwickshire score 604 runs in 80 overs as Surrey win their John Player League match at The Oval by four runs.

Allan Border – warming up for the Test series.

○ Mark Nicholas and Allan Lamb score centuries for MCC against the Australians at Lord's.

### JUNE

○ Australia win the Texaco Trophy series by two matches to one, but at Lord's in the third match David Gower scores a century to end a dismal start to his season and Graham Gooch adds 117 not out to his earlier Texaco scores of 57 and 115.

○ Every seat is sold for all three of the one-day internationals and no one needs an umbrella.

○ Colin Cowdrey opens an indoor Cricket School at the National Sports Centre in Lilleshall.

○ Bill Frindall succeeds the late Gordon Ross as Editor of *The Cricketer Quarterly*.

○ Bernard Thomas announced his retirement from his post as England's physiotherapist after 17 years doing much more than merely bringing on a magic sponge.

Bernard Thomas gives Richard Ellison a helping hand.

○ England win the first Test at Headingley by five wickets . . . Tim Robinson's 175 eclipses Andrew Hilditch's 119 and Gatting, Botham and Downton all make 50 plus to lead England to their 12th highest total against Australia . . . Botham takes three wickets in four balls.

○ Ken McEwan announces his retirement from county cricket from the end of the season.

○ Raman Subba Row is appointed the successor to Charles Palmer as Chairman of the Test and County Cricket Board.

○ A bat used by Jack Hobbs when he broke W. G. Grace's record aggregate is sold at Phillips's auction for £1,338.

○ In the semi-finals of the Benson and Hedges Cup, Essex beat Middlesex at Chelmsford and Kent collapse and lose to Leicestershire by eight wickets at Grace Road.

○ Middlesex take the lead in the Britannic County Championship with Graham Barlow, Wilf Slack and Wayne Daniel all performing well in the absence of the county's Test players, Gloucestershire's David Lawrence and Courtney Walsh bowl out Derbyshire for 82 at Derby in only 24 overs.

○ Viv Richards scores 322 off 258 balls in 294 minutes on the first day of the month for Somerset against Warwickshire at Taunton. But Somerset are unable to bowl Warwickshire out twice.

○ Richard Ellison returns to the Kent side after injury, David Gower returns to form for Leicestershire and Geoff Boycott averages 102 in the Championship for Yorkshire in June.

○ P. G. H. Fender (92) and Len Hopwood (81) pass to more exalted fields.

### JULY

○ Australia win the Second Test at Lord's by four wickets . . . Border makes 196 after being "caught" momentarily between Gatting's legs when 87 . . . McDermott takes six for 70 in England's first innings (Gower 86), Holland takes five for 68 in the second (Botham 85, Gatting 75 not out).

The decisive moment at Lord's as Mike Gatting dives in a vain attempt to retrieve the ball as Border turns to the pavilion.

○ Leicestershire (Peter Willey 86 not out, Les Taylor three for 26) beat Essex by five wickets in the Benson and Hedges Cup Final.

○ Allan Border signs a two-year contract with Essex,

Simon O'Donnell scores the winning run at Lord's to the delight of the Australian balcony.

starting in 1986.

◯ Jon Agnew earns a recall for England with figures of nine for 70 against Kent.

◯ The Australian Cricket Board and the South African Cricket Union announce an out of court settlement by which the SACU were enabled to go ahead with the staging of an unofficial series against Australia later this year provided no further attempts were made to poach players contracted to the ACB.

◯ Graham Dilley (Kent v. Surrey), Paddy Clift (Leicestershire v. Derbyshire), Tony Gray (Surrey v. Yorkshire) and Paul Jarvis (Yorkshire v. Derbyshire) all perform hat-tricks in the County Championship.

◯ Johnny Wardle dies at 62.

◯ Ian Botham scores a century off 50 balls against Warwickshire.

◯ England's 456 (Gower 166) in the Third Cornhill Test at Trent Bridge is countered by Australia's 539 (Wood 172, Ritchie 146) and the game is drawn.

◯ Kent make the running in the John Player League . . . Middlesex continue to lead the Championship with Gloucestershire and Hampshire in hot pursuit.

◯ Geoff Boycott (189) and Martyn Moxon (168) share an opening partnership of 351 against Worcestershire . . . Javed Miandad and Younis Ahmed, both Pakistan born, add 306 for Glamorgan's fourth wicket against the Australians at Neath, the highest stand for any team in Britain against the Australians outside Test cricket.

◯ Oxford have much the better of a drawn university

match as Giles Toogood makes 149 and takes 10 of the 13 Cambridge wickets to fall.

### *University Cricket Match*

# Toogood, 149, has field day

### *By A. S. R. WINLAW at Lord's*

GILES TOOGOOD followed his remarkable best bowling return of eight for 52 in the first innings by hitting ...

◯ David East takes eight catches in the nine Somerset wickets to fall against Essex in the Championship match at Taunton. Graham Gooch's 173 not out in the same match gives Essex a crushing victory despite Ian Botham's 152 scored out of 195 whilst at the wicket.

### *AUGUST/SEPTEMBER*

◯ Australia, helped considerably by rain, draw the Fourth Test at Old Trafford thanks to Allan Border's 146 after England (Gatting 160) had led by 225 on first innings.

◯ Wilf Slack scores a double hundred and Keith Brown a maiden hundred for Middlesex against a fast waning Australian touring team.

◯ As the pace increases for the remaining county prizes, uneasiness becomes apparent at various counties – Yorkshire talk again of hiring overseas players, Nick Cook, Mike Garnham and Gordon Parsons all leave Leicestershire, Graham Johnson departs Kent in unhappy circumstances and the Lancashire coaching staff are reminded that their contracts are not permanent.

◯ England beat Australia by an innings at both Edgbaston and The Oval to regain the Ashes with a real flourish. At Edgbaston Richard Ellison takes six for 70 and four for 27; David Gower scores 215, Tim Robinson 148 and Mike Gatting 100 not out. At The Oval it only takes three-and-a-half days after Gower (157) and Gooch (196, his maiden Test hundred against Australia) have put on 351 in unaccustomed sunshine on a hard, true pitch. Ellison takes seven more wickets, Botham catches anything that moves and, despite a sore toe and a suspect

Tim Robinson – setting up a win for England at Edgbaston.

knee, takes his tally to 31 wickets in the series. Now he plans to walk from John o' Groats to Land's End – then across the sea to Hollywood?

Richard Ellison captures the vital wicket of Allan Border at Edgbaston.

◐ Freuchie win the National Village Championship, Oundle Rovers *The Cricketer* Cup and Old Hill the William Younger Club Knockout.

◐ In a thrilling end to the Championship, Hampshire take the lead by the end of August, with Gloucestershire still hanging on up the final furlong and Middlesex poised to make a late challenge. In the end it is Middlesex, despite a frustrating failure to beat Essex after bowling them out for 92 – Gooch, of course, making a second innings century – who take the title on the season's final day. For Hampshire and Gloucestershire it is a case of "if only" . . . neither have much luck with the weather and Hampshire's season at Southampton ends typically with one wicket needed for victory off the final ball, which is duly hit for six by Harper to give Northants a win instead. Can Northants be champions in 1986 for the first time?

Wayne Daniel bowls Norman Gifford as Middlesex beat Warwickshire to take the County Championship.

◐ The NatWest Final again has the nation on the edge of its seat as Notts need two off the last ball to beat Essex. Randall dies gloriously, Essex have the first leg of a

Ken McEwan (left) with Keith Fletcher and the John Player League trophy at the end of his final season for Essex.

NatWest/John Player double and everyone wonders at how a summer with so much miserable weather could provide us all with so much marvellous entertainment.

# NatWest Bank Trophy Final
## ESSEX v. NOTTINGHAMSHIRE

**20p** **20p**

at Lord's Ground, †Saturday, September 7th, 1985

| ESSEX | | |
|---|---|---|
| 1 G. A. Gooch | b Pick | 91 |
| 2 B. R. Hardie | run out | 110 |
| 3 K. S. McEwan | not out | 46 |
| 4 D. R. Pringle | not out | 29 |
| 5 P. J. Prichard | | |
| ‡6 K. W. R. Fletcher | | |
| 7 A. W. Lilley | | |
| *8 D. E. East | | |
| 9 S. Turner | | |
| 10 I. L. Pont | | |
| 11 J. K. Lever | | |
| | B 1, l-b 3, w , n-b , | ... 4 |
| | | Total... 280 |

FALL OF THE WICKETS

1...202 2...203 3... 4... 5... 6... 7... 8... 9... 10...

| Bowling Analysis | O. | M. | R. | W. | Wd. | N-b |
|---|---|---|---|---|---|---|
| Hadlee | 12 | 4 | 48 | 0 | ... | ... |
| Cooper | 9 | 3 | 27 | 0 | ... | ... |
| Saxelby | 12 | 0 | 73 | 0 | ... | ... |
| Rice | 7 | 0 | 38 | 0 | ... | ... |
| Pick | 8 | 0 | 36 | 1 | ... | ... |
| Hemmings | 12 | 1 | 64 | 0 | ... | ... |

| NOTTINGHAMSHIRE | | |
|---|---|---|
| 1 B. C. Broad | run out | 64 |
| 2 R. T. Robinson | c Hardie b Turner | 80 |
| ‡3 C. E. B. Rice | c Hardie b Turner | 12 |
| 4 D. W. Randall | c Prichard b Pringle | 66 |
| 5 R. J. Hadlee | b Pont | 22 |
| 6 D. J. R. Martindale | not out | 20 |
| *7 B. N. French | | |
| 8 E. E. Hemmings | | |
| 9 R. A. Pick | | |
| 10 K. Saxelby | | |
| 11 K. E. Cooper | | |
| | B , l-b 14 , w , n-b 1, | ... 15 |
| | | Total... 279 |

FALL OF THE WICKETS

1...143 2...153 3...173 4...214 5...279 6... 7... 8... 9... 10...

| Bowling Analysis | O. | M. | R. | W. | Wd. | N-b |
|---|---|---|---|---|---|---|
| Lever | 12 | 2 | 53 | 0 | ... | ... |
| Pont | 12 | 0 | 54 | 1 | ... | 1 |
| Turner | 12 | 1 | 43 | 2 | ... | ... |
| Gooch | 12 | 0 | 47 | 0 | ... | ... |
| Pringle | 12 | 1 | 68 | 1 | ... | ... |

**Any alterations to teams will be announced over the public address system**

RULES—1 The Match will consist of one innings per side and each innings is limited to 60 overs.

2 No one bowler may bowl more than 12 overs in an innings.

3 Hours of play : 10.30 a.m. to 7.10 p.m. In certain circumstances the Umpires may order extra time.

Luncheon Interval 12.45 p.m.—1.25 p.m.      Tea Interval will be 20 minutes and will normally be taken at 4.30 p.m.

‡Captain      *Wicket-keeper

Umpires—D. J. Constant & B. J. Meyer      Scorers—C. F. Driver, L. Beaumont & E. Solomon

†This match is intended to be completed in one day, but three days have been allocated in case of weather interference

## BRITANNIC ASSURANCE COUNTY CHAMPIONSHIP 1985 — FINAL TABLE

Win — 16 points*

| | P | W | L | D | Bonus Pts Btg | Blg | Total |
|---|---|---|---|---|---|---|---|
| 1 MIDDLESEX (3) | 24 | 8 | 4 | 12 | 61 | 85 | 274 |
| 2 Hampshire (15) | 24 | 7 | 2 | 15 | 66 | 78 | 256 |
| 3 Gloucestershire (17) | 23 | 7 | 3 | 13 | 51 | 78 | 241 |
| 4 Essex (1) | 23 | 7 | 2 | 14 | 42 | 70 | 224 |
| 5 Worcestershire (10) | 24 | 5 | 6 | 13 | 65 | 68 | 221 |
| 6 Surrey (8) | 24 | 5 | 5 | 14 | 62 | 76 | 218 |
| 7 Sussex (6) | 23 | 6 | 1 | 16 | 52 | 57 | 205 |
| 8 Nottinghamshire (2) | 24 | 4 | 2 | 18 | 66 | 69 | 199 |
| 9 Kent (5) | 24 | 4 | 5 | 15 | 51 | 71 | 186 |
| 10 Northamptonshire (11) | 24 | 5 | 4 | 15 | 52 | 51 | 183 |
| 11 Yorkshire (14) | 23 | 3 | 4 | 16 | 58 | 59 | 165 |
| 12 Glamorgan (13) | 24 | 4 | 4 | 16 | 41 | 50 | 163 |
| 13 Derbyshire (12) | 24 | 3 | 9 | 12 | 46 | 69 | 163 |
| 14 Lancashire (16) | 24 | 3 | 7 | 14 | 44 | 67 | 159 |
| 15 Warwickshire (9) | 24 | 2 | 8 | 14 | 47 | 74 | 153 |
| 16 Leicestershire (4) | 24 | 2 | 3 | 19 | 48 | 65 | 145 |
| 17 Somerset (7) | 24 | 1 | 7 | 16 | 70 | 45 | 131 |

*1984 final positions are shown in brackets*

*The totals for Worcestershire and Glamorgan include eight points for levelling the scores in drawn matches. Where sides are equal on points, the one with the most wins has priority

The following two matches were abandoned and are not included in the above table May 22, 23, 24 — Yorkshire v Essex at Sheffield. June 22, 24, 25 — Gloucestershire v Sussex at Bristol

## BATTING
(Qualification: 8 innings)

| | M | I | NO | HS | Runs | Avge | 100s | 50s |
|---|---|---|---|---|---|---|---|---|
| I V A Richards | 19 | 24 | 0 | 322 | 1,836 | 76.50 | 9 | 6 |
| G Boycott | 21 | 34 | 12 | 184 | 1,657 | 75.31 | 6 | 9 |
| G A Gooch | 21 | 33 | 2 | 202 | 2,208 | 71.22 | 7 | 9 |
| I T Botham | 19 | 27 | 5 | 152 | 1,530 | 69.54 | 5 | 9 |
| Imran Khan | 14 | 21 | 8 | 117* | 890 | 68.46 | 1 | 6 |
| Younis Ahmed | 22 | 30 | 8 | 177 | 1,421 | 64.59 | 5 | 4 |
| Javed Miandad | 20 | 29 | 6 | 200* | 1,441 | 62.65 | 4 | 8 |
| R T Robinson | 18 | 31 | 4 | 175 | 1,619 | 59.96 | 6 | 9 |
| C L Smith | 23 | 39 | 4 | 143* | 2,000 | 57.14 | 7 | 11 |
| J G Wright | 11 | 16 | 2 | 177* | 797 | 56.92 | 2 | 4 |
| M W Gatting | 23 | 34 | 5 | 160 | 1,650 | 56.89 | 3 | 13 |
| P Bainbridge | 24 | 38 | 9 | 151* | 1,644 | 56.68 | 4 | 11 |
| C E B Rice | 20 | 33 | 8 | 171* | 1,394 | 55.76 | 4 | 6 |
| D I Gower | 21 | 29 | 2 | 215 | 1,477 | 54.70 | 6 | 3 |
| W N Slack | 26 | 43 | 8 | 201* | 1,900 | 54.28 | 4 | 11 |
| D W Randall | 25 | 47 | 7 | 117 | 2,151 | 53.77 | 5 | 14 |
| M A Lynch | 25 | 39 | 7 | 145 | 1,714 | 53.56 | 7 | 6 |
| C T Radley | 27 | 38 | 12 | 200 | 1,375 | 52.88 | 3 | 8 |
| G A Hick | 17 | 25 | 1 | 230 | 1,265 | 52.70 | 4 | 3 |
| D A Thorne | 12 | 20 | 3 | 124 | 849 | 49.94 | 1 | 8 |

## BOWLING
(Qualification: 10 wickets in 10 innings)

| | O | M | R | W | Avge | Best | 5wI |
|---|---|---|---|---|---|---|---|
| R M Ellison | 432.1 | 113 | 1,118 | 65 | 17.20 | 7-87 | 5 |
| R J Hadlee | 473.5 | 136 | 1,026 | 59 | 17.38 | 8-41 | 2 |
| M D Marshall | 698.1 | 193 | 1,680 | 95 | 17.68 | 7-59 | 5 |
| G E Sainsbury | 178.0 | 59 | 481 | 27 | 17.81 | 7-38 | 2 |
| C A Walsh | 560.3 | 132 | 1,706 | 85 | 20.07 | 7-51 | 4 |
| Imran Khan | 422.1 | 114 | 1,040 | 51 | 20.39 | 5-49 | 2 |
| T M Tremlett | 665.5 | 181 | 1,620 | 75 | 21.60 | 5-42 | 2 |
| Kapil Dev | 304.5 | 83 | 805 | 37 | 21.75 | 4-56 | 0 |
| M A Holding | 354.5 | 67 | 1,124 | 50 | 22.48 | 6-65 | 3 |
| P J W Allott | 560.2 | 167 | 1,328 | 58 | 22.89 | 6-71 | 3 |
| L B Taylor | 566.5 | 141 | 1,376 | 60 | 22.93 | 5-45 | 3 |
| N G Cowans | 474.2 | 85 | 1,676 | 73 | 22.95 | 6-31 | 6 |
| A H Gray | 524.0 | 99 | 1,816 | 79 | 22.98 | 8-40 | 6 |
| K M Curran | 469.5 | 104 | 1,419 | 61 | 23.26 | 5-35 | 2 |
| J Garner | 295.4 | 76 | 739 | 31 | 23.83 | 5-46 | 1 |
| D V Lawrence | 544.5 | 66 | 2,093 | 85 | 24.62 | 7-48 | 5 |
| N V Radford | 779.4 | 130 | 2,493 | 101 | 24.68 | 6-45 | 4 |
| D A Graveney | 410.1 | 133 | 1,013 | 41 | 24.70 | 4-91 | 0 |
| R J Doughty | 223.5 | 36 | 867 | 34 | 25.50 | 6-33 | 1 |
| P H Edmonds | 850.1 | 243 | 1,942 | 76 | 25.55 | 6-87 | 2 |

The true worth of England's eventually comfortable victory in the 1985 Ashes series was put to the acid test when David Gower's side travelled to the Caribbean after Christmas and confronted the ultimate test of cricketing courage and skill: a Test series against the West Indies. Even before the First Test their hopes of maintaining the most settled batting combination they had had for years was shattered, literally, when Mike Gatting's nose was broken as he hooked and missed at a bouncer from Malcolm Marshall during the opening one day international at Sabina Park.

England were unfortunate to begin the series on a fast, unreliable wicket and the fearsome quartet of fast bowlers fully lived up to their reputation in demolishing England twice within three days, neither England innings lasting even for 50 overs. The quartet, in fact, had a new member, the tall, long-armed Jamaican Patrick Patterson, who bowled at a ferocious pace in his first Test match and took seven for 73.

In other respects England's worst fears about the tour were not fulfilled. Only when the West Indies Cricket Board had achieved agreement by all the Caribbean Governments concerned, excepting only the Marxist State of Guyana, was the tour given a green light on the grounds that all the England players selected would be welcomed. There were nonetheless, threats of demonstrations against several of the England team who had at various times been to coach and play in South Africa, notably by union leaders in Trinidad, and such was the enormous publicity they received in advance that the mild protests, made by no more than a few hundred determined but disciplined demonstrators when the team actually arrived in Port of Spain, were anti-climactic.

Elsewhere in the 1985–86 winter attention was focussed mainly on Australia, where the still inexperienced home team were beaten by a New Zealand side captained by Jeremy Coney and inspired by Richard Hadlee who took 33 wickets in three Tests, and claimed his 300th Test wicket in a successful return series with Australia soon afterwards. In between, Australia were fortunate to draw a three-Test series against India. The other main theatre of action was Sri Lanka where some more gifted young players emerged in matches against an England "B" touring team and, later, Pakistan. England's "B" tour had also been scheduled to take in Zimbabwe and Bangladesh but deplorable eleventh-hour intervention by the Governments of the two third-world countries prevented these parts of the tour from taking place.

# PICTURE ACKNOWLEDGMENTS

The publishers would like to thank the following sources for their help in
providing the illustrations. (Where there is more than one illustration on
a page, the credits start with the picture furthest to the left and nearest
the top of the page and work down each column.)

All-Sport 151a & b, 153a & b, 154a,
155, 157a & b, 159a, b & c,
163a, 165, 166, 167, 170, 173a
& b, 174a, b & c, 176, 177a, b &
c, 180a, b & c, 181a & c, 183a, b
& c, 184a & b, 186a & b, 187,
189a & b, 191, 193a & b, 195,
196a & b, 197, 198a & b, 199,
200, 203, 205, 206 b & d, 207a,
b & c, 208, 209a, b & c, 211a &
b, 212a & b, 213a, b, c & d,
214c, 215a & b, 216a, b & c

Associated Sports Photography 202

Colorsport 210

The Cricketer 82a, 123, 126a, 139b,
142, 150

Dennis Dobson 154d

Patrick Eagar 18, 23c, 44a, 73a, 81,
86b, 89, 97, 104b, 106a & b,
107a, 112a, 114, 122, 145

Hallawell 64

Hampshire Chronicle 98

George Herringshaw 136b, 171

Ken Kelly 55a, 60b, 78a & b, 79,
84b, 88, 94d, 100b, 109, 115,
121b, 129b, 131b, 136a, 139a,
147, 154b, 168b, 181b, 189c,
206c

Mark Leech 206a

Derek Metson 112b

David Munden 172b

Photosource 9a, 13, 16b, 22, 23a,
24b, 25, 29b, 33, 38a, 39a, 42a
& b, 43, 44b, 55b & c, 58, 65,
66a, 68, 72, 76b, 84a, 87, 93,
94a & b, 108, 111, 113, 116a,
117, 121a, 129a, 132, 163b

Press Association 9b, 17, 29a, 37a,
38b, 45b, 47a, b & c, 76a, 77,
82b & c, 83, 86a, 100a, 102,
104c, 107b, 124, 133a, 135, 141,
143, 148, 154c, 201, 214b

SKR Photos International 92

Bill Smith 113b

Sport & General 8b, 11, 14, 16a, 20a
& b, 24a & d, 26, 28, 34b, 37b,
39b, 41, 45a, 50, 60a, 61, 66b,
73b, 74, 96a, 110, 119, 126b

Sporting Pictures 94c, 96b, 104a,
118, 120, 126d, 128, 131a, 179

Bob Thomas 130, 172a

Universal Pictorial Press 8a, 10b,
13b, 23b, 24c, 30, 36, 59, 63,
70, 116b, 126c

C.E. Woodings 140

All colour photography by Adrian
Murrell/All-Sport

*Back Flap Photos*
John Arlott by Patrick Eagar
Tony Lewis by Universal Pictorial
Press
Mike Brearley by Adrian Murrell
Peter Roebuck by Bob Thomas